VIRGIN REBEL

VIRGIN REBEL

Richard Branson In His Own Words

EDITED BY DANIELLE McLIMORE

AN AGATE IMPRINT

CHICAGO

Printed in the United States.

Library of Congress Cataloging-in-Publication Data

Branson, Richard.
  Virgin rebel : Richard Branson in his own words / edited by Danielle McLimore.
     pages cm. -- (In their own words)
  Summary: "A collection of direct quotes from Richard Branson on topics related to business, entrepreneurship, the Virgin Group, philan-thropy, and life"--Provided by publisher"-- Provided by publisher.
  Includes bibliographical references and index.
  ISBN 978-1-932841-78-7 (pbk.) -- ISBN 1-932841-78-4 (paperback) -- ISBN 978-1-57284-725-5 (ebook)
  1. Branson, Richard--Quotations. 2. Businesspeople--Great Britain--Quotations. 3. Entrepreneurship--Quotations, maxims, etc. 4. Man-agement--Quotations, maxims, etc. I. McLimore, Danielle. II. Title.
  HC252.5.B73A25 2013
  082--dc23

                        2013016978

10 9 8 7 6 5 4 3 2 1

B2 is an imprint of Agate Publishing. Agate books are available in bulk at discount prices. For more information, go to agatepublishing.com.

Whatever we want to be, whatever we want to do, we can do it. Go ahead, take that first step—just do it. The best of luck to you, and have fun along the way.

—RICHARD BRANSON

TABLE OF CONTENTS

Business and Investment

Branding and Marketing

Leadership and Management

Innovation

Air and Space

Personal

Social Responsibility

INTRODUCTION

"Do what you love, and the money will follow"—no person better exemplifies this adage than multibillionaire Richard Branson, who has earned his fortune simply by pursuing his personal interests. His seamless transitions from journalist to record executive to space-travel pioneer have all begun with a natural curiosity and passion, coupled with a well-honed instinct for turning anything into a business.

As you look through Virgin Group's widely varied list of companies (p. 109), you'll be struck by the diversity of businesses. It would seem that they all began with Branson, probably in the bath (he speaks frequently about taking baths), just pondering what he likes to do and how he can make money doing it. Virgin Galactic is a perfect example: Branson wanted to travel to space, and figured he wasn't the only one. Rather than fund the research for consumer space travel entirely out of his own pocket, he created Virgin Galactic; and now, for $200,000, anyone can purchase a trip into suborbital space (whenever the technology is ready).

Branson also knows when to cut his losses—that doing so is just as important as knowing how and when to start a company. When a business or product isn't doing well, rather than hang on in the hopes of a turnaround, he will often just pack it in and move on. Virgin Pulse (a line of electronics), Virgin Brides (a wedding dress retailer), and Virgin Cola (an attempt to take down Coke and Pepsi) were all shut down due to poor sales well before they risked bankruptcy.

Acumen aside, Branson has also had his share of luck. The first album he produced was Mike Oldfield's *Tubular Bells*, which went multiplatinum in the UK and became the theme song for *The Exorcist*. He then sold Virgin Records in 1992 for $1 billion to fund his fledgling airline—a move that seemed completely insane at the time, but looked downright visionary seven years later, as CD sales plummeted and the record industry fought the transition to digital. Branson might still be worth billions of dollars today if not for good fortune such as that, but there's no arguing that these two strokes of luck didn't greatly influence Virgin's health and success.

And what does Branson do with all that money? Aside from buying an island in the Caribbean (which he promptly turned into a luxury resort in addition to his family's personal getaway—

see, making money yet again), he is dedicated to philanthropy. Virgin Unite, the nonprofit arm of Virgin Group, funds a range of initiatives, from reducing carbon emissions to improving healthcare in Africa. With Nelson Mandela and Peter Gabriel, Branson founded the Elders, a group of established global leaders concerned with human rights issues worldwide. Members include Kofi Annan, Jimmy Carter, and Archbishop Desmond Tutu. Branson also founded the Branson Centre of Entrepreneurship, a networking and training program located in South Africa and Jamaica.

Branson isn't afraid to fail, and he knows that in order to succeed, he must find and cultivate talented people. He's never followed the money, but the money has certainly followed him—and above everything, his focus remains squarely on having fun.

Branson's unique style of business is captured in this book. It's an enlightening collection of quotes directly from the man himself. Have fun with it— he certainly would.

ENTREPRENEURSHIP

••

Playfulness

I think entrepreneurship is our natural state—a big adult word that probably boils down to something much more obvious like "playfulness."

—Business Stripped Bare, page 39

••

Virgin of Business

Somebody else laughed… "Why not Virgin? We're all virgins"—hysterical laughter all around. And I suddenly thought, "I am a virgin of business, I might be a virgin of other things as well, and why not Virgin?"

—Bloomberg Game Changers, May 10, 2011

••

Getting Started

We worked out that there was no need for shops to be charging the amount they were for records, so we started a mail-order company that would sell any record, from any record manufacturer, for 10 percent to 25 percent less than their commercial price. For instance, we could buy a record from EMI for 31 shillings, which a shop would sell at 40 shillings. Instead, we sell it for 35 shillings. Virgin Records is helping hundreds and hundreds of young people throughout the country to get records at about 6 shillings cheaper—or 6 to 8 shillings cheaper—than they would anywhere else. At the same time, it's also starting up new groups who have been scorned by some of the big companies. And we're listening to their records and giving them a chance to get going themselves.

—Unnamed documentary, 1971

••

Believing in Yourself

I have no secret. There are no rules to follow in business. I just work hard and, as I always have done, believe I can do it.

—Screw It, Let's Do It, page 30

· ·

Going with Your Gut

Speaking on his "self-professed ignorance" of the music industry (article's words): I know when I like a record and when I don't like a record.

—*New York Times*, June 3, 1984

· ·

Taking Risks

Virgin would not be the company it is today if we had not taken risks along the way. You really do have to believe in what you are doing.

—*Like a Virgin*, page 27

· ·

No Virgin Brides?

Regarding the failure of Virgin Brides, a wedding-dress shop: We couldn't find any customers.

—*TED Talks*, March 2007

· ·

Covering the Costs

Regarding starting Virgin Atlantic: I'm not on
a crusade with this thing.... If we had to pack it
all in, the whole venture wouldn't cost but two
months' profit of the Virgin Group.

—*Wall Street Journal,* August 20, 1984

· ·

Practical Application

I think as much practical experience as people can
have, the better... I'm dyslexic, so I know
that I learn the most from practical experience.
The more one can actually make a school act
practically, the better.

—*"Richard Branson: Talking Management"*
February 16, 2010

· ·

Personalities

Entrepreneurs have the dynamism to get
something started.... Yet an entrepreneur is not
necessarily good at the nuts and bolts of running
a business.

—*Business Stripped Bare,* page 259

••

Excellence

Entrepreneurship is also about excellence. Not excellence measured in awards or other people's approval, but the sort that one achieves for oneself by exploring what the world has to offer.

—*Success*, July 1, 2009

••

Entrepreneurs vs. Managers

As a small-business person, you must immerse yourself 100 percent in everything and learn about the ins and outs of every single department.... And as the business gets bigger, you will have to decide if you're a manager or an entrepreneur. If you're a manager you can stay with that business and help it grow. If you're an entrepreneur, you need to find a manager. Then you should move on, enjoy yourself and then set up your next enterprise.

—*Business Stripped Bare*, pages 260–261

••

Steve Jobs

Who is the entrepreneur I most admire? Steve
Jobs. He is the greatest comeback artist, he has
twice been down and out and fought his way back
and created a brilliant global company. Everything
he does is real class. If he wanted to rename his
company Virgin Apple I'm sure we would be more
than happy to merge!

—*Richard's Blog,* March 30, 2011

••

Bouncing Back

The ability to bounce back after a setback is
probably the single most important trait an
entrepreneurial venture can possess.

—*Like a Virgin,* page 61

••

An Open Mind

Entrepreneurial business favors the open mind.
It favors people whose optimism drives them to
prepare for many possible futures, pretty much
purely for the joy of doing so.

—*Richard's Blog,* December 26, 2012

· ·

Net vs. Gross

We're having a board meeting, and I said something like, "Is that good news or bad news?" and one of the fellow directors said, "Look, Richard, just come outside a minute." And he said, "Look, I don't think you know the difference between 'net' and 'gross' yet." And I said, "Well, yeah, I sort of got away with it for the last 40 years."

—*"Richard Branson: Talking Management"*
February 16, 2010

· ·

Giving It a Try

The challenge is to follow through on a great idea. I think if [you've] got a great idea, you need to just give it a try. And if you fall flat on your face, pick yourself up and try again. Learn from your mistakes. And, remember, you've got to go make a real difference in people's lives if you're going to be successful.

—*Success,* July 1, 2009

···

It's Not about Money

It's rare for me or the team to consider only the money that can be made. I feel it's pointless to approach investing wth the question, "How can I make lots of money?"

—*Like a Virgin,* page 45

···

It's about Making a Difference

I'm not sure that somebody will know that they're an entrepreneur from the beginning. I think they will have a desire to make a difference [in] other peoples' lives, and they'll see that something's frustrating them, there's a gap in the market, they feel they can do it better themselves, and they'll try to fill that gap in the market. And then they almost become an entrepreneur by default. I don't think you can set out to become an entrepreneur. I think you've got to set out to a make a difference to other peoples' lives.

—*I Love Marketing,* July 8, 2011

••

Mixing Friends and Business

There is nothing wrong with doing business with your friends—in fact, I encourage it.... [However, the] fact that your partner is also a friend cannot be an excuse for turning a blind eye.

—*Like a Virgin,* page 126

••

Call Me

How the Sex Pistols were signed to Virgin Records: They were still signed to EMI and when I got back to the office, I rang up the chairman of EMI. I left a message with his secretary saying if that he wanted to get rid of this embarrassment, could he give me a ring. And the secretary gave me quite a curt response, saying that, you know, "We're quite happy with the Sex Pistols, thank you." That night the Sex Pistols went on the Bill Grundy show [called Today] and there were a number of swear words...and I got a call straight after the show saying the chairman himself was on the phone, and could I come over for a 6 o'clock breakfast the next morning, when he'd like to hand over the contract to us. So we ended up sort of getting the Sex Pistols by default.

—*"God Save the Queen—The Sex Pistols Interview,"* September 27, 2012

··

Conventional Schoolwork

I found conventional schoolwork hopeless.... I decided at a very young age that I needed to get out of this environment and carve my own way in life.

—*Big Think*, June 2, 2011

··

Starting a Business

Anyone can start up a new business from home. You can wash windows, take in ironing, or walk dogs. You can be an artist or a writer.... Even the Queen sells her farm produce from Windsor and Sandringham on the Web, as does Prince Charles with his Duchy Originals[.]

—*Screw It, Let's Do It*, pages 44–45

••

Investing for the Future

Regarding a six-month-long drop in profits on the US side of the business: We are investing for the future. We think for the long term, not the short term.

—*Billboard*, June 4, 1988

••

Gut Feelings

I do a lot by gut feeling and a lot by personal experience. I mean, if I relied on accountants to make decisions, I most certainly would have never gone into the airline business. I most certainly would not have gone into the space business, and I certainly wouldn't have gone into most of the businesses that I'm in. So, in hindsight, it seems to have worked pretty well to my advantage.

—*Success*, July 1, 2009

BUSINESS AND INVESTMENT

· ·

What Concerns Us

Business is what concerns us. If you care about
something enough to do something about it,
you're in business.

—Richard's Blog, September 25, 2012

· ·

International Expansion

I want to build Virgin into the greatest entertainment group in the world.... Whatever we are doing
in England, we can do in the rest of the world. We
are in 17 countries worldwide and are growing
very rapidly, with over two-thirds of our income
from overseas.

—Houston Chronicle, July 4, 1980

● ●

Business Requirements

Business requires astute decision-making and leadership. It requires discipline and innovation. It also needs attitude, a good sense of humor, and, dare I say it, luck.

—*Business Stripped Bare*, page 7

● ●

Lost Opportunities

...[A] few opportunities have slipped away. I had the chance to invest in Ryanair...I turned down the chance to invest in Trivial Pursuit and a wind-up radio.

—*Screw It, Let's Do It*, page 59

● ●

Diversifying

Discussing how Virgin Records profits helped pay for Virgin Atlantic's first plane: [Boy George] helped pay for the wings and the tailplane and perhaps one or two of the engines as well.

—*New York Times*, June 3, 1984

••

Community

The beauty of business is that it does not just have one single community.... The businesses that are most successful connect with everyone as an individual, not just as an order number or a transaction.

—*Screw Business As Usual*, page 299

••

Bonkers

Regarding Virgin Atlantic's inability to fly from London to Glasgow, due to a lack of landing slots: It's absolutely bonkers and it makes me angry. We could have achieved so much more in this country [by] creating a massive number of jobs.

—*This Is Money*, April 13, 2013

••

Blowing Away Investors

If a bank or other investor is looking at your business, they have almost certainly looked at your competitors as well. In your presentation, therefore, it's imperative that you understand your competition and irreverently explain why your business will do better. Blow them away! Avoid being overly negative.

—*Like a Virgin*, page 41

• •

Selling the Record Business

People said at the time that we were mad to sell the record company to put the money into an airline. As it turns out, of course, the record industry's collapsed, and the airline industry hasn't done too badly for us.

—Bloomberg Game Changers, May 10, 2011

• •

Going Bust

We've never had a company go bust and we never plan to have a company go bust.

> *Editor's note: This is in fact true, but Branson has shuttered companies before they had the opportunity to go bankrupt. See page 111.*

—Firstpost, October 26, 2012

• •

Cutting Back

Regarding tough times at Virgin in 1976: ...
[W]e cut back on whatever we could: we sold our cars, we closed down the swimming pool at the Manor [Virgin's recording studio], we cut down on the stock in the record shops, we didn't pay ourselves, we dropped a few artists from the record label, and [we] made nine staff redundant.

—Losing My Virginity, page 110

••

Rupert Murdoch

His empire should be looked at by competition authorities, and it should be decided if it's good for democracy that one person has so much influence.

—*Real Business,* July 14, 2011

••

Being Ethical

Regarding his 1971 arrest and conviction for tax evasion: Since then, I've made sure that we've done everything ethically, and without worry that someone's going to come knocking on our door.

—*Bloomberg Game Changers,* May 10, 2011

••

Bankruptcy

There have been times I was almost bankrupt, and I was very glad to see my name in the *Sunday Times* "Rich List," because I thought it would assuage the bank manager. (The figures were often wildly off the mark both ways—but I wasn't complaining.)

—*Business Stripped Bare,* page 325

••

Bureaucracy

I try to keep bureaucracy to a minimum, and remind my teams that business, as well as life, should be fun.

—Entrepreneur, August 27, 2012

••

Calculated Risks

Don't be afraid to take calculated risks. Sometimes they turn out to be less dangerous than the sure thing.

—Like a Virgin, page 59

••

All the Way

I rang up Boeing and I said, "My name's Richard Branson, and I'd like to buy a secondhand 747." And they said, "What did you say your company was called?" I said, "Virgin".... To give them credit they said, "OK look, we'll give you a go. As long as, unlike your name, your airline's going to go the whole way."

—Aspen Ideas Festival, July 5, 2007

● ●

Tough Times

...Virgin America is a great airline and we're very proud of it.... We've been through 9/11, SARS— you name it. And fortunately, we've built up the financial capabilities to deal with these tough years. We're just having to tighten the belt until the good years come again.

—*Time,* September 1, 2009

● ●

Protecting the Downside

Protecting the downside is critical. We'll make bold moves, but we'll also make sure we've got ways out if things go wrong.

—*"Richard Branson: Talking Management"* February 16, 2010

● ●

Limited Liability

Regarding Virgin's status as a set of more than 300 separate private businesses: I think we've proved that a branded group of *separate* businesses, each with limited liability for its own financial affairs, makes sense. We're never going to have a Barings Bank situation where a rogue trader is able to bring down the whole Virgin Group.

—*Business Stripped Bare,* pages 4–5

••

Customers Are Humans, Too

Regarding the phrase, "The customer is always right": It has endured because it sounds wonderful to marketers, but most established companies have learned from experience that it is way too all-encompassing to apply in everyday business. In truth, the customer is only right most of the time—after all, they're only human.

—*Like a Virgin,* page 63

••

Ruthless Capitalism

The music business is a strange combination of real and intangible assets…. The rock business is a prime example of the most ruthless kind of capitalism.

—*Losing My Virginity,* page 61

••

Turning the Big Guys Upside Down

Over the years we've enjoyed taking on the big, fat, bloated companies and trying to turn them upside down…and I like to think we've done it in a fun way, rather than taking ourselves too seriously.

—*Allan Gregg in Conversation,* April 1, 2001

••

Losing Faith

I lost faith in myself only once, and that was
in 1986...I was told I should go public.... I no
longer felt that I was standing on my own two
feet. We doubled our profits, but Virgin shares
started to slip and, for the first time in my life, I
was depressed.

—*Screw It, Let's Do It,* pages 77–80

••

Taking Virgin Public

In many ways, 1987, our year of being a public
company, was Virgin's least creative year. We
spent at least 50 percent of our time heading off
to the City [London's financial district] to explain
to fund managers, financial advisers, and City PR
firms what we were doing, rather than just getting
on and doing it.

—*Losing My Virginity,* page 185

••

Freedom

Regarding reprivatization of Virgin Group:
Freedom is something worth paying for.... All that
time and expense can now be put into dealing
with our artists.

—*Billboard,* October 15, 1988

••

The First Contract

Since Mike Oldfield was the first artist we signed, we had no idea what sort of a contract to offer him. Luckily, Sandy Denny, originally a singer with Fairport Convention who had now gone solo, had recently recorded at the Manor. She had become a friend of mine, and I asked her for a copy of her contract with Island Records. This was apparently a standard Island Records deal, and we retyped it word for word, changing "Island Records" to "Virgin Music," and "Sandy Denny" to "Mike Oldfield."

—*Losing My Virginity,* page 85

BRANDING AND MARKETING

••

Way of Life

The Virgin brand is a guarantee that you'll be treated well, that you'll get a high-quality product which won't dent your bank balance, and you'll get more fun out of your purchase than you expected—*whatever it is*…. No other brand has become a "way-of-life" brand the way Virgin has.

—*Business Stripped Bare*, page 46

••

One Was Cooler

Regarding selecting a celebrity guest to appear at a Virgin Megastore opening in NYC: It was either Marilyn Manson or the mayor, but we decided to pick Marilyn Manson…one was cooler.

—*Late Night with Conan O'Brien*, August 27, 1998

••

Good for the Brand

I get up well before we land to walk the aisles and say hello to our passengers. Showing my face is good for the brand; even more useful, I get to see for myself where we can improve and strengthen our service.

—*Reach for the Skies,* page 160

••

Design

Getting every little bit of the design right is so important…. Great design can be great marketing.

—*Cool Hunting,* October 11, 2012

••

Seat of My Pants

After a marketing stunt gone wrong, in which Branson bungee jumped off the Palms Casino in Las Vegas, hit the side of the building, and split his pants: I've a few bumps and bruises. I never thought I could use the phrase "by the seat of my pants" so literally. But before anyone feels sorry for me, I did have Pamela Anderson waiting at the bottom to mop my brow.

—*Daily Mirror,* October 12, 2007

••

The Pammy

On the Virgin Cola bottle shaped like voluptuous
actress Pamela Anderson: It's called the Pammy.
When we first designed it, it kept on tipping over.

—*Late Night with Conan O'Brien,* August 27, 1998

••

Trustworthy

As nice as it is to read articles that say the
Virgin brand is one of the most powerful in the
world, our corporate goal is to make it one of the
most trusted.

—*Like a Virgin,* page 294

••

Knowing Your Customers

My adventurous side means that I don't get stuck
behind a desk. I make sure that I spend most of
my time out and about, talking to people, asking
questions, making notes, and experiencing my
businesses through the customer's eyes.

—*Screw It, Let's Do It,* page 156

••

Publicity

Publicity is absolutely critical. You have to get your brand out and about, particularly if you're a consumer-oriented brand.... A good PR story is infinitely more effective than a full-page ad, and a damn sight cheaper.

—Business Stripped Bare, page 63

••

Defining Your Brand First

...[B]rands always mean something. If you don't define what the brand means, a competitor will. Apple's adverts contrasting a fit, happy, creative Mac with a fat, glum, nerdy PC tell you all you need to know about how that works. Even in the absence of competition, a betrayed brand can wreak a terrible revenge on a careless company. How many brands do you know mean "shoddy," "late," and "a rip-off"?

—Richard's Blog, October 7, 2008

· ·

Simple Advertising

Strangely, I think my dyslexia has helped...for instance, when we're launching a new company, I need to be able to understand the advertising. If I understand the advertising, I believe that anybody out there can understand the advertising.

—*Time*, 2012

· ·

Staying on the Front Page

You couldn't buy a quarter-page ad on the front of the *New York Times*, but when my sinking speedboat or crashing hot-air balloon just happened to feature the distinctive Virgin logo, there we were!

—*Like a Virgin*, page 35

· ·

Virgin

I like to think it stands for quality...

—*TED Talks*, March 2007

••

Getting It Up

British Airways was sponsoring this giant wheel [the ferris wheel known as the London Eye] on the other side of the House of Commons, and they were having technical problems getting the wheel up, and they had the world's press there to film it as it was going up. We had an airship [blimp] company so I scrambled this airship and...headed it towards this giant wheel, and as it flew over [its] massive banner at the back just simply said, "BA can't get it up." And we had a lot of great coverage at BA's expense for that. And the press loved it, and obviously that helped get Virgin on the map.

—*I Love Marketing,* July 8, 2011

••

Clear Communication

I can't speak for other people, but dyslexia shaped my—and Virgin's—communication style. From the beginning, Virgin used clear, ordinary language. If I could quickly understand a campaign concept, it was good to go. If something can't be explained off the back of an envelope, it's rubbish.

—*Forbes,* October 22, 2012

· ·

Social Media

We soon found that [social media] channels were an amazing tool for reaching our customers and the public. One of the first things we learned was that our new social media accounts gave us a real-time view of how we could improve.

—*CNBC*, September 12, 2012

· ·

Clever Advertising

Regarding whether crossing the world in a hot-air balloon was a good marketing tactic: I think our airline took a full page ad at the time, saying, "Come on, Richard, there are better ways of crossing the Atlantic."

—*TED Talks*, March 2007

· ·

Strong Branding

We have nailed Virgin's colors to the masts of many businesses, so every one of them must pull its weight with our customers.

—*Richard's Blog*, October 7, 2008

··

Fearlessness

Over the years the Virgin brand has earned the reputation of being *bold* and *unafraid*. Isn't it extraordinary how few brands communicate fearlessness?

—*Business Stripped Bare,* page 187

··

Good Tagline

Regarding Virgin's (now-defunct) condom line, Mates: As easy to buy as brown bread.

—*Globe and Mail,* June 27, 1987

··

Creating New Companies

Regarding how he decides to launch a new business or product: There's no point in us going into something unless we can really shake up an industry, make a major difference; unless it's going to enhance the Virgin brand, if there's any danger of damaging the brand in any way, even if it's going to make us a lot of money—you know, cigarette companies or something like that—we just wouldn't do it. And because life's short, we want to enjoy the experience.

—*"Richard Branson: Talking Management"*
February 16, 2010

••

Deserving Free Coverage

I began life as a journalist, and I've always been sensitive to the fact that getting free coverage is one thing; deserving it is quite another.

—Reach for the Skies, page 36

••

High-Quality David vs. Goliath

Virgin is an unusual brand. I mean, most brands specialize in one area.... Virgin is more of a way-of-life brand, and we like to look after people's needs throughout their lives, whether it's their health, or their train travel, or their airline travel, or their music, or so on. And it's very important if you are a way-of-life brand that you don't have, say, one company letting the other companies down. So we strive to be the best in every sector that we take on. We're, generally speaking, the underdog, which is actually a lot more fun than being the Goliath.... We have a lot of fun in what we do, we love to make a difference, and we love to tear down barriers.

—Interview by Tanya Beckett, August 28, 2008

LEADERSHIP AND MANAGEMENT

....

Unprofessional Professional

When I was 21, someone described Virgin as an "unprofessional professional organization," which for my money is just about the best backhanded compliment anyone in business could ever receive.

—*Business Stripped Bare*, page 28

....

People Departments

I hate the descriptor "human resources," by the way...I call them "people departments."

—*HR*, July 12, 2010

• •

Philanthropy

It's important for the staff who work for Virgin to know that the wealth is going to be spent in a constructive way, and that's what we plan to do.

—*Big Think*, June 2, 2011

• •

Brand Ambassadors

Some people might see Virgin's 50,000 employees as a cost to be managed, but I see 50,000 potential passionate brand ambassadors.

—Open Forum by American Express, June 9, 2011

• •

Throwing Parties

Parties are a way of galvanizing teams and allowing people to let their hair down. They have to inclusive and encouraging, and then they are an excellent way of bringing everyone together and forging a great business culture.

—*Business Stripped Bare*, page 257

••

Questioning Leadership

In 2004, I did a program called *The Rebel Billionaire* for Fox Television, where I was nice to people and then had to whittle them down to a winner. In one episode, I told a participant [named Sam Heshmati that] we were going to be the first to go over the Victoria Falls in a barrel.... A split second before we were due to plummet, I shouted: "Stop! Hold on just one moment, I want to show you something."

So we got out. And I showed young Sam the bottom of the falls. I pointed at the rocks below.

"Sam," I admonished him, "you were 10 seconds from certain death. You shouldn't blindly accept a leader's advice. You've got to question leaders on occasions."

—*Richard's Blog,* December 10, 2008

••

Listening and Asking Questions

The ability to listen, and the willingness to stick your neck out and ask the obvious question, are criminally underrated business essentials.

—*Business Stripped Bare,* page 267

••

Firing

There's a machismo about the way some managers talk about hiring and firing that I find downright repugnant.... I think that you should only fire somebody as an act of last resort.

—*Business Stripped Bare,* page 263

••

Collective Responsibility

Our view at Virgin is that collective responsibility bonds teams, and having pride in your work is a far better driver than a hierarchical culture where the boss calls the shots.

—*HR,* July 12, 2010

••

People Motivators

If we're looking for somebody to run one of our companies, we want to be sure that they're fantastic motivators of people; that they love people, genuinely; that they're looking for the best in people; that they praise people; that they never criticize people; that they treat the junior staff as importantly as their fellow directors, if not more importantly—and I think that's what sets a good company apart from a bad company.

—*"Richard Branson: Talking Management,"*
February 16, 2010

· ·

In the Field

Too many people are hiding in dark rooms flipping through too many words on big screens. There's a reason why I avoid boardrooms. I'd rather spend time with people "in the field," where eye contact, genuine conviction, and trustworthiness are in full evidence.

—*Forbes,* October 22, 2012

· ·

Investigation

I leave the day-to-day problems to the other executives in the company's various London offices. It means I can spend my days investigating things.

—*Wall Street Journal,* August 20, 1984

· ·

The Virtues of Telecommuting

The key for me is that in today's world, I do not think it is effective or productive to force your employees [to either work from home or in the office]. Choice empowers people and makes for a more content workforce.

—*Richard's Blog,* March 4, 2013

• •

Good Leadership

The most important thing about running a
company is to remember all the time what a
company is. A company is simply a group of
people. And as a leader of people, you have to be
a great listener, you have to be a great motivator,
[and] you have to be very good at praising and
looking for the best in people.

—Big Think, June 2, 2011

• •

Delegating

For as much as you need a strong personality to
build a business from scratch, you must
also understand the art of delegation. I have to be
willing to step back now. I have to be good at
helping people run the individual businesses—it
can't just be me that sets the culture when we
recruit people.

—HR, July 12, 2010

· ·

"We" vs. "They"

I have always found that an instant barometer to the state of any company's employee relations is the way their people use the words "we" and "they."... Managers and business leaders should watch for this tendency. A company where the staff overuse the word "they" is a company with problems. If employees aren't associating themselves with their company by using "we," it is a sign that people up and down the chain of command aren't communicating—and if that turns out to be the case, you'll usually find secondary problems throughout the company affecting everything from development to customer service.

—*Like a Virgin,* page 52

· ·

A Business Is Its People

What is a business? A business is its people. I can't change a spark plug on a 747 but I think I'm good at finding the right people, the best people, and giving them the freedom to do a good job. And the freedom to make mistakes—not in the engineering department, [but] in other departments!

—*Interview by Tanya Beckett,* August 28, 2008

••

New Virgins

In an address to new employees of Virgin Atlantic:
Who's a new Virgin? We're the only company that
can offer you that.

—A Day in the Life, August 17, 2011

••

People Management

The key to effective people management is
ensuring everyone has a little...people management
in them. It isn't solely Angela's [Smith, Virgin's
then-head of group people management] job to
make our people's policies work at Virgin. It's
everyone's responsibility. We have a [team of
people] who are in essence the custodians of the
Virgin people brand, ensuring there is consistency
throughout the group in key values, behaviors, and
policies. But each business has its own shareholders
and management—this way, we concentrate on the
job at hand rather than [being] part of some
enormous, faceless conglomerate. The process
and approach systems come from the people
management principles, but the brands have a
certain amount of freedom to do what they
want to do.

—HR, July 12, 2010

• •

Courage of Conviction

Empowering employees so that they can make good decisions is one of an entrepreneur's most important tasks. This means that you must build a corporate comfort zone in which your people can confidently express themselves and display the courage of their own convictions.

—Like a Virgin, page 89

• •

Finding the Right People

We went from being a record business into starting an airline, [and] people thought we were mad.... Somebody from the entertainment business running an airline might not be such a bad thing [however], because not only can we find the right people to make sure it runs safely, but we can also find people to entertain our passengers, and they can actually have a pleasant journey.

—Interview by Tanya Beckett, August 28, 2008

••

Bad Reflection

From a young age, if I ever criticized somebody, my parents would make me go and stand in front of the mirror, and they just said, "Look, it's a bad reflection on yourself." Ever since then, in particular if you're running a company, you've just got to look for the best in everybody.... I think if you deal well with people, people will come back and deal with you again.

—*Interview by Michael Buerk,* July 3, 2011

••

Life after Branson

Virgin does work very well without me...when my balloon bursts, Virgin will continue to flourish.

—*Big Think,* June 2, 2011

· ·

Flexibility

Companies need to have a lot more flexibility with their people.... If somebody wants to golf around the world for 2 months, okay, well, maybe on an unpaid basis, let them do it. That sort of flexibility I think is incredibly important because most of our time, we spend at work.

—*"Richard Branson: Talking Management,"*
February 16, 2010

· ·

Taking Care of Employees

We've always had, at our core, a focus on our people and making sure that they are empowered to make decisions and feel part of a company that stands for something beyond making money. I've always believed that by taking care of people in my companies, the rest will take care of itself. This can be something simple, like allowing people to job-share or giving them the chance to run their own show. This has worked for us and has also built a pretty special group of people around the world who are not only passionate about Virgin, but also about making a difference in the world.

—*Screw Business as Usual,* page 17

••

Putting the Phone Away

Way too many executives check their smart-
phones throughout meetings and during their
off-hours. Apart from the fact that it's tantamount
to rudeness in a meeting, it isn't good for anyone's concentration and has a negative impact on
decision-making.

—*Like a Virgin,* page 107-108

••

A Culture of Fun

If it doesn't come from the top down, people from
below have got to shake the people at the top.... I
think it's important for leaders to not worry about
being seen to let your hair down, not worry about
going out and getting drunk with your staff.

—*"Richard Branson: Talking Management,"*
February 16, 2010

INNOVATION

··

Changing the Customer Relationship

When I started Virgin 40 years ago, I wanted
the change the relationship that customers had
with companies.

—"Virgin Mobile Presents: Our Higher Calling™,"
March 14, 2012

··

Customer Relations

If your business proposition is innovative, your
ultimate goal has to be "The customer always
thinks that we are right."

—Like a Virgin, page 66

··

Experimentation and Adaptation

The best, most solid way out of a crisis in a
changing market is through experiment
and adaptation.

—Richard's Blog, November 27, 2008

••

Expansion Can Be Complicated

...[C]omplexity soon gums up the works of an organization as it expands....The separation of day-to-day business from the motive energy that birthed the company does cause problems. Suddenly, innovating is seen as something extra, something special, something separated from the activities the company normally engages in. This is when niggles become endemic, intractable problems; morale declines; and the business begins to lose its way in the market place.

—*Business Stripped Bare,* page 216

••

Virgin Pulse

Regarding the launch of Virgin Pulse, a line of personal electronics that was shut down after two years due to poor sales: Virgin loves to compete, especially in sectors where we feel people have been overcharged. We thought, "We can develop a range of electronics that are stylish and for which we're not charging too much." Virgin has a strong brand and we feel we can give other companies a run for their money.

—*USA Today,* October 14, 2003

· ·

Knowing When to Get Out

So, if things don't work out, don't hesitate: Take that escape hatch. That way, when all's said and done, you will be able to gather your team, discuss what did or did not happen, and then embark on your next venture together. Not much older, but a lot wiser.

—Like a Virgin, page 47

· ·

Too Much Overhead

When asked how he could make air travel so inexpensive: That was just what they asked when I started selling records 20 percent cheaper than anyone else. We went from mail order to basement record stores, then bought a manor near Oxford where bands could play and started producing. The present airlines have just built up too big an overhead.

—New York Times, April 10, 1984

••

The Frontier of Opportunity

Probably the greatest frontier of opportunity is the creation of businesses that protect and harness our natural resources—with the obvious added benefit of reducing our carbon output.

—*Screw Business as Usual,* page 205

••

Online Travel

The Internet has saved the airline business a boatload of money over the years. We were paying 7 to 10 percent commission on every ticket to the travel agents. Cutting the agents out of the business was liberating.

—*Reach for the Skies,* page 181

••

Empty Houses = Business Idea

Regarding the decision to launch Virgin Limited Edition, a small collection of exclusive retreats: Well, it all came about [because] it seemed a shame to have a series of homes around the world that lay empty when I am not there. So, what I have created over the years are some really special homes that we share with other people.

—*Luxury Travel Bible*
http://www.luxurytravelbible.com/Luxury-Hotels.
asp?active_page_id=441

• •

Moving On

I think that the death knell of record labels is pretty well upon us. I had a wonderful time running Virgin Records some years ago, and discovering bands, it was tremendously exciting... but I think that time has moved on and I think record companies are almost a thing of the past.

—*Digg Dialogg*, May 4, 2009

• •

Getting Answers

Innovation can occur when the most elementary questions are asked and employees are given the resources and power to achieve the answers.

—*Business Stripped Bare*, page 220

• •

Things Not Done

I seem to have spent my life—in the aviation business and elsewhere—separating the Things Not Done Because They Don't Work from the Things Not Done Because We Don't Do Them.

—*Reach for the Skies*, page 157

• •

Innovation and Intrapreneurs

Not everybody is cut out to be an entrepreneur.
But that doesn't mean you can't still come up with
new ideas working within an organization. This
is where intrapreneurs come in: They unleash the
power of innovation from inside companies.

—*Richard's Blog,* November 11, 2012

• •

Predicting the Future

...Virgin's success is not down to its crystal-clear
vision of the future. If it were, you'd be Virgining
our company valuations on the Internet rather
than Googling them—and our Megastores would
have been sold off in the eighties.

—*Business Stripped Bare,* page 126

· ·

April Fool's

I'm thrilled to announce that Virgin has created another world-first with the introduction of the technology required to produce the world's first glass-bottomed plane. This technological innovation coincides with the start of Virgin Atlantic Airways' first-ever domestic service to Scotland.

—*Richard's Blog,* April 1, 2013

· ·

Product Tie-Ins

Regarding the 1984 movie Electric Dreams, *which was produced by Virgin Films:* Our publishing company is publishing the book, our distribution company is distributing the film, our record company is putting out the record, our video-game company is putting out the video game, and our video company is putting out the video.... Our studios recorded them, and our shops will be selling them. That's how we maximize profit.

—*Wall Street Journal,* August 20, 1984

••

Virgin Cola

Regarding the decision to launch Virgin Cola: Why should Coca-Cola forever be so dominant? Just the fun of trying to take a bit of that market share away from them, I found, was irresistable. Everybody said it would be impossible, and to an extent, we haven't had the same sort of success [as] we've had with things like the airline business. But we still sold a couple billion cans of cola, and amongst young people in the countries where we've launched it, we managed to keep the youth image…which has been quite important.

—*Allan Gregg in Conversation,* April 1, 2001

••

Improvements

Making changes and improvements is a natural part of business, and for sole [proprietorships] and very small companies, the distinction between innovation and day-to-day delivery is barely noticeable and unimportant. It's all just business, and creative, responsive, flexible business comes easier to you the smaller your operation [is].

—*Richard's Blog,* November 27, 2008

●●●

Trial and Error

Over the years we've pioneered comfortable reclining seats, flat beds, lounges with hairstylists and masseuses, and a motorcycle-and-limo home pickup service. Virgin Atlantic was the first to provide personal video screens in every seatback so our travelers could choose the films and television shows they wanted to watch. These are some of the ideas that worked. There were plenty that didn't. Does anyone remember our live in-flight entertainment?

—Reach for the Skies, page 158

AIR AND SPACE

••

View from Space

Most people hanker for a view of Earth from space. I should know: I'm one of them.

—*Reach for the Skies*, page 20

••

Look Out, NASA

I assumed, having seen the moon landing, that I would be able to go into space in my lifetime, because I was...a teenager at the time. But, you know, decade by decade went by, [and] NASA [wasn't] opening their doors to you and me. So I thought NASA needed some competition.

—*Aspen Ideas Festival*, July 5, 2007

••

Life in Airplanes

I spend a great deal of my life on airplanes. I'm
sometimes exhausted by the routine, as much as
the next business traveler. But there isn't a flight
[that] goes by when I don't stare out of the window
and thank my stars for what I'm seeing
and feeling.

—Reach for the Skies, page 10

••

Launching Virgin Atlantic

I know a lot of people who can't afford to cross
the Atlantic.

—New York Times, April 10, 1984

••

Glamour

One of the most difficult and exciting challenges
of running an airline—and it amazes me how few
airlines take it seriously—is how to maintain the
glamour of air travel.

—Reach for the Skies, page 158

• •

Post-9/11 Security

I have no complaint with extra security; I just don't understand why it has to be done so shoddily. You want to take my mother's knitting needles away? Okay, but why can I still buy a glass bottle full of flammable liquid once I get past security?

—*Reach for the Skies*, pages 158–159

• •

High Demand

Initially, I was very skeptical, but then we looked at the figures. There's an enormous demand from people who want to fly to America cheaply.

—*New York Times*, June 3, 1984

• •

The Airline Industry

I do find it very strange that America is very ser-vice-[oriented], but the American airline industry is so anti-customer, and so uncomfort-able, and really [seems] to herd people on and off like cattle. I think the government's had a hand in that by propping up the largest airlines; they've turned into quite weak companies.

—*USA Today*, October 14, 2003

••

Human Nature

Every day, the industry ties one and a half million people down in narrow metal tubes for hours at a time and insists that they do *exactly what they're told*. For the sake of everyone's safety, we must never forget that we're asking a hell of a lot from human nature.

—*Reach for the Skies*, page 159

••

All About Quality

I mean, when we started 30 years ago with one plane flying out of England, there were 15 American carriers that we were competing with: Pan Am, TWA, Eastern, People Express, etc., etc. Every single one of them...disappeared. And they disappeared because, although we were much smaller than them, their quality was awful.

—*NPR*, October 10, 2012

Government Regulation

The airline business is a strange one in that the American government keeps on jumping in and propping up these ghastly big airlines that offer the consumer next to nothing...I just hope they don't do it again!

—*Interview by Tanya Beckett,* August 28, 2008

Space Travel

We are making fantastic progress on Virgin Galactic's preparations for travel to space. It has been an amazing, [and] at times agonizing, process to get the space program this far, and as the weeks and months pass, we are steadily witnessing more little bits of history.

—*Richard's Blog,* March 5, 2013

Mother-in-Law

Regarding galactic travel: If you've got a mother-in-law, we can always sort out one-way tickets.

— *Aspen Ideas Festival,* July 5, 2007

••

Turning Achievements into Business

Virgin Galactic's job is to [take] the incredible intellectual achievements and acts of personal heroism we've seen lighting up the skies of Mojave and elsewhere and turn them into a business.

Editor's note: Virgin Galactic's research facility is based in Mojave, California.

—*Reach for the Skies,* page 283

••

Coming Down in One Piece

Up until now, flying into space has been like flying into aerial combat: There really has been no sure expectation that you're going to come down again in one piece. Virgin Galactic's launch system will change all that. Our launch system HAS to change all that, or space will be forever out of bounds. No ordinary people will ever go there. Most won't want to. Those who do want to will never be able to afford it.

—*Reach for the Skies,* page 316

First Words in Space

Regarding what his first words would be in space:
Something like, "space is now Virgin territory."

—*Condé Nast Traveler,* July 13, 2010

Virgin Galactic is a US Company

The regulators, for their part, have been tearing
their hair out trying to make this work: Virgin
Galactic—a private company that will fly an
international clientele around on rockets over US
territory—is a project to boggle the legal mind.
The United States is the only country on earth
where such a project could be made real.

—*Reach for the Skies,* pages 316–317

New York–Australia in 30 Minutes

We're then looking at seeing whether we can
develop flights from New York to Australia in
half an hour. It may be unbelievable, but that's the
next stage.

— *Aspen Ideas Festival,* July 5, 2007

• •

Regrets?

Regarding whether he regrets his sense of adventure: I got pulled out of the sea I think six times by helicopters, and each time I didn't expect to come home to tell the tale, so in those moments you certainly wonder what you're doing up there.

—*TED Talks*, March 2007

• •

Control

Regarding his passion for hot air balloons: If you want to excape the world entirely, it's all you need. Nobody can trouble you. Nobody can stop you…. You're not in control.

—*Reach for the Skies*, page 25

• •

Taking Care of All Your Customers

The majority of your customers are going to be traveling in your economy class cabins, and it's extremely unwise not to look after them.

—*Firstpost*, October 26, 2012

....

Waiting to Jump

Regarding a ride in an out-of-control balloon, and gathering the courage to jump out of it and into the ocean: It was a very, very lonely few moments.

—*TED Talks,* March 2007

....

The Seeds of a Business

Our plan was to travel on to Puerto Rico—but when we got to the airport, the flight was canceled and people were roaming about, looking lost. No one was doing anything. So I did—someone had to. Even though I hadn't a clue what I was really doing, with a great deal of aplomb I chartered a plane for $2,000 and divided that by the number of passengers. It came to $39 a head. I borrowed a blackboard and wrote on it: VIRGIN AIRWAYS. $39 SINGLE FLIGHT TO PUERTO RICO. All the tickets were snapped up by grateful passengers. I managed to get two free tickets out of it and even made a small profit! The idea for Virgin Airways was born, right in the middle of a holiday, although the actual airline only properly took off when I was sent a business idea some years later.

—*Screw It, Let's Do It,* pages 39–40

PERSONAL

....

George Clooney

...George Clooney once let slip that he'd swap his life for mine—much to the excitement of my wife!

—*Business Stripped Bare*, page 4

....

Brad Pitt

In response to the question, "Who would play you in the film about your life?" Brad Pitt. He's handsome, sports a good beard, and is a great actor.

—*Guardian*, April 2, 2010

....

Neckties

I don't know why the tie was ever invented. It's about one of the few things that Britain has exported successfully and it completely destroyed those lovely robes that the Japanese used to wear, and now everyone looks the same and dresses the same. I often have a pair of scissors in my top pocket to go cutting people's ties off.

—*Bloomberg Businessweek*, March 7, 2012

••

Basic Needs

You don't need much money to be happy...as long as you can have one breakfast, one lunch, one dinner; as long as you can sort out your family if they're ill.

—*Digg Dialogg,* May 4, 2009

••

Boredom

Would I have been happy without my successes in business? I'd like to think so. But...it depends on what you mean by "business." Would I have been happy had I not found concerns to absorb me and fascinate me and engage me every minute of my life? No, absolutely not, I'd be as miserable as sin.

—*Business Stripped Bare,* page 4

••

Business Should Be Fun

Remember to have fun. There is no point in being in business if it is not fun.

—*Like a Virgin,* page 20

••

Dr. Yes

My colleagues know me as Dr. Yes because I find it hard to say no to new ideas and proposals.

—*Guardian,* April 2, 2010

••

Gumption

Regarding buying Necker Island in 1977: I asked him the price. "Three million pounds," he said. It was far beyond my reach. "I can offer £150,000," I said.... Three months later, I got a call to say the island was mine if I offered £180,000.

—*Screw It, Let's Do It,* pages 39–40

••

Necker Island

I bought it when I was in my twenties.... It's a little jewel. It's the place that we escape to.

—*Digg Dialogg,* May 4, 2009

••

Just Stuff

Regarding the fire that destroyed Branson's Necker Island home on August 22, 2011: It's at moments like these one realizes how unimportant "stuff" is.

—*Screw Business as Usual,* page x

● ●

Mile High

Regarding adding bedrooms to Virgin planes, which didn't actually happen: You can do it in boats, you can do it in your home, why shouldn't you be able to do it on planes?

—*Late Night with Conan O'Brien,* August 27, 1998

● ●

Drug Use

I hate being out of control.... I prefer to have a great time and to keep my wits about me.

—*Losing My Virginity,* page 66

● ●

It Runs in the Family

Regarding his mother: Just the other day she said: "If you throw yourself around, a new hip is the price you pay. The old one looks like a door knocker, so I am going to use it as one." That quote sums up her spirit. She has actually had three new hips and has come back fighting every time. She is, and always has been, a fantastic example to our family.

—*Richard's Blog,* March 26, 2013

•••

Success and Failure

There is a very thin dividing line between success and failure.

—Big Think, June 2, 2011

•••

You Only Live Once

I've always held [on] to the notion that you only live once, and that if you want your life to have any meaning, you simply have to throw yourself into things.

—Reach for the Skies, page 35

•••

Starting So Many Companies

I think it's perhaps quite personal. I just love learning. I love challenging myself. I love challenging the people around me. If I see something that's not being done very well, I'll try to do it better.

—Interview by Michael Buerk, July 3, 2011

••

Daredevil

I do seem to have conceived almost every way known to man to try to kill myself, and I've been very fortunate to be here today to talk about some of these stories.

—*Bloomberg Game Changers*, May 10, 2011

••

Board Meetings

The idea of board meetings horrifies me.

—*New York Times*, June 3, 1984

••

Virginity

I was 15 when I made the name of the company, I was 16 when I actually did it.

—*Late Night with Conan O'Brien*, August 27, 1998

••

It's Just Money

Money's only interesting for what it lets you do. On paper, if I was to sell up my shareholdings in the companies tomorrow, I would have considerable wealth. But where would be the fun in that?

—*Business Stripped Bare*, page 326

· ·

Knighthood

Regarding the utility of knighthood: I suppose if you're having problems getting a booking at a restaurant or something, it might be worth using.

—*TED Talks,* March 2007

· ·

Keeping Your Friends Close...

I've always believed in befriending your enemies.

—*Wall Street Journal,* April 22, 2012

· ·

21

Do you remember when you turned 21? Yours truly was trying to get our record label off the ground, living on a houseboat, and—most importantly—having far too much fun to remember it all too clearly.

—*Richard's Blog,* March 7, 2013

••

It's Your Call

I, for one, would far rather be a nice guy, working with great people, having fun with a small successful business, than a miserable guy heading up a hugely profitable multinational mega-corp. But that's your call.

—*Like a Virgin*, page 21

••

Retiring

It seems very boring.

—*Forbes*, February 14, 2013

••

Natural Interest

I don't work for the money. It's all done out of natural interest and enthusiasm, rather than commercial hard-headedness.

—*Houston Chronicle*, July 4, 1980

••

Shyness

I've trained myself out of a slight shyness.... I used to find it difficult to deal with public speaking.

—*Interview by Michael Buerk*, July 3, 2011

••

Family Teamwork

There was a great sense of teamwork within our family. Whenever we were within Mum's orbit, we had to be busy. If we tried to escape by saying that we had something else to do, we were firmly told we were selfish. As a result, we grew up with a clear priority of putting other people first.

—Losing My Virginity, page 20

••

Dyslexia and Entrepreneurship

Perhaps it was dyslexia that drove me to be entrepreneurial in the first place, because I knew instinctively that I'd never pass exams and go into a profession, such as the law, as my father and his father before him had. I'd never be a teacher, a doctor, or a banker—or so I thought. Ideas and good schemes to set up a business that didn't require much formal learning seemed to be one of my best options.

—Screw Business as Usual, page 55

••

Age

I have always loved the question, "How old would you be if you didn't know how old you are?" My answer to that would be "in my twenties"...

—*Screw Business as Usual,* page 13

••

Advice

Screw it, just get on and do it.

—*Interview by Michael Buerk,* July 3, 2011

SOCIAL RESPONSIBILITY

••

Enlightened Self-Interest

There *is* such a thing as enlightened self-interest, and we should encourage it. It *is* possible to turn a profit while making the world a better place.

—*Business Stripped Bare,* page 289

••

Giving Back

I learned to grasp opportunities and the nettle with equal passion. I learned that if you see a bright idea—go with it. If you see a problem—deal with it. Do good, don't do harm. Give back if you can.

Editor's note: "Grasp the nettle" is a British idiom that means "tackle a problem decisively."

—*Screw Business as Usual,* page 57

••

It Doesn't Take Much

For a relatively small amount of money, you can make a big difference to a lot of people's lives.

—*Big Think*, June 2, 2011

••

They Should Do Something

Too many businesspeople say things like, "They really should do something about developing alternative fuels." Well, we decided we simply couldn't wait for "them," and picked up the ball ourselves.

—*Like a Virgin*, page 119

••

Super Power

When asked, "What would your super power be?" Branson responded: To be able to save our planet.

—*Guardian*, April 2, 2010

••

Jobs

Virgin Galactic and its partner, Scaled Composites, are creating a lot of jobs in a town [Mojave] where they are a scarce commodity, and in a region that currently has a 4 percent higher unemployment rate than the rest of California.

—*Richard's Blog,* December 10, 2009

••

Bees

I love bees because I think that the beehive is a metaphor for the world. Every member of the community is of equal value, although they have different tasks.

—*Screw Business as Usual,* page 220

••

Decriminalizing Drugs

To cut off the flow of money to the top criminals, all we have to do is call a halt to the drug war and decrminialize the use of illegal substances.

—*Like a Virgin,* page 79

••

Centre for Entrepreneurship

...[W]e have set up the Branson School of
Entrepreneurship [now called the Centre of
Entrepreneurship] to help foster budding
entrepreneurs and their fledgling companies.
Most of our students are young men and women,
determined to study hard and build their
businesses. One of the most important things
we impart to them is the importance of enjoying
[their] work.

—*Open Forum by American Express,* August 27, 2010

••

Clean Technology

I was sitting in the bath when it occurred to
me: Why not just divert all the profits made by the
Virgin Group from our carbon-creating
businesses—such as the airlines and trains—and
invest it in developing the cleaner technologies
of the future?

—*Business Stripped Bare,* pages 309–310

• •

40 Years of Failing

The war on drugs has caused so much misery in the world, [and] it's been going on for 40 years; if we'd had a business that had failed for one year, we would have changed tack or we would have closed it down.

—*LinkedIn*, December 11, 2012

• •

Capitalism

Capitalism is the only system that works, but it has its flaws; for one, it brings great wealth to only a few people. That wealth obviously brings extreme responsibility.

—*O*, December 1, 2007

• •

Diversity

The smaller we make the world, the more we have to cherish its richness and diversity.

—*Reach for the Skies*, page 161

••

Changing the World

I constantly meet a growing army of entrepreneurs around the world, and when they ask me if I have one single message which will help them, I tell them it's this: Doing good can help improve your prospects, your profits, and your business; and it can change the world.

—*Screw Business as Usual*, page 2

••

The War on Drugs

We must stop criminalizing drug users. Health and treatment should be offered to drug users—not prison. Bad drug policies affect literally hundreds of thousands of individuals and communities across the world. We need to provide medical help to those that have problematic use—not criminal retribution.

—*Richard's Blog*, December 19, 2011

· ·

Paying It Forward

Those of us who have been fortunate enough to acquire wealth must play a role in looking at how we use these means to make the world a far better place. It's not about martyrdom, it's about balance and compassion and figuring out how we can build new ways to live together, as a truly global village, that allow everyone to prosper.

—*Screw Business as Usual,* page 6

· ·

Climate Change

We know, for sure, that human beings are changing the climate. This surely can't come as a surprise. What other species do you know that starts fires?

—*Reach for the Skies,* page 265

•••

Fracking

The technology exists for fracking to work effectively, but it is up to industry to show leadership and prove they can do fracking safely. It is also up to policy makers to ensure they regulate fracking as responsibly as possible, with accurate pricing.... Gas is much cleaner than coal and oil, and global warming is the number one issue facing the modern world.

—*Richard's Blog*, February 18, 2013

•••

In the Tub

A few years ago, I was enjoying a nice bath at home, in warm water and soft lighting...you can imagine how excited I got as Al Gore walked me through his *Inconvenient Truth* slide show!

—*Forbes*, October 22, 2012

•••

NRA

NRA, NRA, how many kids have you killed today?

—*Richard's Blog*, March 20, 2013

••

Capitalism 24902

On Branson's term for social entrepreneurship: So, what on earth does that [Capitalism 24902] mean? Well, we started talking about how the name had to capture the new level of responsibility that each of us had for others in the global village, and how this needed to be a movement that went beyond a handful of businesses or one country. When someone mentioned that the circumference of the earth is 24,902 miles, Capitalism 24902 was born! Very simple really...every single business person has the responsibility for taking care of the people and planet that make up our global village, all 24,902 circumferential miles of it.

—*Screw Business as Usual,* page 19

••

Using Position Wisely

I was on the phone this morning with the president of the Maldives—there's been a coup there, and I'm trying to see if I can help him not get arrested. I'm in a position where I can make a difference, and think I shouldn't waste that.

—*Entrepreneur,* June 19, 2012

••

Making a Huge Difference

I'm talking about the power of the ordinary, everyday person to become entrepreneurs and change-makers, to set up their own businesses, to seek their own fortune and be in control of their own lives, to say—*screw business as usual, we can do it*! We can turn things upside down and make a huge difference.

—*Screw Business as Usual,* page 6

••

Running a Charity like a Business

I am not a believer in just handing out checks; you should run charity like a business driving change. That is, I believe that most people, even the poorest and most deprived, don't just want to be told what's good for them; they want to be involved in helping to make their own lives better.

—*Screw Business as Usual,* page 33

MILESTONES

1950

Richard Branson is born on July 18 in Blackheath,
a suburb of London.

1966

Branson drops out of school at age 16.

1968

The first issue of *Student* magazine publishes.

1970

Branson launches Virgin as a mail-order record business.
The Virgin Group is founded as the umbrella company to
all future Virgin businesses.

1971

The first Virgin record store opens.
Branson spends a night in prison for tax evasion. He is
convicted of avoiding customs and excise taxes on the
records he is selling.

1972

Virgin opens a recording studio called The Manor.
Branson marries Kristen Tomassi.

1973

Virgin Records and Virgin Music Publishing launch. The first album released is *Tubular Bells*, by Mike Oldfield. The album is a commercial success.

The first track of *Tubular Bells* is used as the theme for the 1973 film *The Exorcist*.

1978

Branson purchases the uninhabited Necker Island, part of the British Virgin Islands.

1979

The first Virgin Megastore opens.
Branson and Tomassi divorce.

1984

Virgin Atlantic launches with a flight from Gatwick to Newark.

1985

Branson attempts the fastest Atlantic Ocean crossing, but the boat capsizes, leading to international media attention.

1986

Virgin Group raises £30 million (about $56 million) by going public.

1988

Branson buys back Virgin Group and makes it private again.

1989

Branson weds Joan Templeman at their home on Necker Island in the Caribbean. The couple's two children, Holly and Sam, are in attendance.

1990

While crossing the Pacific Ocean in a hot-air balloon, the propane gas catches on fire. Branson and crewmate Per Lindstrand make an emergency landing on a frozen lake in Canada.

1992

Branson sells Virgin Records to Thorn EMI for £500,000—about $1 billion.

1998

Branson's attempt to circumnavigate the globe in a hot air balloon ends when the balloon crashes into the Pacific Ocean.

1999

Branson is knighted for his accomplishments in entrepreneurship.

2004

Virgin Unite, a nonprofit foundation, launches.
Virgin Galactic, Branson's commercial space tourism company, launches. The starting price for a trip to space is roughly £130,000 (or $200,000).

2007

Branson, Peter Gabriel, and Nelson Mandela found The Elders, a group of highly esteemed global figures who work together to solve humanitarian issues around the world. 2013 members of the group include Archbishop Desmond Tutu, former US president Jimmy Carter, and former UN Secretary-General Kofi Annan.

2009

The last Virgin Megastores close in the US and Japan. They continue to operate in Australia for another year.

2011

The main house of Branson's Necker Island compound burns down. Actress Kate Winslet, a guest of the family, rescues Branson's mother from the fire.

2012

Virgin Money UK purchases Northern Rock, a British Bank.

At the 54th Grammy Awards, Branson receives the President's Merit Award for his contributions to the music industry.

Virgin Galactic successfully completes its 23rd test flight.

2013

Virgin Active launches its Singapore location, the company's first club in Asia.

Branson announces that Virgin Galactic will be ready for its first passengers by the end of the year or in the first quarter of 2014.

ACTIVE VIRGIN COMPANIES AS OF 2013

Virgin Active Australia
Virgin Active Italia
Virgin Active Portugal
Virgin Active South Africa
Virgin Active Spain
Virgin Active UK
Virgin America
Virgin Atlantic Airways
Virgin Australia
Virgin Balloon Flights
Virgin Books (Ebury Publishing)
Virgin Care
Virgin Connect
Virgin Digital Help UK
Virgin Digital Help US
Virgin Drinks
Virgin Earth Challenge
Virgin Experience Days
Virgin Festivals
Virgin Galactic
Virgin Games
Virgin Gaming
Virgin Green Fund
Virgin Health Bank
Virgin HealthMiles
Virgin Holidays

Virgin Holidays + Hip Hotels
Virgin Holidays Cruises
Virgin Life Care
Virgin Limited Edition
Virgin Limobike
Virgin Media
Virgin Mobile Australia
Virgin Mobile Canada
Virgin Mobile Chile
Virgin Mobile France
Virgin Mobile India
Virgin Mobile Poland
Virgin Mobile South Africa
Virgin Mobile UK
Virgin Mobile USA
Virgin Money Australia
Virgin Money Giving
Virgin Money South Africa
Virgin Money UK
Virgin Produced
Virgin Pure
Virgin Radio International
Virgin Trains
Virgin Unite
Virgin Vacations
The Virgin Voucher
Virgin Wines Australia
Virgin Wines UK
Virgin Wines US

RETIRED OR SOLD VIRGIN PRODUCTS AND COMPANIES

Mates (Condoms)
Radio Free Virgin
Student magazine
Virgin Bikes
Virgin Brides
Virgin Cars
Virgin Charter
Virgin Clothing
Virgin Comics
Virgin Digital
Virgin Express
Virgin Flowers
Virgin Megastores
Virgin Money US
Virgin Play
Virgin Pulse (a line of electronics including a
    digital music player)
Virgin Records
Virgin Spa
Virgin Vie
Virgin Vines
Virgin Vodka
VirginStudent
Virginware

CITATIONS

Epigraph

Richard Branson, *Screw It, Let's Do It*, 2008. London:
Virgin Books. 226.

Playfulness

Richard Branson, *Business Stripped Bare*, 2008. London:
Virgin Books. 39.

Virgin of Business

"Richard Branson Revealed." *Bloomberg Game Changers*
(video), May 10, 2011. http://www.bloomberg.
com/video/69540206-richard-branson-revealed-
bloomberg-game-changers.html.

Getting Started

Unnamed documentary, 1971. http://www.youtube.com/
watch?v=MLSDQFn5w8U&playnext=1&list=PLA5249
FCA83B66EA3&feature=results_main.

Believing in Yourself

Richard Branson, *Screw It, Let's Do It*, 2008. London:
Virgin Books. 30.

Going with Your Gut

Keith H. Hammonds, "A Music Master Takes Flight."
New York Times, June 3, 1984.

Taking Risks

Richard Branson, *Like a Virgin*, 2012. New York: Portfolio/Penguin. 27.

No Virgin Brides?

"Richard Branson: Life at 30,000 Feet." *TED Talks* (video), March 2007. http://www.ted.com/talks/richard_branson_s_life_at_30_000_feet.html.

Covering the Costs

L. Erik Calonius, "How Richard Branson of Virgin Group Ltd. Is Taking Off in Britain—His Unconventional Business Makes Music and Films, and Now Runs an Airline—Some Cues From Sir Freddie." *Wall Street Journal*, August 20, 1984.

Practical Application

"Richard Branson: Talking Management." Interview by Karl Moore (video), February 16, 2010. http://www.youtube.com/watch?v=DCXOnloZyYk.

Personalities

Richard Branson, *Business Stripped Bare*, 2008. London: Virgin Books. 259.

Excellence

"Richard Branson: Virgin Entrepreneur." *Success*, July 1, 2009. http://www.success.com/articles/712-richard-branson-virgin-entrepreneur.

Entrepreneurs vs. Managers

Richard Branson, *Business Stripped Bare*, 2008. London: Virgin Books. 260–261.

Steve Jobs

Richard Branson, "The Entrepreneur I Most Admire."
Richard's Blog, March 30, 2011. http://www.virgin.
com/richard-branson/blog/the-entrepreneur-i-most-
admire.

Bouncing Back

Richard Branson, Like a Virgin, 2012. New York:
Portfolio/Penguin. 61.

An Open Mind

Richard Branson, "Business Favors the Open Mind."
Richard's Blog, December 26, 2012. http://www.virgin.
com/richard-branson/blog/business-favours-the-
open-mind.

Net vs. Gross

"Richard Branson: Talking Management." Interview by
Karl Moore (video), February 16, 2010. http://www.
youtube.com/watch?v=DCXOnloZyYk.

Giving it a Try

"Richard Branson: Virgin Entrepreneur." Success, July 1,
2009. http://www.success.com/articles/712-richard-
branson-virgin-entrepreneur.

It's Not about Money

Richard Branson. *Like a Virgin*, 2012. New York:
Portfolio/Penguin. 45.

It's about Making a Difference

"The One with Richard Branson," Interview by Joe
Polish (video). *I Love Marketing*, July 8, 2011. http://
ilovemarketing.com/episode-025-the-one-with-
richard-branson/.

Mixing Friends and Business

Richard Branson, *Like a Virgin*, 2012. New York: Portfolio/Penguin. 126.

Call Me

"God Save the Queen—The Sex Pistols Interview" (video), September 27, 2012. http://www.youtube.com/watch?v=dauog--DgCI.

Conventional Schoolwork

"Richard Branson: Growing Up Dyslexic," *Big Think* (video), June 2, 2011. http://www.youtube.com/watch?v=TW7t5qXi_dg.

Starting a Business

Richard Branson, *Screw It, Let's Do It*, 2008. London: Virgin Books. 44–45.

Investing for the Future

Nick Robertshaw, "Virgin Group's Pretax Profits Fall by 22%." *Billboard*, June 4, 1988.

Gut Feelings

"Richard Branson: Virgin Entrepreneur." *Success*, July 1, 2009. http://www.success.com/articles/712-richard-branson-virgin-entrepreneur.

What Concerns Us

Richard Branson, *Richard's Blog*, September 25, 2012. http://www.virgin.com/richard-branson/blog/business-is-what-concerns-us.

International Expansion

"Pop Tycoon Branson Is Used to Taking Chances."
Houston Chronicle, July 4, 1980. .

Business Requirements

Richard Branson, *Business Stripped Bare*, 2008. London:
Virgin Books. 7.

Lost Opportunities

Richard Branson, *Screw It, Let's Do It*, 2008. London:
Virgin Books. 59.

Diversifying

Keith H. Hammonds, "A Music Master Takes Flight."
New York Times, June 3, 1984. .

Community

Richard Branson, Screw Business as Usual, 2011. New
York: Penguin. 299.

Bonkers

Richard Harrison, "Richard Branson: I Could Never
Have Become the Billionaire I Am Today without
Maggie's Help." *This Is Money,* April 13,2013. http://
www.thisismoney.co.uk/money/news/article-2308568/
Richard-Branson-I-couldn-t-Maggies-push-
competition-growth.html.

Blowing Away Investors

Richard Branson, *Like a Virgin*, 2012. New York:
Portfolio/Penguin. 41.

Selling the Record Business

"Richard Branson Revealed." *Bloomberg Game Changers* (video), May 10, 2011. http://www.bloomberg. com/video/69540206-richard-branson-revealed-bloomberg-game-changers.html.

Going Bust

"Death of One or Two Indian Airlines Is Necessary: Richard Branson" (video), October 26, 2012. http:// www.firstpost.com/business/why-richard-branson-is-shit-scared-of-indian-carriers-503471.html.

Cutting Back

Richard Branson, *Losing My Virginity*, 1998. Random House. 110.

Rupert Murdoch

Jason Hesse, "Richard Branson: Murdoch Is Getting His Comeuppance." *Real Business,* July 14, 2011. http:// realbusiness.co.uk/article/6321-richard-branson-murdoch-is-getting-his-comeuppance.

Being Ethical

"Richard Branson Revealed." *Bloomberg Game Changers* (video), May 10, 2011. http://www.bloomberg. com/video/69540206-richard-branson-revealed-bloomberg-game-changers.html.

Bankruptcy

Richard Branson, *Business Stripped Bare*, 2008. London: Virgin Books. 325.

Bureaucracy

Richard Branson, "Richard Branson's Tips for Growing
Your Small Business." *Entrepreneur*, August 27, 2012.
http://www.entrepreneur.com/article/224252.

Calculated Risks

Richard Branson, *Like a Virgin*, 2012. New York:
Portfolio/Penguin. 59.

All the Way

"A Conversation with Richard Branson," interview
by Bob Schieffer (video). Aspen Ideas Festival,
July 5, 2007. http://www.aspenideas.org/session/
conversation-richard-branson.

Tough Times

Dan Fletcher, "Q&A: Virgin Founder Richard Branson."
Time, September 1, 2009. http://www.time.com/time/
business/article/0,8599,1919660,00.html.

Protecting the Downside

"Richard Branson: Talking Management." Interview by
Karl Moore (video), February 16, 2010. http://www.
youtube.com/watch?v=DCXOnloZyYk.

Limited Liability

Richard Branson, *Business Stripped Bare*, 2008. London:
Virgin Books. 4-5.

Customers Are Humans, Too

Richard Branson, *Like a Virgin*, 2012. New York:
Portfolio/Penguin. 63.

Ruthless Capitalism

Richard Branson, *Losing My Virginity*, 1998. Random House. 61.

Turning the Big Guys Upside Down

"Allan Gregg: Richard Branson," *Allan Gregg in Conversation* (video), April 1, 2001. http://ww3.tvo. org/video/165195/richard-branson.

Losing Faith

Richard Branson, *Screw It, Let's Do It*, 2008. London: Virgin Books. 77–80.

Taking Virgin Public

Richard Branson, *Losing My Virginity*, 1998. Random House. 185.

Freedom

Edwin Riddell, "Branson, As Expected, to Take Virgin Group Private." *Billboard*, October 15, 1988. .

The First Contract

Richard Branson, *Losing My Virginity*, 1998. Random House. 85.

Way of Life

Richard Branson, *Business Stripped Bare*, 2008. London: Virgin Books. 46.

One Was Cooler

"Salma Hayek, Richard Branson, The Dixie Chicks," Late Night with Conan O'Brien (video), August 27, 1998. http://www.youtube.com/watch?v=5BrKiG1cUPA.

Good for the Brand

Richard Branson, *Reach for the Skies*, 2010. New York: Penguin. 160.

Design

Rod Kurtz, "Interview: Richard Branson on Design." *Cool Hunting*, October 11, 2012. http://www. coolhunting.com/design/richard-branson-interview- on-design.php

Seat of My Pants

Will Payne, "Scrunchee Jump: Branson's Knickers in a Twist as Stunt Backfires." *Daily Mirror*, October 12, 2007. http://www.mirror.co.uk/news/uk-news/ scrunchee-jump-512892.

The Pammy

"Salma Hayek, Richard Branson, The Dixie Chicks," *Late Night with Conan O'Brien* (video), August 27, 1998. http://www.youtube.com/watch?v=5BrKiG1cUPA.

Trustworthy

Richard Branson, *Like a Virgin*, 2012. New York: Portfolio/Penguin. 294.

Knowing Your Customers

Richard Branson, *Screw It, Let's Do It*, 2008. London: Virgin Books. 156.

Publicity

Richard Branson, *Business Stripped Bare*, 2008. London: Virgin Books. 63.

Defining Your Brand First

Richard Branson, "Brand—Flying the Flag." *Richard's Blog*. October 7, 2008. http://www.virgin.com/richard-branson/blog/brand-flying-the-flag.

Simple Advertising

"10 Questions for Richard Branson." *Time* (video), 2012. http://www.time.com/time/video/player/0,32068,1347878415_1721845,00.html

Staying on the Front Page

Richard Branson, *Like a Virgin*, 2012. New York: Portfolio/Penguin. 35.

Virgin

"Richard Branson: Life at 30,000 Feet." *TED Talks* (video), March 2007. http://www.ted.com/talks/richard_branson_s_life_at_30_000_feet.html.

Getting It Up

"The One with Richard Branson," Interview by Joe Polish (video). *I Love Marketing*, July 8, 2011. http://ilovemarketing.com/episode-025-the-one-with-richard-branson/.

Clear Communication

Carmine Gallo, "Richard Branson: If it Can't Fit on the Back of an Envelope, it's Rubbish (an Interview)." *Forbes*, October 22, 2012. http://www.forbes.com/sites/carminegallo/2012/10/22/richard-branson-if-it-cant-fit-on-the-back-of-an-envelope-its-rubbish-interview/2/.

Social Media

Richard Branson, "Richard Branson on How to Leverage Social Media." *CNBC*, September 12, 2012. http://www.cnbc.com/id/49003670/Richard_Branson_on_How_to_Leverage_Social_Media.

Clever Advertising

"Richard Branson: Life at 30,000 Feet." *TED Talks* (video), March 2007. http://www.ted.com/talks/richard_branson_s_life_at_30_000_feet.html.

Strong Branding

Richard Branson, "Brand—Flying the Flag." *Richard's Blog*. October 7, 2008. Richard Branson.

Fearlessness

Richard Branson, *Business Stripped Bare*, 2008. London: Virgin Books. 187.

Good Tagline

"Around the World: Cut-price Condom Offered in Britain." *Globe and Mail*, June 27, 1987.

Creating New Companies

"Richard Branson: Talking Management." Interview by Karl Moore (video), February 16, 2010. http://www.youtube.com/watch?v=DCXOnloZyYk.

Deserving Free Coverage

Richard Branson, *Reach for the Skies*, 2010. New York: Penguin. 36.

High-Quality David vs. Goliath

Interview by Tanya Beckett for the 2008 Lifetime Achievement Stevie Award (video), August 28, 2008. http://www.youtube.com/watch?v=5zsWrOA2ozA&list=PLA5249FCA83B66EA3.

Unprofessional Professional

Richard Branson, *Business Stripped Bare*, 2008. London: Virgin Books. 28.

People Departments

Peter Crush, "Exclusive: Sir Richard Branson talks to *HR* magazine about Leadership." *HR*, July 12, 2010. http://www.hrmagazine.co.uk/hro/features/1018119/exclusive-sir-richard-branson-talks-hr-magazine-leadership.

Philanthropy

"Richard Branson on Philanthropy," *Big Think* (video), June 2, 2011. http://www.youtube.com/watch?v=5wcqdKowpsI.

Brand Ambassadors

Richard Branson, "Make Employees Your Brand Ambassadors." *Open Forum by American Express*, June 9, 2011. http://www.openforum.com/articles/make-employees-your-brand-ambassadors/.

Throwing Parties

Richard Branson, *Business Stripped Bare*, 2008. London: Virgin Books. 257.

Questioning Leadership

Richard Branson, "Entrepreneurs and Leadership." *Richard's Blog*, December 10, 2008. http://www. virgin.com/richard-branson/blog/entrepreneurs-and-leadership.

Listening and Asking Questions

Richard Branson, *Business Stripped Bare*, 2008. London: Virgin Books. 267.

Firing

Richard Branson. *Business Stripped Bare*, 2008. London: Virgin Books. 263.

Collective Responsibility

Peter Crush, "Exclusive: Sir Richard Branson talks to HR magazine about Leadership." *HR*, July 12, 2010. http://www.hrmagazine.co.uk/hro/features/1018119/exclusive-sir-richard-branson-talks-hr-magazine-leadership.

People Motivators

"Richard Branson: Talking Management." Interview by Karl Moore (video), February 16, 2010. http://www. youtube.com/watch?v=DCXOnloZyYk.

In the Field

Carmine Gallo, "Richard Branson: If it Can't Fit on the Back of an Envelope, it's Rubbish (an Interview)." *Forbes*, October 22, 2012. http://www.forbes.com/sites/carminegallo/2012/10/22/richard-branson-if-it-cant-fit-on-the-back-of-an-envelope-its-rubbish-interview/.

Investigation

L. Erik Calonius, "How Richard Branson of Virgin Group Ltd. Is Taking Off in Britain—His Unconventional Business Makes Music and Films, and Now Runs an Airline—Some Cues From Sir Freddie." *Wall Street Journal*, August 20, 1984.

The Virtues of Telecommuting

Richard Branson, "One Day Offices Will Be a Thing of the Past." *Richard's Blog*, March 4, 2013. http://www.virgin.com/richard-branson/blog/one-day-offices-will-be-a-thing-of-the-past.

Good Leadership

"Richard Branson: Advice for Entrepreneurs," *Big Think* (video), June 2, 2011. http://www.youtube.com/watch?v=VH35Iz9veMo.

Delegating

Peter Crush, "Exclusive: Sir Richard Branson talks to *HR* magazine about Leadership." *HR*, July 12, 2010. http://www.hrmagazine.co.uk/hro/features/1018119/exclusive-sir-richard-branson-talks-hr-magazine-leadership.

"We" vs. "They"

Richard Branson, *Like a Virgin*, 2012. New York: Portfolio/Penguin. 52.

A Business Is Its People

Interview by Tanya Beckett for the 2008 Lifetime Achievement Stevie Award (video), August 28, 2008. http://www.youtube.com/watch?v=5zsWrOA2ozA&list=PLA5249FCA83B66EA3.

New Virgins

"Richard Branson," *A Day in the Life* (video), August 17, 2011. http://www.hulu.com/watch/268429.

People Management

Peter Crush, "Exclusive: Sir Richard Branson talks to *HR* magazine about Leadership." *HR*, July 12, 2010. http://www.hrmagazine.co.uk/hro/features/1018119/exclusive-sir-richard-branson-talks-hr-magazine-leadership.

Courage of Conviction

Richard Branson, *Like a Virgin*, 2012. New York: Portfolio/Penguin. 89.

Finding The Right People

Interview by Tanya Beckett for the 2008 Lifetime Achievement Stevie Award (video), August 28, 2008. http://www.youtube.com/watch?v=5zsWrOA2ozA&list=PLA5249FCA83B66EA3.

Bad Reflection

"Sir Richard Branson Full Video Interview 2011—Part 1 of 4," Interview by Michael Buerk (video), July 3, 2011. http://www.youtube.com/watch?v=d6v8bt3UBIg.

Life After Branson

"Richard Branson: Advice for Entrepreneurs," *Big Think* (video), June 2, 2011. http://www.youtube.com/watch?v=VH35Iz9veM0.

Flexibility

"Richard Branson: Talking Management." Interview by Karl Moore (video), February 16, 2010. http://www.youtube.com/watch?v=DCXOnloZyYk.

Taking Care of Employees

Richard Branson, *Screw Business as Usual*, 2011. New York: Penguin. 17.

Putting the Phone Away

Richard Branson, *Like a Virgin*, 2012. New York: Portfolio/Penguin. 107-108.

A Culture of Fun

"Richard Branson: Talking Management." Interview by Karl Moore (video), February 16, 2010. http://www.youtube.com/watch?v=DCXOnloZyYk.

Changing the Customer Relationship

"Virgin Mobile Presents: Our Higher Calling™" (video), March 14, 2012. http://newsroom.virginmobileusa.com/video/virgin-mobile-presents-our-higher-calling.

Customer Relations

Richard Branson, *Like a Virgin*, 2012. New York: Portfolio/Penguin. 66.

Experimentation and Adaptation

Richard Branson, "Innovation—a Driver for Business." *Richard's Blog*, November 27, 2008. http://www.virgin.com/richard-branson/blog/innovation-a-driver-for-business.

Expansion Can Be Complicated

Richard Branson, *Business Stripped Bare*, 2008. London: Virgin Books. 216.

Virgin Pulse

"Virgin Found Richard Branson," interview by Ed Baig. *USA Today*, October 14, 2003. http://cgi1.usatoday. com/mchat/20031015008/tscript.htm.

Knowing When to Get Out

Richard Branson, *Like a Virgin*, 2012. New York: Portfolio/Penguin. 47.

Too Much Overhead

Daniel F. Cuff, "Business People: A Record Entrepreneur Plans Cheap Air Fares." *New York Times*, April 10, 1984.

The Frontier of Opportunity

Richard Branson, *Screw Business as Usual*, 2011. New York: Penguin. 205.

Online Travel

Richard Branson, *Reach for the Skies*, 2010. New York: Penguin. 181.

Empty Houses = Business Idea

"Q&A: Sir Richard Branson, Founder of Virgin." *Luxury Travel Bible.* http://www.luxurytravelbible.com/ Luxury-Hotels.asp?active_page_id=441.

Moving On

"Mile High Chat with Branson and Huffington," *Digg Dialogg* (video), May 4, 2009. http://www.youtube. com/watch?v=tnWZzTudBOg.

Getting Answers

Richard Branson, *Business Stripped Bare*, 2008. London: Virgin Books. 220.

Things Not Done

Richard Branson, *Reach for the Skies*, 2010. New York: Penguin. 157.

Innovation and Intrapreneurs

Richard Branson, "Novak's Up For the Necker Cup." *Richard's Blog*, November 11, 2012. November 11, 2012. http://www.virgin.com/richard-branson/blog/novaks-up-for-the-necker-cup.

Predicting the Future

Richard Branson, *Business Stripped Bare*, 2008. London: Virgin Books. 126.

April Fool's

Richard Branson, "Virgin Atlantic Launches Glass-Bottomed Plane." *Richard's Blog*. April 1, 2013. http://www.virgin.com/richard-branson/blog/virgin-atlantic-launches-worlds-first-ever-glass-bottomed-plane.

Product Tie-Ins

L. Erik Calonius, "How Richard Branson of Virgin Group Ltd. Is Taking Off in Britain—His Unconventional Business Makes Music and Films, and Now Runs an Airline—Some Cues From Sir Freddie." *Wall Street Journal*, August 20, 1984.

Virgin Cola

"Allan Gregg: Richard Branson," *Allan Gregg in Conversation* (video), April 1, 2001. http://ww3.tvo.org/video/165195/richard-branson.

Improvements

Richard Branson, "Innovation—a Driver for Business." *Richard's Blog*, November 27, 2008. http://www.virgin.com/richard-branson/blog/innovation-a-driver-for-business.

Trial and Error

Richard Branson, *Reach for the Skies*, 2010. New York: Penguin. 158.

View from Space

Richard Branson, *Reach for the Skies*, 2010. New York: Penguin. 20.

Look out, NASA

"A Conversation with Richard Branson," interview by Bob Schieffer (video). Aspen Ideas Festival, July 5, 2007. http://www.aspenideas.org/session/conversation-richard-branson.

Life in Airplanes

Richard Branson, *Reach for the Skies*, 2010. New York: Penguin. 10.

Launching Virgin Atlantic

Daniel F. Cuff, "Business People: A Record Entrepreneur Plans Cheap Air Fares." *New York Times*, April 10, 1984.

Glamour

Richard Branson, *Reach for the Skies*, 2010. New York: Penguin. 158.

Post-9/11 Security

Richard Branson, *Reach for the Skies*, 2010. New York: Penguin. 158–159.

High Demand

Keith H. Hammonds, "A Music Master Takes Flight." *New York Times*, June 3, 1984.

The Airline Industry

"Virgin Found Richard Branson," interview by Ed Baig. *USA Today*, October 14, 2003. http://cgi1.usatoday. com/mchat/20031015008/tscript.htm.

Human Nature

Richard Branson, *Reach for the Skies*, 2010. New York: Penguin. 159.

All About Quality

"Virgin's Richard Branson Bares His Business 'Secrets,' *NPR*, October 10, 2012. http://www.npr. org/2012/10/10/162587389/virgins-richard-branson-bares-his-business-secrets.

Government Regulation

Interview by Tanya Beckett for the 2008 Lifetime Achievement Stevie Award (video), August 28, 2008. http://www.youtube.com/watch?v=5zsWrOA2ozA&list=PLA5249FCA83B66EA3.

Space Travel

Richard Branson, "This Isn't Sci-Fi." *Richard's Blog*,
    March 5, 2013. http://www.virgin.com/richard-
    branson/blog/this-isnt-sci-fi.

Mother-in-Law

"A Conversation with Richard Branson," interview
    by Bob Schieffer (video). Aspen Ideas Festival,
    July 5, 2007. http://www.aspenideas.org/session/
    conversation-richard-branson.

Turning Achievements into Business

Richard Branson, *Reach for the Skies*, 2010. New York:
    Penguin. 283.

Coming Down in One Piece

Richard Branson, *Reach for the Skies*, 2010. New York:
    Penguin. 316.

First Words in Space

"Richard Branson's First Words in Space," *Condé Nast
    Traveler* (video), July 13, 2010. http://www.youtube.
    com/watch?v=AmicVs8MVaQ.

Virgin Galactic is a US Company

Richard Branson, *Reach for the Skies*, 2010. New York:
    Penguin. 316–317.

New York–Australia in 30 Minutes

"A Conversation with Richard Branson," interview
    by Bob Schieffer (video). Aspen Ideas Festival,
    July 5, 2007. http://www.aspenideas.org/session/
    conversation-richard-branson.

Regrets?

"Richard Branson: Life at 30,000 Feet." *TED Talks* (video), March 2007. http://www.ted.com/talks/ richard_branson_s_life_at_30_000_feet.html.

Control

Richard Branson, *Reach for the Skies*, 2010. New York: Penguin. 25.

Taking Care of All Your Customers

"Death of One or Two Indian Airlines Is Necessary: Richard Branson" (video), October 26, 2012. http:// www.firstpost.com/business/why-richard-branson-is-shit-scared-of-indian-carriers-503471.html.

Waiting to Jump

"Richard Branson: Life at 30,000 Feet." *TED Talks* (video), March 2007. http://www.ted.com/talks/ richard_branson_s_life_at_30_000_feet.html.

The Seeds of a Business

Richard Branson, *Screw It, Let's Do It*, 2008. London: Virgin Books. 39–40.

George Clooney

Richard Branson, *Business Stripped Bare*, 2008. London: Virgin Books. 4.

Brad Pitt

Rosanna Greenstreet, "Q&A: Richard Branson." *Guardian*, April 2, 2010. http://www.guardian.co.uk/ lifeandstyle/2010/apr/03/richard-branson-interview.

Neckties

Vanessa Wong, "Why Richard Branson Won't Wear a
Tie." *Bloomberg Businessweek*, March 7, 2012. http://
www.businessweek.com/articles/2012-03-07/why-
richard-branson-wont-wear-a-tie.

Basic Needs

"Mile High Chat with Branson and Huffington," *Digg
Dialogg* (video), May 4, 2009. http://www.youtube.
com/watch?v=tnWZzTudBOg.

Boredom

Richard Branson, *Business Stripped Bare*, 2008. London:
Virgin Books. 4.

Business Should Be Fun

Richard Branson, *Like a Virgin*, 2012. New York:
Portfolio/Penguin. 20.

Dr. Yes

Rosanna Greenstreet, "Q&A: Richard Branson."
Guardian, April 2, 2010. http://www.guardian.co.uk/
lifeandstyle/2010/apr/03/richard-branson-interview.

Gumption

Richard Branson, *Screw It, Let's Do It*, 2008. London:
Virgin Books. 39–40.

Necker Island

"Mile High Chat with Branson and Huffington," *Digg
Dialogg* (video), May 4, 2009. http://www.youtube.
com/watch?v=tnWZzTudBOg.

Just Stuff

Richard Branson, *Screw Business as Usual*, 2011. New York: Penguin. x.

Mile High

"Salma Hayek, Richard Branson, The Dixie Chicks," *Late Night with Conan O'Brien* (video), August 27, 1998. http://www.youtube.com/watch?v=5BrKiG1cUPA.

Drug Use

Richard Branson, *Losing My Virginity*, 1998. 66.

It Runs in the Family

Richard Branson, "Don't Forget Your Mum." *Richard's Blog*, March 26, 2013. https://www.virgin.com/richard-branson/blog/dont-forget-your-mum.

Success and Failure

"Richard Branson: Advice for Entrepreneurs," *Big Think* (video), June 2, 2011. http://www.youtube.com/watch?v=VH35Iz9veMo.

You Only Live Once

Richard Branson, *Reach for the Skies*, 2010. New York: Penguin. 35.

Starting So Many Companies

"Sir Richard Branson Full Video Interview 2011—Part 3 of 4," Interview by Michael Buerk (video), July 3, 2011. http://www.youtube.com/watch?v=CLPA25FFpu8.

Daredevil

"Richard Branson Revealed." *Bloomberg Game Changers* (video), May 10, 2011. http://www.bloomberg. com/video/69540206-richard-branson-revealed-bloomberg-game-changers.html.

Board Meetings

Keith H. Hammonds, "A Music Master Takes Flight." *New York Times*, June 3, 1984. .

Virginity

"Salma Hayek, Richard Branson, The Dixie Chicks," *Late Night with Conan O'Brien* (video), August 27, 1998. http://www.youtube.com/watch?v=5BrKiG1cUPA.

It's Just Money

Richard Branson, *Business Stripped Bare*, 2008. London: Virgin Books. 326.

Knighthood

"Richard Branson: Life at 30,000 Feet." *TED Talks* (video), March 2007. http://www.ted.com/talks/richard_branson_s_life_at_30_000_feet.html.

Keep Your Friends Close...

Edited from an interview by Darrell Hartment, "20 Odd Questions: Sir Richard Branson." *Wall Street Journal*, April 22, 2012. http://online.wsj.com/article/SB10001424052702304432704577348122857214042.html.

21

Richard Branson, "21 and Over." *Richard's Blog*, March 7, 2013. https://www.virgin.com/richard-branson/blog/21-and-over.

It's Your Call

Richard Branson, *Like a Virgin*, 2012. New York: Portfolio/Penguin. 21.

Retiring

Michael Noer, "Richard Branson: Retire Like a Rock Star." *Forbes* (video), February 14, 2013. http://www.forbes.com/sites/michaelnoer/2013/02/14/richard-branson-retire-like-a-rock-star/.

Natural Interest

"Pop Tycoon Branson Is Used to Taking Chances." Houston Chronicle, July 4, 1980.

Shyness

"Sir Richard Branson Full Video Interview 2011—Part 1 of 4," Interview by Michael Buerk (video), July 3, 2011. http://www.youtube.com/watch?v=d6v8bt3UBIg.

Family Teamwork

Richard Branson, *Losing My Virginity*, 1998. 20.

Dyslexia and Entrepreneurship

Richard Branson, *Screw Business as Usual*, 2011. New York: Penguin. 55.

Age

Richard Branson, *Screw Business as Usual*, 2011. New York: Penguin. 13.

Advice

"Sir Richard Branson Full Video Interview 2011—Part 4 of 4," Interview by Michael Buerk (video), July 3, 2011. http://www.youtube.com/watch?v=SL-osALf1fs.

Enlightened Self-Interest

Richard Branson. *Business Stripped Bare*, 2008. London: Virgin Books. 289.

Giving Back

Richard Branson, *Screw Business as Usual*, 2011. New York: Penguin. 57.

It Doesn't Take Much

"Richard Branson on Philanthropy," *Big Think* (video), June 2, 2011. http://www.youtube.com/watch?v=5wcqdKowpsI.

They Should Do Something

Richard Branson, *Like a Virgin*, 2012. New York: Portfolio/Penguin. 119.

Super Power

Rosanna Greenstreet, "Q&A: Richard Branson." *Guardian*, April 2, 2010. http://www.guardian.co.uk/lifeandstyle/2010/apr/03/richard-branson-interview.

Jobs

Richard Branson, "Virgin Galactic Ethics." *Richard's Blog*, December 10, 2009.
http://www.virgin.com/richard-branson/blog/virgin-galactic-ethics.

Bees

Richard Branson, *Screw Business as Usual*, 2011. New York: Penguin. 220.

Decriminalizing Drugs

Richard Branson, *Like a Virgin*, 2012. New York: Portfolio/Penguin. 79.

Centre of Entrepreneurship

Richard Branson, "Richard Branson's School of Hard Knocks." *Open Forum by American Express*, August 27, 2010. http://www.openforum.com/articles/s-school-of-hard-knocks-1/.

Clean Technology

Richard Branson, *Business Stripped Bare*, 2008. London: Virgin Books. 309–310.

40 Years of Failing

"Branson's Big Idea for 2013, Presented by LinkedIn," interview by Daniel Roth (video), December 11, 2012. http://www.linkedin.com/today/post/article/20121211003406-204068115-big-idea-2013-this-year-the-war-on-drugs-ends.

Capitalism

"Oprah talks to Richard Branson." *O magazine*, December 1, 2007. http://www.oprah.com/world/Oprah-Interviews-Richard-Branson/2.

Diversity

Richard Branson, *Reach for the Skies*, 2010. New York: Penguin. 161.

Changing the World

Richard Branson, *Screw Business as Usual*, 2011. New York: Penguin. 2.

The War on Drugs

Richard Branson, "Time to End the War on Drugs." *Richard's Blog*, December 19, 2011. http://www.virgin.com/richard-branson/blog/time-to-end-the-war-on-drugs.

Paying It Forward

Richard Branson, *Screw Business as Usual*, 2011. New York: Penguin. 6.

Climate Change

Richard Branson, *Reach for the Skies*, 2010. New York: Penguin.265.

Fracking

Richard Branson, "Good Fracking and Bad Fracking." *Richard's Blog*, February 18, 2013. http://www.virgin.com/richard-branson/blog/good-fracking-and-bad-fracking.

In the Tub

Carmine Gallo, "Richard Branson: If it Can't Fit on the Back of an Envelope, it's Rubbish (an Interview)." *Forbes*, October 22, 2012. http://www.forbes.com/sites/carminegallo/2012/10/22/richard-branson-if-it-cant-fit-on-the-back-of-an-envelope-its-rubbish-interview/2/.

NRA

Richard Branson, "Time to Take a Stand Against the NRA." *Richard's Blog*, March 20, 2013. http://www.virgin.com/richard-branson/blog/time-to-take-a-stand-against-the-nra.

Capitalism 24902

Richard Branson, *Screw Business as Usual*, 2011. New York: Penguin. 19.

Using Position Wisely

Jason Ankeny, "Richard Branson on Building an Empire." *Entrepreneur*, June 19, 2012. http://www.entrepreneur.com/article/223639.

Making a Huge Difference

Richard Branson, *Screw Business as Usual*, 2011. New York: Penguin. 6.

Running a Charity Like a Business

Richard Branson, *Screw Business as Usual*, 2011. New York: Penguin. 33.

A WOMAN'S WAY

When Damaris Fanshawe was accepted by the famous University of Pennsylvania Medical School, she underwent the rigorous training and confronted the raw realities of life and death that were thought too brutal for any female to face.

She was a doctor now, doing what she most wanted to do in the world: tending the sick and suffering, and joining in the search for the cause and cure of the fearful scourge of Yellow Fever that was decimating the cities of the South.

But in the arms of Guy Parrish, son-in-law to the man who held Damaris in his power, and husband to a jealous beauty who would stop at nothing to destroy any rival, Damaris was no longer a doctor . . . she was a woman, with a woman's joy—and a woman's longing. . . .

⊘ SIGNET BOOKS

The Timeless Magic of Romance

The

HAND
of a
WOMAN

by *Diana Brown*

A SIGNET BOOK

NEW AMERICAN LIBRARY

NAL BOOKS ARE AVAILABLE AT QUANTITY DISCOUNTS WHEN USED TO PROMOTE PRODUCTS OR SERVICES. FOR INFORMATION PLEASE WRITE TO PREMIUM MARKETING DIVISION, NEW AMERICAN LIBRARY, 1633 BROADWAY, NEW YORK, NEW YORK 10019.

SIGNET TRADEMARK REG. U.S. PAT. OFF. AND FOREIGN COUNTRIES
REGISTERED TRADEMARK—MARCA REGISTRADA
HECHO EN CHICAGO, U.S.A.

SIGNET, SIGNET CLASSIC, MENTOR, PLUME, MERIDIAN and NAL BOOKS are published by New American Library, 1633 Broadway, New York, New York 10019

First Signet Printing, November, 1985

1 2 3 4 5 6 7 8 9

PRINTED IN THE UNITED STATES OF AMERICA

For my Armenian aunt,
Ashgen Devlet,
and my English aunt,
Maisie Clark,
with great affection.

Contents

*A doctor should have
the eye of a falcon,
the heart of a lion,
and the hand of a woman.*

DUTCH PROVERB

I wish to thank the gracious people of Memphis who were so helpful to me during my visit, especially those at the Memphis Public Library, Jeanne Crawford of the Memphis Chapter of the Association for the Preservation of Tennessee Antiquities, Jane Sanderson of the *Press-Scimitar*, and Melvon W. Swett of the Memphis Cotton Exchange.

I also wish to thank Bill Smart and the Virginia Center for the Creative Arts for allowing me time and a conducive environment in which to work on this novel.

And last, but not least, my thanks to my editor, Hope Dellon, for her painstaking care in following this work to its conclusion.

Diana Brown
February 1984

BOOK ONE

Damaris Fanshawe

The human heart has hidden
    treasures,
  In secret kept, in silence
    sealed;—
The thoughts, the hopes, the
    dreams, the pleasures,
  Whose charms were broken if
    revealed.

                Charlotte Brontë
                "Evening Solace"

ONE

"Come along, Mary, come along. Don't let Augustus dawdle like that. Do see to him. I've never known such a child for getting into everything. Never did any boy cause me half the grief of that one; but then, of course, previously I've only cared for little English gentlemen."

The sharp-edged tones of the solemn woman escorting two small girls along the railroad platform singularly matched her tall frame.

To Damaris Fanshawe, struggling to separate sturdy Augustus Caylew from a pillar he was attempting to climb, she sounded like a jail warden safeguarding inmates, or else a general marshaling forces. How will I ever get on with her? she wondered.

For a five-year-old, Augustus was surprisingly strong. With a child's intuition, he must have recognized her lack of authority and sensed her insecurity in her new position as assistant to an English nanny he despised, for he eluded her grasp. Clinging fast to the post he slowly circled it, all the while carefully making sure that Nanny Wickers's attention remained fixed on his younger sisters.

"Leave go, do, Augustus," Damaris pleaded urgently in a low voice. "Leave go; you're getting covered with grime."

Augustus might have only been five, but he had already assessed that the new nursemaid stood in even greater awe of Nanny Wickers than he did; and he blustered gleefully, though not loudly enough for Nanny to overhear, "Try and make me." And as Damaris again reached to grasp his arm, he shook free with "Don't hurt me, else I'll tell Mama you struck me."

15

"Augustus!" Her tone was shocked. "I would never hurt you or any child, never. Believe me, I could not. Come, give me your hand. The New York train will be here any minute."

Augustus, while not letting go of the post, stuck out his chest in bravado. "I'm a boy. I don't need anyone to hold my hand."

"Then maybe you'll hold mine. I've never been on a train before."

That was true. Damaris Fanshawe had never been farther from her Newport home than Providence. She was only eight years older than Augustus and the prospect of living in New York terrified her. But her candor did little to arouse sympathy in his breast.

"Sissy!" he hissed.

"Mary! What are you doing? Didn't I tell you to get Augustus away from that filthy pole? Aren't you listening to me? How can I expect obedience from the children if I don't get it from one who is paid to give it?"

Mrs. Wickers took one step in their direction, and Augustus immediately released his hold on the post without a word.

"Just look at him, will you? He's filthy, absolutely filthy! You must understand here and now, Mary, that when I give an order it is to be carried out, and carried out with alacrity. Is that quite clear?"

"Yes, I think so, except—" Damaris assented hesitantly.

"There are no exceptions."

Augustus grinned, making sure to turn his head away from Nanny Wickers as he did so. She had boxed his ears more than once; she could, he knew, lunge out quickly, without compunction, and her aim was deadly. Despite his threat to tell on the new nursemaid, he knew his mother not only upheld but applauded Nanny's discipline; the same would probably apply to this new assistant. He put on his blandest smile as he turned back to brush at the dust and grime, smearing it into his coat. He hadn't looked forward to another addition to the nursery staff, fearing the new nursemaid would be a replica of Nanny and further curtail his freedom; but now he'd seen what a ninny she was, he began to think that perhaps it wouldn't be so bad after all.

As Mrs. Wickers turned her attention to Beatrice and Eleanor, arguing over possession of a stuffed bear, Damaris urged, "Augustus, come here and I'll tell you a story until the train comes."

"Bet you only know silly fairy stories, silly girls' stuff!" he goaded, before leaping forward to bend down and put his ear to the railroad track.

"Augustus!" Damaris screamed, leaping after him, her cry joined by a shout from a gentleman standing beside a fashionable lady at some distance from the cluster of children and porters and mountain of baggage.

"Augustus, come back this instant. Do you hear me!" Templeton Caylew thundered.

At the sound of his father's voice, the boy bounded back, leaving Damaris to clamber up after him while he announced in innocent tones, "Mary told me that was how to tell if the train's coming. I was just checking to see if she was right."

Angered stares were trained upon Damaris from Templeton Caylew and his wife, but their looks paled beside the horrified mortification on Mrs. Wickers's face.

"I won't have my son learning such pranks, Mrs. Wickers. See to that."

"No, indeed, sir. Had I only interviewed the young woman before she was taken on . . ." she began reproachfully. "But there, I shall do what I can to train her. I can assure you that such a thing will never happen again."

Though Mr. Caylew nodded, the situation was scarcely alleviated by Augustus's bland cheer as the train pulled in. "There, you see, Mary was right. You *can* tell by listening to the tracks when the train's coming!"

As she helped the children into the special car assigned to the family, Damaris knew that her life in their service was not going to be easy. Still, when had her life ever been easy?

Almost immediately, Augustus, worn out by his pranks, fell asleep, and Damaris reached to draw his head onto her lap so that he might rest more easily. His face was so innocent in sleep that she clung to him, as much for her own reassurance as for his. Beyond his sleeping form, through the window, she could see the sea, the indented shoreline with houses clustered about, people waving, then pastures dotted with cows and trees, all dashing by at an alarming rate, faster than she would ever have believed possible. Receding with all of this was life as she'd known it; ahead lay an unknown existence among people who were virtual strangers.

Had she made a mistake? she wondered, her head swaying back and forth with the motion of the train. But what was the use of such speculation; she was embarked on the course begun by the arrival of that letter the previous fall.

She remembered picking it up from the brass tray in the rectory hall, turning it over in her hands, as instinctively she sensed disaster. She had been tempted to put it away or destroy it, as though, if unread, the news it contained would also disappear. Yet that was the attitude of an ostrich, not only ridiculous but totally unworthy. Steeling herself, Damaris had for the first time taken up her father's letter knife, silver with a jade dragon head, and slit open the envelope, carefully, neatly, almost imperceptibly. How many times when small she had wanted to do just that.

"Damaris, no!" Reverend Fanshawe admonished whenever she had reached for it. "It could hurt you."

The letter contained news that hurt beyond any injury the letter knife could inflict. Couched in carefully guarded phrases, nonetheless sincere in their obvious attempt to temper truth with compassion, Dr. Langmore Hunter, a chaplain with the Army of the Cumberland, serving with her father, informed them of the Reverend Fanshawe's death at the hands of a Confederate cavalryman at the Battle of Chickamauga in a struggle by the South to retain control of Chattanooga. Putting aside all thought of his own safety, he had gone out to rescue a wounded soldier. Before he could reach the man, a cavalryman in hot pursuit of another had cut him down. His gallantry had been commended by General Thomas himself.

It may be small comfort now, [*Dr. Hunter wrote,*] but you have every reason to be proud of Herbert Fanshawe as a husband, as a father, just as I am proud of him as a friend. He did not want the fight, but he went where he was most needed. And he died as he would have wished to die, helping those in need. It is bitter irony that death should have over-taken him on the banks of the Tennessee, in a battle hard-fought for the very state that gave him birth, but this war is filled with bitter irony.

Herbert, I know, deliberated long and hard over the conflict. Like Phinehas and the children of Israel, he asked God, "Shall I battle against my brother?" The Lord told him to go and he went. Now he is gone forever. He would not wish any of us to weep over him; still, I cannot control my tears. Oh, that this sorry business would end! ·

Her eyes glazed over the words—Chickamauga, Chatta-nooga, Tennessee—such names, names from a fairy story; no, not a fairy story but a story of wicked giants and ogres. To think of her father dying in such a place, a place so far away, a place so unlike home. Yet though strange and distant to her, Tennessee was the state of his birth. She remembered his tales of that great river, the Missis-sippi, that bordered Memphis, where he had been raised until nine and his parents died of the fever. Then he had come North to live with a relative who had educated him for the church. Her father had always promised to take her to that distant frontier, and until then she had always been eager to go. Now she hated Tennessee and all its people. They bore responsibility for taking her father's life, the life of a man who had harmed no one, who had gone to comfort, not to fight.

The letter said he had died on the twentieth of Sep-tember. Why, that was close to a month ago! All that time in his book-lined study she and her mother had sat together writing him mundane details of their lives; and all that time he had been dead.

Damaris, rereading Dr. Hunter's words, rebelled at that death as unfair, unjust. She felt anger as much as sadness. Besides, what use were tears? Her mother would cry enough for both of them.

Mathilda Fanshawe had never lived a life of her own; devoted to her own father, she had not married until his death. Being then closer to forty than thirty and in delicate health, she had surprised everyone by bearing a daughter whom Herbert Fanshawe had baptized Damaris after the

Athenian woman converted by St. Paul. Unprepared as they were for a child, indeed unused to the ways of children, each had coped with the addition to their union in his own way: Mathilda continued to live in and for her husband, while he treated his daughter, even from infancy, with kindness but with the respect and reserve more due an adult than a child.

As soon as Damaris was old enough to hold pen in hand and sit in a straight-back chair, she had joined the circle of young gentlemen sent to be tutored by the Reverend Fanshawe. She absorbed their lessons of grammar, reading, arithmetic, and Latin, to be tested upon her learning just as they were, the only difference being that at four o'clock they returned to their homes, whereas she then turned to help her mother with sewing, mending, and sometimes—though not often because her mother considered it frivolous—embroidery. It had been a relief to both parents that their daughter unquestioningly assumed the role to which she had been assigned. Certainly Mathilda Fanshawe's nerves would have stood for no boisterous or childish pranks.

Although only twelve at the time of her father's departure for the war, Damaris had carefully followed his instructions to care for her mother and to place her needs before all else. She eked out the allotments he sent home, making do without the tutorial fees that had always augmented his living, disguising economies so that life for her mother might continue unperturbed. They had been fortunate in that, pending the Reverend Fanshawe's return, the parish allowed them to remain in the spacious, comfortable vine-covered rectory. But Dr. Hunter's news had brought all that to an end. A new rector would be assigned; they would have to move and find some means of income to supplement their meager savings.

Grief became secondary to Damaris as she struggled with the pragmatic realities of her situation. She had become solely responsible for her mother's support. She was strong and willing, she would do anything, but she desperately needed someone to advise her how to go about it.

Then she remembered the day her father had announced from the pulpit his decision to join the Union cause. Though she knew her father had long brooded over the war—born in a state that had seceded from the Union it was a personal as well as a moral conflict—that had been the first intimation that he had decided to go. Without stopping to consider, she had thrown out her arms and had run down the aisle crying, "Why must you go, Papa? Why? Why?"

He had sternly admonished her for her outburst, but wealthy, powerful Templeton Caylew, who kept a summer home at Newport, had come forward to put an arm around her shoulders, comforting her with "Your father's right, little miss. He'll show those Johnny Rebs a thing or two. Don't worry your little head, my dear." And then she heard him turn to assure her father that if his family were ever in need they had but to turn to him. And so she had.

Mr. Caylew's reply to her letter had been cordial. He sent condolences and invited her to call to discuss the situation when next his family was in Newport. While the letter contained no promises, she was comforted by the thought of such an ally.

They had moved from the rectory to a tiny house near the harbor, a small, mean house after the comfort they had been used to, as her mother so constantly reminded her, but all they could afford. Such a drastic change in their manner of living following so closely upon the heels of her father's death only served to sustain her mother's grief, while Damaris, anxiously watching their dwindling resources, impatiently awaited the Caylews' return to Newport.

She would never forget how small, how insecure she had felt on the bright June day she had climbed the wide curved rhododendron-lined carriageway that led to their magnificent mansion. Her hand had trembled so that she had had to rap twice with the gleaming brass knocker on the double portal before a servant responded—then it was only to learn that the Caylews were not at home. Fearing if she left she would lack the courage to return—every step of the way she had wondered whether her letter had been forgotten, whether they might think she was begging rather than asking for honest work—she waited.

Though accustomed to adults, Damaris had never associated with people of the Caylews' social standing. Their opulent, extravagant way of life was foreign to her, almost more frightening than the dire poverty of some parishioners. She waited, sitting stiff and straight on the bench in the marble hall, studying the mural on the opposite wall, a replica of Tintoretto's *Paradiso*, an angel swathed in light driving Adam and Eve from the Garden of Eden. Surely angels would never cause such terror, and why did the angel cast his shadow before rather than behind him?

"Well, well, and what can we do for you, young lady?"

With a start, she heard Mr. Caylew's voice boom upon her reverie. He seemed even more alarming now that his tall figure was before her, his mustachioed face looking down at her, while the light from the lofty skylight above the curved staircase gleamed on his balding pate. No, she thought, her heart pounding, she had not the courage to talk to him.

She smiled in an attempt to cover her alarm and directed her attention to the lofty lady at his side. "I was waiting to speak to Mrs. Caylew, sir."

But the tall lady in the handsome blue drawn-silk bonnet, with low plumes brushing an unsmiling cheek, responded in flat tones, "Templeton, do take care of it, whatever it is. I have a headache."

"Very well, Isabel." He watched for a moment as the lady slowly climbed the wide marble staircase, his brows drawn together, his lips, though fuller than those of his wife, drawn together as tightly as hers had been. Then he turned back to command curtly, "Come along to the study."

Reluctantly she followed him to the oak-paneled room where he seated himself heavily behind a massive mahogany desk, waving her to a stiffly upholstered chair before him. "Now, what is it that I can do for you?"

He examined her briefly, with no particular interest, as she sat down smoothing straight the faded green percale of her skirt before tightly folding her dove-gray-gloved hands in her lap. When she started to speak, he had already turned to the stack of letters set out on the desk. It was not an auspicious beginning.

"I wrote to you some months ago, Mr. Caylew, concerning the death of my father at the Battle of Chickamauga." Noticing his brows furrow in puzzlement, she reminded him quickly but gently, "Reverend Herbert Fanshawe, the rector of this parish."

Mr. Caylew nodded, though he continued to slit open

the letter in his hands. "Ah, yes. My condolences to your mother, and to you, young lady." He shook his head, "It's a terrible war." His eyes strayed back to the letter he had now opened, scanning its contents as he repeated mechanically, "Terrible, terrible."

She waited for him to look back at her, making an effort not to think of the talk in town of the huge sums Templeton Caylew was said to be garnering from government contracts. It was rumored that he supplied, and was well paid for supplying, the Union army with ammunition; but there were also whispers that he aided the Confederate cause by buying up cotton to sell to the English market. "It's an ill wind that blows no one any good" was the more kindly proverb laid at his door.

As he made no further response, seeming lost in the letter in his hands, she cast a glance at his pursed lips, pale face, dark receding hairline, and neatly manicured hands unusually small for a man of his build. She waited silently as he read, until, apprehensive that he had forgotten her existence, she softly cleared her throat.

"Ah, yes." He looked up at last. "As I was saying, please convey Mrs. Caylew's and my own condolences to . . . to your mother, Mrs . . . . Mrs . . . ."

"Mrs. Fanshawe."

"Of course, of course, to Mrs. Fanshawe."

"Thank you, sir, I shall."

"And where was your father killed?"

"At Chickamauga," she reminded, "the battle fought for Chattanooga. He was born in Tennessee, but he went back there to serve as chaplain with the Army of the Cumberland, with General Thomas."

"Terrible!" Mr. Caylew shook his head. "Terrible too when those unholy bas— rebels mow down a man of God just as though he were a common soldier."

Damaris drew herself up. "My father was aware of the danger, Mr. Caylew. He expected no preferential treatment. He knew he would have to be in battle as much as and perhaps even more than most. He, I believe, much more than my mother or myself, was prepared for the fate that befell him. For that I am grateful."

"Well, I'm heartily sorry, nonetheless. You must tell

your mother so. If I can be of any assistance to her or to you I shall be only too happy."

She had hoped he would understand the reason she had come, would be prepared with some advice for her. In a faltering voice she went on to explain their straitened circumstances. "We have had to leave the rectory, for with father gone, so too is our home, our income. There is some talk that in the future there may be pensions for widows, but none is yet available, nor will be until hostilities cease."

"If the country is not by then bankrupt," Mr. Caylew pontificated gloomily.

"Quite so. So you see, with our savings all but gone, we find ourselves in immediate need of life's very essentials."

"I shall be glad to help you, my dear. I presume, however, that there are relatives to turn to for more permanent assistance."

She shook her head. "No, sir, none remain. It was because we have no one that I wrote to you. You had said when my father left for the war to turn to you if in need."

"Of course." He shifted uncomfortably in his chair. "Still, I suppose that the church has been of some help."

Again she shook her head. "Our parish is not wealthy, especially now. The new rector is hard put to serve those in far greater need than ourselves. We would never throw ourselves on the parish." As she saw Mr. Caylew reaching into his coat pocket she added swiftly, with a sense of shocked sensibility, "We do not beg, sir. We neither want nor expect charity. Please understand my purpose in applying to you—to seek your advice on how to earn an income."

"Your mother wishes employment?"

"No!" Damaris was even more shocked by the thought of her mother employed. "But I do."

It was Mr. Caylew's turn to evidence surprise. His dark, thick eyebrows shot up as he asserted, "But you, my dear, are no more than a child."

Holding her chin aloft, Damaris said proudly, "I'm past my thirteenth birthday, and I am strong even though I am slight. I have some learning: I read and write three languages, English, French, and Latin; my arithmetic, my father always said, was quite passable; I play the piano;

and my voice, though lacking in power, is true in tone. I write a fair hand. I can sew and embroider and knit. I bake and cook and—"

"Spare me, spare me, Miss Fanshawe." For the first time he smiled. "You are quite obviously a most accomplished young lady. But because you are a lady, I really don't quite know what you could do."

"I'll do anything . . . anything," she pleaded. "I really don't mind at all. I know you have several children, Mr. Caylew. Perhaps I might be useful as a governess, a nursemaid, anything."

"We already have Mrs. Wickers as nurse—or Nanny, as she insists on being called—to the younger children, and the boys have their tutor." He wrinkled his brow, hesitating. "I suppose she could use help, though goodness knows I pay her enough. Still, Isabel keeps insisting she's no servant. Looks to me as though we have to employ servants to wait on her. I'll be damned if I understand it." He shook his head, muttering half to himself, "She would insist that we hire an English nanny for the young ones. A plain Yankee like me finds little use in such tomfoolery."

Damaris, who remembered her mother's awe at discovering Mrs. Caylew had been a Vandervoort before marriage, while Mr. Caylew's origins remained a mystery, felt an unexpected wave of sympathy. As he rose with an air of finality, she also rose, awkwardly pushing back her chair.

He smiled, perhaps finally sensing her discomfort, and reached over to pat her gloved hand consolingly. "There, Miss Fanshawe, you leave it to me. There will be a place for you somewhere in the Caylew household."

And Mr. Caylew had been as good as his word. Within a week, Damaris Fanshawe received word she had been given a position as assistant nursemaid and should be ready to leave for New York with the family at the end of the summer, with half her annual salary advanced on the appointment. It was a generous gesture; whatever anyone might say of his self-interest, Damaris vowed she would be forever grateful to Templeton Caylew. Since she would receive board and uniforms, practically all her earnings could go to her mother.

Though apprehensive at leaving the only place she had ever known, the solution to what had seemed an insurmountable problem was a great relief. The very idea of New York was terrifying, but in the face of Mathilda Fanshawe's trepidation at being left alone, Damaris put aside her own fears to play the role of comforter, reminding her mother that the Caylews always summered in Newport and she would return there with them each year. Even as she did so, she wondered how it might be to have someone to turn to as Isabel Caylew had turned to her husband with "Templeton, do take care of it, whatever it is." Would she, the comforter, ever be comforted?

Encountering the Caylews at church the Sunday before Damaris was to leave, her mother had effusively thanked Mrs. Caylew, who responded vaguely and had to be reminded by her husband that this was the girl taken on to assist Mrs. Wickers in the nursery.

"Yes, of course." She had smiled distantly. "And your name?"

"Damaris Fanshawe, ma'am."

"Mary—Mary will do."

"Very well, ma'am."

And so, as Mary Fanshawe, she found herself clutching Augustus's head on her lap as the train bearing the Caylew family and the insufferable Mrs. Wickers steamed and groaned its way toward a city with an even louder roar.

TWO

The first time Damaris actually saw Mother Charlotte was the Sunday Augustus Caylew shot one of his speedballs—a messy damp wad of paper—at his Vandervoort cousin, who saw it coming and dodged. She watched in horrified fascination as the missile narrowly missed the man beside him to land squarely on the back of the dark-robed figure in the front pew, who turned in surprise; then her generous lips pursed into a suppressed smile at the sight of Damaris's stricken face, and slowly but quite distinctly Mother Charlotte winked.

As a member of the Caylew household, Damaris regularly attended Sunday service at fashionable St. Stephen's; and from the first she had singled out for special attention the small group of black-robed women who sat in the front pew on the epistle side. Because of their dark habits, decorated only by a heavy crucifix at the neck, their starched square-cut collars, and most particularly because of their high flaring white headdresses, they stood out from the rest of the congregation. They seemed to be nuns—she would have liked to ask them if they were, for she had never heard of an Episcopal order—but they kept to themselves, never even looking around, until that morning when Mother Charlotte winked.

Damaris didn't think Mrs. Wickers, whose expression was anything but amused, had seen the wink; but she knew beyond any doubt she would be in for another lecture when the service was over. Ever since her arrival she'd been in trouble of one sort or another.

She had had a difficult time adjusting to the change, though not because of the city itself. She'd seen virtually

nothing of New York except for a brief glimpse on the ride
from the train station to the Caylews' fashionable establishment on Park Avenue, or these Sunday excursions
to the nearby Fifth Avenue church. Her world was con-
fined to the nursery, to the bare room under the roof that
she shared with two parlormaids, and to the very much
more comfortable premises occupied by Mrs. Wickers,
who commanded not only a bedroom of her own but also a
comfortable sitting room, where she took her meals in
solitary splendor, eschewing all contact with the servants'
quarters.

It was there Damaris reported each morning while Mrs.
Wickers sat tall and erect sipping on tea and spreading her
toast with the orange marmalade sent from England. Once,
when she hadn't been looking, Damaris had tasted a little
from the end of the spoon and found it horribly bitter. No
wonder she enjoys it so, she had thought.

It had not taken Damaris long to discover that Mrs.
Wickers was as heartily disliked by the other servants as
she was by the children, but both servants and children
stood in awe of the English nanny. Neither servant nor
mistress, Mrs. Wickers existed in a limbo that allowed her
no friends but many enemies. If that concerned her, she
gave no sign, treating any amicable overture with scorn at
worst, indifference at best.

Damaris learned to stand silently as she received her
orders for the day, which invariably ended with the statement "I expect implicit obedience both from you and the
children, implicit obedience. Is that understood?"

"Yes, Mrs. Wickers."

"How are you getting along in the servants' hall?"

"Quite well, Mrs. Wickers," she would always reply,
never voicing her humiliation at the taunts and jeers so
often directed at her, none of which she understood. She
suffered through meals, tormented by those who found her
ways too dainty, who chided her for supposing herself
above the rest of them, taunted her if she spoke, accused
her of being sullen if she did not speak. She could please
no one, certainly not the two parlormaids whose room she
shared; they were best friends and never let her forget she
was an intruder.

"And the children, especially that nasty little Augustus, are they behaving equally well when I am not there?"

"Yes, Mrs. Wickers," she would reply again, never owning to the way the children vented all their anger and frustration upon her as soon as the nursery door closed behind Nanny. They took her compassion for weakness. Not only would they refuse to do her bidding, but, organized by Augustus, they would often turn on her, abusing her even to the point of punching and kicking her. She tried to hide the bruises, using her dress for a tent as she undressed each night, but her roommates had noticed the marks on her arms and soon spread the word through the servants' hall that the new nursemaid possessed no authority at all, not even in her own domain over a trio of toddlers.

Had Mrs. Wickers's connections with the servants been closer, she would have known Damaris was lying. But however much the servants might complain of having to wait on her, sniffing, "Thinks she's Queen Victoria, that one," they would never say a word to her face, for Mrs. Wickers had the ear of the mistress. The servants handled her with care, but they made her new assistant their special scapegoat.

"That lot in the nursery may be cunning little bastards, but only a fool would suffer abuse from the little snots" was the general consensus below, but they said nothing to Mrs. Wickers. Nor did Damaris, who suffered in silence.

Her greatest pleasure came in listening to the sermon on Sunday, for the rector of St. Stephen's was Dr. Langmore Hunter, the chaplain who had been her fathers friend. He too had been a casualty of the war, wounded so that he had had to return to civilian life. Damaris vowed one day to tell him who she was, but after the service he was always surrounded by his wealthy and elegant parishioners, and invariably her courage failed her.

It failed her once again that morning, for on rising at the conclusion of the service, a glance toward the gloating faces of the Caylews' servants in the back pews showed that they had seen everything and knew, just as Damaris knew, that she was in even greater disfavor than usual.

"Don't dawdle, Mary. Report to me in my room as soon as we get back," Mrs. Wickers whispered sternly as she grasped Augustus in her iron grip and marched him ahead of her to the waiting carriage, leaving Damaris to take care of Beatrice and Eleanor.

"One thing about Nanny being mad at you, Mary, is she leaves us alone," Eleanor remarked factually.

"Gus'll catch it, though," Beatrice muttered darkly.

"Don't call Augustus 'Gus,' Bee," Eleanor answered primly. "Mama says that's uncouth and common."

"Don't call me 'Bee' then, or else *you'll* catch it," Beatrice threatened.

"I just hope none of you is going to catch it," a sympathetic voice behind put in, and Damaris turned to find beneath the flaring white headdress the kindest face she'd ever seen, calm and clear, with large, lively eyes under straight brows, and a downright cheery smile. "I well remember how bored I used to get in church when I was little. I don't want anyone to be punished on my account. I'm not in the least perturbed by that little incident."

"Are you really a nun?" Damaris blurted out.

"I'm sorry; I should have introduced myself. I'm Mother Charlotte of the Order of St. Catharine, and yes, I am a nun."

"But I thought only Roman Catholics took the veil."

"A thought shared by a number of Episcopalians, too many of whom, I've been led to believe, heartily wish that were so." Mother Charlotte laughed. It was a hearty laugh with nothing ethereal about it, and for that reason it fitted her perfectly. "Dr. Hunter was instrumental in founding this Episcopal order with me, but I'm afraid many wish both him and me at the devil for our pains. Dear me, I really shouldn't say such things in church. Forgive me. One of my many problems is saying whatever is on my mind. Now you know about me, you must tell me who you are."

"Eleanor and Beatrice are the younger daughters of Templeton Caylew." Damaris indicated her charges, adding as an afterthought, "And I'm Damaris Fanshawe."

"Fanshawe?" a voice behind them repeated. "I served with a Fanshawe—Herbert Fanshawe, a dear friend he was too—dead at Chickamauga." The rector caught sight of Damaris's stricken face and added quickly, "No relation of yours, I trust."

"My father," she put in quickly.

"I'm so sorry, so very sorry. But I thought Herbert was from Rhode Island, at least that is where I wrote . . ."

As briefly as she could, Damaris explained her changed circumstances, while Dr. Hunter nodded sympathetically.

"If ever you're in need . . ." he began.

"I don't know about Miss Fanshawe being in need, but we could certainly use one of her obvious capability at Mercy House," Mother Charlotte put in. "Why don't you bring her along some time. Dr. Hunter is the chaplain of our order," she explained.

"How did you ever come to do something so . . . so magnificent as to found an order?"

At the look of awe on Damaris's face, Mother Charlotte laughed again. "It's more often downright onerous than magnificent. As for a reason, though I'd like to say it was piety, very frankly, I'm inclined to believe it was because my younger sister founded Chartwell—that's a Virginia academy for the higher education of young ladies—and I was simply not to be outdone."

"Come, come, that's scarcely fair." Dr. Hunter turned to Damaris. "The work of Mother Charlotte and the sisters of her order speaks entirely for itself. As their chaplain, all too often I feel it is they who should be ministering to me instead of the other way round. Don't take my word for it, though, Miss Fanshawe. Come and see for yourself."

"I'm only free on Wednesday afternoon."

"Wednesday, then, we shall expect you," Mother Charlotte enjoined. "But I warn you, we shan't let you be idle."

There were a thousand questions Damaris wanted to ask, but Beatrice and Eleanor's fidgets were threatening to become rambunctious, and over their heads she caught the cold glare of Mrs. Caylew.

"Till Wednesday, then."

The scene that followed in Mrs. Wickers's sitting room was as unpleasant as any that had gone before it. In addition to other faults, Mrs. Wickers had been mortified by Mrs. Caylew's complaint that Damaris had been conversing after church when she was being paid to look after the children. Mrs. Wickers had explained that undoubtedly she must have been apologizing for Augustus's conduct.

Damaris did not dispute this, although in the excitement of talking with Mother Charlotte she'd all but forgotten the incident that had led to their meeting.

She did, however, apologize to Mrs. Wickers, adding, "I had no idea Augustus would let fly with one of his speedballs."

"Speedballs?" Mrs. Wickers questioned sharply.

"That's what he calls them. He chews up pieces of paper, wads them together, and—"

"Spare me these disgusting details! You knew about this, then?"

"I didn't know he had one with him."

"But you knew he had this revolting practice and you failed to break him of it or bring it to my attention?"

"I didn't encourage him, but he is a child, a little boy, and—"

"This will not do! This simply will not do!" Mrs. Wickers rapped the table sharply with the edge of her hand, as she did when chastising the children. "I did not ask you to explain to me who Augustus is. I'm only too well aware of who—and what—Augustus is."

"I only meant that—"

"I did not ask you what you meant. I do not seek your opinions on anything. I expect you, on the other hand, not only to seek to know mine but to engrave them on your heart. You would do well to remember that, Mary, if you wish to survive in this household."

Damaris nodded, though her blood was rising in anger. It was no wonder that the children despised Nanny. She could even understand their behavior toward her, for to them she represented the Englishwoman's authoritarian rule.

"I'll not have any sulking from you or the children. You will always give me an answer."

Damaris nodded again, but added quietly, "Sulking is not a habit of mine, Mrs. Wickers."

"It's as well, for I loathe that above all. I expect you to carefully observe my manner of handling those children in the nursery, and to ensure that when I am not there you act in precisely the same manner with them. I am attempting to train you to become a good nurse, just as I have trained other young women in England."

She paused, examining Damaris thoughtfully. "I come from a well-to-do family in London. My father is an established tea merchant, a supplier to royalty, and finer by far than most of the so-called gentlemen in this city. You, I am told, are not of the servant class. Your father, I believe, is a clergyman."

"My father is dead, Mrs. Wickers," Damaris said coldly, adding, "and unlike England, in America there are no classes."

"Pish and poppycock! I'll not have any of that equality rubbish from you, Mary. Your much-vaunted equality is nothing but a myth devised to appease the lower orders who pine for it. Do you think Templeton Caylew considers his butler equal to himself? Of course that lazy good-for-nothing is no more equal to Mr. Caylew than Mr. Caylew is the equal of Lord Rossmore, my previous employer. This declaiming of all men being born equal is nonsense. We all know there is only one place where equality exists, and that is in the cemetery."

Had Damaris not been goaded more than usual that morning, she might have continued silent, but Mrs. Wickers had touched on a topic dear to her father's heart, one on which he had preached most firmly both from the pulpit and in the privacy of their home. Deference to her position was thrown to the winds.

"We are all equal before God. The Declaration of Independence states as a self-evident truth that in this country we are born equal."

"I've no patience with that rebellious rhetoric. Self-evident truth, indeed! Just show me two trees that are the same, two blades of grass even. Hold out your hand."

Reluctantly Damaris stretched out her hand, fingers outspread, and Mrs. Wickers triumphed. "There, see for yourself, you have five fingers, but no two are equal, are they?"

But as Damaris began to lower her hand to her side, Mrs. Wickers leaned forward to grasp her wrist.

"What is this?" she demanded, catching sight of a scratch that Beatrice had inflicted the night before as she had fought against going to bed.

"An accident—it's nothing."

But instead of dropping her arm, Mrs. Wickers unbuttoned the starched uniform cuff to pull up the sleeve and reveal the black and blue marks on her arm.

"Nothing! Is this nothing? How did this happen? Tell me. I demand to know the truth." And when Damaris said nothing, she said, "It's those little savages in the nursery, isn't it? How long has this been going on?"

Damaris pulled down her sleeve, and buttoning her cuff she said, "It doesn't hurt."

"I didn't ask if it hurt. That's your business. Order in the nursery is mine. I asked you how long this has been going on. Just answer my question."

"Mrs. Wickers, I'm not one of your charges. You have no right to speak to me like a child."

Damaris's eyes had welled with tears, and surprisingly Mrs. Wickers's voice softened as she responded. "You're little more than a child yourself, Mary, for all your adult airs. And I'm quite sure you never pinched and beat your nurse when you were their age."

"I never had a nurse."

"Well, your mother, then?"

"Of course not!" Her shock at such a question was evident.

"Then why did you allow these little beasts to treat you so? Or at least why did you not tell me, instead of replying, 'Yes, Mrs. Wickers,' whenever I asked if they were behaving?"

"Because they're children. They may be spiteful sometimes, but it is because they know no better."

"Oh, they know better, all right, and that's what is most disturbing to me. I'm not one for sparing the rod and spoiling the child."

"Please, Mrs. Wickers, don't harm them. They're children. Give a child love and eventually the child will give back everything."

"Give a child his will and he'll never thrive," the Englishwoman countered. "I shall see that this never happens again, but you must give me your solemn oath to report any and every infraction of the nursery rules. Certainly striking their nurse is against every principle I stand for. Is that quite clear?"

"Yes, Mrs. Wickers."

"Don't say, 'Yes, Mrs. Wickers,' in that tone. It makes

me think you don't intend to obey any more than those awful children. And they *are* awful children; I assure you they are. I don't believe this Christian twaddle about the perfection of the child. Our renowned poet Pope has said that as the tree is bent so the branches are inclined. I should like you to remember that. Remember too that I hold this position because I have had great experience in raising children of the finest families. I took it only after Mrs. Caylew had agreed to allow me absolute authority in the nursery. She wants these younger ones to grow into ladies and gentlemen, not like those other hoydens of hers; and I intend to accomplish just that, no matter how difficult it may be to instill English culture into them.

"I've no illusions about the difficulty of my task—Mrs. Caylew should have started such discipline at birth—but I intend to accomplish it, and you are here to help me do it. Just look at the older boys, Lawrence and Nathan, disobedient, won't listen to their tutor, won't buckle down and work. I know; he's talked to me about it. It comes of having too much freedom when they were small. I can't think why their father allowed it, but then he seems only to care for his precious Eustacia. She may be a beauty, but she's conceited and spoilt. I regard my position here as a challenge. These three have been following in the footsteps of the others. They're ill-mannered, rambunctious, disobedient, unkind—"

"Perhaps if you didn't tell them all of that quite so often they might not so easily fit the picture you paint of them."

"I daresay you tell them sweet and loving things and get punched and bruised for your kind words by those nasty Yankee brats."

Damaris raised her head sharply. "I'm a Yankee, Mrs. Wickers. I'm proud to be a Yankee. I'll not have anyone run down Yankees."

"Yankees are rough and uncouth. In England we find Southerners far more to our liking in their manners and habits."

Her eyes shining dangerously, Damaris cried out, "You'll take that back, Mrs. Wickers. You've said enough. My father died in the cause of the North. I'll not have you say he died for nothing. There are no good Southern gentlemen, only slaveholding rabble. Do you understand!"

It was the first time Damaris had ever lost her temper. She began striking out at Mrs. Wickers's hard frame, much as Augustus so often struck out at her; but unlike Augustus she did no harm, for just as Mrs. Wickers controlled Beatrice or Eleanor's flailing limbs, so she took hold of both of Damaris's wrists and held them fast.

"Enough, quite enough." The words were quiet, firm, and clearly to be obeyed. Damaris, ashamed of herself, lowered her head and tried not to cry. She had acted like a maniac. She must surely be dismissed for turning on the one she was employed to assist. Indeed, she thought she deserved to be dismissed.

Miserably she stood aside as Mrs. Wickers asked, "Are you quite finished?" before turning to pull the bell rope, which was answered by one of the maids with whom Damaris shared her bedroom. How she would enjoy telling the news of this latest contretemps downstairs! Damaris could just imagine the reception they'd have waiting for her and decided she preferred to go hungry rather than run the gauntlet of their taunts.

"From now on I want two places laid here. Mary will be taking her meals with me. And you can set up a cot in the corner of this room for her. She'll sleep here. This is closer to the nursery than the room upstairs."

The maid's eyes passed from Damaris to Mrs. Wickers with a look of complicit understanding as she replied in a monotone touched with insolence, "Yes, Mrs. Wickers."

"You'll repeat those words in a different tone, young woman, or you can expect a rebuke from your mistress. Do I speak plainly enough?"

"Yes, Mrs. Wickers." This time she spoke without innuendo.

"Then you may go."

"I don't understand," Damaris began as the door closed behind the maid.

"What is it you don't understand?"

"It is I who assaulted you, who was rude to you; the maid said or did nothing objectionable."

"I beg to differ. She's saucy, that one. You, on the other hand, are forthright; and that, though at times dangerous, is not altogether a fault."

"How did you know I was unhappy with the others downstairs at meals and upstairs at night?"

"It's not hard to guess. I started out belowstairs too. No one can be harder on servants than they are on one another. It's plain to me that you are young, innocent, and refined. If anyone is to overcome that refinement, to teach you what you must know, I claim that right."

She smiled. It was the first time Damaris had ever seen her smile; and it was as strange as it was unexpected to see the creases iron out of those perpetually pursed lips to bare teeth, straight enough though yellowed by her unending consumption of tea.

With that smile began a close though uneven association between Damaris and Mrs. Wickers, who instructed her not only on order in the nursery but on anything and everything else: the superior management of English households; the rudeness of American servants; the necessity of keeping all males at arm's length, for all were after you-know-what; the impudence and want of manners in American children compared with their English counterparts; the lack of flavor of American food and its inept preparation (just imagine serving corn, something reserved for animals in England); the elegance and charm of London ladies compared with those in New York, who, though handsome enough, were horribly provincial. The only exception was the Caylews' eldest daughter, but Eustacia had been given her own way too often; she was brash, too sure of herself. She should be sent to London to learn grace.

It was a diatribe of English nationalism, much of it derived from Frances Trollope's *Domestic Manners of the Americans* that served as Mrs. Wickers's bible. Despite Mrs. Wickers's Anglicanism, Damaris often wondered, quite blasphemously, if it weren't Mrs. Trollope she worshipped rather than God.

Nevertheless, from that time on, the relationship between the English nanny and her assistant gradually turned from hostility to friendship. Damaris might still decry Mrs. Wickers's anti-Americanism, but she came to understand the necessity for creating order in the nursery. She could not agree that harsh discipline was preferable to love, but since it had become apparent to the children that Mrs. Wickers would reprimand them for any insults or injuries inflicted on the new nursery maid, their assaults had stopped. They even began to appreciate her kindness, seeking her out, confiding in her, and obeying her instructions more quickly than they did those of Nanny.

Sometimes in the evening before retiring to her cot in the corner and kneeling to say her prayers, a habit she refused to relinquish despite Mrs. Wickers's scoffing, Damaris would be invited to sit before the fire and take the tiniest toddy while Mrs. Wickers read aloud from Mrs. Trollope's virulent diatribe.

"Why does it concern you so; you seem not to be particularly religious?" Damaris asked one night after Mrs. Wickers had read a section on the offensive familiarity of revivalist ministers calling everyone brother and sister, and the mockery they made of worship.

"I hate hypocrisy, Damaris. And here there is so much of it. This man who employs us, what a hypocrite he is, and his wife."

"But surely there are hypocrites in England? Lord and Lady Rossmore, were they without fault?"

"Noblesse oblige, Mary, noblesse oblige."

Damaris sighed. "I find it hard to understand why you ever came to America, since you seem to hate it so."

Mrs. Wickers leaned back in her chair, her glass of port in her hand, staring into the fire, not replying for so long that Damaris thought she must not have heard her. The response, when it came, was the last thing Damaris expected.

"It's not an unusual story, an unfaithful lover."

"Oh, I'm . . . I'm sorry."

"Never trust any one, Mary. They're all liars in the end."

"But not your husband, surely!"

"My husband! I never had a husband," Mrs. Wickers snorted.

"But . . . but I don't understand. You are *Mrs.* Wickers."

"My dear girl, I invented him. I went into service because my father wanted to force me into marriage. He never forgave me for choosing such an alternative to the dolt he had picked out for me. But then I discovered myself considered a fit object for the disgusting attentions of every footman with a well-shaped calf. How I despised their presumption! I'm a determined woman, Mary; you know that. I made myself indispensable to my mistress, and I soon raised myself above the level of the other servants. It caused a lot of jealousy. Does here too, I daresay. But I ignore it. My reputation as a nanny grew. When Lady Rossmore took me away from Lady Carne, whose husband was only a baronet, after all, I simply went as *Mrs.* rather than Miss Wickers. That and the separate quarters I insisted upon satisfactorily took care of any presumptuous ideas on the part of butlers or majordomos. I want you to promise me, Mary, that you will tell me immediately should any one of those louts below try to—"

"To what?"

"To force you to submit to . . . anything. Promise me."

"Of course, Mrs. Wickers, though I'm not sure—"

"And, Mary, when we're alone like this, you may call me Angela, but never in front of the children, and never, ever before the servants."

"Yes, Mrs. . . . . Angela."

Angela Wickers had already returned to Trollope. "She was astute, that woman. She wouldn't compromise with falsehood; that's why they hated her. And your own Mark Twain said she spoke in plain and honest terms without gilding or whitewashing anything. He found her deserving of gratitude rather than resentment. And after all, she didn't dislike everything in America; she said the blackberries here were the finest to be found anywhere, and on that point I must agree with her."

What an enigma she was, Damaris thought, watching the straight outline of her face in the glow of the fire. She longed to ask about the unfaithful lover who had forced Angela Wickers from England. She could never imagine her having a lover, though she was what her mother would have described as a fine-looking woman. Sometimes, as she lay still on her cot before going to sleep, Damaris would quietly observe the doyenne of the nursery as she sat, Mrs. Trollope opened before her in her lap, not reading but dreaming. Was she dreaming of that lover from whom she had fled?

And sometimes Angela Wickers would turn suddenly to stare across at her in a way she could not understand. Her mother had never looked at her so; in fact, no one had ever looked at her quite like that.

THREE

Damaris had gone to Mercy House with Dr. Hunter, as she had promised. The journey to the upper west side of the city, taking the horsecar right to the end of the line, with a two-mile walk beyond, was the first of what was to become a Wednesday afternoon ritual for her.

Mercy House, Dr. Hunter explained, was a mansion that had once known elegance, loaned to the order by a wealthy and sympathetic widow for use as an infirmary until sufficient funds were raised for their goal—a hospital for children. Since the sisters had only the most slender means at their disposal, that goal seemed far distant.

He had the greatest difficulty in finding donors for a sisterhood branded popish by church authorities and laymen alike, criticized for its vows of poverty and chastity, voluntary though they were, for reading the breviary, for observing silence at meals, even for praying too often!

"But I won't give up, Damaris," Dr. Hunter had insisted as they walked. "And you'll understand why after you've seen the sisters at work—and under such difficult conditions. With the barest essentials they care for sick children no one wants: for orphans, for those whose parents are destitute, or for children whose mothers are serving prison terms. And all is done with loving devotion; the more unpleasant and difficult their work, the more cheerful they become. They make of their work a reward in itself—you'll not hear a word of complaint—though it's work no one else will undertake. What difference does it make whether they pray once or seven times a day—or not at all—when their actions speak for their intentions. Here we are. You'll see what I mean."

They hurried up the steps of a dilapidated house that now lacked all former adornment. The sisters had begged and borrowed to convert the lower rooms into a clinic. The walls of the long room, once a ballroom, were lined with beds, squeezed as close to one another as space would allow. Cots and litters were also to be found in every nook and hallway. The sisters lived upstairs, where they had their own refectory, a small chapel, and bedrooms that had been divided into tiny bare cells. They seemed to have precious little time for sleeping, however, for their day began before light dawned and went long into the night.

Dr. Hunter told Damaris he had been chosen as their chaplain partly because he championed their cause, partly because he was distantly related to Mother Charlotte, but mainly, he added laughingly, because no one else would take the job. Mother Charlotte was a paradox who read St. John of the Cross and St. Augustine and Goethe and Voltaire with equal relish. She wrote poetry after the romantic style of Shelley and Keats, yet there was little of the aesthete or romantic about her. She was thoroughly practical, more real than life itself.

Large, capable, and intense, Mother Charlotte was not only an indefatigable worker but also a superb organizer. Damaris had barely been greeted before Mother Charlotte thrust a pan of water, a solid bar of soap, and a washcloth into her hands.

"Wash up, there's a dear, and then clean up little Frank O'Connor's leg, if you will, while I finish taking care of his sister, little Vicky. That watchman turned his dog on them again. I am so very angry. I've told them to avoid him at all costs, for my talks to the man have been useless; he seems not to have a kind or understanding bone in his body. He may be, as he tells me, only doing his job, protecting property; still the methods he uses are inhumane. Don't mind Frank's language now, and be sure to get all the dirt out, so I can dress the leg properly." And then, as an afterthought, she added, "Hope the sight of blood doesn't upset you."

Though Damaris shook her head, she'd never really seen blood, not blood the way it was oozing from the leg of the ragged and bony little urchin.

If she eyed him with awe, his appraisal of her was

distinctly critical. "For Chrissake, do something. Don't just stand there."

He was a frail figure, but the expression on his pale, narrow face was definitely pugnacious. While the sight of his wound sickened her, she realized he must be in great pain and started to work, gingerly at first, then gently but steadily, sponging away at the raw and bleeding flesh, flinching at each groan, each oath he uttered, trying to hide her own qualms with reassurance.

"It'll be all right, Frank. Wait till Mother Charlotte gets it dressed. I've got to get the dirt out, though; otherwise it could get poisoned. Bear with me. I'm new at this. Look at the buttons on my dress; see how bright and shiny they are. Can you count them?"

"What would I want to count'em fer?" he scoffed.

"Can you?" she asked matter-of-factly.

"Course I can."

"Well, do it then," she insisted as she applied herself to her task.

"One, two, three—ouch! Jeeesus!"

"Go on. There are more than that."

"Five—"

"You forgot four," she said, forcing her voice to be calm now that she had reached the deepest, the most raw, most tender part of the wound.

"Ooouch," he yelled, and again, "Ooouch! It hurts like hell, it does. Christ! You're killing me bad as the watchman and his dog almost did."

"It must have been a big dog to cause a gash like this."

"It weren't that old mutt. I could've fended him off, but he held on while that old bastard laid into me with his stick. Got me good this time, he did. Vicky too. Bastard!"

"Oh, Frank!" And then as he groaned again, "Oh, Frank! I'm being as careful as I can, but I know I must be hurting you terribly. I'm sorry. I've just never done anything like this before. Bear with me. Help me, will you?"

"Help you! That's bleedin' rich, that is! You're killin' me and you want me to help you do it!"

His aggression startled her, yet she suspected much of it was bravado. His eyes glistened in pain as much as anger, but she sensed that sympathy would not help, so, still working at the wound, sponging away the dirt from the raw flesh, she reminded him calmly, "You got to four buttons; there are many more than that."

"You're a skitterbrain and no mistake."

"Count!" Damaris ordered firmly.

"Four, then, four and five and blisterin' six . . ."

And as he counted, she proceeded quickly, though not nearly as carefully or as skillfully as she would have wished, to clean up the gash. She worked more swiftly as she gained in sureness, pulling back the torn flesh to discover a huge ugly piece of wood embedded in the heart of the wound.

"There's twelve," he said at last, weakly but with a touch of triumph in his voice.

"You forgot about the ones on my sleeves; but you needn't worry about them. Here comes Mother Charlotte now."

And then Frank, who had resisted her every move, surprised her by pleading, "Don't go away, miss, she kinda scares me."

"Mother Charlotte scares you! But she's going to make you well, Frank."

"I know, but she's different, not like you."

He meant, she supposed, the habit, for no one could have been kinder than Mother Charlotte. Still, she stayed.

"I wouldn't think of going away, not now I've made a friend. I don't have many friends, do you?"

"Only Vicky."

"Vicky? Oh, yes, that's your sister, isn't it?"

"Yes. Least Ma says she's me sister, though our dads is different."

"You have a stepfather then?" Damaris asked.

"No," he snorted. "Ain't got no father at all, least not one I know, nor has Vicky for that matter."

"They're gone to the war?"

"Gone, just gone. Don't expect they'll ever be back, either one of 'em. Bums, Ma says they is."

"I'm sorry. I've got no father either, Frank."

Mother Charlotte, armed with surgical implements that made Frank wince and a box containing gauze and ointment, had begun to examine the wound.

"A good job," she approved. "Damaris, isn't it?"

She nodded.

"A beautiful name, Paul's first convert, first woman convert, that is. You've done a beautiful job of cleaning this mess up. Looks as though you've had some experience. We could certainly use your help at Mercy House anytime you can give it."

As she talked Mother Charlotte had selected a solid plierlike instrument at the sight of which Frank cringed, and as she began probing the wound to remove the large splinter, he pulled away from her.

"Do keep him still, Damaris," she said calmly, paying no undue attention to his sobs of pain as she worked slowly, methodically, far too slowly and methodically for Frank's liking. Having assured Mother Charlotte nothing would give her greater pleasure than to spend as much time as she could at Mercy House, Damaris, her arms around the boy, reminded Frank of the buttons on her sleeve. Still, it took all her prompting and cajoling to make him draw his eyes away from the pliers in Mother Charlotte's hand to the cuffs of the sleeves on the arms that surrounded him.

"Four," he whispered at last.

"That's only one sleeve," she countered.

"You think I'm crackers? There's four there, course."

"That's guessing, not counting. I might have lost a button, how many would it be then?"

He thought for a while, and then said triumphantly, "Seven 'stead of eight."

"But I didn't say which sleeve I might have lost it from. Look." And she turned the other arm while he counted.

"One, two, three—oh!" That last cry accompanied a cry of triumph from Mother Charlotte, who had finally removed and was holding up an ugly and bloodied chunk of wood.

"Where's it from, Frank?" she asked, examining it with interest.

"Off of his night stick," the boy muttered, his face white and drawn.

"How on earth! That's a devil of a man, but how often have I told you and Vicky to stay away from him? Really, Frank, really! You must listen to me."

A flush of guilt suffused his pale face. "I only took an

orange. Ma said she felt like a bit of fruit. I'd do anything for Ma."

"That's very laudable, Frank. How is your mother doing? The baby must be due soon."

"Month or so, she says."

"Then you'd better have her come along and see me. And don't go near that man again. Not just because it's wrong to steal, but next time he may have your leg off, and the law will be on his side. Your Vicky's a delicate little thing. Make sure to bring her in to see me if she's sickly or if she's hungry. Promise?"

"Ma don't want us begging off of you."

"It's not begging. We're here to help those in need. If your mother needs food, she can have ours."

"But you got nothing. Look at you; you live on bread and water like the rest of us."

"The Lord will provide, Frank. Never forget that."

He barely stifled a snort.

"Looks all right now to me." Mother Charlotte was peering into the gash to make sure she had got the whole piece out. "It really should be stitched. We have a few doctors who volunteer their time," she explained to Damaris. "Come by in the morning, Frank. Dr. Weldon usually stops by before going on his rounds. I'd like him to look at it, just to make sure. In the meantime, I'll leave you in Damaris's capable hands."

As she bandaged his leg, Frank triumphed suddenly. "You didn't lose no button, there's four on the other sleeve too."

"Didn't say there weren't, Frank; I only said that it doesn't do to make assumptions. You didn't know for sure they were all there before; now you do."

"Guessed as much, 'cause if it came off you're the kind that'd sew it back on." She bound the gauze firmly, making sure it was not too tight, and he studied her with increased interest. "Why aren't you dressed up funny like the rest?"

"They're nuns. I'm not."

"But they're not proper nuns; least Ma says they're not, 'cause they're not Catholic."

"No, they're Sisters of St. Catharine, an Episcopal order."

"We're Catholic. Do you got the same God as we got?"

"Yes."

"Then why're there different kinds of nuns?"

"You're asking questions that grown men can't answer. It would be so much easier if there were only one religion. But we both know that nothing in this world is simple and easy."

And as she helped him from the table he said shyly, "You smell good."

"Lavender. I always keep a little lavender pinned inside my dress. I'll bring you some if you'd like."

He stood tall, sticking out his chin. "Not me, but I guess Vicky'd like it. She's crazy for flowers, any kind of flowers. Silly really; can't eat flowers." He shuffled awkwardly. "You got nice hands." Questioningly, Damaris spread her fingers. "They feel nice, I mean." He shuffled his feet again before asking, "Will you be here tomorrow if I come back?"

She shook her head. "Not tomorrow, but if the bandage is in need of changing next week at this time, I'll be here."

"Maybe I'll come then." His narrow face grimaced into a kind of half-smile as he added, almost reluctantly, "And . . . er . . . thanks."

"Thank you, Frank, for being such a good patient."

Mother Charlotte, the Sisters of St. Catharine, and the children they cared for at Mercy House became Damaris's family; and the one afternoon a week spent with them became precious to her above all others.

She learned under their expert tutelage to recognize and care for all manner of wounds and ailments. She earned praise from Sister Agnes, whose sense of duty far outdid her sense of humor, by changing linen quickly and efficiently and making beds with clean, square-cut corners. Sister Edith, who laughed a great deal more than Sister Agnes, demonstrated practical things like making lye soap in the ash pit out back. Damaris was pleased when her own hands became as reddened by constant immersion in hot disinfected water as those of the others.

Sometimes they were joined by delicate Sister Emmeline, who came to collect supplies for the shelter for unmarried mothers and prostitutes maintained by the order in the city's notorious Five Points district. The aim of the sisters at Mercy House was to minister to children, yet no one was ever turned away from their doors. They gave not only their time but their own scanty food supplies, as well as clothing and bedding, and when they had it, though that was seldom, money. And always they were collecting discards, pleading for help for others.

"I hate to beg, hate it, hate it, hate it," Mother Charlotte said vehemently one day. "But simply to ask for help is never enough; one has to beg. Perhaps it makes others feel more generous; perhaps they give only to be rid of us. The Lord Himself knows how I hate to be thought importunate, but maybe He's teaching me humility; for if that's what it takes to make those give who can afford to give, then importunate I shall be. Persistence succeeds, Damaris. That I know, but oh, it does demand so much of my time and energy that could be better used elsewhere. Never mind! I thank the Lord I have the strength now and only ask that He will continue to give it to me."

Damaris wondered at that wistful tone. To her, Mother Charlotte appeared to be a tower of strength.

One afternoon as Damaris arrived at Mercy House a group of fashionable, stern-faced ladies swept past her on their way down the steps. Though their mood seemed less than friendly, she asked Sister Agnes, who stood at the top, "Donors?"

"Inspectors," Sister Agnes replied scornfully. "They come at any and every odd hour to interrupt our work with demands to inspect every inch of the house. God only knows what secret immoralities they think to disclose."

"Sister Agnes!" Mother Charlotte, returning inside after bidding farewell to the visitors, admonished sharply.

"Sorry, Reverend Mother, but what's the use of denying it? There's no hope of ever getting those . . . those *ladies* to raise money for a hospital for us when they won't even allow us to carry on our work here without their intervention. And you know it's all because they've been reading that filth."

"That's enough, Sister. I understand your anger. I dislike the surprise visits of these ladies every bit as much, but at least they come. Their intentions in coming are their own, but while they are here let us use these visits to prove our own intentions are above reproach. That the sweetest fruit may have the sourest rind has been taught to me by my sister, Mildred. In founding Chartwell, a college for women in a state where females, like children, are to be seen and not heard, she has been almost as unpopular as I have in founding our sisterhood, and equally at a disadvantage in raising money. But patience, I tell her, patience and persistence eventually will open all doors.''

"Patience, the virtue of fools," Sister Agnes muttered, but only after Mother Charlotte was out of earshot.

"What filth did Sister Agnes mean those ladies had been reading?" Damaris asked Sister Edith later as they folded the clean linen together.

"The dear biddies must have lain their delicate hands on Maria Monk's *Awful Disclosures of the Hotel Dieu Nunnery of Montreal* or perhaps that scurrilous Rebecca Reed's *Six Months in a Convent*."

"Are they awful?"

"Lies, awful lies—those and others. Directed at our Roman Catholic sisters, to be sure, but used to discredit all of us."

"What people won't stoop to to undermine the efforts of others."

"Or to make money. If only others wouldn't buy such smut. That's the only thing that will stop it being written."

Together they shook out the last bedsheet and folded it. "Oh, I know what you're thinking, that I've read them too. Well, I have. Mother Charlotte asked us to, even at the risk of our finding them prurient. She said that undoubtedly these, or things like them, would be leveled against us, and we might as well know what we're accused of. Mother Charlotte says that the tragedy of ignorance is complacency. I daresay now you're grown she might even allow you to know about them."

"Am I grown?" Damaris asked in surprise.

"Course you are. You were such a little runt of a thing that first day you walked in with Dr. Hunter—thin, quiet, and timid—but just look at you now, the way you do everything we do. And look how you've filled out—quite handsomely. You've the finest eyes I've seen in a woman. Now don't let that go to your head. We've got beds to make."

FOUR

While Damaris settled into her new life, her mother's letters continued to be filled with complaints and self-pity, making her daughter think that too much time on one's hands and too little to do provided an unenviable existence. Certainly it was one she had never known; she had always worked and never shirked responsibility, qualities that made her invaluable to both Mother Charlotte and Mrs. Wickers.

Mrs. Wickers might not be as unstinting in her praise as was Mother Charlotte, nevertheless, on those occasions when the third-floor nursery was visited by Mrs. Caylew or on those even fewer and more disturbing occasions when, unannounced, Mr. Caylew arrived to greet his younger children, she often put in a good word for Damaris.

Mr. Caylew obviously felt ill at ease with his younger children; nor for that matter, did he pay much attention to the older ones, except for Eustacia, or Lucy as he called her, a brunette of such startling beauty that whenever Damaris caught sight of her she had to stop herself from staring. Though Eustacia was only two years her senior, it seemed that an age as well as a world separated them. Next to Eustacia came sporty, swaggering Lawrence, a year older than herself, then Nathan, a year younger, who was quieter and inclined to sulk. But these three Damaris saw rarely, only long enough to recognize that they were all self-assured and haughty, that Lawrence resembled his father, while Nathan took after his mother. Both were destined for Harvard College, and Mr. Caylew could often be heard admonishing their tutor to keep their noses in the books.

"A good thing too," Mrs. Wickers murmured sententiously. "Don't want them prowling about up here now you're growing into a young woman. They'll be after what they're all after—you-know-what. Watch out for those two, Mary."

Though unsure exactly what was meant by that oft-repeated caution, from the facial expression that accompanied it Damaris felt sure it must be something distasteful, not to be discussed. It could certainly not be a matter covered by the venerable Mrs. Trollope, or her advice would have been quoted. Whatever it was, Damaris saw little reason for alarm; she was sure the young gentlemen paid no more attention to her than she did to them. Neither they nor Eustacia showed any interest in the happenings of the nursery. Indeed, they were seen so seldom that at times Damaris felt there were two families living in the Park Avenue house—the three older children and their parents in the luxurious apartments below, and she and Mrs. Wickers and the younger ones on the remote third floor.

Damaris was much happier now; since she had ceased to share their table and their rooms, she was no longer subject to the open jeers of the other servants. She often heard whispered taunts of "Wickers's pet" and caught glimpses of arch smiles that accompanied those taunts; but since she had joined Mrs. Wickers in her limbo, she sensed they feared to do more.

As her personal life improved, so at long last was the state of the nation restored to order. At Appomattox one cool gray April afternoon, without a single victorious cheer, General Grant accepted General Lee's sword to bring to an end the war that had decimated the armies of both sides. If the toll of half a million dead were not enough to cast gloom on any jubilation, news came of the President's assassination.

Still, they must never forget which side had won, Templeton Caylew reminded his gathered household as he proposed a toast to their victory. His main concern appeared to be the precarious financial state of the nation.

From the back of the room, studying his tall, commanding barrel-chested figure, his heavily jowled face with its bristling mustache, Damaris saw him as a man to be trusted, respected, though not a little feared. His wife, at his side, was correspondingly tall but distant, ethereal, unapproachable. It was, however, to his lovely Lucy that Caylew first raised his glass in salute, sparing only the barest of nods for his sons Lawrence and Nathan, who stood beside her.

"See how he dotes on that one," Mrs. Wickers whispered. She barely raised her glass in response. She had made little secret of her sympathies with the South, believing perhaps with many of her countrymen that a Southern victory would have increased chances for the reunification of America with England.

Damaris didn't particularly like the taste of the champagne, even though Mrs. Wickers informed her it was Périgord, the very finest. The state of the nation might not be healthy, but life for the Caylew family appeared to remain as sumptuous as ever.

Reminders that she was growing to womanhood came not only from Mrs. Wickers, from the sisters at Mercy House, but from her mother that summer, who pointed out that sixteen was a marriageable age and that it would soon be necessary to find her a husband.

"I'm happy just as I am," Damaris protested. "I don't want to marry."

"Don't be foolish. Every woman must marry."

"Not every woman does." Damaris thought of Mother Charlotte and the other Sisters of St. Catharine, but somehow she suspected her mother would be as mistrustful of their aims as were those worthy ladies of the diocese who conducted regular inspections. Instead, she gave Mrs. Wickers as her example.

"But she's no right to call herself Mrs. Wickers if she's an unmarried woman," Mrs. Fanshawe responded in indignation.

"I can't see that she does any harm by it."

"I can't agree. Marriage is an honorable estate, not to be taken lightly, certainly not to be lied about. If she hides behind that, there has to be a reason," her mother said darkly.

"That's unfair."

"I didn't think you liked her."

"Perhaps I didn't at first, but she's been very kind to me. She's a proud woman, proud of her position. She certainly doesn't consider marriage a woman's only goal in life."

Damaris wasn't sure that Angela Wickers considered marriage a goal at all, but she decided against mentioning that to her mother.

"Hers is to keep someone else's children instead of having her own, is that it? Well, Damaris, it's all right for you to do the same just now, for we're penniless; we need the money you earn. And I quite understand that as you are placed it isn't easy to find a suitable husband. If your father were here, he would have arranged everything; but now you must leave it to me. I've never been one to shirk responsibility." She sighed heavily as she added, "Life's not easy for a poor widow, but I shall see what can be done. I would take it up with the rector, but I can't abide his wife. She called here once and looked down on my poor abode. Perhaps Mr. Caylew might—"

"No, absolutely not, Mother," Damaris replied sharply. "He's done enough in giving me the chance to earn an income."

"It will have to be a man of some means," her mother mused. "I know you'd never take someone who didn't consider the needs of your poor mother."

"I'll always take care of you. You know I will. We're managing quite well as it is."

"You are, living in a fine house. I can quite understand how *you* would be satisfied with things as they are."

Her mother was right; Damaris was satisfied with things as they were. She had no wish to marry. If she could have changed her life it would have been to join the Sisterhood of St. Catharine, but to do so she would have had to be free of all encumbrances; and as long as her mother lived, her care must come first. The sisters, she knew, owed allegiance only to God and to the order.

It was almost a relief that, far from urging her to think of marriage, Angela Wickers continued to warn her of the baser nature of men.

"Watch out for that new footman they've taken on, Mary. I've seen him posing, showing off just because he has a decent shape to his calf. Conceited fool! If he so much as makes a move toward you, you're to tell me. Promise me you will?"

"But he's not so much as looked at me," Damaris protested.

"I sincerely doubt that. You've grown quite lovely. I always knew you would with that coloring and those expressive eyes of yours."

"Do you mean I'm pretty—like Eustacia Caylew?" Damaris's voice expressed incredulity rather than pride.

"Lucy Caylew's not pretty; she's a rare beauty. And she knows it. No one will ever harm that one. I've yet to see such a spoiled, determined young woman in my life. You haven't her looks by any means, but you have something that she doesn't, Mary—an air of innocence that men find irresistible. For that reason you must be even more careful."

Was that why the attitude of the horsecar driver on Wednesday afternoons had changed from indifference to effusive friendliness? Damaris wondered. And could that be the reason that the pale young man who often rode that line had one day missed his own stop and gone all the way to the end of the line? She did nothing to attract attention. Her clothes were plain, her long golden hair pinned neatly back without adornment, yet he had sat looking over at her instead of watching the road for his stop. He'd even tried to talk with her when they got down together, but she wouldn't waste a minute of her Wednesday afternoons in idle conversation. She had things to do and never enough time to do them in.

Apart from boiling up the vat of grease and lye until these unlike ingredients combined to be formed into the cakes of ash-pit soap with which everything and everyone at Mercy House was disinfected, soap so potent that it washed skin away as well as dirt ("I just hope it doesn't wear us away completely," Sister Agnes groaned), there was liniment to be mixed from equal parts of lime water and linseed oil; opodeldoc for the treatment of sprains to be made from camphor dissolved in rectified spirits of wine, adding soap, thinly scraped, and oil of rosemary; and a variety of poultices to be readied for abscesses, from bread and water to mustard and linseed.

Damaris learned that heat would cause dilation in tissues surrounding a wound, that ice packs helped bleeding to subside more quickly, that alternating heat and cold was effective for faster pain relief, and that massage was the best way of relaxing the muscle tension, often the cause of as much pain as the injury itself.

She assisted the doctors who volunteered their services to the sisters in setting limbs with wood splints, watched while they sutured gashes with catgut; she learned how to recognize symptoms of metallic poisoning suffered by many of the tenement children, and how to provide an emetic by forcing down great quantities of arrowroot and water. She applied solutions of carbonate of soda and vinegar to get rid of ringworm, preparing doses of sulphur and treacle to be taken periodically thereafter.

Though the importance of cleanliness was always stressed, not all their efforts met with success. Frank O'Connor had fallen afoul of the watchman again, sustaining a wound far worse than before. At the time it was dressed, the infirmary had been full and they were unable to give him a bed. By the time he returned to have the dressing changed, the leg had become gangrenous and had to be amputated.

He'd been brave. "'S all right." He shrugged, hopping around on his stump. "A wooden pin'll make begging easier."

But his courage had failed when Vicky came down with a cold that, left untended, had turned to pneumonia. Each Wednesday Damaris would find him at his sister's bedside. Remembering Vicky's love of flowers, she took whatever she could find—daisies, carnations—but Vicky's favorites were the little briar roses. She said she preferred them to the big heavy-scented ones because they were so small and delicate. She seemed to know that she would not live and tried to spare others the pain of her death.

Her last words to Damaris had been to thank her for the joy the flowers had brought her. "I'll be waiting for you in heaven with rosebuds, lots and lots of rosebuds."

Just as Vicky had thought of the living, so those at Mercy House had to turn from grief at her death to consoling and caring for those who remained.

As time passed, there was little that Damaris didn't know about the care of common ailments. Yet she was always anxious to learn more. She had asked to be allowed to work with Sister Emmeline at the Magdalen Shelter for Fallen Women in the Five Points district; it was the one request Mother Charlotte refused.

"You've already seen and done enough for your impressionable young mind. Attending the children here can be heartrending—little Vicky's death, Frank's leg—but compared to the desolation of people at Five Points, believe me, this is bearable."

Was it really possible that anything could be worse?

Damaris's skill in the art of healing was to raise her stock with the Caylews' servants at Park Avenue. When Damaris went down to the kitchen for warm milk for Eleanor one day, Cook, who had spilled the turtle soup she was preparing for one of the huge victory celebrations the Caylews were hosting, was cursing her misfortune as she went to cover her burned hand with lard.

"Don't!" Damaris reached over to stop her. "You'll fry the skin."

"Who'd you think you are, telling me what to do?" Cook responded fiercely, her dudgeon aroused by the pain and Damaris's unusually peremptory tone. "I always take care of burns this way, and my mother before me."

"All well and good, but that's no way to treat a burn." Damaris, treating Cook, who weighed close to two hundred pounds, just as though she were a patient of Mercy House, took hold of her scalded hand and held it under running cold water. Then helping herself generously to ice from the wooden tub, she prepared a pan of iced water and held Cook's hand down in it.

"Here, you can't take that ice. Every bit is needed for tonight's lobster gelée," Cook had argued, though she must have been feeling relief, for she stopped trying to wrench her hand free.

Damaris's caustic comment "There won't be any dinner if you can't use this hand, will there?" caused the butler, coming through the swinging kitchen door to put in, "Airs and graces! Haven't we got airs and graces now we're under the wing of that limey bogey? We all know what you two are up to up there in her ladyship's cozy sitting room. Don't we, Cook?"

Damaris longed to ask what he meant; it might explain the sly looks they gave whenever Mrs. Wickers's name was mentioned. She thought to learn something from Cook's response; but Cook, whose hand was feeling much im-

proved for its treatment, said little beyond a muttered word
of assent.

Thereafter, whenever cuts, wounds, or injuries of any
kind were suffered belowstairs, Damaris was sent for. No
one ever questioned how she had learned these things; the
servants were simply relieved to have someone at hand to
render aid.

Mrs. Wickers was the only one to express curiosity after
witnessing Damaris rescue Augustus from choking. Without a word, she had put him across her knee, hit him
sharply between the shoulder blades, and with the boy
turning blue as he struggled for breath, she had reached to
deftly remove the obstruction, a chicken bone, from his
esophagus.

Never having mentioned Mercy House or where she
spent her Wednesday afternoons, perhaps from fear of
disapproval or interference, for there was no denying that
Angela Wickers's penchant to control her every action extended far beyond the nursery, Damaris had brushed off
her surprised inquiry with a shrugged "Just thought that
might work, and it did."

Had Mrs. Wickers not been in such a fine humor that
day, she would probably have pursued the matter. As it
was, she had just learned from Mrs. Caylew that with the
return to peace, Lucy was at last to be given her promised
visit to England the next summer. If his business would
allow, Mr. Caylew would make the journey too.

"But that is not all." Mrs. Wickers's voice rose in
excitement. "I am to go with them!"

Then she had repeated Mrs. Caylew's final words, "It
will give you a chance to see England again, and your
knowledge of the country may be useful to us. It is not yet
certain whether Lawrence and Nathan will be with us.
Lawrence probably will be finishing up at Harvard, but
Nathan is having such difficulties he may have to spend
the summer with a tutor. Of course, the younger children
will stay, but Mary will be there to take care of them. "

Mrs. Wickers had kept to herself her opinions of American colleges—dismal places of learning—or of Lucy's
slim chance, beauty and wealth notwithstanding, of winning a titled suitor. That imperious manner of hers would
never be forgiven in a colonial.

Seeing Damaris respond so quickly to a crisis that might have spelt disaster for Augustus and would most certainly cause Mrs. Caylew to reconsider whether the nursery could spare Nanny's presence, instead of obeying her natural curiosity to find out how Damaris knew something she had not taught her, all Mrs. Wickers said was "Glad to see you're on your toes, Mary, for next summer they'll be your sole responsibility. God forbid anything should happen to any of them. Remember when you're in Newport not to put that mother of yours before the children."

"I wouldn't think of it, Angela."

"I don't suppose you would, but she does take advantage of your good nature. Don't argue now, just because she's your mother. You're loyal and you're reliable; and I can take some of the credit for that, for you knew precious little when you came. Still, I must admit, you've been quick to learn."

"You have helped me a great deal, Angela. I thank you for everything."

Damaris had a certain sympathy for Angela Wickers. She felt that beneath that brusque, imperious manner lay some great unhappiness of which she never spoke. Despite their close quarters and the amount of time they spent together, there was something about her that Damaris did not understand, something with which she was never entirely at ease. The thought of a summer freed from her constant cautions, a summer alone with Augustus, Eleanor, and Beatrice, of whom she'd grown most fond, was appealing. They could run and picnic on the wide sandy beaches without constant admonitions to observe proper table manners, even when they were outdoors, just among themselves. They could pick blackberries without worrying about getting their hands and clothes dirty and play leapfrog without it being called unseemly. Damaris, a child who had known so little of childhood, looked forward to the summer of freedom almost as much as the children did when they heard the news.

That Christmas was an especially busy one for Damaris. She had decided to surprise each of the patients at Mercy House with a present. Having no money, she rummaged through the Caylews' toy box searching out broken toys to repair, old and discarded dolls to refurbish. She made new clothes for them from scraps of material, using trimmings from her own burnished gold hair to supplement shorn wigs.

As she plied needle and thread and glue, Damaris thought of the joy these playthings would bring to children who had never before owned a toy, and her fingers fairly skipped at her task.

She was restuffing a discarded teddy bear—Beatrice had torn it apart in a fit of anger at not being allowed to go down to the celebration of Lucy's eighteenth birthday—when one of the maids hurried in to get her.

"It's Mr. Nathan, he twisted his ankle jumping down from his horse, or broke it. The mistress doesn't know which. She's beside herself. The doctor's been sent for, but he's out on a call. They're looking for him. Mr. Nathan's hurting something fierce and Mrs. Caylew's fit to be tied. I told her you might help, seeing as how you helped Cook and others, and she said to fetch you right away."

"Of course. Bring a pan of hot water and another filled with cold water, some ice, and some heavy bandages, will you please?"

Stopping only to collect a jar of ointment, Damaris made her way to the sitting room, where she found a worried Mrs. Caylew standing beside her second son, who sat in an armchair, his foot resting on a hassock, glowering like a brewing storm. He was quite pleasing in aspect, his face long and narrow, very like his mother's, pale by nature and at that moment far paler than usual, looking far too young for the light mustache that failed to disguise a petulant curve to his lips.

"Oh, there you are, Mary," Mrs. Caylew said in undisguised relief. "Hurry and do something for poor Nathan till the doctor arrives. He's had a fall and is in such awful pain, poor dear."

"Mother, I keep telling you, it wasn't a fall. It was that damnable groom's fault for not holding the horse still. Do please leave me alone. Your fussing only makes matters worse."

"Yes, dear. Well, Mary will take care of you until that doctor is found. They're never there when you want them, are they? Don't worry, though. Father will see to it that you get proper care. He's always good about taking care of these things."

"I can see to things, I don't need Father for everything. When are you going to realize I'm a man? Do leave me alone, please." And as the door closed behind his mother he asked Damaris ungraciously, "Well, now what is it you want?"

"I'd just like to look at your leg, if I may, to see if there's anything I can do to help. I know you must be in pain."

"I don't want anyone except the damned doctor, whenever he decides to grace us with his presence. Useless lot, never around when they're needed."

The maid came in with the two pans of water as Damaris soothed, "I know, but please let me see if I can help relieve your discomfort until he gets here."

"I don't need a midwife," Nathan rasped.

"I'm not a midwife. I work in the nursery."

"Well, what could you know then?" he muttered peevishly.

"I might be able to relieve the pain if you'll allow me to."

"There it is then, the damned nuisance! A fellow has all these plans for the holidays, and now look. I'll probably be laid up nursing the blasted thing and no chance of fun at all."

"It may not be that bad," Damaris consoled as she made to remove his boot.

"For Christ's sake!" he yelled, louder than any child, as she touched it.

"Then I'd better cut the boot off," she said firmly.

"Do what you like; I don't care. Just don't hurt me, that's all."

The maid was sent for a knife, and Damaris knelt before him and set about slitting the fine leather until she was able to free it from his foot, no easy task with its owner groaning at every move and touch. Gently she peeled back the stocking. The ankle was indeed swollen.

"What the hell do you think you're doing!" he yelled as she firmly immersed the foot first in the hot water, then in the cold.

"There, it's just cold. Hold still."

Smoothly but steadily she stroked the swelling, agitating the icy water as she did so, circulating it around the foot. Then she put the foot back in the hot water and repeated the process, changing from hot to cold, cold to hot, talking to him as she worked.

"This will help, really it will, but I know it's awfully uncomfortable," Damaris soothed; and as he groaned again: "All right, just for a little you can take your foot out of the water, and I'll massage it with some of this ointment. I'm quite sure there's nothing broken, it's only a sprain, thank goodness."

"Only a sprain!" he groaned. "You've some nerve. Only a sprain indeed! You've no idea how it hurts."

But as she gently dried his foot and put it on the towel on her lap, and equally gently began to apply the ointment in the inflamed area, as she began to massage the sole of the foot, pressing firmly each section, each joint, he laid his head back and closed his eyes, his breathing becoming easier, his face relaxing at the pressure of her hands, at the steadiness of the motion.

She said nothing as she worked, but when she looked up she saw he had opened his eyes and was watching her from beneath heavy eyelids.

"What's your name?" he asked in a softer, easier voice.

"Mary."

"I haven't seen you around. Where did you say you work?"

"Up in the nursery. I assist Mrs. Wickers."

"Oh, the English witch. I'm glad Mother didn't have any of her ridiculous ideas about English refinement when I was small."

Damaris said nothing but went to put the foot she had been massaging back in the iced water.

"Don't do that. I like the feel of your hands when you touch it that way."

"You want the swelling down, don't you, so you can dance and have fun during the holidays?"

With that she firmly pushed his foot back into the water.

"What perfume is that you're wearing?"

"It's not perfume; it's a sprig of dried lavender."

"Mmmm, I like it." He looked at her with awakened interest. "Where is it?"

"Where is what?"

"The sprig of lavender."

She made no reply, but he obviously enjoyed the flush that rose to her cheeks.

"Are you going to dance and have fun during the holidays?"

She shook her head. "I don't dance."

"Why not?"

She shrugged. "I never learned how."

"I'll be glad to teach you. Oh, damn, I can't—my foot. Well, tell me what you do for fun."

Though she was glad he was forgetting the discomfort of his foot, she disliked these personal remarks and countered with "Tell me about your studies?"

"One word—boring. Tell me about your boy friends. You must have hundreds. You're a real looker with that golden hair of yours. Let me see your eyes. Well, don't look up then; it doesn't matter. I know they're blue, the bluest blue of the southern sea, framed by the darkest, thickest lashes."

She flushed. "You must write poetry."

"I do, as a matter of fact, though I daren't tell Father about it." His face glowered in discontent; then he looked back at her, asking, "Shall I write a poem for you, or would your admirers object?"

"Don't be silly!" she admonished.

"It's not silly. If you were my girl and another fellow wrote a poem to you, I'd object."

She made no reply.

"Do they kiss you in the pantry when no one's looking?"

"For goodness' sake, do stop talking such nonsense. I'm here trying to help you and all you're doing is saying a lot of silly things to upset me."

"I wasn't. I was saying nice things. I like you."

"Well, please stop, or I'll leave."

"You can't." He leaned back smiling. "You work for us and Mother told you to stay till the doctor came."

The fact that this was an irrefutable truth did nothing to lessen Damaris's displeasure, which must have shown on her face, for Nathan leaned forward to apologize. "Sorry," he said quickly. "I just didn't want you to go, that's all."

"All right."

"Would you massage my foot again? It made me feel so much better."

Without a word, she put his foot back on her lap and applied some more ointment before beginning to massage it again.

"You have a wonderful touch," he murmured. "And you're very, very pretty. But you must have heard that dozens of times."

"That's quite enough," she said, thrusting his foot into the bowl of water, and she would have left, except at that moment the door opened to admit Mrs. Caylew accompanied by the doctor, who, rubbing his hands together, began in hearty tones.

"Well, well, well. What have we here."

"It seems to be a sprain, Doctor. I've been bathing the foot alternately in hot and cold water, and I've put on—"

The doctor cut her off without so much as a glance in her direction. "Well, well. Let's see what we have here, shall we?" Damaris stepped aside as he bent down to examine the ankle. She was pleased to see the swelling was already beginning to diminish.

"Well, Mr. Nathan, it's a good thing you called me in."

"It's not broken, is it, Doctor? Mary said—"

"No, you've been lucky. It is my opinion you have a bad sprain, but I intend to leave nothing to chance. I shall bandage it for support, but we'll keep a close watch on it. Can't have any harm coming to Mr. Nathan, now can we! But you're to keep off the foot, young sir. You're to keep it elevated." He shook his head. "No dancing over the holidays, I'm afraid, and I know how that must disappoint you."

"It does, but I suppose I'll have to survive." Nathan glanced over at Damaris as he spoke.

"This bandaged support will help a great deal. I shall call daily."

"I'd like Mary to take care of the dressing, Mother," Nathan said. "She has a light touch. It's felt much easier since she bathed it."

"Has it, dear? That's good." His mother smiled. "Well, I'll talk to Nanny and see what can be done about getting her services put at your disposal."

FIVE

"**B**entley's selling his roan. I'd dearly love to have it, Lucy," Nathan announced to Eustacia as she floated into his room wafting an aroma of tea roses in her train, to lean over and buss his cheek. Of Damaris, who knelt changing his dressing, there was no acknowledgment. That was hardly surprising, for while Damaris noticed everything about the eldest Miss Caylew—the good-morning kisses she bestowed at noon, her manner of interrupting her father for anything or nothing (no matter with whom he was closeted), the never-ending swarm of admirers in constant attendance who seemed strangely encouraged by the disdain with which she received them—Damaris seemed as invisible to Eustacia as the rug underfoot, unless required to fetch or carry for her.

"Then tell Papa," Eustacia said airily, holding up the opal on her finger to the light to better examine it.

"You tell him for me, Lucy, please," Nathan cajoled.

"I'm not a member of the Coaching Club. What would I want with the silly old roan?"

"You might as well be a member. They say a race is never official unless you're there to see them off."

"Sillies!" Still, from the way Eustacia Caylew smiled and the softness of her tone, it was clear that whatever silliness the members of the illustrious Coaching Club may have had it did not extend to their opinion of herself.

"Ask him, Lucy, please! Tell him the horse is a steal. That'll appeal to his sense of a bargain. He's so stingy with me, but he'll give you anything. Go on."

"What will you do in return?"

"Anything," Nathan agreed quickly. Then his face grew

63

glum. "Though given the condition I'm in I can't do much for anyone."

Eustacia's eyes flitted across Damaris as she gazed across the chair behind her and the velvet hangings at the window beyond.

"I do believe that's Sydney Beaufort's carriage." She jumped up, putting her hand to her perfectly coiffed dark hair. "He is naughty to be so early. I mustn't let him see me like this."

"Will you, Lucy?" Nathan called after her.

For reply she blew her brother a kiss.

"She gets everything she wants; it's not fair," Nathan grumbled. "Massage my foot, Mary. It's killing me today."

As she undid the bandage she had just put on, Damaris ventured, "Perhaps if you were to speak to your father yourself in these matters he would react more favorably toward them."

"What business is that of yours?" he snapped.

"None, none at all. I'm sorry. Shall I go?"

"No, stay with me. You make me feel better."

That Nathan had taken a liking to her was obvious, but it was an interest Damaris would gladly have forgone. Boredom, she supposed, was the reason for it, or perhaps having someone at hand to whom he felt superior. Whatever it was, it distressed her, and it was only with reluctance she obeyed his constant summonses to read to him, to run his errands, but mostly just to sit with him. He never did anything untoward, yet he had a manner of studying her that made her feel vulnerable and uneasy. She was sure he would never have looked so at any of Lucy's friends. Somehow his soulful yet unflinching stare distressed her even more than a direct encounter that she could, with reason, have rebuffed.

"Why are you blushing?" he demanded one day as she sat beside him in the conservatory reading from *Moby Dick*. "I'm sure it would surprise Melville that his tale of Ahab's obsession with the great white whale had brought a blush to a maiden's cheek."

"It's not the story," she admitted.

"Then what is it?"

"I don't know," she replied truthfully.

"Is it me? Do I alarm you?"

"Not exactly."

"Do I attract you?"

"Not exactly."

"Why not?" he asked in surprise. "Aren't I a fine-looking gentleman?"

"Quite."

"Quite!" he echoed primly. "But not quite fine enough for Miss Mary, is that it? Not as fine as the swains you hurry away to on Wednesday afternoons."

"I don't have any swains."

"Then where do you disappear to?"

"That is my afternoon to do with as I wish."

"You won't tell me then?"

"I am here to do what I can to help you through a trying recovery. But that doesn't include discussing me or my life."

"You make such a secret of both, you make me want to know more."

"There is really nothing to know."

"Can I not see you on one of those afternoons? We could take tea somewhere, or see a play, go to a museum, or do whatever your heart desires."

"No," she said firmly.

"Don't you like me, Mary, just a bit?"

"I think you're a fine gentleman."

"But I hear reservation in your voice. Why?"

She hesitated. "I'd like you a great deal more if you took it upon yourself to speak up to your father when you needed something instead of getting your sister to do it for you."

His lips tightened. "My relationship with my father is my affair."

"Yes, it is. I'm sorry. It's simply that I believe he would like you a good deal more if you stood up to him as Lucy—as Miss Eustacia does."

"You don't know my father," he said bitterly. "Anyway, I don't want to talk about him. He makes everyone's life a misery, except Lucy's."

"I'm sorry. I shouldn't have said anything." His expression was sulky, and she said to cheer him, "Your

ankle is so much better, you'll be up and about with your
friends very soon.''

"I don't want to be up and about, for then you won't
come and rub the circulation back into my foot anymore.
You work so seriously, and I love to watch you, and I love
the feel of your hands. Your touch is wonderful, light yet
capable. It's exciting to me, sensuous.''

His eyes searched her face as he spoke, then he ran his
tongue lingeringly across his lips as he reached for her
hand. But she eluded his grasp, snapping closed the book
she had been reading, rising abruptly, her heart beating fast,
although she didn't quite know why. Then, with a sense of
relief, she saw his attention was no longer on her. His
expression had changed; his eyes were glued on the door
behind her.

"Getting on all right it would seem, Nathan.'' The
tones of his father's voice were heavy with sarcasm.

"Yes, indeed, sir,'' Nathan responded with feigned
heartiness.

"I shall talk to you about your recovery later. Give my
son his book, Mary. He's no longer in the nursery and
can, I hope, read. Come with me.''

Damaris was upset to be the cause of his displeasure.
Following him from the room, she felt tears come to her
eyes; she blinked several times to keep them from falling.

"Now tell me,'' Mr. Caylew began in cold aloof tones
as he seated himself heavily behind his desk in the library.
"What exactly is going on between you and my son?''

"Nothing, Mr. Caylew, nothing, I assure you.''

"That's not what his words implied just now. You
know, I took you in because you were in need, but I
simply won't have any dalliance under my roof.''

"I have done nothing, sir. I swear I would do nothing to
harm you or any member of your family. I owe you
everything.''

"Very well.'' He appeared to be convinced by the
sincerity of her tone. "But if you are innocent, what of my
son?''

"Mr. Nathan has *done* nothing,'' she stressed.

"But said plenty, from the sound of it, and we all know
where such words lead. To speak of love is to make love.

Remember that, Mary, when young men ply you with blandishments.''

Head down, she nodded.

"And from now on no more changing Mr. Nathan's bandages or massaging his foot or whatever else it is you've been doing that has him inflamed. He's young; his blood runs hot. I believe you when you say you meant nothing by it, but nevertheless he—and you, I might add—are at a dangerous age. I'm surprised at my wife allowing such temptation. I shall have her choose a less pleasing nurse for the remainder of the time he is incapacitated. I'll not countenance untoward behavior in my house.''

Her voice cracked at his vexation. "I'm sorry, really sorry. I wouldn't do anything to cause you displeasure. You've been so kind; I don't know where my mother and I would have been without you. My only aim is to serve you and your family as best I can. I've tried hard; you can ask Mrs. Wickers.''

"No doubt, Mary. I believe you. But serve me, not my sons. Do you understand?''

She nodded.

"I shall have a talk with the young gentleman on this matter. I think I can promise there'll be no more advances from that quarter. In return I expect that should he ever repeat any of those blandishments such as I heard just now you're to come directly to me. Do you understand?''

As she nodded, his eyes assessed her in discriminating measure, and he added in a softer tone, "You've grown into a woman since you arrived in my household, Mary. I hadn't realized that so much time had passed. Now I can understand Nathan's trouble. Just keep out of harm's way. I think you know what I mean.'' As she nodded once again, he got up and put his arm around her, patting her shoulder and allowing his hand to rest there for a moment.

"You've grown very pretty, but you must take extra care for that very reason. I know you had a good upbringing, and the man who has you must be worthy of you. Should you fear anything, from anyone, you're to come directly to me.''

"Oh, thank you, Mr. Caylew.'' Damaris felt so relieved he was convinced of her innocence that she could almost have kissed the hand on her shoulder. "You're so gracious, you've shown such generosity, I shall never forget it. If there is ever anything I can do for you—"

But he cut her short, patting her shoulder. "There, there, that's quite all right, my dear, quite all right."

From that time on, there were no more summonses from Nathan, and for that she was relieved and thankful to his father, who had once again been as good as his word.

As the time approached for the family departure for England, Damaris was glad to be tucked away on the third floor, distant from all the bustle. Occasionally she caught sight of Lucy, beautiful, petulant Lucy, around whom the commotion centered, a fairy-tale princess who stood calm and sedate, removed from the chaos the journey was causing.

"She's a lovely thing," Mrs. Wickers acknowledged as they dined together that last night before Damaris was to leave with the children for Newport. The party for England was setting off later in the week. "Imperious, though. Wants and gets her own way over everything, and her father lets her have it. If she sees some duke to her liking, she'll want Daddy to buy him for her just as he's bought everything else. He has outfitted her in diamonds and furs fit for Queen Victoria herself, but whether he can buy her nobility as well is another story. The way he dotes on her is quite sickening. Women are fine creatures, but not those who are spoiled rotten."

"She is his firstborn."

"I know, but that's why I find it even harder to understand. If she were an eldest son, it would be different, but he treats Lawrence, admittedly a ne'er-do-well, harshly by comparison. And as for Nathan, he's no time for him at all. In girls, from my observation, it is usually the youngest who has the father's eye; but neither Mr. Caylew nor his wife can be bothered with the small ones. You'd think they only had three children instead of six. I've been waiting—"

She broke off, and Damaris prompted, "Waiting for what, Angela?"

"For Mrs. Caylew to be in the family way again. Don't blush about it, Mary. You must realize that Augustus is almost out of the nursery and Eleanor and Beatrice will soon follow him; and with that, there go our positions.

Frankly, I'm concerned. I wonder whether I shouldn't search for something else for us.''

It surpised and touched Damaris that Mrs. Wickers should be concerned with her future as well as her own.

"Thank you, Angela. I hadn't thought of it, but I suppose that will happen. I don't know what I shall do then.''

"Don't worry, Mary. If I move, you'll come with me. Anyway, let's hope Mrs. Caylew's not completely past it by now. Perhaps her absence this summer will bring renewed attentions from her husband, though their separate bedrooms don't provide much hope of a new addition to the nursery.''

"But I thought Mr. Caylew was going to England with you.''

Mrs. Wickers shook her head. "It's trade first with him,'' she muttered tendentiously. "I only hope he doesn't waste his seed on some little floozy while the cat's away.''

And Damaris, finding the discussion unpleasant, was glad when Angela Wickers changed the subject, though the intensity of her sudden "I shall miss you, you know'' was surprising.

Summer in Newport began exactly as Damaris had pictured it. The weather was splendid, perfect for picnics, bathing, beachcombing, lying in the sun, leapfrogging, skipping, making daisy chains. The days became filled with shouts and laughter; there was no one to hush the noise for Damaris's voice was as loud as any. She wore her uniform in the house, but when they went out on rambles she changed into old skirts and blouses. She even fashioned a voluminous bathing dress from an old garment so that she could follow the children into the breakers. She felt better than she ever had; and catching sight of herself in the hallway mirror, she found her face rounded out, her cheeks warm and brown, and an added clarity to her blue eyes.

She did arrange one afternoon for the maid to watch the children while she called on her mother, not altogether a happy interview, for her mother, along with her usual complaints, found her daughter unkempt, even gypsylike with the darkening of her skin by the sun.

Damaris was glad she could not stay long. It was as well she did not, for she returned to find that Mr. Caylew had arrived unexpectedly from New York. He was waiting for her to take the children in to him.

She felt a flush of guilt at being away when he came and was greatly relieved to find him in a pleasant humor. He laughed and joked with Augustus and even went so far as to question Eleanor and Beatrice on their summer. It was the most interest Damaris had ever seen him take in them.

Then he sent for ice cream, which, to Damaris's relief, they managed to consume without accident. After her mother's discontent, she found herself welcoming his geniality.

"Everything going well, Mary, it seems."

"Very well, Mr. Caylew, very well." She smiled at him and he returned that smile.

"You're looking as bright as the children, and not much older. How old are you now?"

"I'll be seventeen in August."

"Seventeen, sweet seventeen, and you've been off dallying with the old boy friends, I'll be bound."

"Oh, no!" She was dismayed that he could think she had been so remiss. "I was visiting my mother. I hadn't seen her since my arrival."

"And no young and handsome swain waylaid you on your way?" he pursued.

Again she hastened to reassure him, "I have no young man, Mr. Caylew, nor do I want one."

"Strange for a pretty girl not to desire a beau. But I can see you're shy. Tell me, how is your mother?"

"Quite well."

"She lives alone?"

"Yes, near the harbor. She finds her house small, not as comfortable as the rectory used to be. She complains sometimes, but she is alone a great deal, and she is getting older."

"Well, I'm sure it must be difficult for her—and for you—a young girl with the responsibility of a mother to care for. She's lucky to have such a loyal and dutiful daughter. I shall have to go along and see her and tell her how happy we are with you."

"Thank you, Mr. Caylew, except—"

"Except?"

"Well, her house is so small, she doesn't like to receive visitors. It makes her feel . . . how much she has come down in the world."

"Well, we shall have to see about that, shan't we?" He smiled, patted her hand, and said they might go.

Though he made no mention of it to her, Mr. Caylew did call on Mrs. Fanshawe, and when next Damaris saw her mother she was full of his praises.

"Damaris, what a kind gentleman your Mr. Caylew is, so very kind, so gracious, and so perceptive."

"He mentioned he might call on you, but I wasn't sure you would like it."

"Not like it! But of course I liked it. He told me how pleased they were with you."

"That was kind of him." And thinking of his concern over Nathan's advances, she added, "He's really kind and has looked out for me in so many ways."

"I really took to him, especially when he looked around and immediately agreed that this place was not at all suitable for a lady like myself—something I've been telling you all along."

"I know, Mother, but there's nothing else—"

"But there is something else. Mr. Caylew owns a house here, a much larger house on Catherine Street. I know the one. It's just come vacant. He said there was no reason why I couldn't move in there."

"But, Mother, Catherine Street—we could never afford it."

"There you're wrong, Damaris. He said it would give him pleasure if I moved in and simply took care of it for him. There would be no rent to pay at all; and there's a housekeeper there, so I could do away with that lazy Mrs. Dodd. Just imagine, a larger house and a better income, for then I wouldn't have to pay out all that I do on rent for this place no bigger than a postage stamp. Oh, Damaris, I walked over to see it yesterday. It's a lovely place, with a decent front garden, and it even has a plum tree in it, just like we had at the rectory, and bow windows in the front parlor, and there would be room to show my furniture to advantage. I wouldn't be crushed and restricted as I am now. I can put my china closet in the hall, and there'll be room to stand back and admire the contents. What good fortune!''

''It sounds wonderful, Mother, but—''

''But what, Damaris? Just think of it, to be able to live like a lady again, to hold my head up high, to receive company and not be ashamed. How wonderful! Do, please, discuss it with Mr. Caylew. He is most anxious to keep you happy. I'm sure that is his reason for offering me the house. Say how much I will enjoy it. He is waiting to hear it from you.''

Despite her mother's effusions, Damaris felt uneasy. ''I really don't know. It sounds like charity.''

''It's not charity that he wants to see me comfortable in my old age. How unkind of you to raise objections! I expected you would do everything in your power to make it possible. It would make me so happy, so very happy.'' Her mouth turned down and her face began to crinkle, a sure prelude to tears, as she finished: ''Do talk to him, I beg of you.''

''Very well, I will,'' Damaris responded dubiously, feeling more uneasy than ever without understanding why. Perhaps it was the fear of becoming indebted, yet to ask her mother to relinquish something on which she had set her heart was well nigh impossible.

''Your offer to my mother of your house on Catherine Street is kind, most kind,'' she told Mr. Caylew when next she saw him.

''I told you I wanted to please you, Mary. You *are* pleased I take it?'' He blew a smoke ring from the thick cigar in his hand and watched it float up toward the lofty ceiling.

''Yes, of course, but—''

''But what?'' he demanded.

''I don't quite know, except I'm unsure that I . . . that she should accept.''

''She doesn't like the house. Is that it?''

''No, she likes it very well.''

''Then why?''

''I . . . I realize you do it as a kindness. It is most kind. But, you see, I may not always be in your employ, and what then would become of Mother? She would be forced to move out.''

"Aha, so I am right. There is a young man on the horizon."

"No. No. Absolutely not. I have no wish, no intention of marrying. I simply meant the children are growing—"

"Mary, Mary." He got up and put his arm around her, squeezing her shoulder gently. "Is that all? You feel indebted, is that it?"

"Yes, yes, I suppose that is it."

Though he'd put his arm around her before, she felt oddly uncomfortable about the way he squeezed her shoulder. She would have liked to shake loose his hold but did not dare.

"Well, don't worry your pretty little head. You want your mother to be comfortable, and so do I. It's as simple as that."

"Thank you, Mr. Caylew, thank you very much."

She moved, forcing him to remove his hand, but he called after her as she left the room, "Come down and have dinner with me. It's getting mighty lonesome being all alone."

"Of course. I'll bring the children."

"Oh, yes, do that."

He looked at her in a way she'd seen others look at her, the driver on the horsecar, the young man who had passed his stop, and Nathan. Yet hadn't Mr. Caylew been the one to warn her of Nathan, the one to protect her from his son? He'd told her to come to him if anything untoward happened. Surely she was wrong to even suspect him of wrong conduct.

Nevertheless that evening she pulled her golden hair back, pinning it in the tightest, least attractive knot. Yet, though ill at ease in being waited on at his table, the evening was not entirely unpleasant. The children were at first afraid to talk to a parent who was a virtual stranger to them, which left Mr. Caylew to carry on the conversation and Damaris to reply. She refused the wine he offered her, but he did not press her to take it. The succulent fresh lobster with peas newly picked and a most scrumptious chocolate mousse with whipped cream were the best she had ever tasted. Still, she breathed a sigh of relief when it was over.

"You must dine with me again," he said as they bade

him good night. "Having you young people around makes me feel young again."

Damaris decided her suspicions of him were unworthy. She had wronged him in thinking he wanted anything more than their company, or that he had had any other motive except to be kind to a lonely widow.

When next she saw her mother she was already ensconced in the house on Catherine Street, with its bow windows and spacious rooms. It was a pretty house, and Damaris, seeing how happy her mother was in her new surroundings, how changed in attitude, felt she would have been wrong to raise any objection.

Her mother was full of plans. "Mrs. Cuddon, the housekeeper, is quite excellent. I can see I shall get along with her famously. She remembers your father, and she is most respectful. And I saw the rector and invited him and his wife to dine next week. You know I didn't care for her, but really she's quite agreeable and never mentions a word about the fact that you are employed, which is a relief. I mean, well, you know what I mean. You do understand, don't you, Damaris?"

Damaris nodded. She did understand her mother. There were times she wished she did not.

"And I've been asked to join the Garden Club. Oh, I nearly forgot. Mr. Caylew called to see how I was getting on, and he's asked me to come to tea on Sunday. He said you would come over in the morning and call for me. We can go to church together, just like old times. He's such a nice gentleman, Damaris, such a a nice, kind gentleman. You know, Damaris, I just think he's the one to select a suitable husband for you. I must speak to him about it."

Her daughter's protests were lost as her mother ushered her outside to show her the plum tree.

"They say the fruit is even finer and sweeter. It's a young tree; young fruit is usually more succulent. It must be so, for the rector's wife asked me if I wouldn't mind saving some for her."

SIX

The ideal summer in Newport became less ideal as Mr. Caylew prolonged his stay. Whenever he dined at home he insisted upon Damaris and the children dining with him, or else he would appear just as they were leaving for the beach, saying he had decided to come with them. He repeatedly said they made him feel like a boy again; yet Damaris found nothing boyish about him, for when he was with them they did just as he wished, she as well as the children. He directed the conversation; he decided the way they should walk and when they should turn back. He did not like blackberries, so they could not stop to pick them.

Still, he had been kind, and Damaris chided herself for waiting so eagerly for the announcement of his return to New York.

Her mother was invited to tea; it was, she told Damaris afterwards, the highlight of her summer. Though Damaris was pleased to find her mother less of a recluse, she was embarrassed by her unceasing thanks and praise for Mr. Caylew, justified though they might be. The effusions did not seem to annoy him, however. He sat back and nodded his acknowledgment, looking over at her as he did so. She sensed he was waiting for her to do more than murmur her affirmation.

Her growing and inexpressible dread at his continued presence in Newport was somehow connected with the kindness he had shown and continued to show to her mother and, by extension, to herself. She remembered Mother Charlotte's words on having to beg for everything. People gave not only to feel magnanimous but because they wanted to be thanked. Yet Damaris had an inchoate suspicion that her mother's repeated thanks to Mr. Caylew were not enough, that he stayed because he was waiting, wanting something more.

It was after dinner one evening—she had been asked to stay and play the piano for him after the children had been sent up to bed—that her suspicion became a certainty.

"I haven't played in so long. I'm not sure I still know how," she protested.

"It doesn't matter. Play anything to soothe the spirits of a lonely man."

So she began "Greensleeves," and after a few bars he asked her to sing too. She did, her voice quavering as she felt his eyes fixed upon her. When he came to stand over her, she faltered and stopped.

"What's wrong, Mary? What is it?"

There was so much concern in his voice that she burst out crying. At that he put his arm around her, asking again, "What is it? You can tell me. What's troubling you?"

And she gulped. "It's the house, the house you gave my mother to live in."

"But she's happy there, isn't she?"

She nodded.

"What's wrong, then?"

Though feeling ashamed, she went on. "I keep wondering why you did it. Please, I know this sounds as though I am an absolute ingrate. I think I am. I know you did it out of the goodness of your heart, yet I feel that you want—"

"Want what?"

"I don't know. I don't know what you could want. It just seems that thanking you is not enough."

She waited for his disclaimer, but none came. He's angry, she thought, and he has every right to be angry.

And his next words conveyed a sense of injustice done. "I want you to be happy, Mary. That's why I gave your mother the house."

"Oh, but I am. Mr. Caylew, I don't want you to misunderstand—"

"I don't want you to misunderstand either, Mary. I've told you that I'm lonely. I want to make you happy. And you have it in your power to make me happy, very happy, if you wish to." He stroked her shoulder gently, adding, "But it is entirely up to you. Only if you wish it."

She felt her heart pounding; her face flushed scarlet. She thought of Angela Wickers's warning: "You have something men want, your innocence." She found herself trapped by Caylew's generosity, but more than that by her mother's new contentment.

"I don't understand," she faltered.

"Don't you, my dear?" He ran his fingers gently down her arm and went to put his arms around her; but she got up, knocking over the piano stool.

"But you told me that Nathan was not to touch me. You told me to come to you."

"I did." He smiled. "It's not a boy you need to teach you this, but a man."

"I'm sorry, Mr. Caylew. I can't."

"Can't or won't? Just think about it. There's plenty of time."

That was the first night she locked the door to her bedroom. She lay in her narrow bed, her cheeks burning, her heart beating fast. She lay there stiff and still, not sleeping. She must go away, run away, but where? Her mother wouldn't believe her; she could almost hear her scoffing at the way her daughter imagined things. Worse yet, Mr. Caylew would probably turn her out of the new home that she loved, while Damaris would be without employment to find her another. Her father had consigned her mother to her care. She would be letting him down.

From Templeton Caylew came nothing but innuendo. "Such a lovely day, isn't it, Mary, but it might have been so much lovelier."

Or else, "How restful Newport is after the pace of the city; yet still I am not relaxing in the way I might, certainly not as I would wish to."

There was, she decided, only one way out, that was to persuade her mother to give up the house. But since the reasons she gave were garbled, her mother was baffled as to why she should forgo something she enjoyed. "But why, Damaris, why should I want to leave here? I don't understand what you mean."

"It's the tie. . . . You see, the Caylew children are

growing. I shan't be employed there forever, in fact I may
not be there much longer at all. I may have to leave."

"Have to leave? You are so mysterious. Why on earth
would you have to leave?"

"I don't know. I don't know," she repeated in agitation.

"Well, I don't know either. One minute Mr. Caylew is
singing your praises, the next you're telling me you may
leave. It doesn't make sense."

"I know it doesn't. Nothing makes sense."

Her mother would never willingly give up the house,
that was quite certain.

The only way out was to find other employment. She
now had experience; training under an English nanny was
a good recommendation. There must be others needing the
services of a nursemaid.

Luck favored her, for she heard from the rector of a
family summering in Newport at a house adjacent to the
Caylews' who had complained when their nurse had argued that five children under seven years of age were too
many for one person to care for. Damaris would be only
too glad to take on such a direct, unencumbered challenge.
Armed with an introduction from the rector, she sought
them out, to be well received. She made no objections to
the workload they proposed, and they, in turn, found her
young and pliable, with the added recommendation of
having been trained by an English nanny. They appeared
to provide the answer to one another's dilemma.

Plucking up courage to face Caylew, she gave him
notice of her desire to take this new position, only to be
rebuffed by an expression of hurt astonishment.

"But why, Mary? Have I not been kind to you? Is this
fair? I have done all I could to help your mother, and now
you repay me by wishing to leave my children to care for
others. I ask you, is it fair?"

"Not when you put it that way, no."

"And how else is there to put it?"

"Mr. Caylew, I have been troubled by your . . . your
suggestion of the other night. That is why I must make this
change."

"And did I do anything to you?"

"No. But you . . . you asked me to . . . to make you
happy," she faltered.

"I see nothing reprehensible in that wish. You know I am lonely. You are without ties; you've told me so yourself."

"It's not a question of that. It's simply more than I can do. And since it is more than I can do, I must leave. I must find work elsewhere."

"I see," he said slowly, repeating, "I see."

She stood still, saying nothing, and his voice changed, softened. She was amazed to see his eyes glistening. Was it anger or sadness? It was hard to tell from the sharp expression of his voice.

"Do you have any idea how you have hurt me, Mary? Can you have any notion of how I have longed all this time to hold you to touch you? But have I ever lifted a finger against you, or tried to make you do anything against your wishes?"

She shook her head.

"Many men in my position would have done so. I could have, but I did not. I have acted honorably; that you cannot deny. I have, it is true, asked for your kindness toward me. I explained my loneliness. I would refuse you nothing. I think you must know that, but you have chosen to refuse me, even though what I ask would rob no one, but it would bring so much happiness. I beg you to think, to be kind."

Inwardly she cringed; it was horrible, horrible. She felt a web spinning around her tighter, tighter, and her own helplessness in its midst.

"I can't, Mr. Caylew. I'm sorry. I can't."

His face grew stern. "Very well. Then you may go."

"I . . . under the circumstances, sir, I think it better that I leave immediately."

"To go where?"

"To the people I spoke to you about—the ones who have offered me employment."

"They won't repeat that offer, I can guarantee you, not without references, they won't. And at the moment I am too hurt, too angered by your attitude to be able to give you any recommendation at all."

"But that's unfair!" she argued hotly. "I've done nothing wrong. My services have been exemplary; you can ask

Mrs. Wickers. Why, you've even said so yourself. You have to give me a reference.''

He stood up, towering over her. "I don't *have* to do anything.'' His voice quivered with suppressed rage. "It's you who *have* to do something to earn it.''

She stood firm, fists clenched, her voice brimming with sarcasm. "At last, Mr. Caylew, you are being frank about your motives. Maybe I should be grateful for even that touch of honesty.''

And then he smiled, his smile far less pleasing to her than his anger. "My dear, there is much more for which you could be grateful if you would only realize it.''

The web had not only tightened, but it had closed. There was no escaping her mother's alarm when Mr. Caylew intimated that her daughter was unhappy and wanted to leave his employ. There was no escape from Mr. Caylew himself, alternately kind and stern, changes of temperament that only served to increase her turmoil.

Returning from a walk with the children the next day, Damaris paused before the replica of Tintoretto's *Paradiso* in the hall with its vengeful angel driving Adam and Eve from the Garden. Now she understood the terror caused by that angel, because she felt that terror in her heart. She knew too why his shadow fell before him, so that his vengeance on those in a state of sin would be clear for all to see.

Lost in her thoughts, in the painting, she hadn't heard Mr. Caylew's approach. His face was unsmiling. "My patience is at an end. You may come to me tonight, Mary, or tomorrow you may leave.''

"But where can I go when you refuse me a reference?''

"That is your concern. And you understand when you leave I shall be forced to ask your mother to vacate my house. You have trifled with me, Mary, and I am not a man to be trifled with. If it is your decision to leave you may do so, or you may decide to make all of us happy. The choice is yours.''

There was no choice; there was no one to turn to for help. To disclose her dilemma to the rector would embarrass all of them; besides, she suspected he would be unwilling to do anything that might offend his most influential parishioner. There was no point in confiding in her mother, who refused to listen to anything she didn't want to hear. Most of all there was no point in crying or pleading with Templeton Caylew himself. She had already done that and recognized by the tone of his voice that he had no more patience for words.

She went to him. She went in shame, but not in trembling. She had decided it was the only way, and she followed a course she deplored with the grim determination that had always been hers.

While in that plush overfurnished bedroom, lying amidst that huge feather-down mattress, she said and did nothing. She wished the deed might have been done in the darkness to which she assigned it in her own mind, but he left the lamp burning, looking long on her nakedness. He was not rough, not unkind; he seemed to go to some length not to hurt her. She only wished he had hurt her far more. The cry that broke from her lips as he entered her was anguish at her situation rather than anguish at any pain he inflicted. That she scarcely felt, for she was virtually numb.

What was it, she wondered after, when she at last made her way back to her own narrow bed, that had made him plead for this sordid, mean, unpleasant act? What made him long for it so? What pleasure had he gained in return for her unhappiness?

Obviously it was something beyond her comprehension, for when she saw him the following day, a meeting she had approached with a sense of loathing, he was relaxed, smiling, complacent.

"It's Sunday tomorrow, Mary," he reminded her. "Don't forget to go in and get your mother. She enjoyed tea here last week. I'm asking Cook to have a coconut cake, for she told me that was her favorite."

Sunday meant church, and taking Communion, and talking to the rector and his wife, just as though nothing had happened. The host burned on her tongue; the wine was bitter as gall. She couldn't stand her mother's endless chatter at tea, or Mr. Caylew acting the part of the genial, gracious host, arranging for her mother to take with her another coconut cake made especially for that purpose.

Damaris pretended not to hear her mother's parting words. "You're such a kind and good gentleman. My daughter and I don't know where we would be without you, do we, Damaris?''

"Your mother seems happy," Templeton Caylew remarked as the carriage pulled away.

"Yes," she said bitterly. Her mother's happiness had had a heavy price.

"And you?"

"I am glad she is happy."

"It will be better tonight," he said as they re-entered the house. "The first time is always most difficult. You'll see."

With a sense of dread, Damaris realized it had not been enough to give up her virginity to him, but that more was expected of her.

If refusal before had been impossible, refusal afterwards was not to be countenanced. He would listen to no arguments. "I won't stand for coyness; I've had enough of that. You're a woman now; you know what it is all about."

Yet as she lay beneath his heaving, laboring form, always she wondered what it was about. She experienced nothing but revulsion each time he touched her, nothing but disgust at his manner of examining her body, at the way his hands moved over her until he was ready to consummate an act that paradoxically gave him relief even as it added to her own tension. She loathed him, but more than she loathed him she loathed herself for not having withstood him, no matter the cost to her mother, to herself.

He had laid siege to her for some time before he took her. Once having gained his end, he seemed satisfied. The battle won, he announced what she had waited so long to hear, his return to New York.

"Discretion is of the utmost importance, Mary. My family will soon be back from England. Word of this must never reach them or anyone. I know I can rely on you as, in return, you can rely on my willingness to continue to care for your mother. You're loyal and dutiful, I know; but even so, I want you to promise me that you will tell no one, no one at all. Promise?"

She turned her head away from him. "I promise." It wasn't hard to do as he asked. Her shame would never allow her to speak of it.

"I've enjoyed this. You've reinvigorated me, made me feel young again. You must understand, though, that in New York I shan't be able to see you in this way. If anything should happen, let me know and I will arrange matters for you."

"Anything should happen?" she repeated dully.

"You know what I mean surely; you're no longer a little innocent. I'm a gentleman of my word. If anything should happen, it will be taken care of, I promise." He stroked her thighs. "You may lack fire, but you've a lovely body. I'll miss you. No," he said as she went to leave his bed. "Not yet. Just once more."

As she lay back beside him she thought of Mother Charlotte saying no Christian could hate because none of God's creatures was deserving of hatred; but Damaris knew she passionately hated Templeton Caylew. If ever fate gave her the opportunity of gaining her revenge upon him, she would do so gladly.

SEVEN

"I have to admit Miss Eustacia Caylew was the toast of London." Mrs. Wickers sniffed. "I heard Mrs. Caylew regaling her husband when he met the boat with tales of her offers. Three knights, a baronet, and a marquess, she claims; though I tend to doubt that last. She was a success, it is true, but so vain; and you can see for yourself, Mary, she's come back with none of them."

Ever since her return, Angela Wickers had talked unceasingly of the sophistication of London and the beauty of the countryside and of Creswell Hall, the estate of Lord Langley where they had stayed, for Eustacia had managed to ingratiate herself with the debutante of the year, Sophia Langley. There had been a detailed account of everything Mrs. Caylew and her daughter had selected for their wardrobes. They'd had to admit that London was the place to find true elegance; and that good-for-nothing Lawrence Caylew, who had joined them, had pronounced English horseflesh the finest in the world.

Yet despite Angela Wickers's unremitting praise for her native land, Damaris sensed she was not sorry to be back. She had apparently not sought employment in England, as Damaris had expected she might, for she had returned with all her personal effects, books, and photographs, with which she proceeded to furnish her sitting room more comfortably in her own style. That indicated that she did not plan to go home again.

Damaris had heartily welcomed back her tall, angular figure.

"And how was your summer, Mary?" she had been asked more than once.

If only she had not gone, Damaris had thought as she avoided a reply, the summer might have been so different. No, rather than different, it would have been the same as in other years. Oh, that it had only been the same! Certainly, had Mrs. Wickers been present, what had happened could never have occurred. And to think she had looked forward to the summer without her, to a summer of freedom that had turned into one of the most horrible bondage imaginable.

"Well, you still haven't told me how it was in Newport, Mary."

"Oh, it was . . ." She gulped, not even wishing to think of how it had been.

"I heard Mr. Caylew say he'd spent some time there with the children."

"Yes, he did."

Mrs. Wickers scrutinized her. "Did something go wrong? Were the children too much for you?"

"No, no. They were good, very good."

"Then what is it? I can see something must have happened. Is that mother of yours complaining again?"

"No, she's much happier now she's moved into a bigger house that she likes very much."

Perhaps it was the reminder of that house, perhaps it was because she felt so low and had done ever since her return, perhaps it was simply because her nerves had been on edge ever since. Whatever it was, she broke into tears and found herself sobbing. Mrs. Wickers's arms were around her, pressing her head into her angular shoulder, stroking her hair with a touch far softer than Damaris would have ever imagined.

"Now, now, Mary," she soothed. "I had a suspicion something happened this summer as soon as I saw you. I know you very well by now, and there's something different. You don't smile in the way you used to; you're less serene. What's wrong, Mary? You know you can trust me. Tell me everything."

But Damaris, feeling the warmth of another's concern and longing to confide her guilt, her grief, remembered Caylew's warning.

"Oh, it's nothing." She wiped her eyes. "Just the wrong time of the month, that's all."

Would that it were the wrong time of the month, she thought when at last she escaped from Angela Wickers's presence, for therein lay her greatest fear. It was due; she knew it must be due, yet it had not come.

She would have prayed for that fear to be unfounded had she been able to pray, but she had not set foot in church since that last Communion taken at Newport. She was in a state of sin; she had so sinned she could not even ask God's forgiveness. If it was as she suspected, if she were with child, surely that must be her punishment.

Her absence from St. Stephen's on Sunday was noticed more by Dr. Hunter than by anyone else. He had especially looked for her since the family's return, for Mother Charlotte had been worried because she had not returned to see them at Mercy House.

One morning, in greeting Mr. Caylew at the end of the service, he asked after her. Having missed seeing her for several Sundays, he wondered whether she was quite well. Mr. Caylew had had great difficulty in placing just who it was the rector was referring to; but Mrs. Caylew, who had overheard the inquiry, reminded her husband that he himself had engaged Mary Fanshawe to help Nanny Wickers.

His wrinkled brow cleared. "Ah, but of course, you mean the young person from Newport."

"She was when you took her on, Templeton, but now she's quite grown. Remember, she took care of Nathan when he hurt his foot last year, and you asked me to find someone else for the job, because you didn't want to tempt fate. I myself hadn't realized until then how much she had grown up."

"Yes, yes, of course. I know who you mean. And you say this . . . this Mary Fanshawe hasn't been attending church, Dr. Hunter? I wasn't aware of that. I shall have to look into it."

"I'll have a talk with her, Dr. Hunter," Mrs. Caylew said firmly. "She'll be here next Sunday."

"Mrs. Caylew, I wouldn't want her to come against her will," the rector put in hastily, while Mr. Caylew, with equal haste, assured his wife. "My dear, you mustn't bother yourself with such trifles. I'll take care of it."

"Would you, Templeton? Really, these servants are a nuisance!"

"I couldn't agree with you more," her husband affirmed in tones of cold fury. "I'll talk to the young woman and straighten her out."

"I wish you would. I wouldn't want her around the children if she's developing any atheistic tendencies."

"Nor would I. It may be better to get rid of her."

"Well, Templeton, you talk to her. I shall rely on your judgment."

So Damaris was sent for.

It was the first time she had faced her persecutor since her return to New York. He sat at his desk, much as he had the first time she had been in his presence. He addressed her in much the same way, reading his mail as he talked.

"Mary, Dr. Hunter tells us you have not been attending church since your return to New York. He is concerned, my wife is concerned, and I can say that I am concerned, and displeased. You will attend service next Sunday. Any absence is to be accounted for to Mrs. Wickers, who will, in turn, report to me. Do you understand?" And when she said nothing, he repeated his question, stressing each word of his final "Do . . . you . . . understand?"

"I shall not return to church, Mr. Caylew," Damaris reponded with quiet dignity.

"You'll do as I say."

"Not anymore."

He put aside all pretense of reading his letters and banged his clenched fist on the desktop. "And why won't you attend church?"

"Because I am in a state of sin."

His face grew red. "If your reference to a state of sin concerns anything that transpired this summer—"

"That is exactly what I mean."

"You gave me your solemn promise never to speak of it."

"Nor have I spoken of it, to anyone. Nevertheless, it has left me in a state of sin, and—"

"And what?"

"I fear I may be with child."

There followed a silence that Caylew broke with a heavy sigh. "I see. Very well. I won't deny my part."

"I was untouched before, and you well know it. You can't deny your part," she scorned.

"Look, my girl. I gave you my word then, as a gentleman, to take care of anything that might happen. As a gentleman I shall keep that word; but I warn you, don't try my patience with your insolence."

"If you're an example, God save me from gentlemen."

His brows furrowed in anger. "I'm willing to help you out of this mess you're in. You'd better thank God for that."

"Just how do you propose to do that?"

"I'll pay for what has to be done. Thousands in my place wouldn't. You came to me, remember. I used no force. But I'm willing to do my part. Go and see Madame Restell. She keeps a house at Fifty-second and Fifth Avenue. She'll take care of it. It will cost fifty dollars, but I'm willing to bear the cost."

"Is that the woman the servants refer to as Madame Killer?"

"I've no idea what they may call her, but she does her job," he rasped in irritation. "It's that or, if aborting goes against your high and mighty principles, perhaps I can arrange for someone to marry you. Your mother asked me to look out for a likely husband for you. The new footman's single, I believe, and not bad-looking. I can't promise, but it may be possible. He's a likely lad; might be able to put some fire in you."

"Thank you. No."

"Well, that's settled then. I've done my part." He reached into his pocket for a roll of bills and began to count them off. "And after this, Mary, I want to hear nothing more from you. Do as you're told and there will be no trouble. Otherwise, I suggest you find yourself other employment."

"I wished to do that earlier," she said bitterly. "You would give no references."

"If you continue to act as you're now acting, I'll be glad to give references just to get rid of you. Rather than being grateful for my generosity to you, and to your mother, I might add, you're biting the hand that feeds you both. Here." He handed her the amount he had counted out. "That's an end to the matter."

"No, Mr. Caylew." As she pocketed the money she drew out a sheet of paper that she set before him. "That's not quite the end. There's the matter of my mother living in a house you own. I don't want to find her dispossessed. You may buy my silence *and* put an end to the matter by signing this document. It guarantees you will allow my mother to freely remain in the house she now occupies for her lifetime; it also promises that you will contribute to her annually the amount I now send her until such time as she is awarded her widow's pension. It will scarcely put you out of pocket; it's a mere pittance to you."

His face grew red as he read the document she had put before him. "This is blackmail!" he bellowed. "I'm not about to be blackmailed by a slut and a whore!"

"Names won't hurt me now; you have hurt me far beyond that. I've given you my terms. As for blackmail, you may be right. But blackmail and coercion were the tactics you employed to induce the condition in which I now find myself. It was not from any warm and generous heart that you went out of your way to please my mother, but to force me into a position where I would have to do your will. You guessed my sense of loyalty to her would come before my own sense of personal honor. I've since realized how wrong I was, but it is done."

"You're right it's done, and the sooner I see the back of you, the better I'll like it. I'll let your mother stay in the house, but I can see no reason why I should pay her an allowance. No, certainly not!"

"You won't have my wages to pay any longer. And you have given me another mouth to feed."

"You're not going to Restell, then?"

She shook her head.

"Well, at least if you're leaving I have to thank God for small mercies. It's worth signing this to be rid of you. Why I ever found you desirable in the first place, I'll never know. Women are always making asses of men, but this'll be the last time."

"Then, if we've both learned something, it may not have been entirely in vain." As he signed the paper, she reached over and blotted the signature and refolded it and put it in her pocket, adding, "I'll keep this carefully."

"I'll just bet you will."

"You're quite fortunate, Mr. Caylew. The world will regard you as a benefactor for caring for a poor widow. Such would not be the case if I demanded care for your child, would it?"

"Slut! Harlot!" he muttered half under his breath as she opened the door and left the room.

Upstairs, Angela Wickers came upon her gathering together her few things.

"What is this, Mary?" she cried in agitation. "Mrs. Caylew has just told me you're leaving. It can't be true. I told her how well the children had got along with you this summer, what an an asset you are to the nursery, but she says you're an atheist. What does she mean?"

"I'm not an atheist, Angela."

"Then tell her, explain. Please, I beg of you."

Damaris turned. She had expected to have to make some explanation, but she had not expected to have to answer such anguished inquiries.

"I . . . it's most likely because, as you pointed out, the children are growing. Augustus is old enough for a tutor. They don't need two of us anymore."

"But why so suddenly, and what is this thing of not going back to church? I told Mrs. Caylew that it was only temporary, that you were simply indisposed. I assured her you're a strong believer, that you're most meticulous in having the children say grace, in listening to their prayers at bedtime. I promised her you would be at St. Stephen's as usual next Sunday. Oh, Mary, what does it cost you to sit through a dull ceremony and make a few meaningless responses. I don't believe, but I go."

"That's the difference between us, Angela. You see, I do believe. That is why I can't go." And fearing she had said too much, Damaris turned back to putting her clothes together.

"Mary, oh, my darling Mary!" Angela Wickers's arms were around her. She pulled her close, stroking her hair, kissing the top of her head again and again as she whispered, "My darling, my dearest one. I can't, I won't let you go. If you go, then I shall go with you. Oh, Mary, don't you understand? I love you. You're the only reason I came back to America." Holding her closer, she raised her voice in an anguished cry. "I love you, Mary, I love you."

"Please, Angela, please," Damaris whispered softly, understanding at last all those sidelong glances from the servants, the grins, the whispers, the innuendos they'd cast at her that had gone over her head. "Please. I didn't know. But please, for your sake, be quiet. They'll hear you."

"I don't care if they do. All this time we've spent together, I've wanted to tell you what was in my heart. And now I have."

But her arms dropped as she spoke, and she stood back turning her head away so that Damaris had to reach over to touch her shoulder, forcing her to turn, to look at her.

"Thank you, Angela. Thank you for telling me. Do you know you're the only person who has ever told me that they loved me? I'll never forget that. I'm grateful to you for many things; that's far from the least of them. I want you to know that I love you too. Not, I suppose, in the same way you love me, but I do love you, nevertheless, and I'll continue to love you always."

"Let me come with you. You're in some trouble; I know you are. I'll take care of you."

Damaris shook her head. "No, it isn't possible. But I shall keep you in my prayers."

BOOK TWO

Colonel Parrish

Know'st thou not, there is but one
  theme for
  ever-enduring bards?
And that is the theme of war, the
  fortune of
  battles,
The making of perfect soldiers?

> Walt Whitman
> "As I Ponder'd in
> Silence"

ONE

Eustacia Caylew had returned from England in love. Not with a duke or a marquess or even a baronet, who, had he been quite as penniless as the man of whom she was enamored, would nevertheless have been entirely acceptable to her family. A title, after all, was worth paying for, but not a run-down cotton plantation.

"A Southerner!" her father had bellowed when his wife had confided the facts of the matter to him on their return.

"Yes, he's from Memphis. I think it's in Louisiana or somewhere equally unthinkable."

"Anywhere outside New York is detestable to you, Isabel. Memphis happens to be in Tennessee, biggest cotton shipping port on the Mississippi River," her husband corrected. "There's nothing wrong with the place. I don't give a damn for that, but I simply won't have Lucy marrying a Southerner. I can't think what came over you, Isabel, not to have watched her more closely. I thought the idea of this trip to England was to find her a titled husband."

"I'm well aware of that, Templeton. As I explained to you, she had not one but several offers from members of the nobility. She wouldn't have any of them. I tried to reason with her, to no avail, and I consider all of this your fault rather than mine. You have spoiled her so; if it had been left to me, I should have demanded far greater compliancy all along."

Her husband ignored her complaint, one obviously heard many times before. "Well, she's not marrying a Southerner, and that's that," he avowed with finality. "I won't hear of her throwing herself away on a worthless rebel, so she might as well put him completely out of her head."

95

Isabel Caylew wavered. "I wouldn't exactly call him a worthless rebel; he is very definitely a gentleman. In fact, in many ways, I find myself forced to admit, he appeared more of a gentleman than some of the titled Englishmen we met."

"That's as may be, but to my way of thinking there are no gentlemen south of the Mason and Dixon, only a bunch of rabble-rousers who wanted things their own way and were prepared to take the country down with them to get it. They almost succeeded in ruining our economy. I'll never welcome one as a son-in-law, so Lucy might as well put him completely from her mind."

"As a matter of fact, Templeton, I think it would be as well if she did. You see, he appears to have no wish to marry Lucy."

Though his heavy eyebrows shot up in surprise, Templeton Caylew growled, "So much the better."

"Still, knowing Lucy, I'm not at all sure the matter ends there. She seems so very smitten and keeps insisting he's the only man she's ever wanted. She says she's determined to have him."

It was true. Colonel Harwood Gaius Parrish was the only man that Eustacia Caylew, the girl desired by so many gentlemen, herself desired; and when Eustacia Caylew desired something, she was prepared to move any impediment, even the bulk and power of Templeton Caylew, to make it hers. In that respect, she resembled her father; in that respect, her father both respected and feared her.

Despite being armed with introductions to the right people, taking a house with a good Mayfair address, and arriving with the set purpose of having London at her feet, Eustacia was soon bored by all of it.

Perhaps it was the ease with which she had conquered that annoyed her. It had all been too effortless. Like her father, she appreciated most those things for which one wrestled and waited. Of course, dowagers might whisper behind their fans of colonial upstarts, of new and questionable money; but news of her fortune, while an obvious asset, was not the only reason that her dance card was filled before any other's. She was lovely, with soft, pouting lips that were so obviously kissable; she was vivacious and breathed an air of newness and freedom that entranced the stuffy gentlemen who frequented London's equally stuffy drawing rooms.

True, that seasons's new debutantes had not been the most exciting. Eustacia had looked them over and decided there was only one worthy of her envy, and she had wisely made a friend of her. The Honorable Sophia Langley, daughter of Lord William Langley, had been the sole star prior to the arrival of Eustacia Caylew. She had at first joined in the snide remarks about the little colonial in their midst, but had responded, perhaps from curiosity, to Eustacia's overtures. The result, surprising to both, had been the development of a close intimacy, if not a firm friendship. Indeed, Eustacia found she often preferred the company of Sophia, with her incisive remarks, to the clip-tongued, all too effete and humorless gentlemen who soon began to haunt her door.

Within a month of her arrival in England, Eustacia had received three proposals of marriage, none of which she had found even tempting. She would, she told her mother, just as soon settle for one of the New York Schuylers, or a Belmont, or even her Vandervoort third cousin.

"Far be it from me to argue that the Vandervoorts are not equally as fine." Her mother was forever praising her superior lineage to her children. "But the title, dear; do think of the title and the effect it would have in New York. A title would clearly put you in a commanding social position."

"I am in a commanding social position, Mama," Eustacia had replied with a toss of her head.

"Yes," her mother agreed, "but it would ensure your keeping it."

"Never fear. I shall."

To ward off boredom there were endless shopping excursions to completely replenish an already overflowing wardrobe. Wide sleeves were in, so all her dresses must have wide sleeves. She eschewed bonnets for the new pert pillbox hats, and her hair was restyled in coronet braids and decorated with flowing ribbons and flower sprays for the unending series of assemblies and balls. But even these amusements, even her long-awaited presentation to the Queen, who had shocked her by appearing less regal than her own mother, all began to pall as the summer months passed. Life became tiresome; even the largest, most splendid gatherings held little hope of amusement. She longed for excitement. She longed to fall in love as others fell in love with her, yet none of the staid, proper, plum-voiced gentlemen, with their immovable upper lips hidden behind bristling mustaches, aroused so much as a quickened heartbeat.

Though bored with London, she hadn't looked forward to her long-promised visit to the Langleys' estate in Hampshire. Sophia was her best friend; but Eustacia found her parents dreary, horsey in the way only English people were horsey, and she guessed that their friends would be cut of the same cloth. Then, too, others might rave about the English countryside, but she found it too wet, too green, entirely too bucolic for her liking.

The first sight of Creswell Hall hadn't improved her humor. A long graystone mansion set amidst an undulating green park, it was bound to be poorly heated, Eustacia thought gloomily. She had brought her new rose amber silk with its ruched satin trim. It had the widest skirt she'd ever worn and the lowest neckline, cut to perfection to frame her soft white shoulders, cut so low, in fact, that her mother had insisted on a wide bertha; still, Eustacia had managed to select one of a lace so fine as to be practically invisible. She hated the cold. It would mean wearing the matching jacket. It was stylish with its frogged lapels and collar, but the dress was not nearly as enticing with it on. Even more gloomily, she supposed there would be no one to entice.

As they drove up the wide approach to the mansion, Lord Langley was just returning from the hunt. With him were several gentlemen, scarlet-clad like himself, except for one; and Eustacia, after scanning the group, saw only that one. He sat in the saddle with an ease that the others did not possess, horse and rider moving as one. She saw at once he did not post for the trot, yet there was no jarred movement, only an easy grace. As they drew closer she noticed his long face and high cheekbones, the slight curl to his dark hair beneath his beaver; closer still, she noticed his deep-set eyes and the generous curve to his lips, all the more obvious because he was the only gentleman among them clean-shaven.

The surprise had come at their introduction. Though his reply, "I'm most happy to make your acquaintance, Miss Caylew," had not differed in content from the others, his voice, with its low accented Southern tones, had been soft and pleasant to her ear.

She had dressed with more than usual care for dinner, throwing caution to the wind despite the cold and donning her new pink dress, but refusing to wear the jacket.

"You'll catch your death unless you take it along, Miss Eustacia," Mrs. Wickers had warned.

But she had shrugged. "I'm perfectly all right. Besides, there's bound to be a fire."

"Even if there is a fire, you shouldn't go too close, not with the width of that skirt. You know how many accidents there've been."

"I know, Wickers. But please don't fuss. I'm not in the nursery, you know."

She had not seated herself close to the fire, not from fear of her dress catching fire, though without Mrs. Wickers's warning she knew that was not an uncommon occurrence, but because *he* did not sit close to the fire. She was sure he must approach her—after all, they were both Americans—but he did not, so she made devious yet purposeful moves until she found a seat beside him, complaining, quite untruthfully, that the fire had been far too warm.

"How do you find life so far from home, Colonel Parrish?" she had asked with only the slightest flutter of her dark lashes. Gentlemen of her acquaintance had swooned at less, but Colonel Parrish gave no sign of swooning; in fact he gave no sign of noticing anything out of the ordinary as he responded, "Gratifyingly peaceful, Miss . . . ma'am."

That had annoyed her. Gentlemen did not forget her name. Had she not found him so appealing, it would have been cause to turn on her heel.

"Miss Caylew, Eustacia Caylew," she reminded him. "Of the New York Caylews. My mother is a Vandervoort."

He acknowledged this with the slightest smile and incline of his head, as though he found her pretentious but not of special interest; and he made no attempt to continue the conversation, so that she was the one to ask, "You have been here long, Colonel?"

"Close on two months, I suppose it must be."

"Then we arrived at the same time. You sailed from New York?"

"Charleston."

His terse replies did nothing to prolong the conversation; still she persevered.

Geography, in fact lessons of any kind, had never held her attention, but she hazarded, "Your home, then, is Georgia?"

"Charleston is in South Carolina, ma'am, but my home is Tennessee—Memphis."

"Memphis. I don't believe I've ever heard of it," and then, for fear he might castigate her ignorance, she added, "That's an unusual name. Indian, I suppose."

"I rather imagine that General Overton, who named it, chose Memphis after the city of ancient Egypt. Originally the area was Indian land, Chickasaw Bluffs. It overlooks the great Mississippi."

"And you live in the city itself, Colonel Parrish?"

"Bellechasse lies on the river south of Memphis, though we have always maintained a house in town." He looked up as a young lady entered, plainly dressed, her hair center-parted but without great style. Immediately Eustacia felt a flash of anger that he should look at anyone else while talking to her, followed by a surge of relief as he went on, "But here is my sister, Lavinia. I am sure she can enlighten you on Memphis just as well as I."

And after introducing the two ladies, he turned to join his host, leaving them alone.

Eustacia was mortified. He had turned away from her, just as she had observed men turn from women who were plain or boring. It was not to be borne. She thought to turn on her heel herself, leaving Miss Parrish to fare for herself, but on second thought she decided to bring this gentleman to heel and one obvious way to accomplish that would be through his young sister.

Lavinia Parrish was shy and retiring, but obviously flattered by Eustacia's interest and delighted to discover a fellow American. She had, Eustacia discovered, been sent to England to stay with her mother's family, the Harwoods, soon after the war began. And far from Eustacia gaining a great deal of information about Memphis, not that she was greatly interested in the subject, it was Lavinia who wished to learn from her about America.

"Do, please, Miss Caylew, tell me how life is there now. Guy says virtually nothing of it; it is most annoying."

"Guy?"

"My brother." And she cast a plainly affectionate glance in his direction.

"But I thought his name was Harwood," Eustacia put in, and then, for fear of having shown too much interest, "Or Harold or something like that."

"You're quite right. How clever of you to remember names; I never do. My brother's name really is Harwood— mother's maiden name, you see—but we've always called him Guy, for Gaius, the name father gave him. You see, he intended Guy for the law, and there was a Roman jurist of that name at the time of Antoninus Pius who had written a treatise that was discovered in Verona when father was a boy. I guess it caused quite a stir; at least father said it was an extraordinary discovery. Guy was sent to England to read law, while Nicholas, my older brother, stayed home with father to learn to manage the plantation."

"He doesn't look much like a lawyer," Eustacia commented, examining Colonel Parrish as he stood nonchalantly leaning against the mantel, glass in hand, following the pontifications of Lord Langley with an amused glint in his eye but with not so much as a glance in her direction. It was most provoking.

"It is as well, for he will no longer follow that profession, with father and Nicholas gone."

Seeing her companion's eyes begin to fill with tears, Eustacia hastened to assuage her curiosity on another point. "If he was studying in England, how does it come about that he is *Colonel* Parrish?"

"Well, you see, mother thought it best that I come to England to stay with her sister during the . . . the conflict. It was foolish, Miss Caylew. I only wish I might have stayed with the others and endured whatever they endured. But I was a child. I could not argue with my parents' decisions, and they did what they considered best for me."

"Just so, just so," Eustacia broke in abruptly. "But I

was wondering how your brother, whom you said was sent here for his education, came to attain the rank of colonel. Or perhaps it is an honorary designation.''

"No, indeed, far from it.'' Vehemently Lavinia Parrish shook her plainly coiffed dark brown head. "As I was explaining, I was sent to England, but Guy was already here engaged in his studies. He was to stay on here, but he refused to do so. He said he must return, no matter the cost.''

"Of interrupting his studies?''

"No, not that. But you see, the conflict placed him in a terrible predicament. Dear me, but I shouldn't speak of this to you, since you are from the North.''

"No, no, please do go on. I am not at all biased; you may express your opinions quite freely with me without any fear.'' Eustacia, in fact, held no opinions on a war that had impinged so little on her own life.

Lavinia smiled. "You're a most generous, kind lady. I'm so very happy you are here and are not bored in my company. I imagine there must be many gentlemen eying my position at your side with no little envy.''

"Not your brother, it would appear,'' Eustacia replied with some asperity. "Does he hold it against me that I come from the North?''

Lavinia shook her head. "I doubt that sincerely. You see, since he studied in England, the conflict in America placed him in a predicament. His ideas had changed; he did not agree on many issues with my father and brother.''

"Then why did he not stay here?''

"Miss Caylew, how he agonized over that. It was a terrible choice, but one he had to make. He said that to stand aside, to have stayed here and completed his studies (they wished him to do that; Father said the South would stand in need of good lawyers), that was cowardice. He went back for the family, not for the cause.''

Again Eustacia appraised the tall Southerner, a man of such easy grace that he made Sophia's brother, whom she'd previously thought not ill-favored, appear decidedly stolid. "He's young, though, to have attained the rank of colonel.''

"Guy says it was more by necessity than military skill,'' Lavinia Parrish replied reluctantly.

"Excuse me, dear Miss Parrish, I had no intention to pry. I simply meant that colonels of my acquaintance are almost all old and crusty."

"Well, I suppose he did rise rapidly; but you see, my brother was killed, and my father died of fever at the end of the war, though I believe it was from grief." Tears rose in Lavinia Parrish's eyes, and Eustacia took her hand, murmuring, "I know, I know. I also lost those close to me. It was a sorry business."

Her face bore such sympathy that it was impossible to tell that all males on both sides of her family had paid commutation fees for exemption from service or had hired substitutes to serve in their stead, all except for one distant cousin whom everyone had agreed was crazy. He had volunteered on the declaration of hostilities; suffering from queasiness of the bowels, he had overdosed himself with calomel and succumbed from a loss of vital fluids. It was an ignoble end to a short military career that never saw conflict. Still, the family had learned to appreciate him in death as they never had while he lived. He became the family hero and with his death prevented anyone from saying they hadn't done their part.

Eustacia spent the rest of the evening, to the annoyance of Sophia, who was also smitten by Colonel Parrish and wanted to whisper about him, close to the side of Lavinia Parrish, someone she might have found beneath her attention had she not been so charmed by her brother. That brother, unfortunately, though seeing to his sister's needs, paid her companion little heed despite all attempts to attract him.

"Colonel Parrish is apparently not a gentleman who is comfortable with ladies," she commented with asperity to Lavinia.

Lavinia laughed for the first time that evening. "Mother would have been surprised to hear you say that. She found him far too comfortable with the ladies. She was always saying thank goodness Father chose to name him Gaius after the jurist rather than Pius after the emperor, for Guy's humor bordered on the irreverent. She worried that he might get up to capricious escapades when he was away, and she was forever reminding my aunt to be sure he kept his nose to the books. Still, I don't think it was Guy's fault, for girls were forever pestering him. Mother always said that of all the young men around he got the most attention and was least deserving of it. She said it only proved that women are perverse creatures. But I do not agree. I am not in the least perverse, nor, I am sure, are you, Miss Caylew."

"Do, please, call me Lucy. My name is Eustacia, but Lucy is the name my family uses; and I should like you, as my dear friend, to use it also."

This was a privilege she had not even granted to Sophia. Lavinia, flushing with pleasure, seemed to realize it was an unusual honor. "Thank you, Lucy. And you will call me Livvy. That is the name Guy has always used for me, though my mother detested it and would never call me anything but Lavinia. I agree that Lavinia is much prettier, but Livvy sounds sweet coming from his lips—as it would from yours."

Eustacia, remembering that Colonel Parrish had not even been able to recall her name, again felt a wave of indignation, which she covered by responding sweetly to Lavinia's numerous inquiries about America.

"I do so hope Guy will allow me to return with him," Lavinia said at last.

"And when does he return?"

"In a month, I believe. He came only to see me, and I believe he hopes to raise money to rebuild Bellechasse."

"Bellechasse?"

"Our plantation. It was rather harshly dealt with by—" Lavinia covered her mouth with her hand. "Oh, I forgot, you are from the North. I am sorry indeed to have mentioned it at all. I have offended you."

"My dear Lavinia . . . Livvy." Eustacia took her hand from her mouth. "How is it possible for one close friend to offend another?"

"Eustacia . . . Lucy"—Lavinia's eyes welled with tears—"how fortunate that we have met."

Before their return to London from Creswell Hall, Eustacia elicited a promise from her mother to invite Lavinia Parrish to stay with them.

"But, Lucy, I really don't understand. She is young and not at all smart or lively, not like Sophia. She doesn't seem the kind of friend you enjoy, and I'm sure I don't want to spend my time entertaining her."

"She's a sweet girl, Mama, and she misses America dreadfully. She is longing to spend more time with us."

"That I don't doubt. But do you really wish to spend more time with her?"

"Of course; otherwise I shouldn't ask that she come," Eustacia replied with a toss of her head.

But knowing her daughter, Isabel Caylew's eyes narrowed. "Or is it that handsome brother of hers, Colonel Parrish, with whom you wish to spend more time?"

"Colonel Parrish has barely spoken five words together to me ever since we've been here. I daresay he's conversed more with you than with me."

That was true. But what had most galled Eustacia was the way that Sophia had flirted with him. She might have expected that, but she had not expected that he would respond after he had treated her own overtures so coldly. Nevertheless, she had come upon them walking together in the park, and neither had seemed to welcome her presence. It was then she had decided that Lavinia must be their guest in London.

Surprisingly an objection was placed upon the proposed visit by Lavinia's brother.

"My sister is young and very impressionable. She does not yet move widely in society. Though I know she might wish to go, I would prefer the invitation not be extended," Colonel Parrish told Mrs. Caylew when she spoke to him.

When this message was carried back to Eustacia, she made haste to inform Lavinia of her wish for her to join them in London, and of her brother's refusal to countenance it.

"I love Guy, but he does make me angry sometimes," Lavinia burst forth. "He thinks I'm a child, because he is ten years older than me; and because Father's no longer living, he thinks he must protect me and be more father than brother. I shall explain to him how important this is to me, how I want more than anything to be with you, Lucy."

She had done so with apparent success, for Colonel Parrish had relented; and when the Caylews returned to London, Lavinia Parrish went with them.

TWO

*B*efore meeting Colonel Harwood Gaius Parrish, Eustacia Caylew had believed herself in love hundreds of times. She had been in love, that is, until she discovered the gentleman spoke too much, or too little; his laugh was too loud, or else he had no sense of humor; the nose she had thought aquiline appeared on further examination far too long; or he was supplanted by one superior from his position as crack whip of the fashionable Coaching Club. Upon discovering the fatal flaw—whatever it might be— Eustacia fell out of love as quickly as she had fallen in; and the gentlemen thus discarded became known as Eustacia's Castoffs. Derogatory though the term might seem, only the very best gentlemen earned the title, so they wore it proudly and continued, even though supplanted, to walk in her train.

That was the case until Colonel Parrish crossed her path, until she felt his presence in a room by the quickening of her heartbeat, by the sudden somersault her stomach took on catching sight of his tall figure, so easy to distinguish from all others by its ease of carriage. She noticed he held his head high, yet without arrogance; he wore his clothes well, choosing gray where others wore black; his hands were well shaped, with long fingers and square-cut nails; and there was that twist to his mouth whenever he began to smile. But how seldom he smiled at her! She noticed everything about him, everything he did and said, just as others had always done with her. And in much the same manner as she had acknowledged those gentlemen with an air of distant restraint, even disdain, so Colonel Parrish acknowledged her.

It was frustrating; it was not to be borne. Were Lavinia Parrish not a guest in their Mayfair house, she doubted he would have called there at all.

Why was it? she wondered. He was fine-looking, but then so had all the others been. He was witty, but unlike the others he wasted precious little of his wit upon her. She had learned from his sister that it would be four years until he attained thirty, yet his eyes and his demeanor had the aspect of one much wiser, much more assured, than others she had known. Perhaps that stemmed from the war, from having assumed a commanding position at such an early age. Whatever it was, it seemed to her a most romantic quality. He was, she decided, a man in a way that none of her previous admirers had been; more than that, he appeared to be a man without a fatal flaw.

"Your brother is not engaged to anyone, is he, Livvy?" Diffidently she put the question that had been burning in her thoughts as she and Lavinia sat at their tambour frames. Eustacia did not care for embroidery, but Lavinia did. She had taken it up not so much to please her guest—with whom as time passed she discovered she had less and less in common—as to please her guest's brother, who often called in the afternoon. He was excessively fond of his sister, and for that reason Eustacia took care not to show that Lavinia was anything less than her greatest delight; thus she put up with boring poetry readings and the embroidery that Lavinia had always at hand. She even said prayers nightly with Lavinia. With that, she felt, she had stretched her forbearance to its utter limits.

"To Mother's displeasure, when he was only seventeen he wanted to propose to Miranda Crawley—she then only fifteen. Poor dear, I hear now she is dead of the fever. And for a time it seemed something would develop with Felice Blanchard. My parents would have approved of that, but then my cousin Dorothea arrived from England for a visit, and she commanded every moment of his time. Mother always said that wherever Guy was there was bound to be a young lady close by."

"Your cousin Dorothea, I have not met her."

"I daresay you will. Now Guy is in London, she is bound to come."

"There is some arrangement between them?"

Lavinia shook her head. "No arrangement, but there is
no doubt that Dorothea likes Guy; but he teases her as
much as he does me, and it's my belief he thinks of her in
much the same way. Apart from that, they are cousins; so
there is no thought of marriage, on his side at least.
Besides, Guy will not marry unless—" Lavinia broke off,
flushing.

"Unless what?" Eustacia pressed with avid curiosity.

"No, no." Livvy shook her dark head vehemently.
"You're likely to misunderstand."

"I won't. I promise I won't. We are best friends, are we
not? Do best friends misunderstand one another?"

"Well . . . I mean"—she leaned lower over her work—
"I don't believe Guy will marry unless it is advantageous
for him to do so."

"Money?" Eustacia prompted immediately.

"Now you're shocked; I can see that you are." In actual
fact, nothing could have shocked Eustacia less; she had
been brought up to understand and appreciate the importance of money. In the case of Colonel Parrish, however,
she began to think his lack of it might be used to her
advantage.

"You must not think him mercenary, though, Lucy,"
Lavinia went on, "because I assure you he is not. But you
see, Bellechasse, our home, means so much to him. Father
worked so hard for it, he was so proud of it, and it has
been left in a shambles; at least, so Guy tells me. He feels
bound to restore it in honor of Father. I haven't seen it
since . . ." Lavinia's eyes filled with tears. "It was
wrong. They should not have spared me by sending me
away. I am not weak; I could have borne what they had to
bear."

"There, of course you could." Eustacia patted her hand,
wondering what compelled some girls to cry so often (she
never did), before returning immediately to the subject at
hand: "And he has prospects for an advantageous marriage, your brother?"

"I really don't know; he does not confide in me a great
deal anymore. I only wish that he did talk of those things
that concern him. Perhaps when he takes me home, when
we are together all the time . . . And I am determined to
go, Lucy. America is my home. I will not stay here!"

Her voice grew tremulous, so that Eustacia, fearing she would cry again, hastened to reassure her. "Never fear, Livvy. If your brother will not take you with him, then I shall get Mama to invite you to stay with us."

"I would dearly love that, but you live in . . . in New York, do you not?"

"And your brother is still in a state of war with the North?"

"No, no, I would not say that; though with Reconstruction, with our parents dead, our brother gone, he particularly feels the consequences of this War between the States."

"I'm afraid that he does."

Little more was said on the subject. When Colonel Parrish arrived later that afternoon, Eustacia remained at her tambour frame, examining him closely from time to time. Apart from general remarks paid to all of those present—her mother had come in as well as Lawrence, who had arrived quite unexpectedly the day previously—as usual Colonel Parrish did not single her out until, after rising to leave, he came over to examine her work. Then only did she wish she had employed more of her time at needlecraft, for the results of her stitchery were poor indeed compared with those of his sister.

He smiled. "I see we have something in common, Miss Caylew."

"What is that?"

She didn't know whether to be pleased or annoyed by his reply. "Stitchery is not my forte either; and I see no reason why it should be yours, for you obviously don't enjoy it." He leaned over as though to examine her work more closely, adding in lowered tones, "Do I perhaps have a spot on the end of my nose, or has the scratch I made on my chin while shaving this morning begun to bleed?"

She looked up swiftly, "No, not at all. But why do you ask?"

"You have studied me so oddly, I felt sure it could only be because of some blemish."

Yet from his look Eustacia guessed that he knew exactly why she had been looking at him; and she, who had teased

others so often, found herself flushing. That did not stop
her pressing what she felt was her first advantage.

"Will you be at the Langleys' ball tomorrow?"

"I have an invitation."

"You will go," she implored.

"I probably shall."

"Then I shall save you a waltz," she announced boldly,
and he bowed his acknowledgment.

He was already at the Langleys' when they arrived.
They were late because her mother had insisted upon
Lawrence attending, and he had had other amusements
planned that he had hated to relinquish.

Still, Lawrence was enjoying himself long before Eustacia, who, although immediately besieged by admirers,
was not besieged by the one she most wanted. In fact, she
saw him dance twice with Sophia Langley before she
signaled him with an imperious gesture of her fan.

"Miss Caylew." He bowed.

"I have saved you the next waltz, Colonel Parrish, as I
told you I would."

"Dear Miss Caylew, I do wish you had reminded me
earlier of that, for I should certainly not have signed Miss
Vernon's card for that dance if I had remembered."

It was mortifying; had she not been so attracted to him,
she would gladly have detested him. She looked across the
room at Miss Vernon, who always had someone in tow,
not because of her attributes—she was tall and angular,
without particular charm, and spoke in a high voice Eustacia
likened to the braying of an ass—but because of her
oft-mentioned inheritance.

Tapping her fan on her white-gloved hand, Eustacia
quipped indignantly, "You must, indeed, be in this country seeking your fortune, Colonel Parrish."

But he seemed not in the least perturbed by her im-
putation. "And you, Miss Caylew?" He smiled. "Since
you have your fortune, may I presume you have come to
find a title?"

"I have been offered that more than once since my
arrival," she retorted with asperity, elevating her chin to
indicate her disdain and at the same time outline the fine
line of her white throat.

"And you turned it down. Not of high enough rank

perhaps? Would a marquess appeal?'' He nodded in the direction of the other side of the room. ''The Marquess of Gilvray is here, I see. No money, of course, but you have no need of that; and an Irish peerage is not as highly regarded as some. Still, no one back in New York would know the difference.''

''You are insufferable, Colonel Parrish. How dare you talk to me in such a fashion?''

''I dared by the same means that you dared call me a fortune hunter.'' And then, seeing her flush, he said, ''It is simply that we have recognized one another, that is all. And for that honesty, it would give me the greatest pleasure if you would save me the last waltz of the evening.''

She wished she had the fortitude to refuse him, but she did not. Handing him her card to sign, she bent her wrist to give more brilliance to the heavy diamond-encrusted emerald bracelet her father had given her on her eighteenth birthday. Its center emerald alone weighed almost ten carats; Tiffany's, with restrained dignity, had labeled it a highly important piece.

''I scarcely believe England is the place to seek a fortune,'' she remarked pointedly.

''You may be right, Miss Caylew,'' he agreed with a half-smile. ''Your emeralds are as fine as any here tonight.''

''They are finer, Colonel Parrish,'' she snapped.

''Your taste, ma'am, as well as your means, are to be commended.'' Again he smiled enigmatically.

Neither that taste nor that means, however, prevented him from turning on his heel to join Miss Vernon, who, Eustacia thought bitterly, smiled upon him more sweetly than she had her other partners, and whose braying laugh appeared less noticeable than before. She saw too that he was deep in conversation with her again after supper.

''He is nice, your colonel.'' Sophia had come upon her without her noticing.

''Why do you call him *my* colonel?'' she asked quickly.

''Well, I had supposed that your only reason for inviting that dull sister of his to stay with you was to pin him to your side.''

''That's unfair. Livvy's—''

''Dull, and you know it, Eustacia. Thank goodness for your brother; otherwise I don't suppose she would have anyone to dance with, and she would be hanging on your skirts.''

"She's sweet, but very shy. And Lawrence is being kind.''

"*Your* brother is being kind, that I can't deny; but is *her* brother being likewise?''

"There could hardly be any necessity for him to be kind in the same manner. I'm sure I have more partners than I know what to do with.''

"I don't deny that. I simply had the distinct impression that you thought him rather nice.''

"He is nice enough, I suppose.'' Eustacia was determined not to reveal herself too plainly. Sophia had singled him out more than once herself; she was no pauper, and a beauty to boot. To show her own interest would likely make him seem even more desirable. Looking over to where Colonel Parrish stood talking to the Marquess of Gilvray, she said, "But he's not nearly as handsome as his companion.''

"Oh, Jack!'' Sophia dismissed the Marquess of Gilvray with a shrug. "He'll be delighted to know you think so; he's been after an introduction to you. In fact, if I'm not mistaken, here it comes now.''

The introduction came from no less a person than Colonel Parrish, who prefaced it by "Miss Caylew, Lord Gilvray has been telling me that there is only one lady for whom he has had eyes all evening. I assured him that I, for one, did not consider his Irish gallantry extreme in the least.'' Yet from the mocking gleam in his eyes, Eustacia was not at all sure this was so. She was further annoyed to find him pressing the suit of another as he went on: "Perhaps you might honor him with the dance that he desires.''

Turning her most brilliant smile on the Marquess, who was not unpleasing—she might even have found him attractive had she not been so smitten by his companion—Eustacia dismissed Colonel Parrish and made up her mind to ignore him from then on. She was incensed to see him care not one whit for her coldness, thoroughly enjoying himself with Sophia Langley without turning a single glance in her direction. Still, she was not sufficiently incensed to refuse him the waltz on her card when he came to claim it. Even then his thoughts seemed less on her than on his sister, who was dancing with Lawrence. He directed the conversation toward her brother, until she broke in with an indignant, "Colonel Parrish, you really are insufferable."

"What for? Wanting to protect my sister from a possible philanderer? You must excuse me. Your brother is charming, but obviously a thoroughly worldly young gentleman with far too much money at his disposal; and Livvy is very impressionable, very young, and without sophistication. I should not wish her to be hurt."

"Your sister must not get hurt, but you care nothing for whether you hurt others."

His voice was serious. "I would not willingly hurt anyone, Miss Caylew. I hope you are not implying that I have inadvertently injured your feelings in some way."

She pouted, making her soft lips more kissable than ever. "You dance with me and then talk of no one but my brother. And you're forever trying to arrange my life for me," she complained.

"Arrange your life, Miss Caylew?" His eyebrows rose.

"Introducing me to the Marquess of Gilvray."

"He wanted to meet you; I had the opportunity of doing him a service. I found him a fine fellow. Was he not equally charming to you? I had thought that he would be."

"He is nice enough."

"And he is a marquess," he reminded her quite seriously, though she detected a glint of amusement in his eyes.

"I know that," she snapped, "but I shall deem it a great pleasure if you will desist from introducing me to other gentlemen."

"You mean, you want to find your own marquess?"

"I don't mean that at all. I really don't give a fig for a title."

"But Daddy does. Or is it Mummy?" He glanced in the direction of Mrs. Caylew.

"Papa lets me do exactly as I please, and Mama is . . . well, since Papa decides everything, it really doesn't matter what Mama wants, does it?" She smiled up at him, regretting that the dance would soon end, that she would soon lose the grasp of his fingers on hers, the touch of his hand at the back of her waist.

"Goodness, I have danced simply the whole evening long." She sighed.

And his murmured response—"So I've noticed"—pleased her and allowed her to venture, "I would so enjoy a breath of air."

"You have but to ask, my lady."

Once on the terrace, he guided her deftly, without a moment's hesitation, into the shadows of the privet hedge and, without a word, took her in his arms and kissed her.

It was, of course, exactly what she had hoped he would do; it was what she had wanted. The kiss too was everything she could have wished it to be. She had longed to feel those lips on which her eyes had so often rested possess her own as they did, without hesitation, with the confidence of one who knew what he wanted and would take it, with more passion than tenderness. She had longed to have his arms pressing her to him as he did, not gently but purposefully. She who conquered all was at last conquered, and she clung to him, not wanting him to release her. Yet when at last he did, rather than let him think it was quite the most satisfying kiss she had ever known, afraid her own response had betrayed her, she murmured, "Colonel, you really are insufferable."

Again he raised an eyebrow, to repeat with mock solemnity, "Insufferable, Miss Caylew? But why? I don't understand."

"For taking advantage of me in that way."

"My dear Miss Caylew," he expostulated. "Spare me your protestations of modesty. It was you who suggested coming out on the terrace, and in my experience ladies who express such a wish want exactly what just took place between us. I see nothing wrong with it. I enjoyed it immensely and was of the opinion that you did also. I probably should have not come out here with you had I not suspected as much. If, however, I have misjudged you, allow me to extend my most sincere apologies for my behavior."

Even in the dark she could see his half-smile. He knew how she felt about him. If he hadn't before, it must have been obvious from the way she had clung to him. Even in her protestation she had made no attempt to draw away.

"You could at least have pretended, or made to admire the moon first." She pouted.

"I rarely dissimulate, Miss Caylew. Besides, there is no moon tonight. Apart from that, my dear"—he kissed her forehead gently before taking her elbow to guide her back toward the lighted room—"there wasn't time. The dance is almost at an end. If we were to be discovered here, that might cause talk, something I am sure neither of us desires."

THREE

*E*ustacia was prepared to be cool toward Colonel Parrish, to indicate that his behavior on the terrace had been beyond the pale of a gentleman's conduct, that she would not condone further advances. Principled though this intention might have been, it proved, however, to be quite unnecessary. Though he might cast an occasional smile across at her in what she haughtily considered an entirely too perceptive manner, he made no attempt to approach her unless in the company of his sister or others. Worse than that, she thought he spent entirely too much time in the company of that plain Miss Vernon, intrigued, undoubtedly, by her much-discussed fortune.

"What else does the poor girl have to offer?" she said to Livvy one day, interrupting her reading out loud a recently published essay on what she had insisted was a most important topic for women.

"Men do not want solely the obedience of women; they want their sentiments. All men, except the most brutish, desire to have, in the woman most nearly connected with them, not a forced slave but a willing one, not a slave merely, but a favorite. They . . .' " Lavinia read on, unheedingly.

"For goodness' sake, Livvy, I was talking about that horse-faced Miss Vernon. She isn't obedient to anyone with her thirty thousand a year. She'll always be leading some man around by the nose, the way she's leading your brother around now, and I hope he realizes that."

Lavinia Parrish looked up, her gentle mouth unexpectedly firm. "She won't, Lucy, not Guy. Besides, that's just the point of Mill's essay. No matter what fortune a woman

116

has, as soon as she marries she becomes subject to her husband's rule. But, you see, John Stuart Mill maintains that it's only common sense to say that women are different from men, but—"

"But I think Mill's a bore, Livvy, and whatever he says doesn't answer the fact that Colonel Parrish is spending far more time with Miss Vernon than anyone else. Has he mentioned her to you, Livvy?"

She had to repeat the question twice, for Lavinia Parrish had already returned to Mill's essay.

"Well, yes, he has," she replied, reluctantly pulling her eyes from the page. "He says she is not without charm."

"Not without thirty thousand charms!" Eustacia retorted.

"Lucy!"

"Well, Livvy, you told me he had said he would marry only for money."

"I said no such thing, Lucy, only that . . . that it would help matters at Bellechasse if he did. You mustn't think him a cool fortune hunter. That's unfair!" Lavinia's tone was heated, more vociferous than Eustacia had ever before heard; she hastened to sweeten her own words and was relieved by the arrival of Lawrence, who always held Lavinia's attention.

"Do listen to this essay that Livvy insists is at the root of all women's problems, Lawrence, and give us your opinion."

And despite Lavinia's vigorously shaking her head, she made her begin reading all over again, not herself listening to a word but deciding very firmly that something must be done about Miss Vernon and Colonel Parrish.

It proved, after all, not to be difficult. Her mother was very receptive to her opinion that a penniless American should not be allowed to cast snares for an English fortune, an idea Isabel Caylew carried boldly to Lady Langley in an effort to show her that principles held sway over national bonds.

"I realize that we are American also, from the North of our country, to be sure, Lady Langley; but I would not want it to be said that Miss Vernon had not been warned by those who know. Colonel Parrish is, I understand, without a sou. We took pity on his young sister, who, you know, is staying with us. She talks a great deal of their plantation, Bellechasse; but I understand, from what her brother has let fall, that the place requires a fortune to restore it after the . . . the vicissitudes of war and all that business. It may well be Miss Vernon's fortune that he has in mind to perform that task.''

"Of course, Mrs. Caylew. I thank you for mentioning it. I shall speak to Miss Vernon's uncle and tell him what you have said.''

Mrs. Caylew smiled. Sir Frank Vernon was a miserable soul who had so far refused to acknowledge her existence, but perhaps now his attitude toward her might change.

It did. The next time she saw him he smiled in her direction; at least she took the changed grimace on his features for a smile. Even if it were not, there could be no doubt that that was definitely a half-bow he extended to her. She beamed. Eustacia beamed when she saw that Colonel Parrish was no longer close to Miss Vernon's side. It had been so easy.

Yet though she had separated him from Miss Vernon, that did not bring him immediately to her heels. She saw the half-smile still when he looked in her direction, but it was a half-smile tinged with gall. And he had insisted that Lavinia's London visit had been quite long enough, that she should return without delay to the bosom of the Harwood family.

For that Eustacia was not altogether sorry. Lavinia's serious nature, her espousal of causes, her poetry and embroidery, were all tedious to her. And truly the object of inviting her to stay in the first place—to further her acquaintance with her brother—had not transpired as she had planned. All the regrets at parting were on Lavinia's side, though that was not apparent by the pains Eustacia took in planning a farewell dinner for her.

"It really is not necessary, Lucy dear. I would so much more enjoy being with you and Mrs. Caylew, and—''

"And my brother. I do believe you're rather sweet on Lawrence, Livvy.'' And the answering blush convinced Lucy that she had been right. "But you know he'll never go along with those advanced ideas of yours on women's subjection or whatever silly thing that is.''

"It's not silly. Mill's essay makes a great deal of sense.

And I have discussed it with Law—Mr. Lawrence, and while he may not agree with me—"

"I'll be bound he doesn't. Dear me"—Eustacia looked up from the dinner invitations she was writing—"perhaps I should not send a card to Miss Vernon, for she no longer seems to be a favorite of your brother's. At least from my observation, they are never in one another's company anymore. Was there some disagreement between them?"

She caught Lavinia's deepened blush. So, she conjectured, it must have been a subject of discussion between brother and sister. What wouldn't she have given to have overheard it. If only Lavinia weren't so close-mouthed about things. She never gossiped; that was what made her so boring.

But Eustacia didn't realize quite how clearly her own role had been divined until Colonel Parrish, on the evening of the dinner, sought her out to confront her with the matter.

"My dear Miss Caylew, allow me to extend to you my congratuations."

"Congratulations, Colonel Parrish? I'm afraid I don't understand."

"For saving me from Miss Vernon's grasp," he answered lightly.

"For saving *you?*" she responded swiftly. "I would hardly put it like that."

"Then how would you put it?"

And when, opening her fan to hide her confusion, she made to leave what was proving an unexpectedly difficult situation, he caught hold of her wrist, his hold hidden by the fan, to repeat firmly, "Just how would you put it, Miss Caylew?"

"I really don't know what you're talking about."

"But I think that you very well know. I have it on the very best authority that you told Miss Vernon I was after her fortune."

"I did no such thing! It was Mama."

"Your mother, who got it from you, you knowing full well that she would carry such a tale to Miss Vernon."

"She didn't speak a word to Miss Vernon."

"No, only to friends, who relayed every word of what I

planned to do with her fortune. That is the sort of interference I don't tolerate. You owe me an apology.''

"You're hurting my wrist."

"Then apologize."

"Very well, then. But I don't see why I should apologize for something you yourself have admitted."

"I admitted nothing."

"You didn't deny it!"

"I didn't deny it in the sense that you did not deny wishing to marry a title. You didn't wish me to arrange your life in that direction; you chided me for introducing you to the Marquess of Gilvray. I have an equal right to chide you for spreading a very ugly rumor, and one quite untrue."

"You were not going to offer for Miss Vernon, then?"

He shook his head. "Bellechasse means a great deal to me, but the price of daily facing Miss Vernon across the breakfast table is a price too high."

Eustacia smiled her prettiest smile. "I thought you found her attractive."

"You thought no such thing."

"But you were seeing a great deal of her."

"Was I?" he quizzed.

"Well, I mean, there was beginning to be talk."

"Talk?"

"Well, Livvy said you were not indifferent."

He looked across at his sister, deep in conversation with Lawrence Caylew. "It seems I am removing my sister just in time."

Mrs. Caylew, overhearing this last remark, hastened to put in, "Your sister's feminist ideas do not come from this household, Colonel Parrish; that I can assure you. Eustacia would no more think of embracing the liberal ideas of that man Mill than of joining those terrible militants in New York. Mad, frustrated women all of them. If I were you, Colonel Parrish, I would squelch any ideas Lavinia might have of becoming in any way like them."

Though he smiled in response, she found his reply quite enigmatic. "My dear Mrs. Caylew, I quite understand that the attitude adopted by you and your daughter differs widely from their exceedingly brash and forthright approach."

It left Mrs. Caylew with the uncomfortable feeling that Colonel Parrish knew every word she had spoken to Lady Langley about him. She tossed her head. Well, the man was a fortune hunter after all. It had been only right to warn Miss Vernon's guardian. She would have expected the same thing if he had been dawdling around Eustacia. Thank goodness she had no problems in that regard. Unlike most gentlemen, Colonel Parrish evinced no special interest in her daughter.

FOUR

With Lavinia's departure from the Caylew household, Eustacia Caylew and Colonel Parrish met seldom in London; and on those occasions when they did, he was polite, nothing more. Lavinia's parting had been tearful, with promises to write and insistence from Eustacia that Lavinia should visit her in New York.

"And remember, Livvy, if your brother does not take you back to America, then I shall," she promised.

But when next she heard from Lavinia it was to say that she would be returning to Bellechasse with Guy. And to Eustacia's relief, following Colonel Parrish's fall from Miss Vernon's favor, his name was not linked with any other.

Though her own pursuit of him had gained nothing except a single kiss, still that had been sufficient to ensure he remained in her mind and in her heart. His very aloofness, rather than disenchanting her, served to determine her course.

She returned to New York with one single idea. Colonel Harwood Gaius Parrish was the man that she wanted; she was determined to have him.

Her father, as she had suspected might be the case, was furious.

"I will not have you wasting yourself on some worthless rebel, some poverty-stricken, money-grubbing planter who probably can't keep soul and cotton boll together without an assist from us in the North. Well, he'll not get it from me. That I can assure you, my girl, and that's what he's after. You're a prize, Lucy, a prize far beyond his reach. You can have anyone. I know that, and you do too.

Any gentleman of distinction in New York will come running at the crook of your little finger.''

"Colonel Parrish is a gentleman of distinction, and he is the one that I choose, Papa,'' Eustacia replied firmly. "I'll not change my mind.''

"Nor shall I. I wouldn't have a Southerner for a son-in-law! Why, it's him and others tarred with the same brush that came close to costing us our fortune. Had it not been for my perspicacity, we might have ended up ruined. Unsuccessful in that, now he thinks to marry my hard-earned cash.''

"As a matter of fact, Papa, he does not want to marry it. He has not even asked me to marry him—yet—but I assure you that he will.''

"A ploy, my girl, a ploy that I can plainly see, even if he has blinded you with his charms. A fortune hunter. Your mother told me how she went to great lengths to save one of those moneyed Englishwomen from his grasp, though why she wasted her efforts I don't know. He might have been safely married to someone else by now.''

Eustacia smiled. "It wasn't Mama, really, it was me who got her to do it. I wouldn't have him waste himself on that horsey Miss Vernon. He agreed with me; he said she was too high a price to pay for Bellechasse.''

"Bellechasse?''

"His plantation.''

"Well!'' Templeton Caylew expostulated. "There, you can see for yourself. He as much as admits it's money he's after.''

"What if it is, Papa? I don't care. And the money settled on me is mine by rights. You've often said I mustn't be beholden. If I want to use it to obtain Colonel Parrish, why should you object?'' She leaned over to grasp her father's arm. "I want him. Don't you understand what it is to want something so much you can think of nothing else?''

Templeton Caylew shifted uncomfortably in his chair.

"That's all very well, but those things don't last. You want it, you have it, that's that. But marriage—in that case you'll have him for life.''

"That's exactly what I want.''

"Well, I don't want this Parrish for a son-in-law, and

that's flat. I mean it, Lucy. I don't have to remind you there is a matter of parental consent to consider."

"His parents are dead."

"I don't give a damn for his parents, wherever they may be," he exploded, not at all appeased by Eustacia's curving arm placed affectionately around his shoulders. "It's my consent that's required, and that I'll never give."

"Oh, Papa, you're such a wonderful man. There's really no one like you, no one at all. You can do anything you set your mind to. Nothing is unreachable to you. That's what's so wonderful about you." She kissed him on the cheek. "Get him for me, Papa. Please, please get Colonel Harwood Gaius Parrish for me."

"Lucy! You ask too much of me."

Lightly she kissed his cheek again. "Nothing is ever too much for the great Wizard of Wall Street. Please, Papa, get him for me."

"I'll do no such thing, Lucy. Cajole as much as you wish, you little minx, I won't relent."

Nevertheless, two weeks later Templeton Caylew instructed his wife to write to Colonel Parrish inviting him and his sister to visit them in New York.

"I'm not giving in," he insisted. "I intend to expose him. I'll show my little Lucy just how worthless this fortune hunter she has set her heart on really is. When I've finished she'll be thanking me for saving her from him."

"I don't know that will answer, Templeton." His wife, taking paper from the drawer of her delicate Sheraton writing table with its pure gold fittings, paused. "The man really is a charmer."

"For God's sake, Isabel, don't tell me you fell for him also."

Isabel Caylew looked shocked. "Templeton, I'd no more think of looking at another man in that way than you would at another woman; but many of the English ladies I met did not have similar principles. Old World decadence, I suppose. Anyway, I heard him remarked upon many times in most flattering terms."

Templeton Caylew turned away, responding gruffly, "Well, just do as I say, will you?"

Both Templeton and Isabel Caylew were relieved by the reply to this letter. Couched in fine prose, written in a firm hand, Colonel Parrish sent his appreciation of their invitation but insisted that pressure of business at Bellechasse prevented his leaving the plantation at that time. His sister, however, would be delighted to come North, and he had no objection to her doing so as long as the visit was not of long duration. He did most particularly request them to bear in mind that Lavinia Parrish was still young and quite unused to society.

"Should Lavinia come North," he concluded, "I am sure I can rely upon Mrs. Caylew's good judgment. I am aware that she is most capable in preventing ladies of genteel birth from becoming the object of attention from unworthy sources."

"The damnable nerve of the man!" Templeton Caylew, reading the response, was infuriated. His wife wholeheartedly concurred in his sentiments, though she was less vociferous in stating her opinion. Still, while the letter annoyed, it also pleased. They had invited him and he had not wished to come. It was an end to the matter.

Templeton Caylew flourished the letter before his daughter with an airy "Well, I'm a man of my word. I tried, but he can't come North, though he'll allow you to entertain his sister."

"I don't want to entertain that foolish Livvy, embroidering, reading prosy poems, and studying silly feminist tracts!" Eustacia snapped.

"I don't think there can be such a thing as prosy poems," her mother put in calmly.

"Oh, Mama, for goodness' sake, you know very well what I mean. She's boring, boring, boring." She stamped her foot at each repetition of the word.

"Well, dear, if I'd known how you felt, I shouldn't have invited her at all."

"Mama, don't be obtuse. You know very well it was him, not his sister, that I wanted to come."

Her mother raised her eyebrows. "I suggested as much in London, but you would have it that you dearly loved her. I said she was not at all the sort of person you usually took to and—"

"Now, now, Isabel, don't rub it in. Lucy's disappointed, that's all; but it's an end to the matter."

"It is, Templeton. I shall write to Colonel Parrish and

tell him we've had a change of plans. I'm sure it won't displease him, for he seems not at all anxious for his sister to come to New York. It was probably her idea, for I believe she was the one who insisted upon staying with us in London. As I remember it, he was not at all keen about that either.''

"No, Mama," Eustacia put in hastily, "you're not to turn her away on my account. In fact, I want her to come. But I do wish Papa would do something to make Colonel Parrish come with her."

"I really don't know what you expect me to do, Lucy. Against my better judgment, I had your mother invite him, and he has refused. I shan't plead with him to change his mind, and I'm not about to go down there to force him to come."

"Look, Papa," Eustacia cajoled, sharpening his pens as she spoke (he always said that no one could sharpen them quite as well), "you know that during the war you bought up as much cotton as anyone; in fact, General Sherman complained that your money was going to help the South by allowing them to buy guns."

"I won't have you repeating that falsehood, Lucy. I just won't have it. I bought cotton from licensed agents and freed slaves. Whose cotton it was, and where the money for it went was not my affair. I'm a businessman, not a politician or a military man, and I told General Sherman that quite plainly."

"I don't give a d—"

"Lucy!" her mother reproved sharply.

"I don't give a damson for that, or for General Sherman, Papa." Quite deliberately Eustacia turned her back on her mother. "And you're quite right, Papa. You are a man of business; and because you're a man of business, I should have thought you would have wanted to lay hands on fine Southern cotton now that trade is open again.

"I have, my girl, I have."

"But not of the quality grown at Bellechasse. Why, Livvy told me it was quite the finest anywhere. Her father had won prizes with it, she said, and buyers were always pestering for it. She said the region is noted for the quality of its cotton, but none surpassed theirs. And the prices it fetched in England, where they need it for the finest of cotton goods, were quite astounding, she told me.''

"I had no notion you were so interested in the market, Lucy." Her father grinned. "But cotton is cotton."

"Oh, Papa, don't you think it would be worth your while to go and judge for yourself?"

"Me—go all the way to Memphis!"

"It's not really so far, Papa. I've already made inquiries. There's a good railroad connection."

"But I'm not even interested in purchasing cotton, let alone journeying all the way into the hinterland for it. Can you explain to me why I would go all the way to Memphis when there's nothing there that I want?"

Eustacia pouted prettily, smoothing the wide lapels of her father's coat. "But there is something there that I very much want, Papa. I'll come with you. I learned a new form of whist in London that I shall teach you on the train. I promise you'll be amused and the journey will pass in no time, you'll see."

FIVE

*E*ustacia didn't notice the overgrowth on the wide drive leading to the long porticoed white mansion, or the copper beech that towered over the dry, weed-choked lawn surrounding it. Nor did she have eyes for the crumbling exterior stonework or the peeling paint. Inside, she barely glanced at the heavy gouging on the parquet floors, the damaged oil paintings, the sparse furnishing. All she felt was a sense of disappointment that *he* wasn't anxiously awaiting their arrival with his sister.

"Lucy, Lucy! I couldn't believe it when you said you would come. You're an angel, a positive angel, to come all this way to see me after Guy made so many silly stipulations about my going North. And, Mr. Caylew, excuse me for not greeting you first." Here Lavinia extended a gentle hand that Templeton Caylew barely touched.

Unlike his daughter, he had seen all too clearly the overgrowth and weeds that covered the approach; he saw the broken steps, the peeling paint, the damaged flooring, the threadworn drapes—where there were any window drapes—the barest of furnishings, the bookcases bereft of books; all of that he saw, knowing right down to the last cent what it would cost to put things to rights. But beyond all that, what he saw most clearly, and what he most disliked, was the oil painting in a battered gilt frame placed centrally above the mantel of the room into which they had been shown, a painting slashed clear across as though by a saber. Yet that slash, disastrous though it had been, had done nothing to obliterate the likeness of its subject.

So . . . Lucy's Colonel Parrish was of the clan of that

devil Parrish, that renegade, that ferocious, brutal, malevolent, cloven-hoofed General Bentham Phineas Parrish, the scoundrel who had tweaked Sherman's beard and got away with it and who, with his handful of men, had vowed to save the South single-handedly if necessary. And he'd almost done it, riding openly through occupied territory, recruiting men, taking supplies, getting information, just as though it had been his own land still. He'd fought like a demon in battle. Twenty-nine horses were said to have been shot from beneath him, he'd been reported wounded a dozen times, yet no one ever managed to pick him off. He had been the South's most hated, most feared general.

Though Templeton Caylew did not lack patriotism, he had throughout the war placed his own economic security first; a man was a fool who did not. To show the world that his heart was with his country, though, he had contributed generously to the reward for the man who would bring in General Parrish, dead or alive.

He hadn't had to give up that contribution, however, for though General Parrish had died, no Northern bullet had brought him down. He had survived almost up until the end, and then been brought to his bed by yellow fever rather than the hand of the North. He had been given a hero's burial right under the eyes of Sherman's men—a last act of defiance.

Caylew had been angry with those in the North who looked upon General Parrish's exploits as heroism, and there were many who did. A damned rebel, the worst of the lot of them, had been his own description of him, knowing that the longer hostilities were prolonged the more his fortunes might be jeopardized, knowing too it was General Parrish and his band who were almost alone in prolonging those hostilities.

And to think his dearest Lucy had chosen a connection with one of the family of that devil Parrish. He had been determined to squelch the match; his intention in acquiescing to her pleas to come South had been to allow her to see how impossible such a match would be. He had felt a sense of elation at the state in which they'd found Bellechasse. Surely Lucy, used to every luxury that money could provide, would never consent to live in such surroundings.

But when at last Colonel Parrish made his appearance, when he saw the way his daughter looked with such clear pleasure at the man who so obviously resembled that devil of the painting above the carved mantel—the same long face, the same deep-set gray eyes, the same taunting downturn to the lips, the same dark hair curling slightly over the collar of his coarse cotton Garibaldi-style shirt (he'd obviously been working in the fields like a common hand), the only difference being that the man in the portrait was mustachioed while the man before him was clean-shaven—all Templeton Caylew's misgivings returned. And Eustacia, who put such store by outward appearance, seemed not in the least disturbed by Colonel Parrish's tanned skin and loose open-necked shirt. She greeted him with a smile that her father had never seen before.

Dinner was served in a large dining hall bereft of everything except a long oak table and sadly scuffed chairs. The food was plain—barbecued rabbit, stewed calves' feet, and roasted sweet potatoes—looking all the more plain in contrast with the ornate silverware on which it was served, silverware that had surprised Templeton Caylew by being as good as or better, in fact, than any he owned. It was not from Colonel Parrish, who made only the most general conversation, but from his sister that he learned the silver had been buried by their mother.

"Buried it, but why?" Eustacia asked unthinkingly. She had forgotten the war; she had forgotten everything but the object of her visit.

"To prevent a midnight requisition, Miss Caylew," that object of her attention replied evenly.

"I don't understand."

"Colonel Parrish undoubtedly means it was buried to prevent looting, Lucy. I'm quite sure, had the situation been reversed, that the same would have happened with our own property," her father put in, determined to squelch any sympathy.

It was not his daughter but Colonel Parrish who responded swiftly. "I quite agree with you, Mr. Caylew. It is amazing how quickly all veneer of civilization becomes lost in war. Perhaps Miss Caylew's pianoforte would have been used for firewood, as was my mother's. Perhaps the main rooms of your New York home would have served as horse stables, as did these main rooms of Bellechasse, though for the life of me the efficacy of that will forever escape me when there were perfectly habitable stables outside that remained unused. And why some cavalryman should have chosen to try to ride his horse upstairs and break the balustrade''—he shrugged—''sport, perhaps, though it's hard not to believe there was a desire to desecrate.''

''And if such were the case, it was not entirely un- natural, given the owner of this house,'' Templeton Caylew rasped.

''Perhaps.'' Colonel Parrish nodded gravely. ''Perhaps that was the reason my mother, armed only with her paint box, was shot by a marauder. Or maybe that had nothing to do with Bellechasse being owned by General Parrish but was simply a vile act of greed.''

There was silence, broken by Colonel Parrish's apol- ogies for raising such an issue. ''If you will permit it, though,'' he added raising his glass, ''I should much like to toast that gentleman's memory.'' And sensing Caylew's reluctance, he went on: ''You are the first Northerners to be entertained at Bellechasse. The toast is not only to his memory but to a sense of peace between us.''

It was Eustacia Caylew who raised her glass—''To General Parrish''—and who, before she sipped from it, prompted her father to do likewise. Then, turning to Colo- nel Parrish as she drank, she looked over the rim of the glass with such clear admiration that her father's ire was further aroused.

That chagrin grew as the ladies withdrew after dinner, leaving the two gentlemen to take port together.

''It was a custom my father firmly adhered to, though I suspect he would be sorely upset to see it carried on with such inferior port. Our own cellar was quite naturally emptied.''

''Not to be wondered at.''

''No, not at all,'' Colonel Parrish responded, refusing the cigar offered him by Caylew, but settling back to ask, ''And what brings you to our part of the country, Mr. Caylew?''

''Business—cotton, mainly.''

''You're buying, then?''

Caylew nodded.

"Well, you're doing it in a good year. It's a particularly fine crop. No rain to discolor the bolls, just as good as I've ever seen."

"You undoubtedly are selling. I might be willing to look it over," Caylew conceded begrudgingly.

But Parrish shook his head. "No, sir, I have nothing left to sell. I made my arrangements directly with buyers at the English mills."

"I see. Well, I should still like to see the quality of your cotton. I understand it is quite good."

"I believe you already know that it is particularly fine, Caylew," Parrish replied evenly.

"Why, what do you mean?" His companion sat back, drawing hard on his cigar.

"It was to you, I understand, that during the war all the Bellechasse cotton was sent."

Templeton Caylew drew himself up in his chair. "How dare you, sir, imply that I pillaged your plantation! That I categorically deny, and I demand an apology. I have never been south of the Mason-Dixon line, nor ever wanted to, I would have you know."

"No, but your agents were well known on the Memphis waterfront."

"See here, Parrish, I deal in any number of commodities, cotton among them, but whatever I might have got, I paid for with good, hard Yankee cash."

"You paid nothing to the people who owned the goods, Caylew, only to scalawags the like of which we find ourselves surrounded with today. Apart from that, I've made it my business to find out exactly how much you paid for it—a pittance compared with its worth—and that pittance was paid to people who had no legal right to sell, a fact that could not have escaped you."

"How dare you, sir, how dare you! I could have taken it without paying a penny had I wished, and you know it."

"True, you could have. It was being done every day. But since my family saw nothing of what you paid, doesn't it amount to the same thing?" And seeing Templeton Caylew's face grow red, he went on: "You must excuse me, sir. I have no wish to insult a guest in my house; but the cuts, like the gouges from the hoofs of the Union cavalry mounts in this floor, go deep. Still they are not irreparable. Your visit indicates that.''

"My visit, Colonel Parrish," Templeton Caylew exploded, "is by no means a profferred olive branch. I have not come here in order to repair your floor or your fortunes."

"Undoubtedly not. But, sir, without impertinence intended, may I ask just why you have come?"

Templeton Caylew floundered. He would never willingly have this man as a son-in-law, and particularly not as husband for his own favorite. Lucy must be made to see reason.

He hesitated before retorting, "It was so my daughter could see your sister. She had formed some attachment to her in London."

"Livvy is also much attached to Miss Caylew. Your paternal affection in making such a long trip to bring them together is appreciated not only by my sister but by me also—for making Livvy happy. It has not been easy for her, this return to the ghost of Bellechasse."

"Well, if you've suffered losses, I presume you have put in a claim for recompense."

Colonel Parrish laughed sharply. "A claim, a mountain of paperwork, an exercise in futility, but yes, I along with my neighbors have done so."

"Then I expect in due course something will come of it."

"I doubt it."

"Then how do you plan to rebuild—hard work?"

"Hard work, yes, but that alone won't do it. I require good fortune also."

"Someone else's fortune," Caylew hazarded smugly.

Colonel Parrish raised his eyebrows. "Forgive me, I don't follow."

"I'm not one for gossip, but my wife did mention there was some talk of you being after an heiress when you were in England."

"Ah, you must mean Miss Vernon," Colonel Parrish responded blandly. "Yes, that is so. It did cross my mind; but as I explained to your daughter, it really would not have worked. Miss Vernon is a well-meaning lady but, I suspect, devoid of the charm, the humor that would make for happiness in marriage."

"So, you won't be satisfied with just any heiress, but she must be a beautiful heiress, eh Parrish?"

"That would certainly be a winning combination," he replied evenly, picking up the decanter to refill their glasses.

"You have the bare-faced gall to admit, with all your much-vaunted Southern gallantry and sense of honor, that you're an outright fortune hunter."

"You might say so, but only in the same way that your daughter seeks a title in marriage. Obviously that would supply Miss Caylew with something that her money cannot buy, just as marrying an heiress would be advantageous to the future of Bellechasse."

"Well . . . just wait until Lucy hears of this!"

"But Miss Caylew has, sir, from me. We have been most frank with one another. That is what I have truly appreciated in her."

"How far have matters gone between you?" Caylew demanded.

Colonel Parrish wrinkled his brow. "I'm sorry, I don't understand. There is nothing between Miss Caylew and myself."

"Come now, you don't fool me for a minute, though you may have fooled her. You went out of your way to infatuate my daughter with your pretended indifference. You'd set your sights on her, and knowing men fall head over heels at first sight of her, you resolved to be cold, inattentive. You challenged her with your feigned disinterest. Well, I saw through you right away, and you might as well know I'll never allow her to marry you. What do you have to say to that?"

"Only that I have not asked Miss Caylew to marry me, sir. Indeed, if in fact I had any intention of it—something I cannot maintain to be the case—I should never think of doing so without first consulting you as her father. I would point out that *you* have come to me. I have not sought out either you or your daughter. Knowing your dislike, even had I such ideas in mind, I would never do anything to promote a match to which you so obviously object. I reiterate, the idea is yours and not mine."

"Then stop going out of your way to make my daughter fall in love with you," Caylew exploded.

Parrish shrugged. "I've done nothing, nor was I aware

your daughter was in love with me, though I admit to sensing a certain infatuation on her part. She is a very charming, a very lovely young lady, and I would do nothing to harm her."

"Then leave her alone."

"Perhaps I should point out again, sir, that I did not go to New York, though I was invited to your house, but that you came to mine. I should also point out that were our positions reversed, had I a daughter who wished to marry where I did not choose, I should hardly travel a great distance to put her in proximity to a gentleman disliked by me but the object of her fancy."

"Gentleman, huh! I wanted her to see for herself the sort of person you really are—a gold-raking gigolo with nothing, I repeat, nothing to offer in return. You'll never have my daughter for your wife, sir, never!"

Colonel Parrish rose. "I shall overlook your insults and your outburst, Caylew. But to put your obviously troubled mind at rest, I can promise you I have no intention of offering for Miss Caylew. I think it is long past time to rejoin the ladies."

SIX

"Well, Father?" Eustacia had demanded as soon as they were alone.

"What do you mean by 'Well, Father'?" Templeton Caylew replied with irritation.

"You know perfectly well what I mean."

"Well, my dear, what I mean is that we are leaving this house tomorrow, and we are never going to return."

Eustacia seemed unaffected by this outburst, replying calmly, "We shall leave, Papa, when Colonel Parrish has proposed marriage to me and when I have accepted him, not a moment before."

"Lucy, I have his word that he's not about to do that."

Eustacia's calm was broken. "Why not? There is no impediment. He is not engaged elsewhere; I know that."

"It's not a case of there being someone else. It is simply that I don't want him as a son-in-law, and he has promised me he will not proceed without my approval. The matter is at an end."

Unexpectedly Eustacia smiled, breathing a sigh of relief.

"Ah, so you discussed it, then. Good, I'm glad you did something while you were closeted together all that time. When I am mistress at Bellechasse I shall certainly not separate the gentlemen from the ladies after dinner, a boorish custom that gives the gentlemen by far the best part of the bargain. Really, Livvy gets on my nerves with all her causes—education for women. Next she'll be out for the vote."

"Well, I don't care for him any more than you care for her."

"But *I* care for him, Papa. I care for him very much,

136

and that is why we are here. I have no intention of leaving until the matter is settled."

"It is settled. He does not wish to marry you."

"Then I shall change that," she said with a determined shake of her dark curls.

"Lucy! You'll do no such thing."

"I mean to have him, Papa. I have told you that. And you promised me you would help me get him."

"I promised you nothing of the sort."

"Then why did we come all this way?"

It was the question Colonel Parrish had put to him earlier, and Templeton Caylew was placed in the unusual position of feeling himself trapped. It was not a position he was used to, though it was one he liked to exert over others. For the first time it seemed that he, the spinner of webs designed to entrap, had a web inexorably closing around him, a web from which he was having great difficulty extricating himself. He was not enjoying the experience.

Because Lucy refused to acknowledge defeat, they remained at Bellechasse. Her father argued with her, he threatened, he entreated, he cajoled, he attempted to bribe her to change her mind; but nothing would sway her from the object of her wishes.

Throughout all of this, Caylew was treated most civilly by his host. The cotton season was about to begin, but Colonel Parrish set aside his work to conduct his guest around the green-gold Bellechasse lands, high along the bluffs bordering the wide brown river.

He bent down to pick up a handful of the rich alluvial soil and held it out to Caylew, allowing some of it to run through his fingers.

"See for yourself. It's the soil that made West Tennessee into the power it once was; it's the soil that will make it so again. We were the last section of the state to be settled, yet we became its largest cotton producer. Four-fifths of Tennessee's cotton is grown in Shelby County. It's long staple, Bender grade, the very best. My father was not a man to deal in superlatives; still he was particularly proud it was his cotton, Bellechasse cotton, that received the medal at the 1851 London Exposition as the best cotton in the world."

As he scattered the remainder of the dirt from his hand back onto the field, Caylew said, "No doubt he raised you to follow in his footsteps."

Parrish shook his head. "No, Nicholas, my elder brother was the one. I guess Father felt closer to him, he being the firstborn. Advocacy was my field until . . . Well, now they're both gone, but before my father died I promised him I'd bring Bellechasse back, and I will. Not only to its pre-war standard, either; I'm determined to surpass it."

"With no knowledge and no one to work in the fields, how can you expect to do that?"

Parrish nodded toward a small group of men tilling the long field. "They haven't all deserted the place, and I work beside them. There's no better way for me to learn, Caylew."

They entered the warehouse where the cotton bales were kept before being hauled to the Memphis wharfs for shipment. Seeing Caylew brushing the lint from the sleeve of his dark coat, Parrish said lightly, "Lint on a gentleman's coat, Caylew, is a sign of honor, a sign down here that you belong."

Caylew continued to brush his sleeve. "I don't wish to belong to any place that relied on labor bought body and soul. You'd have none of this without slaves working it for you."

Caylew had in fact been no abolitionist; he appreciated far too well the importance of property. Nevertheless, it was an effective argument to use against a man whom he heartily wished to dislike, yet for whom he was beginning to develop the sort of regard he felt for one who would study the odds and then be willing to buck them in order to succeed.

Parrish's nodded assent took the wind from the sails of his argument, however. "You're right, Caylew; I can't deny it. To say that those of Bellechasse were well treated would beg the question; but you and I both know it was a political war we fought, of secession versus union. Abolition was only one of the tools used by the North. I'm not saying it wasn't a good one. Tennessee was a divided state. Many of its sons had to decide between family loyalty and their own beliefs, no easy decision. You in the North may have given impetus to abolishing a peculiar as well as a particularly distasteful institution; but having freed the blacks, you've left them to fend for themselves. Where we're able, we at least give them a living. But the battle was fought; it's over. Come, let me take you into Memphis to dinner at the Peabody. You'll meet planters and factors. We're planning a cotton exchange. I'll tell Livvy so she won't wait dinner for us.''

As they walked toward the stables, Parrish looked out over the wide fields. ''I'd like you to come back in ten years and see what I've done with this. I keep looking at the cottonseed, thinking there must be a more reliable way to extract the oil as well as make better use of the residue. I intend to find it.'' He laughed suddenly. ''My father used to call me a wastrel; now I waste nothing.''

Templeton Caylew might not like Parrish, but he couldn't help but think that whatever he was determined to do he would do. Had his daughter not conceived such an infatuation for him, he might even have acknowledged a sneaking regard for a man with his determination—rebel or not.

Eustacia had acquiesced without argument to the time her father spent with Colonel Parrish, believing that was the only means to achieve her ends. Besides, she had no wish to tramp around fields and warehouses, soiling her fine leather shoes. Instead, she toured the house with Lavinia, making notes in her mind of the improvements she would make when she became mistress.

But when she discovered her father still expected her to return North with him, with no word spoken, nothing decided, she adamantly refused. Lavinia, she argued, had invited her to stay at Bellechasse for as long as she wished, and she fully intended to remain.

It was an impasse that at last forced Templeton Caylew to admit defeat. Though Parrish was not the man he would have chosen for his daughter, he was only too plainly Lucy's choice, and he was a choice for which she was willing to fight. In his daughter's intransigence, in her determination to reach her object no matter the odds, he couldn't help but feel a tinge of paternal pride; it was the stuff of which he himself was made. It was that, together with his wife's fortune, that had earned him the title of the ''Wizard of Wall Street.''

Well, if it was Colonel Parrish Lucy wanted, Colonel

Parrish she should have. He only hoped that once her object was gained Parrish would prove worthy of her. Still, Lucy was only too well aware of his opinion in the matter. He'd get her the man she wanted; after that it was her affair.

As they sat at port that evening, Caylew handed Colonel Parrish one of his cherished Havanas; and as Colonel Parrish for the first time accepted it, Caylew began expansively: "I want to apologize for my attitude on my arrival, Parrish. I fear I acted in a hasty manner, that I lacked understanding; but during the week here at Bellechasse the opinion I held of you has changed considerably. You are, sir, a gentleman."

He was only slightly irritated by his host's "I had never supposed myself to be anything but."

Caylew went on to affirm, "You are, Colonel Parrish, a gentleman whom I no longer object to having in my own family. I can say no more than that. You have my approval, sir, to address my daughter."

Colonel Parrish inhaled deeply; then looking down at the cigar in his hand, he wrinkled his brow, as though something were not altogether to his liking, and made no reply.

"Did I make myself clear?" Caylew prompted. "You have my permission; you may address Lucy."

"I regret that I find myself rather confused, sir, and not a little embarrassed, since I have made no request to address your daughter."

Caylew was not as much put out by the disclaimer as by the fact that Colonel Parrish looked not in the least embarrassed in uttering it.

"Let's not beat around the bush anymore, Parrish. Lucy's in love with you and you well know it."

"I'm aware that Miss Parrish is not indifferent to me. Whether that is love I cannot say, for, of course, the subject has never been discussed between us. I told you it was not my object to promote any such alliance, and I have been good to my word."

"Well, take my word for it, she loves you and wants to marry you; and I am willing to let bygones be bygones and to allow that to come about."

"I see."

But what Colonel Parrish saw he kept to himself as again he drew firmly on the cigar Caylew had given him, and then intently studied the resulting ash.

"I don't mind admitting, you are not my choice of husband for Lucy, who's as fine a woman as any man could want; but you are her choice, and that's what counts."

"I see," Colonel Parrish repeated once again.

"Well, don't keep saying, 'I see,' " Caylew growled in irritation. "Just what is it that you see?"

"I see, Caylew, that you have given me permission for something that I have not requested, namely to ask your daughter to marry me."

"You mean you don't want to marry Lucy!" Caylew exploded.

"That I did not say. I am perfectly willing to marry Miss Caylew. It is only that before I should make such an offer there are certain things that should be decided between us."

"Just what do you mean?" Caylew asked cautiously, with growing suspicion in his eyes. "You don't mean to tell me you expect *me* to pay *you* for the privilege above and beyond the comfortable dowry she brings with her! You call yourself a gentleman—a gentleman with a price, is that it!"

Colonel Parrish's lips tightened; his eyes grew dark and then, just as suddenly as he had angered, he relaxed to break into a terse laugh.

"Perhaps that is the sort of gentleman I am, Caylew. Every man, it would appear, has his price. I should expect to be paid by you for the cotton you took from Belle-chasse. In the season of 1863-64 alone, fifty thousand bales were shipped from Memphis by Yankee pedlars, long white staple, Caylew, selling at a dollar a pound. Over half of that came from Bellechasse, and I'd like to be paid for it—all of it—and not in worthless paper, either, but in gold."

Caylew's face had grown red. "You damned swine, I owe you nothing."

"I believe I can prove otherwise," Parrish continued smoothly. "I should also like reparation on my claim with the North for property damage. You are, I know, a friend of Grant's cronies. You have influence and can use that influence as you see fit. As well as myself, I have neighbors who could use such influence. And in the matter of—''

"This, Parrish, is nothing short of blackmail," Caylew bellowed.

"Blackmail, sir," Parrish responded blandly. "I'm afraid I don't quite understand."

"Oh, but you do. Besides, you have no right to make terms in marrying my daughter. It is rather I, as her father, who should make terms. You can see for yourself she hardly comes penniless; she brings a good dowry."

From his inner coat pocket Caylew drew forth a folded sheet of paper which he put in front of Parrish, who pushed it aside without looking at it.

"No, Caylew, that's not what I want. Whatever money Miss Caylew has is hers to use as she would wish, for it is all too plain that I have none to offer her. But from you I demand what is mine. I demand the recompense that is mine by right, not a gift or favor to be supplicated." He picked up the decanter to refill the glass Caylew had the moment before emptied in one gulp. "But sir, this is hardly convivial conversation for gentlemen over a rather indifferent port but quite superior cigars. May I suggest these business terms be decided under proper conditions in my office tomorrow, if you are still of a mind."

"Tomorrow, Parrish, you may go to the devil!"

"I shall not return the wish to one to whom I may become related," Colonel Parrish replied coolly.

"His terms are extortionate," Caylew complained to his daughter later. "I've told you before, as has your mother, the man's nothing but a fortune hunter, after your money. I should have thought any woman with a sense of her own worth wouldn't want anything to do with such a man. I hate to say it, for I'm not partial to the English, but that Miss Vernon showed better sense than you, Lucy."

"You'd never say as much if you'd seen her, Papa; you'd like her no better than Harwood did. As for me, I have not the slightest doubt of my worth. If Harwood wants to put a price on it, then let it be as high as possible."

"Harwood!"

"Yes, I've decided I prefer that to Guy. I think it far

more fitting. Eustacia and Harwood Parrish—yes, I like it very well indeed.''

The next day found Templeton Caylew closeted with Colonel Parrish in his office, and the day after that. During the time they spent together, his regard for the man undoubtedly destined to become his favorite daughter's husband rose rather than diminished. Parrish drove as hard a bargain as Templeton Caylew had ever driven. He might growl about it to Lucy, but there was a sneaking sense of pride that his daughter had chosen well. Colonel Parrish would be a man to be reckoned with. When at last their talks concluded, though publicly he bemoaned their outcome, Caylew experienced a sense of inner pride. He had been able, at a price, to give Lucy what she wanted; and oddly enough, he felt that she was, after all, aligning herself with one worthy of both of them.

SEVEN

*E*ustacia had been unusually forbearing with her father's rantings, certain that in the end she would succeed. He might say what he liked as long as he got her what she wanted. She had been patient too with Lavinia, in whose company she had been forced to spend hours while her father was where she most wished to be, at the side of Colonel Parrish.

She had barely listened to her companion, whose soft voice had been unusually firm in confiding her reactions to the abysmal state of women's education in the South, particularly noticeable to her after living in England. It was not a matter that concerned Eustacia in the least, and she had nothing to add to Lavinia's ideas on the Episcopal school for girls that the Bishop of Tennessee was considering for Memphis.

Yet despite her boredom, Eustacia had made no effort to change to a subject more pleasing. Indeed, the only time she had managed to draw Lavinia from her lofty arguments was when she had read aloud a letter from her mother that contained the news that Lawrence was to be sent down from Harvard College for a year for inattention to studies and too much attention to other Cambridge pursuits.

Quite surprisingly, far from abhorring Lawrence's conduct as did his mother, Lavinia had sided with him.

"It must be difficult for a young man of his lively nature to concentrate when so many other attractions are at hand. It is not for want of intelligence, for your brother has a bright and eager mind. His tutors are much to blame in not teaching proper study habits."

Eustacia, convinced that Lawrence was at heart lazy,

did not agree; but infatuation, she knew, had a tendency to impair judgment, and she was quite sure, though Lavinia said nothing, that she was attracted to her brother. Thus she accepted Lavinia's statement without comment, which was unusual for one who enjoyed the supremacy of her own opinions. Yet for once it seemed unimportant. All she waited to hear were the words that finally came from her father.

"Well, Lucy, it is settled. Colonel Parrish will ask for your hand."

"Oh, Papa!" Her face lit with a triumphant smile, then she threw her arms around him and hugged him. "Oh, Papa, you did it. I knew you could."

"Well, I knew I could too," he responded without his usual conviction, for it had been surprisingly difficult and had caused him to swallow his pride more than once to make reparations where he did not feel them due. But what did it matter? After all, his Lucy would benefit, and it was for her he was reconstructing this corner of the South, not for any of its rebellious inhabitants.

Eustacia waited that evening, feeling Colonel Parrish's eyes upon her more often than had been his wont, looking unusually serious in response to her smiling encouragement. But not until the following afternoon did he ask her to walk with him to the belvedere looking down onto the river that General Parrish had built for his wife.

It was a low building constructed of logs, with large windows on either side, one overlooking the river, the other facing the path and gently sloping lawn that led back to the house.

"My mother and father were quite different, you know. Mother had been born in England and was determined to retain her own culture. She would take tea here every afternoon at four, and Father often joined her, even though he hated the stuff. Father was a son of Tennessee—tough, resourceful, determined. His preferred brew was Jack Daniel's, not Ceylon's finest. With his father he built Belle-chasse; it was everything in the world to him. I think Mother was the only person who came from outside that world that he ever completely tolerated, and her he worshipped. Yet though he loved her, he never overwhelmed her with that love. He recognized that she was not only his wife but also an individual with ideas of her own. That's why he built this place for her. This was hers alone, and no one, not even my father, came here without an invitation. Here she would read, or paint. She was fond of watercoloring, though she said she found the colors here too dazzling; they lacked the delicacy needed for watercolors."

He ran his hand over the carving on a straightbacked mahogany chair slowly as he spoke. "I'm glad this place escaped. I found it quite untouched. If only she'd been here that day; but 'if only' is pie in the sky. Everything you see here was hers. I come here sometimes when I want to think, and sometimes I see her resting on the chaise over there, looking at the river." He turned to look back toward the house. "It's heavenly here in the spring when the dogwood is in bloom, though Mother always preferred the maple and birch in all their glory in the fall, just as they are now, and her own copper beech, the one she planted in front of the house the day they married."

"You loved her a great deal."

He nodded. "She talked to me about everything, perhaps because I was like her, or perhaps because my elder brother was always at Father's side." He seemed to shake himself mentally, for he turned to look fully at Eustacia. "I tell you all this because I wanted you to know that this place is very special to me, and I have asked you here for that reason."

Eustacia's eyes throughout had been firmly fixed upon him, barely noticing the stretch of wide river or the riot of color on the bank beyond. She had waited for this moment; and now he began: "You must be aware of the matter that has been under discussion between myself and your father these past days."

"I am not totally unaware." She smiled invitingly.

"If you are not fully aware, Miss . . . Eustacia, then I must explain to you why I made the demands upon him that I did."

"I don't give a fig for any of that, Harwood. Papa has plenty, and whatever you asked he can supply; and he did nothing, gave nothing, that I did not want him to give. You need explain nothing to me on that score."

"Nevertheless, it must be clear to you. I won't want you to believe me mercenary without cause."

"My dear Harwood, that matter was settled when I saw Miss Vernon out of your life."

"Then you admit to interceding there?"

"Of course, but you knew it. Admit that you knew I did, Harwood; admit you knew why," she demanded in triumph.

He smiled ruefully. "I had strong suspicions."

He turned away for a moment, and she felt growing impatience. All she wanted was that he would kiss her as he had kissed her on the Langleys' terrace that night; but he stood apart from her, far too serious, and his voice as he turned back was far too concerned.

"You must know that I am going to ask you a question that will mean much to the future of both of us, that I intend to ask you to be my wife; but before I do so there are some things we must discuss, things that must be clearly understood between us."

"Oh, Harwood, there is nothing to say, nothing, that is, except—"

"Except 'I love you.' Is that it?"

She nodded.

"That is part of what we must talk about, Eustacia." As he saw her face cloud over, he hastened to add, "It's not that there is anyone else, or ever has been seriously. I don't deny enjoying female companionship. When I was younger there were infatuations, many of them; but that, I suppose, is part of growing up. I've never had a serious affair of the heart; I've never had to give up someone I loved. My heart is unscathed." For a moment his eyes looked pensively beyond her. "Perhaps too unscathed."

"It's been much the same with me, Harwood, all too one-sided—until now, that is." She stroked the lapels of his coat possessively. "And you mustn't talk about being young as though it's all in the dark and dismal past. You're still young."

"I may be young in years, but so often I feel that I've seen enough, too much of life, Eustacia, that I shall never again know what youth is about. There are times when I feel that, though I survived when others fell, some vital part of me lies buried with my brother at Chickamauga, or with my parents down at Elmwood. You see, Eustacia''—he took her hand—''you must not only know but try to understand this, for if we are to begin life together there can be no dishonesty between us.''

He paused, then went on with difficulty: ''My feelings seem to be locked away; it's as though I'm afraid of tenderness, afraid of love. Even my own sister tells me I've changed, that I'm unbending, that I don't laugh and tease as I used to. I care for her deeply, yet I'm not sure I know how to love, not even little Livvy. Eustacia, I'm not sure that I can truly love at all.''

He ran his hands through his hair impatiently. ''I'm making a mess of this. It's just not easy to say; but I want to be honest with you, and I most desperately want you to understand. You're lovely, more than lovely; you're a beautiful woman. I'm most horribly flattered that you want me, and I should be less than human if I did not react to you as a man must to a woman like you. To see you is to want you. I do want you, very much, but I'm not certain that is enough. It is not, I think, love. And you deserve love.''

''Oh, Harwood, I do love you.''

''I believe you do, Eustacia. That is why I want you to know my fears. Everyone I loved was taken—''

''But I shan't ever leave you, Harwood,'' Eustacia protested.

''I don't believe you would, Eustacia, but you must try to understand that my feelings are not as they used to be.''

''Harwood, I love you. There's nothing more to be said.''

''Only that Bellechasse is my home; my roots are more firmly planted here after . . . after what happened than they ever were. I want to build it back into the way it once was. No, I want to make it better than it ever was. But I know it must be strange to you, as it was to my mother. Your home is in the North. You must be free to go back whenever you wish.''

''The war is over, Harwood. I would hope you will come too. You may find the North equally to your liking.''

''I'll never move there, Eustacia. Don't marry me thinking that I would. My place is here, at Bellechasse. This is a working plantation, and a planter can't up and leave at will. I should willingly visit whenever I have the time, but I have precious little for pleasure trips. You must know that now. You must understand, though, that I shall never stand in your way of visiting your home, your friends, or following your own inclinations. I would want you to be free, just as my mother was free, to make your own friends, to enjoy your pursuits. This will be a strange world to you. It's not fashionable or sophisticated, particularly not now when so many people are simply struggling to survive. You must think carefully of all I've said before you give me your answer."

"I intend to make Bellechasse the showplace of the South. It won't only be the talk of Tennessee but of New York as well. I have plans, Harwood." Lovingly she ran her hands along the lapels of his coat.

"I can't keep you in the luxury you have been used to; that must be obvious. I know you have your own fortune; that is yours to do with as you wish. Renovation of the house is something I intend eventually to undertake, but it can't be done at the expense of the plantation. The first thing I must do is to make that profitable once again. Will you be satisfied with a husband who spends all day in the fields, who will not be always at your side?"

"I want you for a husband, Harwood," Eustacia said with determination. "Let's not talk anymore about who does what. If my fortune is my own to do with as I wish, then I will use it on Bellechasse. And as for spending your days in the fields, I shall overlook that just as long as your nights are spent with me."

"Oh, Eustacia, you do humble me with your love."

She smiled and put her arms around his neck. "Be humble, my darling. And put your fears aside. I love you enough for both of us."

He looked down at her, putting his arms around her. "I do believe that's so." He smiled. "You know, I'll probably look back on this day and wonder how I ever dared to put up so many disclaimers. I might have lost you."

"You'll never lose me, Harwood, never."

"Eustacia, my darling, Eustacia!"

And at last he did what she had been waiting for him to do ever since they entered the belvedere. He bent down to kiss her as he had that evening on the Langleys' terrace, the same kiss except this time there was more tenderness in it; this time there was no dance to interrupt its course.

Their dance had only just begun.

BOOK THREE

Lavinia Parrish

A nun hath no nation.
Wherever man suffers, or woman
may soothe,
There her land, there her kindred.

E. R. Bulwer-Lytton
Lucile

ONE

$\mathcal{T}$wo events happened in the summer of 1873 that were to change the life of Lavinia Parrish forever. An epidemic of yellow fever struck Memphis, and she first met Sister Serene.

Ever since Guy Parrish had married Eustacia, Livvy's life at Bellechasse had grown increasingly difficult. She had eagerly looked forward to the event, believing a wife's love might bind her brother's inner wounds and that Lucy would become the sister she had never had.

That Lucy was spoiled, even petulant, had become apparent at her tantrum over Guy's refusal to marry until late in the spring, after the cotton season was over. She had pouted and fumed, demanding the wedding take place immediately. Only when she realized Guy was not to be moved had she placed a finger to his lips, and expressed her acquiescence.

"Very well, my master, so be it. Till spring then. We shall have the most magnificent wedding New York has ever seen. Papa has promised me it will outshine all others."

"If that's what you want, Eustacia, and your father wants it for you, I shan't object. A wedding belongs to the bride."

It had indeed been Eustacia's day. Her father had been as good as his promise; and Livvy, surveying all from the Caylews' pew at St. Stephen's, was not the only one to think she had never witnessed anything as lavish. It was a scene from a fairy story. And as in any good fairy story, it had its prince and princess.

As the organ swelled to the notes of Mendelssohn, Guy

Parrish waited, tall and erect, before an altar banked with white roses entwined with fuchsia and japonica, roses so numerous that the air was heavy with their perfume, while the altar rail had been turned into a hedge of white lilies over which hovered a canopy of smilax ferns. He was dressed in gray rather than black, which had been the cause of some controversy. Caylew had objected that gray was too reminiscent of the Confederate cause, but Guy had been firm, and more than ever Caylew realized he was giving his daughter to a man as determined in his convictions as he himself.

Journeying North, Livvy had been full of anticipation, excited at the prospect of seeing Lawrence Caylew again. Guy and Nicholas had promised to stand as best man for one another, but Nicholas was gone, and Guy had invited Lawrence to fill that office.

She had been jolted from her complacency when, after changing trains at Louisville, and jolting on to cross that fateful line dividing South from North, Guy had voiced previously unspoken misgivings.

"I hope I'm doing right, Livvy." He had turned away to stare out the window. "I just hope it's right."

"But of course it is, Guy. Lucy's mad for you."

"You've chosen the right word, Livvy. I feel she's mad for me, but it's a sort of feeling I don't understand, not one I return, at least not in the same way."

"She loves you, Guy. She'll make a wonderful wife."

"I guess you're right, Livvy." He smiled and put his arm through hers, going on as though to convince himself: "And she'll not only make a wonderful wife for me but a wonderful sister for you. She'll be a comfort to you in a way I have not."

"Oh, Guy, you're the best brother a girl ever had. I couldn't be more fortunate. You, and now Lu—Oh, dear, I must get used to calling her Eustacia."

Yet watching Eustacia, dazzling but somehow unreal in her beauty and elegance—wearing white satin bordered with fresh orange blossom, the diamond crown that held her veil in place decorated with the same blossom that formed a perfumed cloud around her as she advanced down the aisle—for the first time Lavinia wondered whether Eustacia was any more real than the picture she presented.

Her glow outshone even the priceless necklace she wore, a gift from her father described in that morning's *Tribune* as composed of 226 triangular and square-cut diamonds supporting five pear-shaped emeralds weighing ten carats. The necklace was real enough, of course; but beyond its glitter, was it any more than hard, cold rock?

Could one who placed such store on appearances, on material possessions, really be like a sister to her? In London, Livvy had thought it possible; but since the engagement Eustacia all but ignored her, making her feel insignificant, even unwanted, particularly when they were alone together. Livvy wondered whether Eustacia could be jealous of Guy's obvious affection for her, whether she disliked sharing him with anyone. Still, she did love Guy, of that Livvy was certain, and that was really all that mattered.

The ceremony was performed by the rector, Dr. Hunter, before a congregation of those Four Hundred that made up the Caylews' world. Amidst all the finery, one group stood out from the rest—a small knot of women dressed in black with flaring white starched headdresses. Nuns of the Episcopal Order of St. Catharine, Livvy was told, an order of which Dr. Hunter was chaplain, and of which Mrs. Caylew, at his recommendation, had become a patron. As a mark of her endorsement, they had been invited to attend, perhaps also because their marked austerity in the midst of opulence provided a striking contrast in a carefully orchestrated event. To Livvy, the nuns were the only reminder of the religious significance of the ceremony. While the rest of the congregation irreverently chattered, assessing everything as though imminently due for the auction block, they alone silently observed the sacrament.

Guests at the reception were greeted in the wide hall of the Caylews' Park Avenue mansion by yet another enormous floral tribute entwining the initials E with H. Two hundred sat down to consume oysters, consommé de volaille, green turtle au Madeira, bass à la Normandie, brook trout, vol-au-vent à la Toulouse, squab, filet de boeuf en croûte, Westphalian ham, widgeon, lobster salad, lemon ice, cheeses, fruits and nuts, and the largest wedding cake ever made by Habermeyer's. There followed toast after toast in French champagne served from Austrian crystal, while

congratulatory messages from across the country and around
the world were read.

Afterwards, the panoply of wedding gifts, entirely filling one room on the main floor, was viewed: seven sets of
china—from Dresden to Limoges—gold goblets and bronze
urns, antique carved ivory figurines, a magnificent epergne
from the Caylews to be set on the Sheraton inlaid mahogany dining table already dispatched to Bellechasse, an
enameled pendant watch for the bride, gold and opal cuff
links for the groom. Livvy searched in vain for the leather-
bound Bible that had been her present, given to replace
their own mutilated family copy, and at last found it
hidden behind a silver tea service from Mrs. Vandervoort.
She sensed her brother's dismay not only at this meretri-
cious display but at the event as a whole. But it was, as he
had said, the bride's day, and Eustacia shone.

Livvy had felt lost and alone after the bridal pair left to
spend their first few days in Newport before sailing from
Boston for a honeymoon in Europe. Then Lawrence had
come to console her, plying her with champagne, so she
remembered little except the kiss he stole from her in the
billiard room. She was quite sure she should not have
kissed him back, at least not as fervently as she did; he
had, after all, been flirting with any number of pretty girls
that day.

Back at Bellechasse, Livvy spent her time unpacking
and arranging everything for the return of the newlywed
couple. An army of workmen, commissioned by Eustacia's
father, arrived to renovate the house, painting and plaster-
ing, refinishing the floors and woodwork. One elderly
craftsman was assigned to repair their paintings, but Livvy
removed that of General Parrish until he was gone, and
then replaced it, still battered and mutilated, on the freshly
painted wall over the mantel.

It was the first thing Eustacia noticed on her return.

"Why was that not repaired, Lavinia? I simply can't
understand how it was overlooked. It must be taken down.
I bought a wonderful Gainsborough in England; Guy thought
the subject very much like me. It will look very well there.
That awful relic can go upstairs."

Then Eustacia had turned her attention to the furnishings.
Nothing was where she wanted it to be. Surely Lavinia

must have realized that Hepplewhite chair was intended for
their bedroom rather than the salon. And why had she
placed the gilt mirror in the dining room rather than the
hall?

Livvy was confused. Rather than being praised for her
efforts, as she had expected, she found herself being casti-
gated. She hid her consternation in her brother's shoulder
when he came in to hug her.

"Oh, Livvy, it's so good to be home. You've done
wonderfully, hasn't she, Eustacia? Bellechasse is looking
. . . well, different, but quite magnificent." He had
glanced at the portrait over the mantel, squeezing her hand
gently. "And thank goodness you knew to leave that just
as it is."

Eustacia had not mentioned the painting again, nor was
it moved. In the weeks that followed, however, she busied
herself in turning everything around, having the walls in
the salon repainted until exactly the shade of duck-egg
blue she had admired at the Langleys' was achieved.

Watching the refurbishment of the home in which she
had been born and bred, Livvy found herself less at ease in
the new elegance than in the sparsity and decay that had
greeted her on her return to Bellechasse. She felt increasingly a stranger in a house that was rapidly becoming a
replica of the Caylews' Park Avenue mansion, perfect
though their taste might be.

Increasingly she sought comfort in her mother's summer
house, where family pieces rejected by the new mistress of
Bellechasse had been relegated. Even so, she knew she
could not hide herself away forever.

Memphis had welcomed Eustacia with cordiality if not
with warmth; but then, Eustacia, a formal person herself,
probably found that preferable. Their attitude had not dis-
couraged her from planning a housewarming for Bellechasse
more opulent than anything seen in Tennessee for a decade. The wide magnolia-lined drive, bordered with col-
ored lanterns, led up to a colonnaded, flower-strewn portico.
Inside, English antiques and French tapestries, beveled
mirrors and fine china, created less interest than the bath-
room, one of the first in the state with indoor plumbing.
The manufacturer from Baltimore had been summoned to

install it, complete with covered tub and gold faucets for the running water.

Eustacia, wealthy victor in a conquered land, was shrewd enough to realize that her display was likely to invite envy. She found the Tennesseans crude and unsophisticated, but these were her husband's people, and she was determined to do anything to shine more brightly in his eyes. So she made it her business to learn individual tastes; and while there were trays of champagne, canapés of caviar, and the finest Chesapeake oysters, there were also mint juleps and Jack Daniel's whiskey for men like Frank Johnson and Dr. Tom Mitchum, who would drink nothing else. They were Harwood's friends; otherwise she would never have had them under her roof, for they were known to frequent that notorious Palace of Cleopatra on Gayoso Street.

She had sent for the entire orchestra of the New York Academy of Music, of which her parents were sponsors, and for famed singer Minnie Hawk; but she had also invited Cleopatra's local musicians to perform their own wild and cacophonous, sometimes slow and dirgeful sounds. She found it dreadful, but Harwood liked it; he said it was the sound of the future. If that were so, she would certainly keep up with the times. No one would ever be able to say Eustacia Parrish didn't know how to throw a party.

Guy had demurred at the extravagance; but Eustacia, pouting, reminded him it was her money, and hadn't he told her she might do with it just as she wished? Well, then, what she wished was to entertain their neighbors and friends. He had not spoken of it again. Only Livvy realized how much he hated the fuss, the pretentiousness, the extravagance, and unrestrained squandering of wealth when so many were in need. A vulgar display of Yankee wealth was what people would say. Guy could imagine his father's horror.

If only Eustacia hadn't been so obvious in her local touches—the condescension of those heart-shaped hush puppies served from silver platters, the catfish prepared in vintage Madeira. She'd even produced sheet music of Chopin waltzes for the pianist from Cleopatra's to play between his own music, not realizing that, besides never having heard of Chopin, he couldn't read music; he played from the heart.

There were so many things Eustacia didn't understand, but Guy was learning to tread carefully; for she would construe the most innocent remark as criticism and was likely to pout and sulk for hours. Even worse were the effusions and tears that followed, the apologies, the insistence on dragging him away from his work to make up. How he wished her feelings for him were less obsessive.

But that must be overlooked now that she was to have a child. In the midst of her preparations for the party, Eustacia had mentioned this important event to her husband with cold reluctance. She seemed to resent his happiness, making him promise not to speak of it. Still, sensing Livvy's uneasiness, Guy had confided the news to her.

"I'm sure Eustacia plans to tell you herself, Livvy, when she's adjusted to the idea. Just don't let her know you've heard it already for she probably wants to surprise you. I told you only so you might forgive her illhumor. I've noticed how you hide yourself away."

Though Livvy was puzzled by the idea of a woman "adjusting" to the joy of giving birth, she was relieved to learn there was an explanation for Eustacia's behavior.

"Guy, I'm sorry. I didn't know. But should she be so busy with this entertainment just now?"

"I don't know. But this party of hers keeps her mind off things. She seems pleased by it."

It was odd, Livvy thought, that the party was at Bellechasse, the guests were Parrish family friends, yet both of them realized it was Eustacia's event.

"I must find something to do, some life for myself, especially now you're starting a family."

Guy looked up from his ledgers. "You're not thinking of going away, Livvy. I won't have it. Wait till the child comes. Things will change; I'm sure they will."

"I'll be here for that." She kissed his cheek. "Then we'll see."

The answer to Livvy's dilemma had come from their father's old friend James Turner, the Episcopal priest who had baptized and confirmed the Parrish children, whose exploits during the war had earned him the title of Chaplain of the Confederacy, and who had been the natural choice for elevation when the office of Bishop of Tennessee was established.

He had spoken before of establishing a school for girls in Memphis, but now he came seeking to use the Parrishes' Memphis house as a shelter for children still homeless from the war. The Sisters of St. Catharine were to organize it. Since Mrs. Caylew was their patron, he supposed Eustacia wouldn't object. Discovering that Livvy was unhappy, he suggested she use her creative efforts and join them.

"What do you think, Livvy? Would you help?" His bright eyes gleamed. "I'm sure you'd get along with the sisters; there's nothing sanctimonious about them. Their superior, Mother Charlotte, is not a bit stuffy or self-righteous. I wouldn't suggest anything nauseously pious; you know me well enough for that."

Livvy had been caught up in his excitement, but she hesitated. "I'd never want to be a nun."

"I wasn't suggesting that."

"And I'd have to have Guy's permission. I'll talk to him, but not now. After the baby comes. Oh!" she clapped her hand over her mouth. "That's supposed to be a secret."

Bishop Turner laughed. "Can't keep something like that a secret for long."

Bishop Turner had provided Livvy with an option, and her good humor was not to be shaken, even when Eustacia complained bitterly that Guy was paying too much attention to Felice Blanchard at the party.

"I don't know why he smiles at her so. She has no style at all."

"He smiles at Felice Blanchard because he likes her—as a family friend. And she's brave too, for Guy said that in the War between the States, she—" Livvy broke off abruptly.

"In the Civil War she did what?" Eustacia demanded.

"Something about. . . I don't remember. I was just trying to explain that the Blanchards have been friends and neighbors for a long time; that's all they are to both of us, friends." Livvy suddenly sensed Eustacia's insecurity and added gently, "Guy smiles at others because they are guests in his house, but he smiles at you, Eustacia, because you are beautiful. Everyone is saying so."

"Are they, Lavinia? Are they really? All I've heard them admire, after all the trouble I've gone to, is that awful painting over the mantel, the one of your father. If only you'd had the man repair it it wouldn't be quite so bad. But the people here are so odd, I just can't figure them out."

"Guy's a Tennessean, Eustacia."

"I understand my husband perfectly. He's not like them, nor you, either," she added as an afterthought, shooting a glance of critical satisfaction across at the reflection of herself in the gilt-edged mirror in the hallway, running a hand over her tiny waist. "I do hope that childbearing won't completely ruin my figure. I couldn't stand that."

"Of course it won't."

Eustacia shot a sharp glance at "Lavinia, you knew!" she said accusingly.

"Guy told me. I'm very happy, for both of you."

Then Eustacia repeated what Bishop Turner had said. "Everyone will have to know sooner or later, I suppose." And she smiled at Livvy, and Livvy felt glad, hoping they might be friends—Lucy and Livvy—as they had been at the beginning. And maybe she wouldn't insist on calling her brother Harwood instead of Guy, and they'd be happy together, and Livvy wouldn't go away after all.

That spring Eustacia bore a daughter. If Guy was disappointed that it was not a son, he gave no sign. He seemed only glad it was over for his wife's sake, for if Eustacia had hated the pregnancy, how much more had she loathed what she was later to describe as the utter indignity of giving birth.

Livvy overheard Dr. Mitchum, who attended the birth, complaining to Guy, "I've never known a lady less able to help things along. The birth canal seems wide enough, but she's insisting on chloroform. She says the Queen of England had it, as though that gives it the mark of approval. I'm against it; it will render her completely lifeless, and we need her participation. She seems to think we can get this baby into the world for her, but I can't use forceps until she uses the contractions to push the child down. I'm not in favor of husbands around at a time like this, Parrish, but under the circumstances, since you're the only one who has any influence with the lady—she is, if you'll pardon me saying so, very strong-willed—I'd appre-

ciate having you in there with me. Believe me, you're the
only one she'll listen to."

Guy got up in relief. "Anything, Mitchum, except sitting here like a helpless dolt."

"I do think it only fair to warn you that I am concerned
about the amount of constriction Mrs. Parrish has placed
on that critical area, wearing those tight stays of hers. I
spoke to her about it several times, but she didn't listen. I
should have had you tell her. Just hope there's no damage
done."

Nevertheless, Isabella Lavinia Parrish, born two hours
later, though small, had lusty lungs and a fine color. Guy,
the first to hold her, glowed with pleasure. "She's grand,
perfect, a lovely little lady. I'm so proud of you, Eustacia,
proud of both of you."

"I won't go through it again, Harwood. It was absolutely disgusting, apart from being the worst pain I've ever
known. If I have to have another, it's going to make that
part of marriage hateful to me. I adore it when you make
love to me, but I can't stand this."

Still holding the baby, Guy stroked his wife's hair.
"Don't worry, Eustacia. I didn't intend to talk of it yet,
but Dr. Mitchum tells me it's unlikely that you'll be able
to have another child."

"Thank God!" Eustacia breathed a sigh of relief.

"We're fortunate. You're going to be all right, and we
have little Bella."

"We have one another, Harwood; that's what's most
important. Right now, all I want to do is rest and get my
figure back to the way it was. This business turned me into
a monstrosity. I must look a horrible sight now, after that
ordeal I've been through."

"You look lovelier at this moment than you ever did.
And just look at little Bella. Isn't she adorable?"

He held out the baby to her, but Eustacia turned her
head.

"Do go away, Harwood, and get the nurse to take care
of the baby. That's what she's paid for. Come back when
I'm rested and sit with me. What an agony! And to think
Mother went through it six times!"

Templeton and Isabel Caylew arrived for the baptism,
loaded with gifts. Livvy sensed her brother's sadness that

this would be his only child, that there would be no son to succeed him, but Templeton Caylew shared his daughter's relief.

"She's always been a delicate thing, Parrish. It's a nasty business; I'm only glad she came through it all right. I was worried, I have to admit it. I wanted her to be with us at the time, but she wouldn't leave you."

"I am her husband, and this is her home," Guy answered with a touch of asperity.

"New York's her home too; besides, we could have got her the best care there. My Lucy should never have anything but the best."

"She's quite well, Caylew. Dr. Mitchum is a fine physician who's brought hundreds of babies into the world. He assures me there's no need for concern."

Caylew's frown remained. "I'd still like her to see a New York specialist, just to make sure."

Lawrence came for the christening, handsome and worldly, standing as godfather beside Livvy, who was godmother to the child. He teased and flirted with Livvy, who was little used to such exciting attention. When Livvy told him she would wait to go North with Guy, who was occupied with Frank Johnson in planning the establishment of a cotton exchange in Memphis, he said he could hardly wait to see her again and promised to show her a fine time.

It was after the christening that Bishop Turner first spoke to Guy of his plans. While Guy had no objection to the use of their Adams Street house for an orphanage, he strongly objected to his sister working with the sisters.

"I won't have her in Memphis. Livvy's place is here."

"I wish you would reconsider. She does want to come, and we need her. Its not just the matter of setting up the orphanage, but since I shall be spending most of my time in Sewanee reorganizing the University of the South, I shall be giving over my house by the Cathedral for use as a girls' school. We really could use Livvy's help. I can assure you she'd come to no harm."

"I'm sorry, sir, but I won't have my sister serving alongside women who choose such an unnatural, I may say even an abnormal, life. What sort of women can they be? Frustrated, canting Pope Joans. God gets only those women no man wants; they can't be like Livvy, young and charming with all of her life ahead of her. No, I won't allow it.''

Bishop Turner shook his head. ''I can't agree with you about the sisters, Guy. They're fine women. But you are Livvy's guardian, and I must respect your wishes.''

''I want to go,'' Livvy protested. ''I need something to do. I'd be in our own house, and it's not as though I'd be far off, not like being in England, half way around the world.''

''That was different, Livvy. There was a reason for your being there. There's no reason now for you to move away.''

''But I want and need something to do.''

''You're young; you should be enjoying yourself. I wish now you had gone North with Eustacia and not waited for me.''

''So do I,'' replied Livvy, not thinking of Eustacia but of Lawrence.

By the time Guy was ready to leave for New York, the summer was almost over and Lawrence had left to tour Europe with the Schuylers. Before they returned to Bellechasse, Livvy heard rumors of an engagement between Lawrence and Drusilla Schuyler, and that made her think she had been foolish in waiting to travel with Guy. Lawrence was the only man she had ever liked; still, he wrote her a postcard saying he would see her at Bellechasse in the spring.

In the meantime, with Eustacia home again, Livvy's unhappiness returned. Once more she approached the subject of the orphanage.

''We've already discussed it, Livvy. You know how I feel. Besides, we need you here. Don't we, Eustacia?''

Support for her plan came from an unexpected source. Eustacia interceded on her behalf. ''I love having Lavinia with us, Harwood, but I can see how she feels. Goodness knows no one wants her to leave Bellechasse less than I, but we must consider the fact that she wants to serve a worthy charitable cause. Why, even Mama supports the Order of St. Catharine.''

''Bellechasse is Livvy's home, Eustacia, and there are plenty of worthy things she can do right here, if that's what she wants.''

"Eustacia's right, Guy. I need something more than I can do here, especially just now."

"I won't have you in Memphis on your own, and that's that."

"But, Guy, I shan't be ten miles away. And how could I possibly be safer than surrounded by nuns? What harm could there be in it? Bishop Turner approves of them."

Her brother's face grew grim. "I like and respect Bishop Turner, but you were here when he spoke to me; you heard my feelings on the sort of women who adopt such a life."

"Harwood! Mama would never give them her support if there were anything questionable about them. She's made every effort to raise money for their children's hospital. She would never do that if they hadn't been thoroughly investigated by the Diocese."

"Perhaps. But whatever they're like, I don't want a young and impressionable girl becoming enamored with their odd way of life. That's what they'll try to do, and I won't allow it."

"It's only until she is ready to marry, Harwood. Isn't it, Lavinia?"

"Till the spring, Guy, just till the spring."

Guy looked at his sister searchingly. Both knew Lawrence Caylew was expected at Bellechasse in the spring.

"All right," he agreed reluctantly, "just till the spring, then."

Livvy found work with the sisters absorbing, exhilarating; best of all, she was needed. The sisters came to rely on her. She knew the city on the bluffs of the Mississippi to which they were complete strangers; where they were often rebuffed by the Memphians, a member of the Parrish family was accepted. Where the sisters' assurances that the daughters of Memphis would receive the best possible education at the new St. Catharine's School were disregarded—either because they were Yankees or because they were nuns, it was hard to tell which was held most in suspicion—the same assurances from Livvy were met with sympathy and interest. Livvy loved being wanted. Though Sister Agnes tended to be officious, Sister Bertha was always working, and she found it difficult to overcome Sister Luellen's shyness, still she was needed in Memphis in a way she was not at Bellechasse. And they had accomplished much in a few short months. Not only had they set up a curriculum for the school, but twelve orphans had rapidly become twenty-seven, no easy task, for despite the $1,400 raised in New York, they were constantly short not only of funds but of help.

Though happy, Livvy still looked expectantly for Lawrence Caylew's visit. It came as a blow when, the following spring, Eustacia received news of his engagement to Drusilla Schuyler. While it was true that she and Lawrence hadn't known one another well, and Livvy had no assurance he would ever have proposed marriage to her, she had been attracted to him. The news left her deeply depressed.

She was glad to be busy and away from Bellechasse and Eustacia's repetitious detailing of plans for the wedding, perhaps because Eustacia feared there might be a greater celebration for Lawrence's marriage than there had been for her own. Maintaining outward indifference, for she would never want it known that her hopes had been crushed, Livvy was relieved that Eustacia, usually acute in such matters, did not guess.

Still, when Livvy demurred at attending the wedding, Eustacia argued, "Not go, Lavinia! But of course you must. Lawrence will wonder why. He's quite fond of you, you know. Look at all the trouble he took to entertain you when we were in England. Besides, I'm sure Mama will consider it an affront."

It was Guy who came to her rescue, supplying her with an excuse that she never expected to come from him.

"I daresay the sisters need your help, Livvy. They will appreciate it if you decide to stay behind. They must really have their hands full what with the orphanage and now the school. They've come to rely on you. I'm proud of all you've done to help them out. I don't think I've told you that before, but I am, really proud."

And he hugged her close, closer than he had for a long time; and she knew that he knew, that he felt for her, that he loved her. That was a comfort in a bleak and what was to turn into a hot and disastrous summer—the summer of the yellow fever, yet also the summer of Sister Serene.

TWO

Father Quayle, priest of the Roman Catholic church in the Pinch, the squalid shantytown at the water's edge, teeming with men, women, and children, dogs and cats, rats and mice, flies and mosquitoes, as well as all manner of dregs from the river, was the first to bring them word that two sailors, dropped off in Memphis from a steamer heading from New Orleans, were dead of yellow fever.

The news was received just as the sisters were rejoicing in the promised increase in enrollment at St. Catharine's School in the fall. Education of females was hardly a matter of priority in the multitude of troubles facing the community under Reconstruction; but despite the school's shaky start in Bishop Turner's house next to the Cathedral, hope for the future ran high.

Livvy had been glad of the challenge, glad to be needed in Memphis, and the last thing she or the sisters wanted to hear was Father Quayle's advice to leave town immediately.

"No telling how fast it will spread, sisters, but it's already got beyond the Pinch. Best get the children out and yourselves with them."

"But what exactly is yellow fever?" Sister Agnes asked. "Some sort of jaundice?"

"It certainly has elements of jaundice, yes." Father Quayle nodded. "But it's jaundice of a most virulent type. Its victims turn yellow, all right, an ugly sort of yellow. That's not the worst of it, though; I only wish it were. The Spanish have another name for the fever that better describes it. *Negro Vomito*, they call it, after the vile black vomit its victims spew forth in the late stages of the disease. Never in my life have I smelled anything to equal that foul odor, like the disgusting stench of decaying flesh.''

Sister Bertha turned away, and Livvy saw Sister Luellen shudder; but Sister Agnes remained resolute, demanding factually, ''They die then?''

''Most of them. See, the yellow jack only runs a short span. Begins with a fever like many other diseases and lasts anywhere from twenty-four hours to five days after that, during which time its victim suffers both chills and fever, severe pains in the head and back, then subnormal temperatures and pulse. That's when we begin to think the worst is likely to be over; yet that's when the wretched thing is only just beginning, for then comes the vomiting of blood and stomach acids.'' He saw Sister Luellen put her hand to her mouth and wrinkle her nose and he apologized. ''Sorry, Sister. It's a vile thing, I know.''

Sister Agnes frowned at Sister Luellen before prompting Father Quayle. ''That is the end then, the vomiting?''

''Like I said, just when the worst seems over, comes this awful vomiting.'' He threw an apologetic glance at Sister Luellen. ''That vomiting is the only true sign that the disease really is yellow fever and not dengue, the breakbone fever. They're often confused up to that point. And within hours of the vomiting it's either complete recovery or, all too often, death.''

''You've seen it before, I take it?''

''The sting of yellow jack has struck Memphis any number of times. We had quite an epidemic in '67, and there was another back in '28, before my time, that one carried off a third of its victims. They're fearing this may be quite as bad. That's why I'm urging you to leave.''

''And you, Father, are you leaving?''

''Of course not.'' He jutted forth his blunt jaw. ''My place is here to do what I can to help.''

''Then so is ours,'' Sister Agnes replied just as firmly.

''But you know nothing of it. You've never been exposed to the fever,'' the priest protested.

''Looks like we'll learn quickly enough, and if it's spreading as fast as you say, there'll be no difficulty about becoming exposed. Now how does it spread exactly?''

"There's the trouble. If only we knew what caused it, we might be able to do something to prevent it other than simply running away like the rich folks do. We can't say with any degree of certainty how it spreads. We only know it goes like wildfire once it starts, and we presume it's contagious; that's why anyone with the means leaves the area until after the first frost, when the disease disappears as quickly as it came.

"Those that remain take whatever precautions they can, but it's not easy. Some think the miasma—the air around us—carries the contagion. Memphis is a dirty city; not around here where you are, perhaps, but over in the Pinch there's filth everywhere—refuse, stagnant water, pollution of all kinds. Why, a traveler from a riverboat once said to me, 'I've been to Cairo and there's dirt for you,' he said, and Cologne would make any man back away from the stench, but there's nowhere that's as putrid as Memphis.' "

"We'll never get the city cleaned up overnight," Sister Agnes said. "We'd better concentrate on doing whatever we can to help fever victims and then see about improving conditions after the disease passes."

"Well"—the priest tugged at his ear—"if you're determined to stay, Sister, I'd best let the Howard Association know. They'll be organizing aid for the victims, sectioning up the city. Maybe you'll be able to care for the area around the Cathedral."

"Of course, we'll do so gladly."

"Very well then, Sister; I wish you luck. And pray for an early frost."

Apart from informing the Mother Superior and Bishop Turner of her action, Sister Agnes immediately set aside work with the school to turn all her own energies and those of Sisters Bertha and Luellen to answering the call. Even their housekeeper was assigned tasks, but not Livvy.

"You must leave, Lavinia," she said firmly. "It was noble of you to stay and help us with your brother and his wife off to that big wedding; now you'll have the opportunity to join them after all."

"But I don't want to go to the wedding. I never did."

"Well, go home, back to Bellechasse, then. Wait there until it's all over."

"Go, when Memphis is my home? Go, while the rest of

you risk your lives? I should think not! I shall stay and help too.''

"I can't allow it, Lavinia. Colonel Parrish would be furious. I know he's not overly pleased to have you here at the best of times. He'll accuse us of negligence if we allow you to stay here at such a time.''

"But you're staying, and Sister Bertha and Sister Luellen. Why should you risk your lives?''

"It's our duty to stay. Our purpose is to help those in need, to nurse the sick; it's our reason for being. For you, though, it's different.''

"But these are my people.''

"They're our people too, Lavinia. Please do go. If I allow you to stay now, like as not your brother will call you away and never let you come back. Just think how we'd miss you. Do please go, for our sakes if not your own.''

"But there are so few of you to take care of this large area, and the fever is spreading.''

"I've written to Mother Charlotte; she's sending help.''

"Then I insist upon waiting until that help comes.''

"Oh, Lavinia.'' Sister Agnes shook her head. "I know you mean so well, but I just can't take the responsibility for your well-being, not if this fever is as Father Quayle describes it.''

"I refuse to leave, at least until help comes.'' Seeing Sister Agnes's worried frown, she added, "Then I'll go to Bellechasse.''

Livvy had meant to do just that; but when help arrived in the form of Sister Serene she forgot all about her intention.

There was something about Sister Serene that impressed Livvy beyond anyone she'd ever known. Livvy liked and respected Sister Agnes, yet she had never felt entirely at ease with her; she found her too cool, too exacting. Sister Bertha was sweet but muddled, while Sister Luellen was devoted but quite timid, so Livvy was never sure she understood her or was understood. But Sister Serene was everything that Lavinia would like to be.

She was tall, though not overly tall, and her face framed in her coif reflected the serenity of her name. It was difficult to tell her age; Livvy was sure she was still young, but how young she could not say. She had a quiet confidence, indicated in movements made without haste but with clear intention, yet she also had a thoroughly feminine aura, emphasized by the soft scent Livvy always noticed when she entered a room.

Sister Luellen said she had been sent to Memphis because of her superior medical knowledge; there was even talk of training Sister Serene as a physician. But she brought so much more than her knowledge; it was her decisive presence, her quick understanding that made all turn to her. And though she was obviously a Northerner, unlike the others, who, try though they might, were never thoroughly accepted, from the start it was apparent that Sister Serene belonged.

It was apparent too, though Sister Agnes remained nominally in charge of the mission, that Sister Serene had taken over. She organized the supplies, adapted both the orphanage and school into makeshift hospitals, and saw that everything was scoured, cleaned, and disinfected to help prevent contagion. She insisted that each of them wear beneath her clothes, folded across the chest, a heavy cloth soaked in carbolic.

"I've talked to the doctors, I've read everything I can lay my hands on about this fever, but there's no way to know for sure how it's transmitted. We must take every precaution we can; and carbolic is better than the cologne and rosewater I see others using for immunity. As for those little bags of asafetida some tie around their necks for protection, I fear that's no more effective in preventing contagion than the bag of lavender I've always worn simply because I like its perfume. Still, if they'll use soap and water and common sense along with the asafetida, it can do no harm, and may even help. Belief is a marvelous tool in making things happen—or not happen."

Sister Serene, unlike Sister Agnes, accepted Livvy's presence without question. When Sister Agnes reminded Livvy that she had promised to leave, Livvy appealed to Sister Serene, who assuaged Sister Agnes's worries with "Miss Parrish is no fool; she knows her own mind. If she wishes to assist, I'm only too glad. I feel it's not for us to dissuade her."

"Colonel Parrish won't like having his sister here at a time like this," Sister Agnes warned.

"But *I* want to stay. I promise to take every precaution."

After Sister Agnes left, still shaking her head, Sister Serene said, "Frankly, Miss Parrish, I'm glad you're here. You've the coolest head of any of us, I do believe."

Lavinia felt herself glow with pride. "Please, Sister Serene, call me Lavinia or Livvy. That's what my brother calls me."

"Your brother is here, Livvy?" Sister Serene asked as she began scrubbing out the cabinet where they planned to store their supply of sulphur.

"Here, let me do that," Lavinia insisted.

"No, most certainly not. You've all had more than your fair share of cleaning before my arrival. But I shall be most grateful if you will stay and keep me company for a while."

"Of course." Lavinia perched on the edge of a chair. "What do you want to know? About Guy, my brother, he's in New York with his wife. They went to attend the wedding of her brother Lawrence." She paused as she uttered his name, realizing she had almost forgotten about him in the flurry of activity.

She found Sister Serene's eyes fixed upon her. "Did you like him very much?"

"How did you guess that I liked him?"

"The way your voice changed at the mention of his name."

"Mmmm, I thought I did, but now I'm not sure."

"You're very young. There will be many young men who will come your way."

"Did none come yours, Sister?" And then Lavinia flushed. She'd never have said such a thing to any of the others. She was sure they would have been embarrassed by it; but Sister Serene responded openly and matter-of-factly, "No, none ever did; but my life, I am quite sure, has been very different from yours. Tell me all about how it was for a girl growing up in the South."

So Lavinia did, all she remembered of her father and mother, of going to England to stay with her aunt during the War between the States, and of how much she had hated it, how she had longed to come home. And about

Nicholas, but mostly about Guy, whom she'd known most and loved best.

"Oh, Sister Serene, when I stepped off the boat in Charleston, it seemed like heaven. It was awful to see what had happened to Bellechasse, everything ruined, and then to visit the grave in Elmwood where Mother and Father are buried; but I had to see that to know in my heart they were dead. I'd always thought that sometime I'd waken and find it was all a dream. I hated to see Bellechasse like that, empty, ghostly. It hurt me, though not, I think, as much as it hurt Guy. It was odd, though, for even in my sadness I couldn't help thinking how grand it was to be back."

"Bellechasse is your home?"

"It's our plantation. My father's father started growing cotton there even before Memphis was founded. After the war it was left in a terrible state, close to ruin, but Guy's done wonders in bringing it back. He's worked the fields with his own hands. If only Father could see him, I've often thought. You see, Father used to chide Guy for being too fine to be a planter. He favored Nicholas to follow him, and Guy was sent off to study law. But Guy's most like Father, really; he's adaptive and inventive, and he has such a good head for working things out. And like Father, he's absolutely dedicated in what he does. I wish I were more like that."

"You like your brother very much, that's plain to see." Sister Serene smiled. "Makes me wish I'd had a brother like that."

"No sisters either?"

"No natural ones, but now I'm lucky. I have many of them, and I love them all."

"How is it possible to love them all?" Lavinia frowned. "I mean there must be some you prefer to others."

"Loving and liking are quite different things, Livvy. While I love all of them, I may not necessarily like them equally. Quite frankly, I don't. But you see, I'm human and I have preferences and can choose those I like. But loving is different. We're asked to love one another. Each one of us is a child of God, and for that reason it's possible to love even those we don't really like."

Lavinia lowered her eyes shyly. "I hope, then, Sister Serene, that you *like* me."

Sister Serene put aside her scrubbing brush to fix her clear eyes on the younger girl's face. "Livvy, I both like and love you, very much indeed. It was something I knew as soon as we met."

Lavinia laughed self-consciously. "I'm glad. I don't think I could stand it if you didn't." Then she added as Sister Serene went back to her task, "You are most aptly named. I've never seen such a serene expression on anyone's face."

"It wasn't always so; but I found my place, my purpose, and I suppose that is all any of us can ask of life. I feel particularly fortunate for that reason."

Lavinia grew thoughtful. "You know, Sister Serene, I didn't think so at first, but I'm coming to believe I'd like to be a Sister of St. Catharine."

"Now I didn't say that to persuade you that it is the only way for a woman, Livvy. Many, many find their fulfillment in marriage and raising a family. Thank goodness they do, for what on earth would become of the human race otherwise?" She turned her back on Lavinia as she continued, "Motherhood is the highest calling a woman can have. There'll be another young man to come along for you, quite as good as this Lawrence, I don't doubt. Does your brother have a large family?"

"One daughter, Bella. She's just turned two."

"Well, undoubtedly there'll soon be others."

Livvy shook her head. "No, his wife can't have other children. Between us, I don't believe she's sorry about it."

"I seriously doubt that, Livvy. It's a tragedy when a woman can't have children."

"When she wants them, it is; but I'm not even sure that she wanted Bella, let alone any more."

"Since I don't know her, it seems wrong for me to talk about her. Would you help me with these bottles of carbolic, Livvy? Just pass them up to me." Sister Serene had climbed on a chair and wouldn't allow Livvy to take her place.

As she passed the bottles one by one, Livvy pursued: "I really do want to be a sister, just like you, Sister Serene."

"Perhaps you will, but this is no time for such decisions. It's enough that you are here and willing to help. And you must remember that your life is ahead of you, and there are many other gentlemen of equal virtue to the one who has chosen to marry someone else. Rather than feel sorry for you, I feel sorry for him in that he has missed having you as a wife."

Though Livvy said no more, when Sister Serene smiled down at her, she was quite determined that she wanted to marry no one; her only aim was to follow the path of Sister Serene.

Livvy did wish that she might have been allowed to share equally with the sisters the care of the sick. As summer turned to fall without any change in the hot, humid weather, the task grew daily more onerous. Though Sister Serene had insisted that she be allowed to remain, she would not hear of Livvy accompanying them into the city to seek out and nurse those stricken. Livvy knew of the horror that confronted them only by its reflection in their eyes. To her care came only those who were convalescing, or children who had escaped the disease.

When she complained, Sister Serene wouldn't agree that she was being unduly protected. "You do more than enough, Livvy, seeing to it that there's food, clean linen, and taking care of the children. I just don't know who would do all that if you weren't here."

"It's not that I mind, but it's unfair. You're taking all the risks; I want to share those with you too."

"Livvy." Sister Serene paused in scrubbing down her hands and arms. "Every day when I come back I look for Sister Agnes and Sister Bertha and Sister Luellen. I'm so afraid of losing one of them not because any of us is one bit more important than those who are dying but because we're needed to help those struggling to survive. And as they need us, we need you here—someone to come back to. How can you doubt the importance of what you're doing? Because of you, we don't have to worry about the children, or about those who've been through the worst stages of this terrible disease. We know they have the best possible care."

"But it's not the same as nursing those really in need,

as you do. And look at you, Sister; you're so tired you can hardly stand.''

"Livvy! I'm no more tired than anyone else. I'm only glad that I have the strength.''

"You won't if you don't stop and rest. Let me go with you tomorrow, please.''

Sister Serene shook her head as she reached for a clean towel.

"You make me feel—''

"Feel what, Livvy?''

"Well, staying here, it makes me feel different, less than the rest of you.''

"Oh, Livvy, you are not in any way less than any one of us. Never think that for a moment.'' Sister Serene paused before adding slowly, "You've told me you want to join the order, to be a nun like Sister Agnes, like me. If that's so, you should know there is the matter of obedience to one's superiors that has to be undertaken. It's not easy at all; it's much more difficult than giving up worldly goods or promising to be chaste. Think of this as a test of your ability to give unquestioning obedience.''

"But I thought you said we were equal, that no one was less than the other.''

"Let me explain, Livvy. Superior does not mean superior in intellect or worth, merely anyone who has been with the order longer. Sister Agnes is my superior, for she joined before I did. I must obey her.''

"But she seems to take instruction from you.''

"Only in matters where she believes my knowledge to exceed hers—I have greater medical training than Sister Agnes. It would not be sensible to exert one's will arbitrarily.''

Then suddenly she smiled that quiet luminous smile. "I do, however, confess to using persuasion occasionally, such as pressing that you be allowed to remain with us. You have shown that judgment to have been correct, but were you—a young lady of great gentility, of great generosity, but also of great innocence—to go about the streets as we do to deal every day with the dead and dying, not only the old, but the young, the very young . . .'' Just as suddenly as she had smiled, Sister Serene's eyes glistened with tears, and she whispered, "No, Livvy, if you were exposed to all of that now, I should feel I had been wrong in persuading Sister Agnes to allow you to remain in Memphis."

THREE

Whenever they could find a celebrant to administer the host, the sisters took Communion and Lavinia joined them. She joined in too at those other times when they prayed together for the souls of victims of the fever, for the recovery of those in the throes of the disease, and, most importantly, for an early frost that would free Memphis from its dreaded sting.

They prayed in a small room at the top of the house that had been consecrated as a chapel. They prayed when they could, for prayer was a part of their life; yet, though it was never forgotten, it was often undertaken hastily, though no less sincerely, before falling into bed close to exhaustion, or sometimes early, very early, before the work of the day began. They prayed earnestly but silently, a small band of women intent in their purpose, strong in their sisterhood, sincere in their belief.

Livvy was there one morning—praying with more than her usual fervor because Sister Serene had been called out the previous night and had not returned—when the housekeeper came up to tell her she was wanted below. News of Sister Serene, she hoped fervently as she hurried toward the winding staircase; then, looking down, she saw one she had not expected.

"Guy! But what are you doing here? I thought you were still up North?"

But his face showed no answering smile; like his voice as he answered her, it conveyed utter displeasure. "I might ask, Livvy, what are you doing here at all? I wrote to you as soon as I found out about the outbreak, and from your reply I thought you to be at Bellechasse." Under his

stern scrutiny, his sister flushed. It was a piece of decep-
tion that she had practiced, knowing he would insist on her
leaving Memphis if he realized she had stayed behind.

"But I didn't *say* I was at Bellechasse," Lavinia
demurred.

"You know damned well you implied it, Livvy, so
don't prevaricate."

"But what are you doing here? You said that you and
Eustacia would remain North at least until the end of
September."

"I came when I received no reply to my telegraph."

"Telegraph?"

"The telegraph I sent to Bellechasse instructing you to
join us. The reports we've been getting of this outbreak
have not made pleasant reading; and when Mrs. Caylew
heard from the Mother Superior of this order that nuns
here were assisting victims, I reread your letter and realized you hadn't actually said in so many words that you
were at home. I am most annoyed and upset that the sisters
allowed you to remain. It shows a lack of due concern on
their part."

Sister Agnes, who had followed Livvy downstairs, flushed
at his censure and intervened with "Colonel Parrish, I
pleaded with your sister to leave, but she was adamant
about staying. Indeed, I wouldn't have allowed it, had it
not been for—"

"For what?"

"Your sister wanted so much to be of help, and Sister
Serene, who has a greater knowledge of these matters than
I do, felt it would be all right if she were to remain here in
the house. I can assure you she has not left it, and Sister
has made us all take the greatest precautions."

"Sister Serene, whoever she may be, has no right to
decide on what is right for my sister, no right to expose
her to such danger." And turning to Livvy, he said, "I am
here to take you home."

"Oh, Guy, I can't go; I really can't."

"What do you mean, Livvy, you can't! I'm telling you
I'm taking you home now, this minute. I don't want to be
any more heavy-handed than I have to be; but remember, I
am your guardian."

"Your brother is right," Sister Agnes put in quickly.

"But I can't." Livvy turned to her. "Not until I know that Sister Serene is safe. Does anyone have any idea of just where she went?"

"No. It was just as she was about to retire for the night when a woman came saying she was needed right away. So she put her cloak back on and left. She said she'd be back as soon as she could. I don't believe she knew where the woman was taking her."

"I'm so worried. She was gone all day, and now she's been out all night. She's only human. If she doesn't succumb to the disease, she may be downed by exhaustion. I think she would have sent word if she was all right."

"Look, Livvy," her brother said firmly, "I don't know who this Sister Serene is, except since she's the one who's responsible for your remaining here and being exposed to such danger, I cannot say I think highly of her sense of judgment."

"Guy, I've never been exposed to the danger that she has, not at any time."

"That's not the point at issue," Guy exploded. "Unlike you, Sister Serene has been sent here for that purpose. You know full well, Livvy, I wasn't at all happy about your leaving Bellechasse to come here in the first place, even without this epidemic."

"Do go, Livvy," Sister Agnes urged. "Your brother has a right to be angry."

"I won't move an inch until I know that Sister Serene is all right."

"Sister Serene! Sister Serene! Who is this Sister Serene that she is all important to you?"

"She is the most wonderful person in all the world, Guy; and she may be sick, even dying." Livvy's lower lip quivered as she said the word.

"Look, Livvy, I'm very sorry that Sister Serene may have met with misfortune; but if she's paid no more attention to her own welfare than she has to yours, then I can't feel great sympathy for her. In fact, to be quite frank, I think she has acted irresponsibly and unwisely throughout."

"She's not irresponsible, Guy, she's—" Livvy broke off her protest, looking beyond her brother toward the door that had opened. Her face cleared. "Sister Serene, there you are at last! Are you all right?"

They all turned to the doorway, where Sister Serene, pale with fatigue and strain, was standing holding the hand of a wan and bedraggled child.

"There you are, Sister!" Sister Agnes echoed, evidencing relief at the sight of the newcomer, before reproaching, "You really should have called us, not gone out alone, and without telling anyone where you were going."

"I didn't know where I was going; and anyway, when I got there, there was nothing that I could do." She knelt down beside the small boy, putting her arm around him, holding him close. "This is Arnaud. Don't you think he's a big boy for his five years?"

The boy clung to her as she introduced the others until, coming to Colonel Parrish, she stopped.

"This is Colonel Parrish, Lavinia's brother," Sister Agnes explained. "I'm afraid he's quite upset that we allowed Lavinia to remain here. And I suppose he has reason in wishing his sister had not stayed in Memphis at such a time." Despite herself, Sister Agnes's voice conveyed a certain unctuous tone, as though to remind Sister Serene that that had been her recommendation.

"I'm at fault, Colonel Parrish. Sister Agnes is completely blameless; she wanted your sister to leave."

"So I understand, Sister. She should never have been allowed to remain, never; and if Livvy refused to go, you should most certainly have advised me without delay."

"That's unfair, Guy," Livvy began, but Sister Serene silenced her with "Your brother is complaining of my negligence, Livvy, more than yours. While I understand your concern, Colonel Parrish, your sister is a person who does have a mind of her own. She's a capable and intelligent young woman, and she's done nothing to endanger herself unduly."

"Being here is danger enough."

"She chose it, sir; and while you may wish her to follow your wishes, she must have some say in her own destiny."

"My sister is young, too young to make choices of life and death, Sister."

"Many young men not too long ago made choices just as final."

"Please, Sister, no one knows that better than I; but you seek to deflect the issue. Anyone with a grain of common sense should have realized that my sister should have been sent home immediately. Sister Agnes's advice was sound. I only wish you had listened to it. If you sisters choose to remain, that is your own affair. Nursing the sick is a worthwhile endeavor. I've no doubt you've done good work here, though what you propose to accomplish with your prayers is beyond me. Do you think if there really were a God that He would allow the yellow jack to run rampant, leaving its swath of death and suffering in this city? Never! As much as anything else, I object to your encouraging my sister to believe in myth over reality."

No one spoke. Three pairs of eyes were fixed upon him in stunned dismay until Sister Serene, drawing the child she knelt beside still closer to her, said softly, "You must be famished, Arnaud, and very tired. We've a cook who makes the best johnnycakes, and then we'll find a clean bed for you." Turning back to the others, she said, "He really must be starved."

"I'll take him, Sister Serene," Livvy said at once, but her brother interrupted sharply.

"No, you won't, Livvy. You're coming home with me."

"I'll take care of him," Sister Agnes interceded firmly; and picking up the little boy, she left the room.

Only then did Sister Serene turn to Guy Parrish, her face filled only with compassion. "You have suffered, Colonel Parrish; you have suffered deeply. Only one who has suffered so could deny the existence of God."

"I didn't come to Memphis to engage in a philosophical argument, ma'am," he retorted. "My suffering—or lack thereof—is my concern, mine only. I came for my sister, only to find you've filled her with platitudes."

"Colonel Parrish, each of us believes, each of us acts, as we see fit, according to our belief. It is not for any of us to tear down the beliefs of another," she responded with quiet dignity.

"That is so. Nor is it for anyone to intervene in the life of another, as you have intervened in my sister's. The life you and these other ladies have chosen is abhorrent to me. Those who seek such a peculiar existence are not, nor can ever be, fully women. The cloister is only for those afraid to live. I won't have my sister, a girl flowering into womanhood, tempted to hide herself behind a veil. I won't allow you to influence her any longer. I won't have you speaking for her, or making her decisions for her, do you understand?''

"Guy! You've no right to speak to Sister Serene that way,'' Livvy rebuked. It was the first time she could ever remember being angry with her brother.

But if Lavinia was angry, Sister Serene's reply was unusually soft. "But he does, Livvy. He has as much right to speak as I have. And remember, he speaks so only because he is your brother and he loves you dearly. If he considers you are better off away from here, you must go. He thinks only of your well-being.''

"I don't require you to persuade my sister to do as I bid her.'' Guy Parrish eyed Sister Serene with rancor, adding coldly, "I am my sister's guardian, not you, Sister Serene. Put on a cloak, Livvy, and come with me.''

"I'll go, Guy, but only against my will, because you force me to,'' his sister responded frigidly.

It was the first rift they had ever experienced, and as they stared angrily at one another it was plain that each was shaken by it.

"Livvy.'' A certain anguish was detectable behind the ire in Guy Parrish's voice. "I just wish you'd try to understand. It's not only because I'm your guardian that I want you to leave; I'm thinking of you and of myself as well. I've seen Nicholas die, and I've buried Mother and Father. Don't you see, I couldn't stand it if you were taken away too.''

"Oh, Guy, don't!'' Lavinia's eyes filled with tears as she put her arms around him. "I won't do anything to hurt you; you know that.'' Then she turned back to Sister Serene. "I guess I must go, then.''

Sister Serene nodded and then said quickly, softly, "I'm sorry, really sorry, Colonel Parrish. Maybe I shouldn't have let Livvy stay; but she was so sincere in her desire to help, and she's really been absolutely invaluable. We shall miss her. I can assure you that pains were taken to see she was not exposed to the worst virulence of this fever, though I know there is no place in this city that is completely safe. We did our best to care for her, for as much as to you, she is dear to us. We wouldn't want any harm coming to her. All of us, myself especially, are proud of her. She's an admirable young woman. You're fortunate to have such a sister."

But if Sister Serene's tone was soft, Colonel Parrish showed no similar conciliation as he abruptly reminded his sister, "Your cloak?"

"I shan't need it."

"Yes, you will, Livvy," Sister Serene insisted, smiling for the first time. "The early morning is chilly. I don't doubt that frost we've all been praying for will soon be here."

FOUR

Frost came early that year to the western section of Tennessee, and to the fever-infested waterfront city of Memphis. Livvy breathed a great sigh of relief and sent up a prayer of thanks when she saw the crystal-white covering on the huge copper beech on the lawn, on the dogwood bushes, on the roof of her mother's belvedere. She thought of the frost's significance in order of descending benefits. It would mean the end of the fever, but it would also mean that Sister Serene would go North and she might never see her again. It would mean too that Eustacia would return to Bellechasse.

Livvy had missed Sister Serene, the others too, though not to the same degree. Ever since she'd returned to Bellechasse she'd tried without success not to brood on what was happening in Memphis. She worried about all of them, but about Sister Serene she worried most of all. Yet she couldn't speak of it to Guy. She knew he'd never really approved of the sisters and especially not of Sister Serene, and that saddened her. She did so want the brother she loved to share her admiration for her new friend, but whenever Livvy spoke of Sister Serene, Guy was noncommittal. When she had pressed him for a response, he'd called her a "veiled Florence Nightingale," with a touch of asperity in his voice; and once he'd even gone so far as to label her an interfering Sarah Gamp.

"You're so unkind to Sister Serene, Guy," Livvy had objected hotly. "She's good, and smart, and capable. She wouldn't harm anyone. I can't understand why you don't like her."

"With you to like and defend her, Livvy, she's no need of my support."

"But she likes you, Guy; she told me so."

"She doesn't know me," he said flatly.

"Yes, she does—through me. She said she'd give anything to have had a brother like you."

But Guy was not to be won over to Sister Serene's side.

Her brother's open declaration of disbelief in God had come as a shock to Livvy. It was true that the Parrishes had never been noted for their religious fervor, but whatever they may have wanted in devout piety they had certainly made up for in solemn observation of rites. Guy had been married in church. Had his vows meant nothing to him? To come right out and say there was no God—why, that was worse than heresy. It was blasphemy!

Livvy wished he would talk to her about it. She tried more than once to raise the subject, but his replies were always terse. "I'm not discouraging you from believing, Livvy, if you use common sense. By the same token, you mustn't preach to me the stuff this Sister Serene has filled you with. You know my opinion of it, and of her."

Then he'd turn affably to comment on Bella's progress, or the exceptional glory of the leaves of the copper beech their mother had planted; or if she tried to turn the conversation back to what was foremost on her mind he would accuse her of being as grave as a barnyard owl.

"Do let's be gay, Livvy. Life's only as pleasant as we make it. Read to me from one of the books I brought you. Not Dickens, no; I'm tired of social reform. The one by the Boston journalist, maybe, about that mixed-up Mrs. Partridge, or whatever the woman is called."

"Mrs. Partington—*The Life and Sayings of Mrs. Partington.*" And so she'd take up Shillaber's book and read of the redoubtable "poor widowless body," as Mrs. Partington called herself, giving advice on the drought: "I think a little rain might help as much as anything"; acting piously stricken on being told there was a nave in the new church; admiring the "cemetery" of her own features in a daguerreotype; or complaining because her landlord had called her "a termagrunt" but vowing she'd not "bear mallets."

They'd laugh together over Mrs. Partington's pretentious absurdities which Guy found every bit as amusing as Mrs. Malaprop's and Livvy supported because she was not only funny but epitomized the American free spirit; and they'd talk of Mrs. Partington, a fictitious character, but not of Sister Serene, who was all too real. While Guy would thus avoid discussing how and why he had ceased to believe in God, Livvy was also precluded from mentioning that matter she had spoken of to Sister Serene, her wish to join the Order of St. Catharine. Since her brother didn't want her to return to the school in Memphis, even though the fever had abated, how would he ever allow her to go to New York for the purpose of joining the sisterhood?

Livvy had written to Sister Serene and from her reply knew that she would soon be returning North; but just as she was wondering whether she could persuade Guy to be hospitable to her if she were to invite her friend to Bellechasse, her brother announced that Sister Serene was coming.

"Sister Serene, coming here?"

"That's what I said." He continued with his breakfast without looking up from the *Daily Appeal*.

"But how? I don't understand. I thought you didn't like her?"

"I don't particularly. But I thought you did."

"You know I do. It still doesn't explain—"

"Sister Serene wrote to me asking if she might stop here before going North. I agreed, Livvy, only because of your fondness for her; but if her purpose is to proselyte you for that order of hers, then I promise I shan't deal kindly with her."

"Sister Serene would never proselyte."

"Sister Serene is a very determined woman."

"I thought you liked determined women, Guy. Eustacia is determined, isn't she?"

But Guy had gone back to his paper. Livvy had found there were many things he'd never discuss since the war, and that list seemed to be lengthening—his lack of faith, and now his wife. He'd never spoken a word of complaint about Eustacia; but then, Livvy realized, he never spoke fondly of her either. Was he unhappy? she wondered, examining his long, tanned face until, turning the page, he

looked over at her to ask teasingly if he had smudged
newsprint on his face.

She smiled, shaking her head. "Thank you, Guy."

"For what?"

"For asking Sister Serene to come."

He shook out the pages of the newspaper. "She rather
asked herself. I simply agreed to it."

For Livvy, who had known Sister Serene for less than a
month, it was like the arrival of an old and valued friend;
more than that, it was like being reunited with a blood
relation, a true sister.

"It's over at last, that terrible scourge," Livvy greeted
her with relief.

"Over for this year, at least," Guy responded.

"Let's pray it never comes again, not like that, at
least," Sister Serene said with fervor. "The Howard Organization calculates five thousand must have been stricken,
and two thousand of those died—a terrible toll—mostly
white, many of them Irish Catholics, Father Quayle tells
us, down by the riverside in the Pinch. If only we knew
the cause."

"You should ask your God, Sister. Blessed are they that
do hunger and thirst after righteousness."

Sister Serene was less perturbed than Livvy at this clear
indication that past hostilities were not forgotten. She smiled.
"I'm glad to see you know your Testament, Colonel. The
Beatitudes are especially fine reminders for us all."

"It wouldn't do for one lacking faith to be ignorant of
what it is that he does not believe, Sister."

Despite this caustic beginning, the visit progressed well.
Livvy took Sister Serene everywhere, showed her everything: the house, the grounds, the offices, the fields, and
the machinery, which Guy, distant but polite, explained to
their visitor.

Sister Serene asked so many questions, evinced such
obvious interest and understanding, that Lavinia was happy
to see her brother's attitude thaw as his own enthusiasm
waxed in describing something of importance to him.

"Cotton determines our lives here in this region of
Tennessee; it always has. The Southeast has indigo and
rice; there's sugar in Louisiana and tobacco in the border
states, but here it's cotton." He looked across the newly

harvested fields, then back to the long white staple being readied for shipment. "We've the land to raise it, ample storage, and pretty soon we'll have organized in Memphis the best cotton exchange in the country, a place where people not only know their crop but understand its worth on the world market. And above all else, we have that grand old river to ship it on."

"You've every right to be proud, Colonel. You've a marvelous place here. Do you know, in spite of the horror of the epidemic we've just been through, I shall be leaving here with a sense of regret? I developed a strong affinity for Memphis and a high regard for its people."

"It's a fine city, though that's not to say it can't be a lot finer. We're growing, but as we do we're inheriting the vices of large cities—overcrowding, dirt, poverty. Still, along with those we're gathering benefits too, building our own mills so we won't have to rely on others to spin our cotton. We've also discovered a more effective way of separating the kernel from the cottonseed hull to extract the oil. And while we're at it, we don't waste a thing. The linters are used for stuffing and the remainder goes for cattlefeed."

He handed Sister Serene a clump of cotton from an open bale; lint fell on the black sleeve of her habit as he did so, but she made no motion to brush it off.

"We're lucky here at Bellechasse," he went on. "We've managed to remain independent and not fall under the thumb of factors."

"Factors?" Sister Serene questioned.

"Many of our neighbors have been forced to raise their crops on credit, with the factor in control of production rather than the planter. I'm not saying all factors are bad, because they're not. They provide a service, and some do it honestly and well. But for me, it's no way to run a plantation. I must do things in my own fashion. That's not getting any easier, though; for apart from the tax on land, and the federal levy of three cents a pound on cotton, and buyers in the North (where the money is) cutting prices, there's always the risk of a bad crop and having everything end up in the hands of bankers. That won't happen this year, but it has before and will again, I've no doubt. A planter can be wiped out overnight, the plantation put on the auction block, everything gone. That's been the fate of too many of my friends. No wonder they turn to factors to cover them.''

"It is to your credit that Bellechasse has done so well, Colonel Parrish.''

"Not entirely.''

Again he looked out across the land, still and silent for a moment, before going on, a slight smile playing on his lips, "I married money, ma'am, Yankee money.''

It was the first time Lavinia had ever seen Sister Serene disconcerted.

"I see,'' she said hesitantly.

"I'm quite sure you don't see, Sister, but no matter.''

It was yet another note of controversy; still, Livvy was delighted that her brother and the friend she held most dear were, if not friends, at least no longer at complete odds.

And when they were alone together, how they talked, until Livvy, seeing her friend rest her head in her hands, whispered, "You're tired, Sister Serene. You must rest.''

"Tired, yes, but the fatigue comes from a feeling of helplessness, of not having been able to do more.''

"You did everything.''

"But they died anyway, Livvy, two thousand of them. Mother Charlotte talks of sending me to train as a physician. Perhaps I could learn something to prevent people dying as Arnaud's mother did. Oh, Livvy, I didn't tell you how I found her; she was quite alone, lying on a filthy couch, covered in her own vomit. By the time I got there, she was almost dead. Someone had heard the little boy crying. They didn't know how long he'd been there with her; no one knew they were there. They thought the house was closed up. It was filthy inside; he'd been there without food, watching his mother go through the agony of the fever, seeing everything. He didn't move when I went in; he just sat there on the floor in the filth of the vomit. And there were rats and vermin everywhere.'' Sister Serene's voice broke.

"What she must have suffered!''

"Yes, but it's what he suffered that concerns me, for he is the one who lives, poor little soul! I did what I could for him while I was there; but, well, Arnaud's the reason I wrote to your brother. I was wondering if he would take him here for a while. The boy has no one, I gather. From what his mother was able to tell me before she died, he has no father.''

''He is dead too?''

''She was never married.'' Sister Serene paused. ''What do you think, Livvy? Would Colonel Parrish allow him to remain here, for a time anyway, until something else might be arranged for him? I know he could stay on at the orphanage. It's just that for some reason, perhaps because I found him, I feel so personally responsible for him. I want him to have a home, to be cared for.''

''Guy is good, really he is. He'd help anyone. He never talks of it, but I've heard so many stories of things he did in the war for others—from them, never from him. People are always coming by to thank him. I'm sure he'll help Arnaud too in any way that he can.''

''I don't quite know how to broach it to him, though. He seems not to like me.''

Livvy shook her head. ''I don't know. It's not like him, but since the war he's so uncommunicative. It's hard to know what is bothering him. You should have known him before. Mother always said he didn't have a serious bone in his body. Now he so seldom laughs.''

''I like him very much. And I like you very much, Livvy; you know that.''

''I know. And I guess you must know how much I admire you. Oh, Sister Serene, you live such a good, such a useful life. I want to be just like you.''

''No, you don't, Livvy.'' Sister Serene smiled that smile that lit her face and lightened her clear blue eyes. ''You want to be yourself, totally, wholly yourself.''

''But what I mean is I want to go back to New York with you. Guy's wife will return to Bellechasse soon; and I'm going to hate staying, because she really doesn't want me here, and Guy doesn't want me to go back to Memphis.''

''Where do you want to be, Livvy?''

''I want to be with you, in New York. I want to join the order and be a Sister of St. Catharine, like you.''

Sister Serene was silent for what seemed an eternity to Livvy before saying, ''Think carefully, Livvy, and tell me just why you want to join with us.''

''I want to be like you, to serve others the way you do,

and Sister Agnes and the others too. But, oh, Sister Serene, you're so sure, so calm; that's how I want to be. I want God to shine through me the way He shines through you.''

''But He can, Livvy; you don't have to be a nun for that to happen.''

''But that's the way I want it to happen for me,'' Livvy replied simply.

Sister Serene stood up. ''It's not an easy life, Livvy; it's downright difficult, even onerous at times. Up till now you've had a life of relative ease. All that would be gone. You would never marry, never have a family of your own or see a great deal of your own family; your allegiance would be to God, then to the sisterhood. It means cutting yourself off from all you know. It means wearing a habit as an outward sign of your profession. It means a life of poverty, obedience, and chastity. It means praying to be filled with the Christ's love while being aware you're only too frail, only too human, just as I feel at this moment in trying to tell you what it's like to be a Sister of St. Catharine.''

Livvy's eyes remained fixed on her face as she replied, ''I want to join, Sister Serene. I still want to join.''

''Your brother won't like it, but I'm sure you must know that. Can you live with his unhappiness?''

''I don't know.'' It was the first time Livvy had looked away; and when she turned back, her eyes were troubled. ''Would you speak to him for me, Sister Serene?''

Sister Serene shook her head. ''No, Livvy, I can't do that. But while I can't speak to him for you, I can and shall speak to him with you.''

''Tonight, then.''

''It must be tonight, for I leave for New York tomorrow.

FIVE

After dinner, while trying to think how to raise the matter with her brother, Livvy had taken up Mrs. Partington to read aloud.

She began with the tale of Mrs. Partington settling her 250-pound person most solemnly on the apothecary's new castor.

" ' "For heaven's sake, old woman, get off my hat!" ' " Livvy quoted in incensed tones, before changing to Mrs. Partington's aggrieved " ' "Old woman!" ' How ungallant, though the circumstances seemed to justify the epithet, the hat being the pride of the apothecary's existence. The opera,' " she concluded, " 'is very destructive to hats—if they're not thrown at the singers they're sat upon.' "

Guy laughed. Livvy was pleased to see him in good humor; and looking over at Sister Serene, she moved to set aside the book. But Guy pressed, "Do give us another, Livvy; and act it out just like that. You'd make an admirable actress. Don't you agree, Sister?"

"Whatever Livvy chooses, she will do well."

"One more, then." Livvy turned the pages. "What about this one? " ' "Where's the fire?" asked Mrs. Partington of a fireman from an upper window as the bells awoke her with their clangor.

" ' "In——" was the ungallant response, naming the hottest place of perpetual warmth.' " Livvy paused.

"In hell," her brother supplied.

" ' "Dear me!" said the old lady, "is it so far off! I wish it was nearer for your sake, but I'm sure you'll be there soon enough.' " Livvy's voice faltered; she looked over at her brother and closed the book.

"Look, Livvy," Guy said firmly, "if I'm not worried about going to hell, I don't want you—or your friend—to worry about it for me. Well, are you going on with the story?" Livvy shook her head. "Then let's see what news we have from New York."

He picked up a still-sealed letter from Eustacia that had come that morning and slit open the envelope. "Ah, she's coming back; be here before Thanksgiving, she says." He read on, omitting sections that were obviously too intimate, going on to Eustacia's minute descriptions of clothes she had bought, parties she'd attended. The letter was full of gossip.

"It's too bad we don't know these people; it might make it more amusing. Ah, here's someone I know. She says Bella's been fussing a great deal, and they believe the cause to be another tooth pushing through."

"But I thought she was over that by now—at least the worst of it."

He looked at his sister with a rueful grin. "Mrs. Wickers says it is teething, and you know that paragon of the nursery is never wrong."

"Mrs. Wickers?" Sister Serene had stopped short in her task of unraveling the embroidery yarn that Lavinia's cat with great elation had mingled into a multicolored ball.

"Mrs. Wickers is what is known in England as a nanny—a mainstay of every English noble or would-be-noble dwelling. I believe she still hangs on to the title here, just as strongly as visiting knights and baronets do theirs.

"You know, even though this country prides itself on being egalitarian, I'm afraid most Americans still revel in the world of English aristocracy as much as, perhaps even more than, the English do themselves. Maybe I'm overgeneralizing. There *was* one who came intent on founding a state of perfect equality—not too far from here, as a matter of fact. She called it Nashoba. Ever hear of Fanny Wright, Sister?

"She was the darling of Lafayette and believed in absolute freedom, free speech, free love; and she attempted to establish a colony based on those principles. It didn't last, alas. We might be a country built upon liberty and declare our freedoms; but I fear free love went beyond the limits of the Founding Fathers, and beyond the understanding of the local populace. It wasn't only they who decried Nashoba, but even Miss Wright's fellow countrywoman Mrs. Trollope, found it disreputable. She's the one who vented her scorn upon life on this side of the Atlantic in *Domestic Manners of the Americans*. You may have read it perhaps."

"I've heard of it. Do you think the lady was wrong, Colonel?"

"Fanny Wright was probably ahead of her time."

"I meant Mrs. Trollope."

He smiled. "Acerbic, perhaps, outspoken certainly, but not necessarily wrong. You must remember that for one of her upbringing, Ohio in the 1820s must have seemed a barbarous place, and western Tennessee even worse. She was a lady who was free with her barbs, but I found her book quite humorous. Not her intent, I suppose. She probably would have felt quite at home with the authoritative Mrs. Wickers."

Sister Serene made no comment, nor did she look up from her task.

"Ah, this concerns you, Sister," Guy went on. *"Ma belle-mère* is planning a benefit ball to raise money for a children's hospital for your order. My wife says it is to be the event of the season." He threw the letter aside, "Well, if that's the case, and her family exerts the sort of pressure that they well know how to on the illustrious Four Hundred, perhaps she'll realize enough for you to build your hospital."

"Perhaps," Sister Serene responded laconically.

"I thought that would make you happy, Sister," he pressed. It seemed to Livvy that her brother was determined to make their visitor look up; and when she did, he examined her solemn face so earnestly that she seemed embarrassed by the scrutiny and immediately took up the tangled yarn again.

"We are fortunate that they've chosen to adopt the order as a cause."

"God does not always provide, does He, Sister? Not, at least, without a little help."

"But He does, Colonel Parrish. It is only necessary to see the hands that do the work as instruments of His will."

He laughed suddenly. "I wonder how Templeton Caylew would feel at being called an instrument of God."

"Templeton Caylew?"

Livvy, perhaps fearing that the sharpness of Sister Serene's voice prefaced another acrimonious exchange, chose that moment to broach the topic that had been on her mind all evening, the topic she wished were under discussion rather than Eustacia's letter.

"I suppose you must know the family, Sister Serene," Livvy began.

"What makes you say so?" There was a sharp edge to the question that took Livvy off guard.

"Since Mrs. Caylew is the patroness of the order. But if you are unacquainted, I shall make it a point to introduce you when we are in New York."

Sister Serene had returned to her unraveling.

"I know something of the family. I hadn't realized until now that you were acquainted with them."

"Eustacia Caylew is my wife," Parrish stated.

"You're fortunate to have such a beautiful and charming lady for a wife," Sister Serene commented after an imperceptible pause.

"So I am often told," he agreed coldly; then, as though to change the subject, he turned to his sister. "But I thought you had forsworn New York, Livvy. You said you never wanted to go there again. I hadn't realized that you'd change your mind."

Livvy took a deep breath. "I am going to New York when Sister Serene returns—to join the Order of St. Catharine, Guy; and nothing you say will stop me."

There was silence, a long, stony silence, during which Guy Parrish stared alternately from his sister to Sister Serene, who had set aside the embroidery yarn and returned his gaze equally unflinchingly.

"Livvy, would you leave us? I'd like to talk to Sister Serene alone."

"But this concerns me, Guy. I should be here."

"What I have to say concerns Sister Serene. I'd rather say it to her in private." Livvy looked over at Sister Serene questioningly and only after she nodded did she rise and leave the room.

Guy Parrish waited until the door closed before turning accusingly with "This is your doing, isn't it?"

"No, it is not my doing," Sister Serene responded acerbically. "I talked to your sister at some length when she told me what she wanted to do. I told her in all honesty the difficulties of such a choice. By doing so, I thought to dissuade her should she have any romantic notions about the life we lead. It is often far from pleasant. She is most sincere, Colonel. I am thoroughly persuaded that she is not speaking lightly, that this is what she wants to do with her life."

"You're not going to try and tell me that God has called her as He undoubtedly called you, are you, Sister?" he rasped.

She shook her head. "God didn't call me, Colonel Parrish. Such a specific sort of calling, a hearing of voices like that accorded to St. Joan, is no requisite to becoming a nun."

"If no voices, what then was it that made you join?"

She hesitated. "It was a choice I made, just as your sister is making a choice."

"Did you make it, as my sister is now making it, because you were crossed in love?"

The question was as deliberate as it was unexpectd. "You speak of the young gentleman who married someone else—Lawrence, I think is his name."

"Lawrence Caylew, my wife's brother. So she told you of him."

"She did talk of a Lawrence. But I am quite certain that though there was a time when she liked him, she is no longer despondent over his having chosen to marry someone else."

"And you, Sister, did you remain despondent?"

"We're not here to discuss me, Colonel; but if it is of any importance, I did not join the order because I was crossed in love. I was never in love. But that does not necessarily mean that you're right in supposing, as Livvy has told me you do, that God gets only those women no man wants." She leveled her gaze with the directness of her words, making a flush rise in his cheeks. "We are all quite normal women, sir. Since a woman's life is usually one of service, we have chosen to serve God rather than some man; that is all. It does not mean that we are wanting in any way."

"You don't wish to talk about what led you to your decision, is that it?"

"Any discussion of why I joined the order is irrelevant. It is your sister's desire to join that is at issue."

"I shan't allow it." His response was terse. "I am her guardian."

"You are also her brother; she loves you dearly, and I am quite sure you love her in the same way, that you have only her good at heart. And if I am right in that, you won't oppose her now. To do so may alienate her from you forever. Livvy's no child, not anymore; she's a young woman and she has a right to make her own choices, just as you did."

"There is such a thing as family loyalty, Sister; that too is a choice. Sometimes it may lead us to do things we would rather not do. Family loyalty took me into the War between the States; it forced me to fight against friends and for a cause in which I did not wholly believe, but I could not bring myself to take up arms against my own father and brother. Those are choices too, Sister, that we have to make, between moral and personal convictions."

"I well know what you mean, Colonel." Her face had grown grave. "I understand that anguish, the grief it causes. Who can ever say what is truly right in such situations? We each have to make our own decisions. We can only go by what is in the heart. I know what it means; believe me, I know."

He shrugged impatiently. "If we're not here to discuss you, we're certainly not here to discuss me. I don't know why I spoke of it."

"There are times when it helps to speak of such things, when we can't remain silent any longer."

"I suppose, Sister, I can't blame you for pleading your cause, for proselyting—"

"I am not proselyting, Colonel. That was not my reason for coming."

"Then why did you come?"

She shook her head. "I'm not sure it's any use broaching the matter now."

"You might just as well. You don't seem a woman whose courage fails easily."

"Sometimes it does. But anyway. Do you remember the little boy I brought back with me the day you came to Memphis, when you were so angry because you felt I had allowed your sister to be endangered? His name is Arnaud. His mother brought him from New Orleans. She died in the most miserable circumstances imaginable; he watched her die." She saw Colonel Parrish's grip on the letter opener in his hands tighten. "He's without a home, Colonel. I wondered if you might take him in for a time at least. He has no one."

She saw the question in his eyes and went on: "He has no father, no legal father. There is little possibility that his natural father can be found. Even if it were possible, it would take time and effort; and there would be no guarantee that, once found, the father would take him in. Women seem to bear the responsibilities of such misfortunes."

Guy Parrish examined her face intently before asking with all deliberation, "You really want this, Sister?"

"Yes, I do. The little boy is very special to me. I've spent a lot of time with him. I can't bear to think of him in the orphanage, or given I don't know where."

He raised his eyebrows. "You'd prefer to leave him with a disbeliever?"

"You're a good man, Colonel Parrish. I know Livvy would never love you as she does if you weren't."

"Suppose," he said slowly, "that I were to take Arnaud. Would you be willing to persuade Livvy to give up this foolish notion?"

There was silence, a silence in which they studied one another assessingly, uneasily. Then Sister Serene shook her head. "I'm sorry; I can't promise to do that."

"I didn't think you would."

"Then why did you ask me to?"

"I suppose it was to find out the sort of person you really are. I suspect that, like me, you only allow part of yourself to be known. Because you could not choose something you want over something someone else wants makes me think myself wrong in believing you were here to proselyte. I apologize."

"There's no need, Colonel. I believe each of us loves Livvy and has her good at heart."

"And you're unwilling to tell her to give this up, that being a nun is an abnormal existence for a woman."

"I am not abnormal, Colonel Parrish," she replied quietly.

"Aren't you, Sister?"

His words were deliberate. He caught the steady gaze from her clear blue eyes, studying her perceptively, not allowing her to look away, as the air grew deep and still.

"All right, then, Sister," he said at last. "I'll go into Memphis tomorrow and bring Arnaud back to Bellechasse."

"And Livvy?"

"I still think she's running away, if not from Lawrence Caylew, then from someone she's not yet met. Just as I think you have hidden yourself away for some similar reason. But you're a persuasive woman, Sister Serene, and will give my consent to her going back with you if only to get the idea out of her system. But I want her taking no lifelong vows. Is that clearly understood?"

"I am professed, but I have taken no lifelong vows. We are not required to do so. Mother Charlotte says she wants no compulsion placed upon us, only our personal willingness."

"I am sure, were I to ask, I would learn no more about why you chose not to take those vows than I have about why you decided to become a nun in the first place, so I shan't. I do want you to promise to let me know how Livvy is faring, to tell me frankly, honestly. Will you promise me that?"

"I will."

"Then she may go, if that's what she wants. She may try your life, but she must be completely free to leave it. And I won't give my agreement to her profession unless I am completely certain in my own heart that she is completely happy."

"I should not for a moment wish Livvy to be there if she weren't happy, Colonel." Sister Serene rose. "I'll tell Livvy to come in and talk to you."

At the door, she turned back. "I wish, when I was growing up, I'd had a brother like you, Colonel Parrish."

He knew he did not return her wish. As the door closed, leaving behind her the delicate scent of the lavender that his mother had with great difficulty and diligent care managed to transplant to her garden—"I fear the climate is too harsh for it," she used to say—Guy wondered if the same were not true of Sister Serene. He had felt her sensitivity; she had touched on some deep and buried part of him on which he allowed no one to intrude. His reactions during their talk had changed from acute annoyance to begrudging admiration, and he was left with the discomforting knowledge that, while he no longer disliked her, his feelings were far from fraternal.

SIX

"Really, Sister Serene, I do wish you would come with me to the Caylews' at least once. Each time I go they ask me, 'Where is this famous Sister Serene of yours?' Each time you say, 'I'll come next time,' and then find some pressing reason that prevents you from doing so. I told you at Bellechasse that I wanted to introduce you to Eustacia's family, and here I've been at Mercy House for more than four months and I've yet to be able to do so. Even that lavish Christmas party they gave for the sisters, you were the only one to stay behind."

"Someone had to, and it was no sacrifice, because I hate large gatherings. From all I heard, it must have been splendid, though." Sister Serene glanced up from the heavy copy of Gibson's *Anatomy* she had been poring over and looked at her friend's disappointed face. "Dear, dear Sister Livvy. You know I must study. It won't be easy gaining admittance to Pennsylvania University's Medical School. They've yet to allow a woman into their hallowed halls; though, as a nun, I may have an advantage in that they—as your brother does—may consider me some sort of an aberration: certainly not a man, but also not a woman."

"I don't know that you're right about Guy," Lavinia replied thoughtfully. "He's not really opposed to women doing things on their own behalf. My mother, you know, had more freedom to pursue her own interests than most of her friends. She had her own place and time to herself to spend as she wished. It was the cause of some comment, as I remember it; but we grew up knowing her as a

woman, not simply our mother, and certainly not a reflection of Father.

"Guy has tried to do as much with Eustacia, but she
seems not to like that at all; she wants to be forever
following him around, interested only in whatever interests
him. I am sure he wishes she had her own pursuits when
she's at Bellechasse, as she has in New York, for when
she is at home she seems concerned with nothing but him.
Little Bella hardly commands any of her attention." She
paused before concluding, "Guy's objections to my coming here arose from religious grounds, you know, more
than anything else."

"Did he always feel so?" Sister Serene queried, setting
aside the book.

"No, I don't think so. He attended church with the
family, but of course that was mandatory. I don't believe
he took it seriously; but, then, Guy never used to take
anything seriously. I remember once his calling Father a
lip-serving Episcopalian, which earned him a thrashing.
He told me once that Father was a man to cover all
eventualities; that was why he prayed and why he fought
so successfully in the war."

"Your brother did also; he must have to have attained
that rank."

"I believe it was only after Mother was killed that he
really fought hard. He was in battle with Nicholas when he
fell. Father had relied a great deal on Nicholas; it was only
after he died that he turned to Guy. I believe he was
critical of him; he thought England had made him effete.
Nothing he did was ever as good as Nicholas would have
done it. Then Mother was killed—shot in her own home—
and that changed Guy. They said from the moment he
heard that it was as though he set out to out-Nicholas
Nicholas. My own opinion is that it wasn't till then that he
declared war on the North. Guy's never been one to do
things by half, not once he's made up his mind. Until then
he mulls things over; but once he's set on a course,
nothing's going to stop him. That's been obvious at
Bellechasse. You should have seen it the way it was when
he took it over." She paused. "I'm really troubled by his
loss of faith, though. I pray for him daily."

"So do I," Sister Serene declared softly. "Arnaud seems

to be getting along famously with him. Your brother sent me some drawings he'd done of the puppy he got for Christmas. From what he writes, he and your brother sound inseparable.''

''I believe they are, and that doesn't sit well with Eustacia.''

''Oh, dear!'' Sister Serene shook her head, and then took up the book she'd put aside.

Before she could immerse herself in it again, Lavinia intervened. ''Do please come with me, just this once, I implore you. I've told Mrs. Caylew about you, about the plans Mother Charlotte has for you to study as a physician. She couldn't imagine a woman would want to do that, but she really does want to meet you.''

''I too wish you would go, Sister Serene.''

Both Sisters turned at the hearty voice of Mother Charlotte, whose stalwart figure had paused at the open door to the library.

''I wish you would meet Mrs. Caylew,'' Mother Charlotte repeated. ''She told me that she would persuade her husband to write to a friend of his at the University Medical School. His support would help immeasurably in your being accepted. People do things to oblige friends that they would never do on grounds of merit alone, I'm sorry to say. I really think, Sister Serene, that it's time you went and pleaded the case yourself.''

''I really am trying to finish this section on the anatomy of the foot, Mother Charlotte. I must memorize everything, for Dr. Weldon says questions on the foot, a dissection even, are often required in gaining entrance. Though he has been kind in lending me his books and in explaining the parts that I simply can't understand on my own, the foot with its great number of bones is an area where I feel least sure of myself. Dr. Weldon promised to go over it with me; but if I haven't thoroughly studied the section, I'll never be able to ask pertinent questions. I must try to have it clear in my head. For instance, this part on—''

''Dear Sister Serene, spare me. It's you who's to study medicine, not I. I simply do what I can in a practical way in providing care for the children.''

''Better than any of the rest of us, Mother.''

''I doubt that, but practice rather than theory has always

been my forte. Don't embarrass me with your questions. But to go back to the matter at hand, I do think it time that you meet with Mrs. Caylew. You know full well how supportive she has been of the order. She's planning that lavish event to raise funds for the hospital; we've a lot to be grateful to her for. Talk to her about our work, about what you could accomplish as a trained physician. Help her to understand.''

"Of course, Mother Charlotte, if that is your wish." Sister Serene closed her book, her face expressionless.

"Now, Sister Serene," Mother Charlotte reproved, "I don't want you to go simply from a sense of cadaver obedience.''

"No, Mother, no. I go willingly."

"Very well, then. And how are you getting along, Sister Lavinia?"

Though Livvy had settled down well to life at Mercy House under Sister Serene's guidance, she still felt a pang of trepidation whenever the Mother Superior addressed her directly, perhaps because of the cadaver obedience—the blind obedience—that had made Sister Serene put aside her book. It wasn't that she had been one to strive to have her own way, like Sister Edwina, who had come into the order soon after her and had great difficulty in adjusting because she questioned everything in the Rule.

Perhaps Livvy had settled well because Sister Serene was her novice mistress and she explained everything so carefully, so patiently, not only the requirements but the reasons for them, and all with such good humor. If Livvy made a mistake in reciting commemorations, Sister Serene would correct her, but take away any sting of rebuke by reminding her of the Buddhist definition of a novice—a creature who breaks crockery, spills oil, and giggles.

And if grave Sister Louise glared at them for giggling together, Mother Charlotte would say, "Why shouldn't they laugh, Sister Louise? After all, aren't we all on our way to heaven?"

Still, cadaver obedience did not come easily to Livvy, even though she knew it was necessary. But she had to admit it had its uses if that was the reason that Sister Serene consented at last to come with her that blustery March afternoon to visit the Caylews.

Mrs. Caylew was at tea in the conservatory when they
arrived. Though Livvy believed her well-meaning, she
never found her easy to converse with and much preferred
it when the younger children were present. She was, however, quite alone that afternoon. Her look of habitual
boredom momentarily vanished at the sight of visitors who
promised to relieve her of the onerous task of having to
entertain herself.

"Ah, so this is the Sister Serene of whom I've heard so
much from Mother Charlotte, as well as from you, Lavinia.
I understand you are quite brilliant. Sit down and tell me
all about yourself."

Sister Serene, who had taken a chair in the corner near
the door quite remote from her hostess, acknowledged the
greeting only with a nod of her flaring starched headpiece,
but that seemed not to perturb Mrs. Caylew, who went on
without pause. "I know that when I was young my mother
insisted that I had the brains with which my brother should
have been endowed.

"I was a Vandervoort before my marriage, you know,
an old New York name. You must have heard of the
family; my great-great-grandfather Vandervoort bought Man-
hattan land from the Indians; that's how far we go back.
Anyway, my mother always said I was the one with the
brains, but of course ladies had no use for brains. She
would occasionally mourn the fact that my brother seemed,
well, not dull—I won't say Harry was dull, but he's never
been what you would call brilliant. Luckily for him, he
inherited, so he didn't need brains. My husband, however,
thinks it essential in a man—not a woman."

She looked pointedly in Sister Serene's direction for a
brief moment. "Mr. Caylew is quite brilliant; he's often
referred to as the Wizard of Wall Street, but I've no doubt
you've heard of that also. Being a financier is not to be
confused for a moment with being in trade. All of our
children, in their own ways, are gifted, Sister Serene; but I
suppose that is only as it should be. We have six. I
suppose I shouldn't refer to them as children, for they are
all quite grown, even the baby.

"Nanny Wickers was reminding me that Sunday is Eleanor's twelfth birthday. Twelve—I could hardly credit

that my youngest is twelve. And here I am, a grandmother already once, and soon to be twice.''

She turned to Lavinia to announce in confidential tones, ''Drusilla is in the family way. I told her I thought that she should take on Nanny Wickers. I wanted Eustacia to have her for Bella, but Nanny was adamant against leaving New York. That surprised me, for originally she hadn't a good word for it.'' Mrs. Caylew hadn't stopped talking since their arrival. She served them tea, and all that was required of her visitors was an occasional nod to indicate that they were listening.

But she paused at last to sip from her own cup, and then turned to demand of Lavinia, ''Now tell me everything you have been doing, Lavinia, and how are you liking this life of yours? Eustacia writes that your brother is still not at all happy with it. I can't say I blame him. I know that it's a fine thing; I wouldn't support the sisters' work as I do if I didn't believe that. I do think it preferable to lend one's name to a charity that helps the poor, rather than something like Mrs. Vandervoort's orchestral society. I know it means she can give parties before performances, but I can guarantee you that nothing is going to surpass the charity event I have planned to raise money for the hospital.''

''I hope you've told Eustacia that I'm happy. I keep writing as much to Guy, but he might better believe it hearing it from another source. I gave him my promise before I came that I wouldn't make profession without his consent.''

''Your brother, Lavinia,'' Mrs. Caylew intoned sententiously, ''must be the most persuasive gentleman that ever was. I never believed there was a man on this earth over whom Eustacia couldn't gain ultimate ascendancy. I said as much to Templeton when they married. Eustacia would have him, you know, even though my husband was not in favor of the match. 'It won't last, Templeton,' I said when he told me it was arranged. 'I give it a year, no more. She'll hate it down there on the edge of nowhere.'

''Well, I still don't believe she cares for it at all. She's glad to come back to civilization each and every year, and each and every year I think she's going to stay on; but she always has to get back to her dear Harwood. I declare she's as infatuated with him today as on the day she

married him. Of course, it's no secret that her ultimate
wish is that he will come North. Templeton has said he
would not be at all opposed to taking Harwood in with
him. My husband respects your brother's ability, Lavinia.
He has a good, clear head, Templeton says."

"Guy would never move North," Lavinia declared firmly.

"Well, we shall see. When Eustacia sets her mind on
something, it rarely eludes her for long."

"Guy is every bit as determined, Mrs. Caylew."

"I daresay that's why Eustacia finds him irresistible.
Well, how are you enjoying living up here, Lavinia?"

"I'm very satisfied. Do let Eustacia know that when
you write."

"I know Eustacia feels much as I do; it's a woman's
duty to marry and—however onerous it may be—to produce children. Poor dear, she did have such a time with
little Bella. I'm relieved that she can have no more. She
did her duty; she did what was required of her, just as a
woman should. Where would the world be if women chose
to escape their responsibilities as you and Sister Serene
did?

"I make no secret of my reservation about your order on
that score. I've spoken of it to Mother Charlotte; it was
one of the reasons that I held grave doubts about our
Episcopalian ladies taking the veil. There's not only the
smack of popishness about it, but also I felt it a form of
cowardice—women seeking to absolve themselves of the
God-given if rather disgusting requirement of bearing
children.

"Still, as Mother Charlotte pointed out to me, if the
sisters were to marry they couldn't give their undivided
attention to the order; and knowing the restrictions family
life places on a woman, I have to agree." Mrs. Caylew
sighed heavily. "I think it good for maiden ladies whose
prime years are behind them, those who have been passed
over for marriage. But I'm really not in favor of it for
young ladies like yourself, Lavinia. It is one point on
which I am in agreement with Harwood. How old are you,
Sister Serene?"

"Twenty-four."

"Well, you're getting to that point where it would be
unlikely that you would marry, but Lavinia's only eighteen."

"I'm nineteen," Livvy corrected.

"Well, nineteen, then. You still have several years to go before you can be considered an old maid. And you're nice enough to look at. I've always thought it was only the plainest women who spoke out on suffrage issues or women's education."

She glanced over toward the corner where Sister Serene had seated herself, as though in confirmation of this fact, when her attention was diverted by the arrival of her husband.

"There you are, Templeton. I'm glad you stopped in, for Lavinia has brought Sister Serene with her. She is the one on whose behalf Mother Charlotte would like you to write to Dr. McChord at the Pennsylvania Medical School. You remember, dear; I've spoken to you of it any number of times. Mother Charlotte wishes her to train as a physician."

"Well, Isabel, you know my views on that. I certainly wouldn't want—" Templeton Caylew, crossing the room to the corner where Sister Serene sat, stopped suddenly and turned back to greet Lavinia, who found him oddly discomposed.

Mrs. Caylew had poured him tea, and he took the cup she offered him but went to the other side of the room, taking up the newspaper from the chair.

"Don't read now, Templeton, not while visitors are here," his wife commanded. "Well, dear, are you willing to write to Dr. McChord?"

"I don't know." His irritation was obvious. "I suppose so."

"Perhaps you will furnish my husband with pertinent details of your background, Sister Serene. Why don't you take her into the library, Templeton, and find out whatever you need to put in your letter; you might as well while she is here. I've asked Lavinia on several occasions to bring her, but it appears she's a busy young woman who can't always favor us with her presence."

"That won't be necessary," Templeton Caylew and Sister Serene replied almost in unison, and then stopped.

"I can write down whatever information is necessary and give it to Mother Charlotte to pass along to Mr. Caylew," Sister Serene finished quickly.

"My goodness, I'm sure you've nothing to fear from my husband, Sister," Mrs. Caylew noted with some acerbity.

"I'm quite sure I've not," Sister Serene responded.

"She's right, though, Isabel. That will do perfectly," Caylew agreed.

"Very well." Mrs. Caylew clearly disliked any changes in ideas she put forward; and Lavinia wondered why Sister Serene, who made a practice of obedience in every matter and had come that afternoon for the express purpose of strengthening the Caylews' advocacy of her medical training, had demurred.

It was, Lavinia found, her least successful visit to the Caylews, when she had so hoped it would go well. She wanted the Caylews to support her in her vocation; it would help to win Guy over to her side. She had hoped Sister Serene would put any doubts they might have to rest, but she'd hardly said a word; and since the arrival of Mr. Caylew the atmosphere had become even more strained. After a short exchange with Sister Serene about the hospital, he sat apart, and Sister Serene said nothing at all. Lavinia had never seen her look as solemn as she did that afternoon, her face almost as forbidding as Mother Charlotte's was on occasion.

"I should like to wish Eleanor a happy birthday before we go," she said at last, as a means of signaling their departure.

"I am quite sure Eleanor will be delighted that you thought of her, Lavinia," Mrs. Caylew approved as she rang for her youngest daughter to be brought down. "Lawrence and Drusilla are back from Paris, you know." She lowered her voice. "As I indicated earlier, she is in the family way, and of course we are hoping for our second grandchild to be a boy, aren't we, Templeton?"

Her husband, his face buried in the *Daily Tribune*, did not appear to hear her, and when she repeated her remark, he only grunted noncommittally, causing his wife to remark, "You really are less than pleasing today, Templeton."

But since he made no response, she turned back to her visitors. "We were delighted, of course, with the arrival of little Bella, particularly Templeton, who found her just like his Lucy at that age, though I see more of Harwood in her. Of course, I dote upon children; still, feeling in my prime, it is hard for me to think myself old enough to be a grandmother. I daresay Harwood would have preferred a boy, especially since Bella is likely to be their only child. That may be why he has taken so to that orphan. I understand it was at your instigation, Sister, that he took the boy in.''

The look fixed upon Sister Serene was less than agreeable, but she replied quite calmly, "Yes, I did ask Colonel Parrish to take Arnaud. I was pleased that he agreed to do so.''

"Well, my daughter is none too happy about it. I think she should have been consulted first.''

"I'm sorry. I would have done that, but Mrs. Parrish wasn't at Bellechasse at the time.''

"Guy loves little Bella to distraction, Mrs. Caylew,'' Livvy put in. "He just wanted to help the little boy. He'd been left quite alone, you see.''

"Well, he certainly wasn't Harwood's responsibility,'' Mrs. Caylew rebuked as her youngest daughter came into the room. "Ah, there you are, Eleanor. Lavinia wanted to wish you a happy birthday. Say hello prettily to her, and to her friend Sister Serene.''

"I would have brought you a little present had I known, Eleanor.'' Lavinia kissed the cheek of the darkhaired girl, immaculately attired in a short crinoline that showed the edge of her matching lace petticoat and set off her soft kidskin side-buttoned boots. "How smart you are, and how grown. Why, you're almost as tall as I am. Twelve is getting to be a very responsible age, isn't it, Sister Serene?''

She looked across at Sister Serene for agreement, but Sister Serene's attention was caught by the angular lady who had accompanied Eleanor into the room and whose eyes were fixed with even greater scrutiny on Sister Serene in a look of shocked recognition.

"This is Mrs. Wickers, Sister, Nanny Wickers, of whom I've spoken,'' Lavinia put in, since Mrs. Caylew made no attempt at introduction.

Sister Serene nodded, rising in some agitation from her chair. "Yes, yes, I know.''

Livvy, on seeing her friend get up, also rose to begin her leave-taking.

That was interrupted by an anguished cry from the lips of the tall English nanny: "Mary!" And then again, "Oh, Mary! I never thought to see you again."

BOOK FOUR

Sister Serene

Whenever it is proper to introduce women
as patients, there also it is in accordance
with the instinct of truest womanhood
for women to appear as physicians and
students.

Dr. Ann Preston
U.S. physician and
educator
1813–1872

ONE

More than five years had passed since she had thought of herself as anything except Sister Serene, five years in which she had become a woman so completely changed, so utterly disjoined from everything she had previously been that, while she might have experienced a qualm of trepidation at the sight of the Caylews' grandiose and oppressive Park Avenue mansion, having once crossed its threshold, she was not unduly disturbed by either her first meeting with Mrs. Caylew, who so obviously did not recognize her, or her subsequent encounter with Templeton Caylew, who equally obviously did. Only Angela Wickers's cry of that name the Caylews had given her—Mary—had served fully to bring back the past.

Even then it was Lavinia's astonished glance that held her attention as Mrs. Caylew broke in with a start of recognition. "Mary? Why I do believe you're right, Wickers; it is Mary—Mary who used to help out in the nursery. My goodness, I'd never have known it, would you, Templeton?" There was a certain note of reserve, even disdain, in the words.

Templeton Caylew responded with a weak smile. "No, no, my dear, I most certainly would not. Well, I never. Well, well, this is a surprise."

Yet whatever surprise he felt was reserved for the words alone, not for the tone of his voice or for the sheepish expression that crossed his face as he spoke them. To those, however, his wife paid no heed. Turning to Sister Serene, she demanded, "But why did you not say something immediately?"

Why hadn't she indeed? The question was far from

spurious; it was one she had often put to herself. Why
hadn't she spoken, not necessarily to the Caylews, to
whom she believed she owed nothing, not even the courtesy of recognition, but to Lavinia, to Mother Charlotte,
both of whom had pressed her into coming, both of whom
deserved from her nothing but her absolute integrity? Was
it because she wished to forget the past? Or did she seek to
hide from it behind her habit?

For a time, perhaps, that had been so, though she had
always known it was impossible to escape entirely from
the misty and bottomless pit of the past. Eventually it must
force itself upon her, as it had that afternoon in the Caylews'
conservatory.

In the order it was Mother Charlotte who knew most of
her past, though even she did not know everything. And it
was that fact that made the situation increasingly difficult,
particularly after Mrs. Caylew had adopted the order as her
own special charity, becoming its principal benefactor.

Then Mother Charlotte had grown increasingly insistent
that she make her presence in the order known. "Sister
Serene, you must meet her; at some point your paths are
bound to cross. If God has forgiven you the past, as I
know full well He has, if the order does not censure the
fact that you fell, then why should the Caylews not show
equal Christian charity?"

Knowing full well why they—or at least one of them—
might not, Sister Serene could only shake her head. "Not
yet, dear Mother; not yet, I beg you."

A direct order from her superior she could not have
refused, but Mother Charlotte had not become Mother
Superior only because she had been instrumental in founding the order; she was a woman who knew when to impose
her will, which was but the will of God, after all, and
when to bide her time. Sister Serene had been thankful that
she had, until that day, chosen the latter course.

Though Mother Charlotte might know the circumstances
in which she had left the Caylews' house—had she not
been the one to rescue her from surroundings that resembled nothing more than a living Hades?—yet Sister Serene
had never divulged the identity of the man who had placed
her in the predicament that had led her there. Initially she
felt it was of no importance; it was in the past, and Mother

Charlotte had not pressed the matter. She would let it die. Later, as the Caylews came to be the order's greatest supporters, Sister Serene knew she could never speak of it without placing Mother Charlotte in a quandary.

Besides, Sister Serene had cause to realize that the hand of God moved in strange ways. Mrs. Caylew had personally organized the Friends of the Sisters of St. Catharine to lead the drive to construct and equip a hospital for children, so long the order's goal as well as Mother Charlotte's personal dream. Whatever Mrs. Caylew's motives, social or charitable, she had made the construction of St. Catharine's Hospital for Children a personal challenge; to jeopardize her help in any way was unthinkable. Sister Serene would never disclose Templeton Caylew's role in her past: She never wanted to; his very name was odious to her, and she much preferred never to mention it again in any context.

Yet she knew her past would find her someday, and so it had in the ponderous, dominating form of the man who crossed the room to greet the nun whom he had been asked to assist in gaining admission to the country's finest medical school. She watched the beneficent but condescending smile fade from his features as—unlike his wife, who had spared her only the most cursory glance—he looked directly into her face. She raised her chin just a trifle as their eyes met, enough to prevent any suspicion that she feared discovery; and as she did, the smile faded from his lips to be replaced by a frown of confused recognition. Would he speak? she wondered. But she might have guessed he would not.

Her black serge robes armored her like the shell protecting a tortoise from predators. She stood forever beyond his grasp. Even Templeton Caylew would not dare to transgress that inviolate shroud. He infringed only upon the rights of those so small, so insignificant, that they could never endanger his position in this world or the salvation of his soul in the next.

They regarded one another squarely. True, she still felt repugnance at the sight of his heavy lips, his jutting chin, his pale but determined features; yet knowing herself encased in the outward sign of inward grace, knowing he would never dare inflict himself on her, he no longer resembled that ogre who had panted with lust over her innocent body, but only a man so wanting in decency that he was unable to keep a rein on his desires whatever the cost to his victims.

"Mary" she might have been, but "Mary" she was no more; and she made that decisively clear by refusing to acknowledge that past existence, speaking factually, succinctly, of funding for the hospital, the necessity of staffing it with qualified people, and the benefit of having one of the order trained as a physician, to be on call whenever required.

"You refer to yourself, Sister . . . Sister . . .?"

"Sister Serene," she furnished, wondering whether he had forgotten the name by design.

"Of course, Sister Serene." Templeton Caylew, who appeared equally anxious to overlook the past, repeated it with care, as though to remember it in the future.

"My candidacy has been suggested. Where the training should take place remains undecided. Pennsylvania Medical School, the most prestigious in the country, has yet to admit a woman."

"I've no time for women meddling in men's affairs, studying unsavory material. But a nun can hardly be counted as a woman."

"Let us hope that the medical school authorities may be as enlightened as yourself in making that distinction," Sister Serene responded blandly. The hand of God did, indeed, move in strange ways; she began to suspect that Caylew would bring his influence to bear to have her admitted, if only to remove her presence from New York, for a time at least.

"Dr. Elizabeth Blackwell, with whom Mother Charlotte has corresponded on the subject, was unable to gain admittance some few years ago, but she seems to feel that the climate is changing and that their refusal may not now be absolute."

"I can promise nothing, but something may be arranged." Stroking his whiskers, he had returned to his chair to bury himself in his newspaper. The visit would pass without incident; Sister Serene breathed a sigh of relief. But the entrance of Mrs. Wickers changed that; her cry of recognition caused Mrs. Caylew to scrutinize Sister Serene's face and recognize in the nun her former nursemaid.

Apart from her surprise that Sister Serene hadn't announced her identity immediately, it was soon obvious the discovery did not altogether please Mrs. Caylew. The order she supported was, she had always believed, composed solely of gentlewomen, in reduced circumstances perhaps, but gentlewomen nevertheless. Could a nursemaid, albeit a clergyman's daughter, be counted as such? Could she be received as a guest in her house? Mrs. Caylew's dilemma showed clearly on her face.

"I remember how you cared for Nathan when he sprained his ankle that Christmas," Mrs. Caylew conceded, as though seeking some mitigating circumstance. "You were most useful."

"I'm glad you found me so." Sister Serene nodded and insisted they must leave. The scene had played its course. She cast a momentary glance at her companion, the only one whose opinion she really cared about, seeing the unanswered questions still in her eyes. They were to be avoided no longer. "We should be going. We have a long journey before us and the cars are quite infrequent."

She was glad that Lavinia joined her in refusing the offer of Templeton Caylew's carriage. The walk to the horsecar and the ride in a public conveyance would clear her head and leave less opportunity for intimate conversation.

Nevertheless, as they hurried along in the brisk late afternoon, pulling their heavy cloaks around them to seal off the March winds, she knew she must speak.

"I suppose I should have told you before that I once worked for the Caylews," she began.

Lavinia's reply was stiff. "It was your prerogative not to mention it."

"True, but it must have seemed odd that I did not. The fact is, I said nothing because . . . because it brought back memories, painful memories, memories I would rather forget. I was young then, very young when I went with them, and—" There was a crack in her voice, and she broke off.

"You need say nothing," Lavinia put in quickly; but

despite the disclaimer, Sister Serene noted the hurt in her voice.

"No, I should have spoken of it. It was wrong not to have done so. You see, my mother and I were left without means of support. My father, an Episcopal clergyman, served as chaplain with the Union army and was killed in battle. We were left virtually penniless. I applied to Mr. Caylew for a position." She paused imperceptibly this time. "He was kind enough to find one for me assisting in the nursery."

"He is really kind, kind and thoughtful; at least he has always been most kind to me, most gentlemanly, though sometimes I believe Guy thinks otherwise."

"He has said so?" Sister Serene spoke quickly. Was it possible that men understood one another in a way women did not?

"No, no. I daresay it is simply that he confronts Mr. Caylew more often in the world of commerce, a world where they both excel, each in quite a different way. Father was a planter; Guy's not only a planter but he understands cotton as a commodity in a way Father never did. It has stood him in good stead through difficulties that Father never had to face. That is probably why he sees Eustacia's father in a different way. Kindness and commerce may not go hand in hand."

"Probably not."

They stood on Eighth Avenue waiting for the horsecar, two dark cloaked figures standing close together to ward off the gusting wind. A young girl vending hot chestnuts rounded the corner, closely followed by a stout gentleman who, at the sight of the sisters, touched his rakishly tilted tall hat and turned his head away as he hurried past the girl, who had slowed her steps to stop beside them. "Thanks, sisters," she murmured.

"For what?" Lavinia asked in puzzlement.

"The dandy, he wouldn't leave me alone. Pretending to give me money for charity, but I know what he wants. Police don't do nothing about it, neither. They say if we hawks wares on the streets we're fair game for that sort of thing; but I don't open my legs for money, not for his sort at least. I don't have to, not like some."

Livvy flushed at such frankness, but Sister Serene af-

firmed forcefully, "You most certainly do not. Come to
Mercy House, to me, or to any of us there whenever
you're afraid or in need or in any sort of peril. Do come,
please do. We're there to help you. And tell the same to
other young women you know who find themselves in
similar straits."

"Pity." The young girl shrugged. "But I'm not no
Catholic."

"Nor are we."

"But I thought you was nuns!" Her cry was triumphant.
"You're dressed up just like you was. What are you up to
then—panhandling?"

"But we are nuns—Sisters of St. Catharine. It's an
Episcopal order."

"Everyone knows only Catholics is sisters, real sisters,
that is. You're just pretending to be nuns. You're no better
than that old gent just now, stuffing a hand in my bosom,
saying it was for charity, and getting a good feel while he
was about it." She reached into her dress and stared down
at the bill in her hand. "Still, a dollar and all, it was worth
it."

With that, she picked up her basket, slung it over her
arm, and stalked off down the avenue, swinging her hips
and singing out, "Chestnuts, hot chestnuts!"

Lavinia shuddered. "How awful to allow something like
that—just for money."

Sister Serene, her eyes searching the mass of horse-
drawn vehicles on Eighth Avenue, appeared not to have
heard. "There, I think that's our car coming now" was all
she said.

TWO

"How awful to allow something like that—just for money!"

Livvy's words kept echoing in her head. How awful! How awful indeed.

She had in her heart always blamed Templeton Caylew for what had happened, yet Livvy's words gave her cause to remember his assertion that he had forced her to do nothing. She had not wanted it to happen, but she had allowed it. And if she had not herself profited from that disgusting act, if she had almost died from its consequences, there was no denying that she had allowed it so as to benefit one close to her. Altruistic, some might say, though she had since realized that however justifiable the reason for committing a wrong seemed, it could never make that wrong right. She had put loyalty to her mother above what she knew to be morally right, and she had had to suffer the consequences.

She had tried so hard to put it from her mind. She would not allow herself to think of it. Even the sight of the tormentor whom she still detested and for whom no amount of Christian charity could make her feel compassion, even that had not inflicted the mortification of Livvy's words: "How awful to allow something like that—just for money!"

Livvy was right, Sister Serene had thought as she watched the retreating figure of the young chestnut seller, seeing in her slight form Damaris Fanshawe as she had been when she had left the haven of Park Avenue to venture into New York.

She had never known the city until then. Oh, she had known her way to Mercy House, of course, but she did not go there. She could never allow Mother Charlotte and the sisters she so admired to know of her degradation, her shame.

Not for one moment did it occur to her to return to Rhode Island, to her mother, where the fifty dollars in her possession might have bought ample food and shelter. Her mother treasured respectability above life itself. To have a wayward, pregnant daughter turn up on her doorstep would mortify her reputation beyond redemption. No welcome for a wanton child was to be expected there, only distraught fear and frantic desperation to keep the truth from becoming known—an impossibility given the size of Newport. If her shame haunted Damaris in New York, where she was unknown, how much greater would that guilt be in her mother's house, Caylew's house, the house that had been the cause of her downfall? No succor could be found there. She could never go back; she would take her chances in the tumult of the great city which gave her its greatest gift—anonymity.

So she stayed, finding lodging at a boardinghouse just off lower Broadway. For the first time in her life she had lied, saying she had just arrived from the country looking for work. At the beginning her landlady had been courteous, the food had been plain but good, the room minuscule but reasonably clean. After breakfast each day she had walked and walked, exploring a different section of the city, even venturing as far as Brooklyn and Staten Island. It was a holiday, a holiday such as she had never had; yet as soon as she relaxed to enjoy the river or take in the commotion of the marketplace, a prompting deep inside would remind her that this could not last. Nor did it.

After initial sympathetic inquiries about her inability to find employment, the landlady had offered suggestions, even seeking the help of other boarders.

"I can see you've had some work with the books." She nodded her head approvingly, making her heavy jowls quiver. "You're quiet and well-spoken. No reason why you won't do very well in a shipping office like Mr. Switzer's. Can't you recommend her there, Mr. Switzer?"

Damaris knew the landlady meant well. She loved to organize the lives of others, but she did want to help. How Damaris wished just to be left alone, though, especially when she was pressed to move while the iron was hot after Mr. Switzer assured her his employer would be glad to talk to a steady, respectable person, just as long as her references were impeccable.

If only they weren't so helpful. Their attempts to mitigate her circumstances only made them worse. She could not go and see Mr. Switzer's employer. Even if she were able to overcome the lack of references and receive an offer of employment, she could only keep it for a month or two, by which time her condition would become obvious.

At some time it must be known. She lived in daily dread of that time, especially as her girth increased and she had to keep letting out the seams of her dress. Someone would notice. The landlady had eagle eyes. Outside she could bundle herself up in a cape against the midwinter cold, but inside she was constantly teased for doing the same.

And then one morning as she was hurrying along the narrow hall from the water closet, she had bumped into the landlady and the loose robe she wore had parted, clearly revealing the telltale bulge.

"So that's it!" her landlady had triumphed. "I might have known. Looking for work indeed. You've had the work done on you long since, and no mistake. And I thought you a decent girl. I'm not often mistaken, but you had me fooled with your quiet air. My husband always used to say, 'Beware of a silent dog and still water.' Well, I run a respectable house, *miss*. You'll be off, and off today. I won't keep none of your sort around."

Arguing had been to no avail; worse yet, the landlady had refused to refund the balance of the month's room and board. Damaris had left, not knowing where to go. Hotels were far too expensive, so there had followed a series of sleazy rooms that had increased in sleaziness as the fifty dollars Caylew had given her had dwindled. She could at any time have turned to the nearby Magdalen Shelter run by the Sisters of St. Catharine. She knew they would have helped her; but though she had gone as far as to walk past the shelter, her pride would not allow her to enter its doors.

She saved, pinned in her bodice, ten dollars for the midwife when her time came. After that, she reasoned, she would lie, do anything to find work to support her child and herself.

As her time approached and with her money almost gone, she had drifted from the part of the city in which some sense of decency prevailed to the notorious Five Points district, where the dregs who could drift no further congregated. There was no longer a question of a room to herself; she had to be content with a corner to roll out her mat, making sure to cover her face and hands at night to protect herself from the rats that roamed at will. Sanitary inspectors came but rarely; and when they did, they hurried through as though the devil were at their heels, a cloth held to the face to guard against the stench-filled air.

One night, close to her term and also close to starvation, but still refusing to touch the money in her bodice, she had for the first time accepted an offer of charity—bread and weak tea from a new arrival. The next morning she awoke after an unusually long, deep sleep to find both the donor of the tea and the money for the midwife torn from her bodice, gone.

For the first time she had given in, allowing herself to wallow in her misery. Her courage deserted her, and she cried bitter tears. She had dragged herself up and gone out on the streets, walking unwillingly toward the Magdalen Shelter, hating to do so; but there was nothing else she could think to do. Her child must not die. Then on the path before her—she'd almost bumped into her, she was crying so hard—stood a young prostitute, a girl she'd seen many times who always smiled and waved, a friendly girl, still fresh and comely, and for that reason obviously new to her trade.

"Well, well, well, what have we here? Down on your luck, are you, dearie?"

Damaris nodded, wiping her face with the back of her hand. These were the only kind words she'd heard in weeks. She found herself pouring out her plight.

"What're you going to do then?"

"I'm going to the Magdalen Shelter. I don't know anywhere else to go. I'm sure they'll help me."

"Oh, they'll help, all right. And fill you with religion and likely take your baby away when it comes."

"They wouldn't!"

"Wouldn't they just? Did just that with a friend of mine. Called her an unfit mother, said the babe was better off without her."

"I don't believe they would." Still, Damaris's voice had grown dubious. "Anyway, I've no money; there's nothing else I can do."

The girl had scrutinized her. "How old are you?"

"Seventeen."

"This your first time, I'd guess."

Damaris nodded.

"Look, tell you what I'll do. I feel sorry for you, see. I'm only a year older than you, but I know a sight more about life than you do, and that's a fact. Enough not to get in the fix you are, I can tell you. I'll let the boys play, but there are precautions I demand. I can, you see, 'cause they know they won't get nothing else. Too bad you didn't meet up with me earlier. Still"—her face brightened with enthusiasm—"I'll take you in, and I'll see you through this fix. Don't you worry."

"But how would I ever repay you?"

"I don't know. We'll think of something when the time comes."

"Oh, you're an angel, a real angel!" Damaris smiled at this unexpected new friend.

"Angel I'm not. Let's get that straight for starters. And for next, what's your name?"

"Thank you, thank you so much. My name's Damaris Fanshawe."

"Mine's Katharine Duvere. That's my business name; real name's Katie Framp, and that don't sound too good. Come on, I'll take care of you. Only thing is you'll have to leave the room when I need it, but we'll work things out together."

"It's great to find a friend."

"Friends are partners. Let's look forward to a long partnership."

Perhaps because she was still young, perhaps because, as she often told Damaris, she believed in giving her clients (with great dignity she so called the motley crew that visited her) full value for money received, Katie's business was brisk. At any hour of the day or night Damaris would be forced to quit the room while Katie plied her trade. At these times, Damaris would walk and walk until she felt sure the man would be gone, but as her time grew close, she simply waited outside, watching for him to leave.

"After you get rid of that bulge, you'll be able to make a bundle too," Katie said one night as she sat on the bed counting her money. "We'll be partners. We'll make a good team the two of us. Young, fresh, nice-looking— that's the way they like them. And we won't have to go into no house, nor get ourselves no pimp to collect our earnings and keep them for hisself neither. We'll keep the old bed rocking and the cash flowing in. You'll see, Dam." She sat back, her arms clasped around her bent knees. "One day I'm going to run a house myself; that's my ambition. It's going to be real nice. It'll have a fancy name like Buckingham Palace, and I'll run the whole show and only work when I feel like it. Maybe I'll meet me some fellow I like. Who knows?"

"Katie, Katie, stop, I didn't know—"

"Don't worry, it won't be a while yet."

"I don't mean that. I mean . . . what I mean is I didn't know you were counting on me, that you thought I would join you. . . . I couldn't. I just couldn't!" Damaris's voice rose in heated denial.

"You couldn't what?" Unperturbed by the outburst, Katie finished counting her money before folding it into a small wad to hide in a place known only to herself.

"I couldn't do it—what you want me to do afterwards."

"What do you mean, you couldn't do it, Dam?" Far from being annoyed, Katie laughed out loud. "You already done it, ain't you? Don't go putting on airs with me. You said you was going to repay me; you can't go back on your word."

"I know I did, and I will. But I never meant doing it like that."

"What was you planning on, robbing a bank?"

"No, but after, I thought I'd get a job of some kind."

"Course! It'll be a piece of cake getting a job, tugging the young'un along, and no man in the picture. What sort of job d'you think you'd be offered? Same as I'm offering you, that's what, and not on such damned fine conditions, I'll be bound. I don't doubt you were a decent one who took the wrong path. Could say the same for meself. Only thing after that happens is to make the best of it.''

"But I can't, Katie. I can't and I won't. I mean that."

"But I said we'd be partners and you agreed."

"I didn't think you meant like that."

"How did you think I meant it, then? Think we were going partners in stock brokering?'' Katie sprang up from the bed, straightening the bedclothes in quick movements. "Your type makes me sick. Come and take a person's hospitality and help and won't offer to do nothing in return.''

"I'll do something, Katie, but not that. Look, you're a fine person, the only one who's shown me any kindness. I'll never forget you, and I will repay you; I promise I will. Don't get mad at me, not now, please." Damaris jumped up in great agitation and almost as swiftly sat down again. "Oh, Katie, Katie, something's happening! I think it's coming. The baby's coming.''

"Don't panic, Dam. Sit there. It's just the waters, the bag the baby's in; it broke, that's all. It'll be hours yet, a first one doesn't come like that. Look, don't get all excited. I'm not one to hold hard feelings. After it's all over, I'll show you what to do so it don't keep happening to you. It ruins business.''

And as her labor pains mounted one on the other, Damaris had no strength to argue with Katie about the future. All she worried about was getting her child into the world.

"Get the midwife, Katie, please," she groaned.

"Not time yet, Dam. I've got a medical student I know who'll come and help you through it, in return for certain favors; but he's warned me not to fetch him until the last minute. He don't have no time to waste.''

"Katie, please, are you sure it's going to be all right?"

"Don't moan, Dam. Tying up my place this way is costing me a fortune; I hope you realize that.'' Katie got up and put on her cloak.

"Don't leave me, please."

"Nothing's going to happen for a while. I'll bring Johnny Medic back with me when I come. He'll take care of everything. Meantime, maybe I can turn a trick or two someplace else.''

Katie was gone, not to return for what seemed like an eternity, by which time the pains had increased beyond anything Damaris had ever endured before. Then they had receded, just as Damaris's strength and endurance had receded. She was scared, scared that the baby was dead. She was tired, too tired even to cry, though she did manage a sob of relief as the door opened and Katie came in with a young man.

"Oh, Katie, I thought you'd never come back."

"I said I would. I'm as good as my word. This is the Johnny Medic I told you about." Katie walked over to draw back the covers, and the two of them viewed her dispassionately. "He'll take care of it, but you gotta push, Dam, to get it out. My room's no labor ward. Go on, you gotta push, and you gotta push hard."

"Just tell me, is the baby alive?" Damaris's voice was so weak she had to repeat the question twice before the student understood what she was saying.

"Think so. Hard to tell, the position it's in," he answered laconically, listening through his stethoscope for a heartbeat. Then he got down to peer at the opening. "Push; do your bit so I can get the forceps round the head. Push! Can't you do better than that?"

It was no good. He stood up and took an envelope from his pocket, then asked for a cup of hot water into which he stirred the powder from the envelope. When it cooled, he handed it to Damaris.

"Here, drink it."

"What is it?"

"Ergot. Don't worry; I only gave you ten grains. It'll bring on the labor again; but the minute you feel a contraction, push just as hard as you can."

The pains did begin again, but pains more violent than any before so that Katie held her hand over Damaris's mouth to stifle her screams.

"Hush, for God's sake, or you'll get me evicted for sure."

"Chrissake, she'd better not go into convulsions. If she does, I'm leaving. I don't want to be mixed up in any complications. You didn't tell me it was going to be this difficult," the student groaned, prodding the opening with his forceps.

"There's not going to be any. Just get the kid out. I'll make it worth your while."

And when Damaris had given up all hope, when she was convinced that she and the child were both done for, she prayed. For the first time in months she prayed. And then he came, a tiny frail thing all covered in a slimy white mucus. She felt his satin smooth skin, the grip of his tiny hand on hers, and she smiled, forgetting everything except that her baby was there and alive. And nestling him to her breast, she lay back oblivious to everything, even to Katie's ceaseless complaints.

"Let me rest, just a little. Let me rest, please, Katie."

She didn't know how long she slept, an uneasy sleep, but she awoke with Katie shaking her.

"You got to get him out of here. Look at him; he's not going to make it. Get rid of him, and you can come back."

"Get rid of him! My child!"

"Well, see for yourself. He's almost gone without help from anyone."

Damaris looked down at the baby at her breast. It was true; he was barely moving, and his color was unhealthily blue, not the glowing pink she'd thought belonged to all newborns. She worried that there was not enough nourishment in her emaciated body to sustain him. Still, he was warm. She hugged him closer, pulling the soiled blanket closer around both of them. Though she could not see clearly—her head felt light yet heavy at the same time— when she focused her eyes on him again she was struck by his unhealthy color. What if he were to die without baptism? It was a terrible thought that he might die at all, but that he might die unbaptized was worse still.

"He's not going to make it; you can see that, Dam. Here, I'll help you get rid of him. Poor little tyke, never had a chance. Put him in this box and I'll take him down to the river. Then we'll get you cleaned up and you'll be right as rain in a trivet, ready to go. Come on, dearie. Don't just lie there. Do it or you got to go, both of you. I don't want to be cruel, but it's my livelihood, you know. And I can't stand for anyone dying on me. There'll be police around and everything."

Damaris's voice rose in agitation. "No, Katie, you're wrong. He will make it, he will. He has to!"

Yet what if he didn't? What if he were to die without baptism? Her father had always said that was the church's most important rite; to die unbaptized meant purgatory forever.

"Go and get Mother Charlotte for me, Katie," she whispered. "Please, get Mother Charlotte."

"A fine time to want your mother. Should have gone to her long ago."

"No. Mother Charlotte. Ask at the shelter; they'll know where she is. Tell her I need her badly."

"I'm not having no nun here. Worse than calling in a policeman."

"Please, Katie, get her for me. I'll leave then, but not before. I swear I won't move until you do."

"Fine way you're repaying me for all I've done. I don't want to go to that place. They'll be wanting to reform me or out to make me collect alms for them or something degrading like that."

"Please, Katie. I'm sorry. This is the last thing I'll ever ask of you."

"Last time I ever stick my neck out and do a good deed for anyone," she grumbled as she slammed the door.

In the dark, empty room Damaris dozed fitfully, holding the baby close to her as though to contain his life, waking now and then from the peace of sleep to the nightmare of the real world, feeling her child to make sure he was still warm, listening to hear if he continued to breathe. Though she tried to remain awake to watch over him, she felt herself growing hot, feverish, and she fell into that limbo between waking and sleep, between life and death, her eyes sharply flickering open now and then, certain if she let go of life her baby must die too.

Suddenly her eyes opened wide. She thought the figure before her with the huge halo of white around the head must be an angel.

"Where am I? Is this heaven? Is my baby here with me?"

"It's me, Damaris, Mother Charlotte."

It was the closest thing to an angel on earth at that

moment. "Please, Mother, take him, have him baptized, then bring him back to me."

"I will, Damaris, I will. Let go of him. I'll take care of both of you."

When next Damaris saw Mother Charlotte it was from a bed in a hospital ward. She didn't know how she had got there, but there was only one thought in her mind as she looked around and saw bassinets beside the other beds but not hers.

"My baby! My baby! Where's my baby? What have they done with my baby?"

A nurse came at the cry. Something was pushed between her lips; something bitter that she was forced to swallow. She felt too weak to cry out anymore; all she could do was sob to herself over and over again. "My baby, my baby!"

When next she woke, she saw the dark robes and flaring white headdress of Mother Charlotte at her bedside.

"My baby?" she whispered.

"He's gone, Damaris, gone to God's care."

"Oh, no!"

Mother Charlotte sat by her holding her hand. "We tried everything, Damaris, but it was impossible. He was just too weak. You've barely survived a terrible case of puerperal fever. All you must think about now is getting yourself well again."

"I don't care about living anymore. You should have let me die too."

"Damaris, don't! You've been given life; it's wrong to talk of giving it up."

"But he was given life. Why was it taken from him? Why am I still alive when I don't want to be? Tell me, Mother Charlotte, explain it to me."

"I don't know, Damaris. There are many things I don't know—why one lives, another dies. I don't know. It is God's will."

Damaris was silent.

"Your life has been spared for some reason, though."

"But without my child I don't want to live."

"We're not always given what we want, Damaris, but what we need. Your life has been saved for some reason; it's for you to discover what that reason is."

And though she made not the slightest effort to do so, live she did. When she was sufficiently recovered, Mother Charlotte arranged for her to convalesce at a shelter the order maintained on the shores of Long Island. There in the brisk sea air she walked and walked on the long sandy beaches, watching the breakers follow one another into the shore, the gulls flying overhead.

Why had her child died? Why did she live? Questions with no answers haunted her until one day she turned her steps from the sandy shore into the cold water, walking till it reached her waist, pushing on with the outgoing tide that carried her further still until her feet could no longer touch bottom and the sea engulfed her. It was cold, icy cold, as cold as her heart; it was fitting to die in that icy grave. She gave herself up to it willingly; it would be such a relief when she was gone. If there was an afterlife, her child would be there. She could care for him. She was so entranced with this thought that the fisherman who picked her up for dead, saw the smile still on her face.

"Why can't people leave me alone? Why did he save me? I wanted to die. My life is mine. It's all I have that is mine. Why can't I do with it as I will?" she wailed to Mother Charlotte, who came as soon as she heard.

"I've told you, Damaris, there are many things I don't understand," Mother Charlotte said. "I refuse to plead with you not to do this again. All I ask is that you stop to think that your life has been spared not once but twice. Why, do you suppose?"

"An irony of fate, that's why," Damaris raged. "I'm spared because I want to die. I want to die," she reiterated bitterly. "Can you understand that, or are you too removed from the mundane world to understand that it is filthy, rotten, that there is no good, no decency in it? I hate living; I want to die. I want to die," she sobbed over and over again.

Instead of sympathizing, Mother Charlotte passed her wrap to Damaris. "Come along. We're going for a walk. If you want to die, you might as well do it while I'm here, then I won't have to waste my time wondering when it will happen. Hurry up; I haven't all day. I have work to do in New York."

They set out along the beach in silence. All that was

heard was the roar of the breakers, the cry of the gulls, and the trudging of their feet on the wet sand. Still they kept walking, farther along the beach than Damaris had ever been.

Then suddenly Mother Charlotte stopped. "I have to rest a minute; I'm not as young as you are."

She began talking of the gulls scavenging for food, of the scurrying clouds that showed the change in the wind. Then she went on from talk of the world around them to the problems facing her in New York. A plan was afoot to open another school for girls; there were proposals to send sisters west as far as Ohio, even Illinois. And always there was her dream, the hospital for children. Money, money, money; there was never enough to do all the things she hoped and planned for, nor enough willing hands to help.

"Oh, Damaris, pride is a terrible sin. I only hope it's not pride that forces me on even when I think I can go no further. I hope it is my genuine willingness to serve. I can never be sure. It is so hard for us ever to understand our motives. I'm sorry; I shouldn't be burdening you with this. It's just that I have no one to talk to; the sisters are overtaxed as it is. I don't want to inflict my troubles on them, and I shouldn't on you. I know you have troubles of your own that are far more pressing."

Keeping her eyes on the gray line where the sea met the sky, Damaris made no reply.

"You know, you said just now that I didn't understand the world; you made me sound like some idealist. You're wrong. I'm a very practical person and always was. I was the eldest of the family. My mother died early; and as was expected, I took her place, helping to raise my two brothers and my sister. I never thought of becoming a nun. We were staunch Episcopalians, and there was no such thing in this country then as a veiled order. My sister opened Chartwell, an academy for girls in Virginia. I helped her. I thought that would be my life, helping others to complete their tasks. I never expected to have a task all my own.

"Then Dr. Hunter came to visit. We're related, you know. He talked of the wonderful work that the Roman Catholic Daughters of Charity and the Poor Clares were doing and said he couldn't see why our church had nothing comparable. I said I couldn't understand why we didn't either, and he said, 'Well, then, why don't you do something about it!' So I did. Dr. Hunter was very brave in suggesting it. It was he, not I, who persuaded the Bishop to agree to found the order. I can assure you his task as our chaplain has been an unenviable one. Apart from dealing with all manner of complaints and criticisms, including some quite awful personal attacks—he's even been called Father Ignatius because he helped to write up our rules—there have been cries of ritualism and protests that if women become nuns what's to prevent them from becoming priests?

"I've said this to no one, Damaris, and if it were ever repeated I should deny having said it; but with the exception of Dr. Hunter and a few others, I think we could do quite as well as most of them. Though who would want that burden I don't know. I certainly wouldn't. The order is more than enough for me."

She stopped and put out her hand. "It's beginning to rain, Damaris. You won't have to worry about getting wet whenever you decide to walk into the water. You mustn't mind if I keep on talking. I have to because I suspect I am wrong in aiding and abetting this act of yours. The law says suicide is wrong, though it does occur in the Bible."

"Judas Iscariot, you mean?" These were the first words Damaris had spoken since they started out.

"Well, yes, Judas did commit suicide. I suppose there was nothing else for him to do really. That's usually the way it is; when a person has nothing to offer life, then death is the only way. I feel sorry for people who reach that conclusion, but it's a personal decision; there is little anyone can do to dissuade them. I know I shall go on until the end, because I have to. I may decry the difficulties I have taken on with the order, but they're what keep me alive. I love the order, Damaris. I used to think that you loved it too, and in much the same way. Well, I mustn't hold you up any longer. I'll just stand here if you don't mind." Mother Charlotte tucked her hands into the wide sleeves of her robes. "Dear me, it's getting cold."

Damaris took a step toward the water, then another; then she stopped and looked back accusingly at Mother Charlotte. "The tide has changed. It's coming in now. You knew that. You kept talking and talking."

"And you kept listening, Damaris." Mother Charlotte smiled. "Tell me honestly, do you want to put an end to your life? I promise you, I'll never stop you, not now, not when the tide changes, not ever." She turned back toward the retreat, and Damaris fell into step beside her.

"You do so remind me of myself at your age." She saw Damaris's look of inquiry and shook her head. "No, I was never pregnant, and I can't recall ever wanting to take my own life. But when you used to come and help us I always thought you the most calm, most practical person there. You could pick up and carry on, no matter what. I was like that, but you always did so with a serene smile that I lacked."

"I'm not the way I used to be, Mother Charlotte. I've changed inside. Maybe it comes from being exposed to life as it is, but as I never suspected it to be."

"Yes, life is hard. Perhaps you're right; perhaps death is easier than facing the challenge of it."

"You're making a coward of me!" Damaris argued hotly.

"Well"—Mother Charlotte turned to face her—"aren't you?"

"No, I'm not."

"Prove it then."

"How?"

"Come and join us. I ask it quite selfishly; I need your help. Come temporarily if you wish, until you decide whether you want to live or die . . . or marry."

"I shall never marry."

"Well, that sounds quite definite. Can I count on your help then?"

"How could I! You know all about me. You may overlook or forgive, but just think of the ladies of the diocese who are always inspecting you so closely. If they found you harboring a Magdalen in your midst it could cost you all the goodwill you've so carefully built. And how could I ever take a vow of chastity?"

"It's true that those who've joined us have all been single ladies without the trace of a blemish in their past. It's true that if it were known I'd have a great deal of explaining to do; but I'm the only one who does know. The only way anyone need ever hear of it is from you, and

I don't guess you'd want to talk of it. As for the vows, they are and always have been optional in St. Catharine's. I don't believe in compulsion.''

Damaris stopped, feeling the ocean spray in her face. She was wanted. She would never be alone again; she would have a mother who cared and sisters, lots of sisters. She would be safe from harm. And maybe she would one day save lives, as hers had been saved. She was being given a chance, perhaps the only one she would ever have.

''Well?'' Mother Charlotte questioned.

''Did you know this would happen when we started out?'' Damaris asked. ''That instead of drowning myself I'd walk back with you and into the Order of St. Catharine?''

Mother Charlotte shook her head, laughing. ''You credit me with far more power than I have. But I do confess I prayed a little.''

''I've done little enough of that of late.'' Her eyes grew dark as she remembered the last time she had prayed, right before her baby was born. She'd prayed for him to be born alive.

''Because your prayers have not been answered?'' Mother Charlotte questioned gently.

''In a way, in an ironical sort of way, they were.'' Damaris shook herself as though to brush away the memory and said briskly, ''If I should come with you, it won't be from a sense of calling.''

''My dear girl, come for whatever reason you wish. As I told you, I'm asking you for purely selfish reasons. You're a capable nurse; you're patient, and though at the moment you may deny it, you're gentle and kind.''

Damaris smiled. ''Thank you, Mother.''

''For what?''

''For my life, I guess. I'll make you proud of me.''

''Good! I do have one request to make of you, though.''

''What is that?''

''I should like you to take the name of Sister Serene.''

''But that would be a farce. There is no serenity in me.''

''It was there once. It will be again. You'll see.''

THREE

And so Damaris Fanshawe became Sister Serene of the Order of St. Catharine, an order that gradually became so completely her life that there were times when she seemed to have known no other.

Mother Charlotte had been right. Serenity did return to her. Though she never forgot the child she had borne, and never would, as she devoted herself to the care of the children at Mercy House, the memory lost much of its bitterness and she was able to give to others the love she would have given to the son she was never able to know. She might never achieve that "peace that passes all understanding" promised at each Communion, but she came to possess a sense of security in recognizing her own worth and a satisfaction in having found a meaning for her life. Those who met her were instantly aware of her inner strength.

It was Mother Charlotte who had given her reason for being; it was to the order that she belonged. She had nothing beyond that.

There was her mother, of course. She had written to tell her of her intention, as a courtesy rather than expecting approval. Her mother's reply made clear how little regard she had for the choice. If God had intended women to become nuns, He would have so indicated, but where was it to be found in the Bible? There was Mary Magdalen, of course, of whom the less said the better, and Mary and Martha—Martha the dutiful, she'd deserved greater mention. There was Mary, the mother of Christ, but Episcopalians abhorred Mariolatry. Priests were another matter; there were clearly twelve appointed disciples, but for women to take the veil smacked of popishness. She only hoped Damaris harbored no foolish ideas. The whole business seemed to Mrs. Fanshawe an unseemly desire to enter the world of the church, a world belonging only to men.

Damaris had considered explaining to her mother that profession as a sister incurred no laying on of hands, no episcopal or apostolic contact such as a priest received at ordination. Hands might be raised, folded, crossed, or shaken; but they were never imposed. There was no desire and no thought of usurping the priest's position. But her mother, she guessed, would never understand. She had grown up at a different time, in different circumstances. Perhaps it was even wrong of her to expect her to understand. Their letters, though regular, became filled with trivialities; nevertheless, they served to assure Damaris of her mother's well-being; Templeton Caylew was living up to the terms of his agreement; in addition, the award of pensions to war widows was under way.

It may have been her total dedication to the order coupled with her own inner fortitude that made her ideal in caring for the sick. She was cool and able to get to the root of the problem no matter how garbled the patient's story might be. She remained calm in the face of the worst emergencies and was able to attend to the goriest wounds without flinching. To see a child in pain, in anguish, to see small bodies distorted, young flesh cut and bruised—sometimes even intentionally by others—was beyond the endurance of many of the sisters; yet having faced the death of her own child seemed to have equipped Sister Serene to approach even the most hopeless situation with a strong, almost obsessive determination not only to alleviate suffering but also to fight for survival against all odds, as though each and every life at stake was that of her own lost child.

Dr. Weldon and his equally elderly partner, as well as those few other dedicated physicians who donated time to attend children at Mercy House, were always relieved to find Sister Serene on duty. She was quick, resourceful, energetic, and she always seemed to know exactly what they needed done. Often they would leave matters entirely to her, satisfied she would look for their assistance only when absolutely essential. Thus when Mother Charlotte

decided one of their number must train as a physician, she
did not have to look far before deciding on the most
suitable candidate.

It wasn't long after her visit to the Caylews that Sister
Serene was summoned to her superior's office.

"Well, the appointment to the University Medical School
is almost certainly yours. Mr. Caylew has written that you
are to go and see Dr. McChord. If he approves of you—as
I am quite sure he will—they will allow you to train there
among their august student body, all male, as we know;
but I have no fear of your letting our sex down."

Though Sister Serene's face lit up at the news, she
couldn't help expressing her qualms. "Oh, Mother Charlotte,
I only wish I had your faith."

"My dear sister, you have faith enough for both of us.
Don't allow Dr. McChord or anyone else to intimidate
you; just be yourself and all will be well. I know it; God
knows it. Learn well and hurry back to us with your
knowledge."

Sister Serene said nothing. Over the years of working
and praying together, their silences had become quite as
meaningful as their words. Mother Charlotte came over
and put her arms around her, and for a moment Sister
Serene clung to her. "God brought you into our lives,
whatever the manner, and I never cease to thank Him for
it."

"And where might I be had it not been for you, Mother
Charlotte?"

"You would have been all right, Sister Serene. I've
never really had to worry about you as I have some of the
others who sometimes seem not to know which foot to put
forward without being told. Being a superior is no easy
task; remember that when your time comes."

"My time! But I shall never—"

"We'll see. A great part of the job is judgment of
others, and here is your first chance to exercise that judgment." Mother Charlotte put on her spectacles and picked
up a letter from her desk. "I have heard from a lady who
says she is known to you, a Mrs. Angela Wickers. You are
acquainted with her, are you?"

"Of course. I worked with her at the Caylews'. They

brought her from England as a nurse for their children. I was her assistant."

"Then you must know her quite well."

"Very well."

"Then give me your opinion of her."

"Let me see." Sister Serene hesitated. "She's a strong Anglophile, and tended at first to dislike things American. But she's very efficient and uses great common sense. She will put up with no nonsense from her charges. She knows what she wants and makes sure it is done."

"That is her attitude toward children. But toward others, other women, yourself, for instance?"

"Well"—Sister Serene hesitated a little longer this time—"she was very kind to me. She taught me a great deal. She was protective toward me. I was very young when I went to the Caylews' and I had never been out in the world. She did her best to keep me from harm."

"We know she did not quite succeed in that, but no matter."

"Mrs. Wickers was in England that summer when . . . when that happened. Had she not been, I think it might never . . . But as you say, no matter."

"Then you recommend her, this Angela Wickers?"

"Recommend her for what, Mother?"

"To join the order. She wishes to become a Sister of St. Catharine. From what you tell me, she would do very well. Her work with children would be of great benefit, and she says it has long been her wish to serve God more fully."

Sister Serene bowed her head. She could never remember any inclination on the part of Angela Wickers to serve God, nor any strong religious convictions at all. In fact, looking back to that last scene together, she distinctly remembered words to the contrary.

"I am glad that she is known to you, for now I need have no qualms about the moral conduct of Angela Wickers. You must understand how careful I have to be. The order, as you know, is constantly being scrutinized for the slightest sign of immorality. We all stand suspect. There are times when the Friends of the Order seem more inquisitors than allies, though they mean well, goodness knows, and it's through them and their efforts to raise money for us that we're going to be able to build our hospital at long last. God is a busy worker; but He does love help, and it's not for us to question the source of that help. But dear me, sometimes I do wonder at their constant search for wrong-doing or unspeakable vices within our walls."

"I've never understood exactly what they are looking for. Surely they can't suspect Dr. Weldon and his colleagues of ulterior designs! Is their kindness suspect? Poor souls, they're getting so old that I sometimes feel we should be nursing them along with the children. That leaves only Dr. Hunter, who is most respectably married. What unspeakable vice could they possibly consider occurs among us?"

"My dear sister, it's not that. Any time a group of people live in a different way, there are always those who will suggest they do so in order to indulge in some sort of reprehensible conduct. We are women living alone, something not done in our society. We are fortunate in that, unlike the Catholic orders, our priests marry. With no unmarried clerics living adjacent to us we aren't accused of licentious meetings. So, robbed of that speculation, they turn their attention to any particular friendships that might develop between us."

"Particular friendships?" Sister Serene knit her brows. "Do you mean like the one between myself and Livvy?"

"That is a true sisterly, loving affection, and not at all the sort of thing they look for; but I am sure you can conjecture what I mean." She saw Sister Serene's look of puzzlement become flustered and hastened to add, "It's unnatural, I know, quite disgusting and not a topic one wants to discuss; but it is not something that can be ignored. Remember that when you sit in this chair, as I am quite sure that one day you will."

"Mother Charlotte—" she began hesitantly.

"No, don't protest. I am quite sure that you will, but not yet. First comes your medical training. Besides, I am still hale and relatively hearty. You'll have to wait a goodly number of years before I'll be put out to pasture. Nevertheless, you must train for it every day, for if there is one among us who can do it, it is you."

"But Mother Charlotte—"

"No more buts. You have plenty to take care of, I

know, but I am going to ask you to go over the speech I've been working on for Mrs. Caylew's hospital building fund dinner. Did you know the state legislature has agreed to match every dollar the Friends of the Order raise? Add any thoughts of your own, Sister. I never was an elegant speaker, and that is what we need—someone to touch their hearts as well as their pocketbooks.''

"Your sincerity will do that, Mother Charlotte."

"Sincerity is all well and good, but I'm not at all convinced that that alone will do for that fashionable throng, who by the time the speech is to be given will undoubtedly have overimbibed as well as overeaten. They're all too likely to fall asleep. Strong and stirring words will be necessary."

"Conciliatory words also," Sister Serene reminded her. "You must make them feel important, make them feel that the task and the rewards are theirs. Appeal to their hearts; but more importantly, appeal to their consciences."

"There, that's it! That's just why I'm asking for your help. Now I won't keep you any longer. Dr. McChord says he's willing to see you tomorrow at three. I am going to rely on Sister Lavinia to fill your shoes while you're away from us. Her postulancy will soon be over, but she still has much growing to do. What is your opinion?"

"Oh, Livvy will without a doubt be entirely excellent," Sister Serene affirmed. She only wished she felt the same unquestioning enthusiasm for the entrance into the order of Angela Wickers.

FOUR

Sister Serene had heard of Dr. McChord's research in diseases of the skin, so on the train to Philadelphia she buried herself in Robert Willan's treatise *On Cutaneous Diseases*. She studied the section on eczema, trying hard to memorize the way in which he had grouped various forms of dermatitis, yet again and again her mind would wander from the text to the matter of Angela Wickers.

Had she been right in not confessing to Mother Charlotte all she knew, or at least had reason to suspect, of Angela Wickers's nature? To have done so in the light of the Friends' suspicions concerning particular friendships would most certainly have ended all hope of her postulancy. Yet had she the right to deny that opportunity to Angela Wickers, who had truly done her no harm and had, in fact, acted to protect her? She had distinctly said it was her wish to serve God; and God, as Sister Serene knew, worked in strange ways. She had prayed for Angela Wickers, as she had said she would. Perhaps this was God's way of answering that prayer. Yet she owed everything to Mother Charlotte; she could never allow anything to happen that might place the order she had founded in jeopardy.

She went back to her memorization of Willan's definitions. Tubercle: a small hard superficial tumor, circumscribed and permanent. Wheal: a rounded or longitudinal elevation of the cuticle with a white summit. She had to be prepared. She must be prepared.

But it was not Robert Willan's treatise that was on Dr. McChord's mind when she arrived. She observed him as she entered: a man of slight build, for which he compensated with an all too obvious pomposity. His elaborately pomaded wavy hair was styled in such a way as to add at least three inches to his height; yet even so, as he momentarily rose to greet her, Sister Serene realized she was by far the taller of the two. That did not augur well.

He did not immediately offer to let her sit down, allowing her to stand before him while he sat studying Templeton Caylew's letter and the application that she had submitted. Only then did he motion her to the chair in front of his desk.

"Why do you wish to become a physician?" he asked abruptly, removing his glasses and holding them up to the light, then taking a handkerchief from his pocket and meticulously cleaning them. Round and round his fingers went, with Sister Serene following their progress as she explained her own aptitude and the greater service she would be able to render to the order's hospital as a resident physician.

"All very fine," he answered, putting his spectacles back on and adjusting them on his nose. "But you yourself, why do *you* wish to take on a man's profession? For it is a profession for a man. I do not approve of women in the field, nor will I ever, and I make no bones on that score. I do not feel it necessary to apologize for my opinion."

"You are most certainly entitled to hold your beliefs, as I am mine," she replied with an air of finality that clearly did not please him.

"Well, out with it, what is your reason, Sister . . . Sister— What is your name?" he asked testily. "There appear to be two here."

"Sister Serene is the name I took at postulancy; Damaris Fanshawe is the name with which I was baptized. My reason, Dr. McChord, probably differs little from yours when you took your oath. There is a need, I wish to fill it, and I believe I have the capability to do so. My background may be weak in some areas—I know little of chemistry, for instance—but I am willing to devote all my time and effort to proving myself a worthy student if you will but give me the opportunity."

"There was a woman—Blackwell, I believe was her name—who was most persistent in petitioning for admittance some time ago. The faculty strongly opposed her application. I believe she did finally train, but at some small inferior school in upstate New York. Since then, each year we have been importuned by a series of young women, all too brash in my humble opinion, seeking to succeed where she failed. We have resisted all attempts to open our doors to students of the female sex. My only reason for considering you at all is the high recommendation from a worthy gentleman and a good friend of mine, who, I might mention, shares my views, but asks that I consider you nevertheless.

"Coupled with the desire to accommodate a worthy friend is my own sense of charity. You are a nun, after all, rather than a woman; for that reason you should not prove as great a distraction to the other students. But were I to allow your entrance, and I'm not saying that I shall, I should warn you I would most certainly expect more of you than I do of them. Nor would I hesitate to curtail your studies if they were not completed in a superior manner. I make plain that I am not in favor of such an experiment. Should I take you—and again I reiterate that I am not saying I shall—you would indeed receive an education such as no other woman in this field has ever had. But were I to allow you admittance, it would not be setting a precedent; it would be nothing more than an experiment."

He studied her as he might a laboratory specimen, and she returned his gaze unflinchingly. That did not altogether please him. He concluded petulantly, "More than for you, or for your order, as I have already told you, I wish to accommodate my friend Mr. Templeton Caylew. You are fortunate in having him as a champion."

He leaned back in his chair, sighing almost inaudibly, an indication perhaps that while he cherished Caylew's friendship, at times it imposed hardships upon him. Passing a delicate hand over, but not quite touching, his pomaded head of hair, he asked in measured tones, "Well, Sister Serene, tell me what you know of puerperal fever?"

She blanched, her calm exterior shaken at last. That seemed to please Dr. McChord, for he settled back, crossing his arms across his chest, as he demanded, "Come along, you should at least be able to define it for me. I don't expect much of you at this stage, but tell me what kind of a disease it is. You've mentioned your aptitude, and Caylew's letter indicates you've been performing some sort of nursing functions in this infirmary of yours. Surely you know something, even at an elementary level. What sort of a disease is puerperal fever? Is it contagious?''

Sister Serene passed her tongue across her dry lips as pointedly he took a gold watch from his waistcoat pocket and studied its face. ''Come along. I haven't all day.''

''It is a disease generally known as childbed fever, for it afflicts women in childbirth,'' she began unsteadily. Then remembering how in studying Gull's merciless descriptions of cretinoid states in women, she had managed to separate the terrible changes in a certain Miss B after the cessation of the catamenial period—rose-purple complexion, thickened and folded skin, broad thick tongue too large for her mouth, heavy lips, guttural voice, depressed nose, spadelike hands—from her feelings for the poor woman who was so afflicted, she forced herself to separate what had happened to her from the clinical description of puerperal fever.

She went on with increasing assurance, finishing, ''Two British physicians, Gordon and White, have studied its contagious nature. Their findings show it to be carried from patient to patient by midwives, or whoever might be attending the birth . . .'' Her voice broke momentarily, remembering; then she inhaled deeply, sat tall in her chair, and continued, flatly but firmly, with a precise description of Oliver Wendell Holmes's paper on methods of prevention, which cautioned that those attending births should never take part in postmortems, as medical students often did, going directly from the postmortem room to the labor ward, taking the contagion with them, examining women in labor without so much as washing their hands. Holmes had recommended disinfecting the hands with chloride of lime and assiduous scrubbing with a nail brush, though Lister had employed carbolic acid and found that more successful as an antisepsis.

Her last remarks re-emphasized her own beliefs on the importance of asepsis in preventing puerperal fever, the use of carbolic acid spray to disinfect the air, especially in operating or delivery rooms, and the necessity of all attendants keeping clothing as well as hands and nails scrupulously clean.

''Thank you, Sister Serene.'' Dr. McChord's nasal voice

sounded not entirely happy. "That is quite enough. You've told me more than I need to know. I asked you specifically about puerperal fever. You did not confine yourself to my question."

"You did ask if it was contagious," she reminded him.

He pursed his lips in displeasure. "You will have to learn not to answer back, and not to make a display of your knowledge. Is that clearly understood?"

A sharp retort died from her lips as she sensed his last remark indicated her acceptance. "I'm sorry, sir. It won't happen again."

"Very well then," he said abruptly. Then with an air of having brooded and reached a momentous though not particularly palatable conclusion: "You will begin in the dissection room. When you come, you are to be prepared with needles, forceps, scissors, a blowpipe, hooks both single and double, and knives of course." He picked up a slender knife, holding it to allow the light to glisten on its keen blade. "Get several; you will be using them a great deal. I take it you'll have no difficulty handling a cadaver."

A cadaver; that had as little similarity to the human body filled with the spirit as a bird nest after the birds had flown. Yet suddenly she shuddered, remembering her son. She'd never thought of his tiny body ever being a cadaver. Was it possible it had served for such a purpose? Across from her she saw a sneer cross Dr. McChord's face, making her respond briskly, "No, Dr. McChord, no difficulty at all."

"I shall expect you to train under your given name, whichever that is, Miss . . . Miss—"

"Miss Fanshawe, Damaris Fanshawe," she supplied.

"And don't expect the other students to like you. I warn you they will not. In fact, I shouldn't be surprised if they make your life a hell. Don't come crying to me if they do. My sympathies will be with them. I know how incensed I would have been in training to find a nun cluttering up the operating room."

"I understand, sir."

Her placid air of acceptance seemed to irritate him further. "And I won't have you wearing that great wimple or headdress or whatever you call that thing on your head. It will get in the way of others."

"I shall remove my coif." Dr. McChord's ill-humor was not improved by Sister Serene's smiled thanks. "I do appreciate your overcoming your own inclination against the admittance of a woman to this school."

"Don't give me cause to regret it."

"I'll do everything in my power to prove worthy of this school's superior training, an education, as you have pointed out, such as no other of my sex has yet been privileged to receive."

FIVE

Sister Serene was gratified and relieved to find Angela Wickers settling well, proving to have a cool head in emergencies, never standing on her dignity as had been her wont on Park Avenue but taking her fair share of whatever was expected of a novice with true humility, washing the floors, serving in the refectory.

"You're a good judge of character," Mother Charlotte approved. "If you know any more like Sister Angela I hope you will imbue them with the same spirit of service and send them to see me. You're a great example, Sister Serene. Sister Lavinia is always saying she wants to be just like you, and now Sister Angela tells me if it weren't for you she would never have thought of joining us."

Sister Serene was relieved, but she hoped that it was for a higher reason that Sister Angela had come to Mercy House. She wished too that Sister Angela would not single her out for special attention; she seemed always to be watching, waiting upon her every move, fetching and carrying things for her. It was more than any of them did for their Mother Superior, the only one deserving of such deference.

There was also the difficulty she had in persuading Sister Angela to call her anything but Mary.

"I am Sister Serene now," she would remind her, in an effort to stress their new relationship, yet without success.

"I'm sorry. It's just that I never think of you as anything but Mary."

They had seldom been alone together, but one afternoon as Sister Serene was in their small library working on

Mother Charlotte's speech Sister Angela came in to see her.

"Do I disturb you, Mary?"

"No, I've finished. It's just I'm dissatisfied. This speech is simply not good enough for its intended purpose."

"I'm sure it is if you've written it, Mary," Sister Angela replied, yet her praise, rather than encouraging Sister Serene, served to aggravate.

"Please, Sister Angela, I've asked you so many times; do try to remember that I'm Sister Serene now."

"I'm sorry. I just don't think of you that way." Even though Sister Serene had taken up her pen again, Sister Angela stayed sitting and watching her until at last Sister Serene looked up.

"Is there something else you wanted, Sister Angela?"

"Yes. You see, Ma— Sister, ever since you packed and left the Caylews, not a day passed without my thinking of you, wondering what had happened, how you were faring. I searched for you. I searched everywhere, for I sensed you were in trouble. What was wrong? Surely you can tell me now that it's all in the past."

"I appreciate your concern. You were very kind to me. I shall never forget that. But you're right in saying it's all in the past. I don't think about it. I'm very happy here. I hope you will be just as satisfied, Sister Angela."

"I am satisfied simply being under the same roof as you."

"The satisfaction comes from our work, serving others, serving God," Sister Serene reminded her sharply.

"I know, but surely I may serve you as well. I see nothing wrong with that." Sensing Sister Serene was about to argue the point, she reiterated her original question, "Was it because something happened to you, Mary? Did anyone do you any harm? Was that why you went away? I do wish you would tell me."

But Sister Serene shook her head. "It's all so far in the past now; whatever it was is finished, done with."

Yet Sister Angela refused to leave it at that. "Was it because of some man that Mrs. Caylew insisted on your leaving so suddenly? I'm sure it could not have been to come here. Otherwise why would she have been so vociferous about your not believing in God?"

"Do you, Sister Angela?" Sister Serene scrutinized her companion's face, its angularity emphasized by the coif. "Do you believe in God?"

Sister Angela shrugged aside the inquiry with "Would I be here otherwise?"

"I don't know. Would you? Is that your only reason for being here?"

Sister Angela turned, her face tense, her lips quivering. She deliberated for a moment, then burst forth, "All right, Mary, if you want me to be frank, *you* are the reason I'm here; it's because of you I came, but you must have realized that."

The color fled from Sister Serene's cheeks. She stood up and began to pace the floor. "Since you're being frank, Sister, then I must be also. I've been troubled ever since Mother Charlotte told me you had asked to be admitted to the order, troubled because of those things you said to me just before I left the Caylews. Mother Charlotte asked my advice when you wrote to her, she asked me to tell what I knew of you; and I said nothing, hoping I was wrong in my suspicions and that the reason you gave, to serve God, was really why you wanted to be here." She paused, then shook her head. "It's wrong, Sister Angela, totally wrong. You mustn't stay. If Mother Charlotte were to know . . . I would have to tell her—"

"But Mother Charlotte does know that you're the reason I came; I told her as much."

"But not in the way you've told me."

"Oh, Mary, Mary. Listen to me. When I saw you again after all that time, so calm, so pristine, when I'd imagined all sorts of horrors that might have befallen you, I did thank God for keeping you safe. So you see I'm not beyond redemption. You know, Mrs. Caylew had been pestering me to go down to Memphis and take care of that haughty Eustacia's child, but I wouldn't go for fear of being further than ever from you. I wonder if I had gone whether our paths might not have crossed sooner. But that's academic. Now we are together again, that's what matters. How I missed you, Mary. Don't send me away. Please don't send me away."

Angela Wickers was a tall woman, but at that moment

she looked small, even weak, and so vulnerable; despite her misgivings, Sister Serene's heart melted.

"It's not for me to decide; it's for Mother Charlotte. I have to tell her."

"Don't, Mary. What harm does it do? I promise you I would do nothing. I've missed you so. I used to see you sitting opposite me while I read from Mrs. Trollope, your sad, sensitive face. I cried over the cot you used to sleep in, and I kept the comforter you used on my own bed because it smelled of your fragrance."

"Sister Angela! Don't, please stop. You mustn't; you can't speak of me as though you were speaking of a—"

"Of a lover," Sister Angela finished. "But I do love you, Mary; you know I do."

Sister Serene grew pale. "You must never say that, never."

"But you've told me that we are here to love one another."

"That's true, Sister Angela, but you know very well I don't mean in that way."

"You do love me, though?" Sister Angela persisted.

"I love you in the way I love everyone here, no more, no less," Sister Serene said firmly.

"Then I must be satisfied with that."

Sister Serene was silent. "It's not that simple. You mustn't stay; it's not right. It could endanger everything Mother Charlotte has worked for."

"I've given up everything to be here near to you, Mary," Sister Angela said quietly. "I've been frank with you about my feelings; I've told you what has for so long been in my heart. I promise I'll never repeat it again, not to you or to anyone. No living soul will ever know it." Then she cried in anguish, "Please, don't condemn me for being as I am. Don't hate me. Try to understand even if you can't return my affection in the same way."

"I certainly don't hate you, Angela. You must know that, though I confess it's difficult for me to understand one woman loving another in that way. Yet I could never condemn what I don't understand. I feel for you deeply; I sense your tragedy. Nevertheless, if it were ever to come to light, for whatever reason, it could mean the end of everything—the hospital Mother Charlotte has worked for,

this house, the order itself. That would kill Mother Charlotte. I can't take that risk. I must tell her and let her
decide.''

"No one will ever know," Sister Angela promised fervently. "Not unless it comes from you, and you'll be in
Philadelphia in training. I'm needed here. There aren't
enough for the work; you know that. Mother Charlotte is
pleased to have me; she's said as much, often. You may
have been the reason I came, but that's not to say I don't
also fulfill a purpose. Please, Mary, let me stay. I'll do no
one any harm. If you make me leave, I must warn you I
won't go on living. Please don't blame me for loving as I
do; we don't choose where we love.''

Sister Angela had begun to cry; it was the first time that
Sister Serene had ever seen her cry. She thought of the
resolute nanny she'd first met. Was it possible that this
unhappy, sobbing woman was the same martinet who had
held sway over the Caylew nursery and servants alike?

"Oh, Sister Angela!" Sister Serene's anguished voice,
her gesture of regret as she reached over to touch the
sleeve of her companion, were noticed by one who had
just come into the room.

"Is something wrong?" Mother Charlotte looked from
Sister Serene's startled face to Sister Angela wiping away
her tears.

Sister Serene knew she should, indeed she must, say
something of what was no longer a suspicion but a fact.

"Sister Angela has been talking to me about the circumstances that prompted her to join the order," she
faltered. Seeing Sister Angela's eyes on her, pleading, she
remembered her own wish to die that had brought her into
the order, and how her life had changed. Might it not be
the same with Angela Wickers? God worked in strange
ways. She saw the relief on Sister Angela's face as she
finished awkwardly, "And we were catching up on old
times.''

"Reminiscing can be emotional business. I know how it
is on those occasions when my sister Mildred and I are
together. I'm sorry to interrupt your confidences, but I
simply must find out how you're getting along with that
speech, Sister Serene. The dinner is next week.''

"It's finished, Mother Charlotte, all but the final touches."

"That's splendid! Then rather than our usual reflection, perhaps you'll read it to us during the evening meal."

So that evening in place of the novice usually assigned to the task Sister Serene sat on a high stool at the head of the long trestle table where the nuns ate their plain fare in complete silence, and she read a speech aimed at New York's wealthiest, most sophisticated audience.

"It is not the thanks of the Sisters of Saint Catharine you will receive for your contribution," Sister Serene concluded, "though you will have our heartfelt thanks. It is not the thanks of the Episcopal Church, though those will most certainly be yours. It is not salvation in heaven that you buy with each dollar given for a replica of a hospital brick. Though there can be no doubt that when the day arrives that our deeds on this earth are counted, each paper brick must surely be credited in your favor. It is rather the thanks of the poor, the destitute children of our city who, sick, friendless, often homeless, have no source to which to turn in their dire need. I ask you to give for them. Remember that it is in giving we receive, that God loves a cheerful giver. The hand that gives, gathers. The truly generous is the truly wise."

As she finished, the silence that had lasted throughout the meal remained unbroken.

She looked around but was unable to tell what her fellow sisters thought of the speech. She was herself dissatisfied in a way she could not define; it was too precise, filled to overflowing with proverbial wisdom that somehow lacked spontaneity.

"It's not right, is it? It's too much, or not enough. I can't tell which," she said dubiously.

"It is far better than anything I could do, Sister Serene," Mother Charlotte praised. "But I have only one request to make."

"Yes, Mother, do tell me. I shall do whatever it is to the best of my ability. I know it needs improvement."

"It needs nothing except for *you* to give it at the benefit dinner just as you have given it to us this evening."

"Oh, but I can't. I've never ever spoken in public."

"You said you would do anything to the best of your

ability, Sister,'' Mother Charlotte reminded her. ''Spare me and give the speech yourself, just as you did just now. Give it not because I ask it but give it for those poor dear children who will benefit from the new hospital.'' She smiled. ''Remember your own words: 'It is in giving we receive.' God does indeed love a cheerful giver. You give the speech, Sister Serene.''

SIX

It was the first time that a hotel had ever been considered suitable for a social occasion of such magnitude. When the owner of the new establishment at Fifth Avenue and Thirty-third Street had sought out Mrs. Caylew suggesting a benefit for her favorite charity, she had been dubious. Such affairs were exclusive and never held in public places.

She had not allowed herself to be persuaded, but had consulted other doyennes of society, particularly Mrs. Vandervoort. She had pointed out possible advantages to such an arrangement, such as the simplicity of catering and the greater numbers that might be accommodated, thus making it a far more consequential affair, which, she had added almost as an afterthought, would make it possible to raise a far larger sum. She only hoped, she told Mrs. Caylew sternly, that her charity would prove sufficiently worthy; for there was nothing like a worthy cause to justify lavish entertainment. Only then had Isabel Caylew given her gracious nod of consent to the owner of the new Waldorf Hotel. Equally graciously, she had allowed the hotel to absorb many of the costs of the benefit for her personal charity, the Order of St. Catharine.

The New York Symphony under Leopold Damrosch was to play for the guests within the white terra-cotta walls of the Waldorf's interior garden court, blending Brahms with its fountains and flowers.

Fifteen hundred guests were to dance and dine in the Empire Hall, modeled after the grand salon of King Ludwig's palace in Munich.

And especially for the occasion, Oscar, the chef, had created an unusual combination of chopped apples, wal-

nuts, celery, and mayonnaise that the guests were to savor
with both pleasure and puzzlement. Was it a fruit dish or a
salad?

The most illustrious of New York's Four Hundred had
clamored to be patronesses for the event, lending not only
favor but, more importantly, prestige, to the twelve-story
hotel with its Turkish smoking room and Marie Antoinette
parlor.

And it was not only New York society that placed its
stamp of approval on the event, for the Biddles, the Drexels,
and the Lippincotts came from Philadelphia; the Lowells,
the Sargents, the Lawrences, and the Peabodys came from
Boston; and from far Chicago came Mrs. Potter Palmer.

While the benefit to raise funds for St. Catharine's
Hospital for Children was not the only event of the year, it
was certainly *the* event of the year, if not of the century.
The magnificence of the background was rivaled by the
splendor of the distinguished array of guests and the glitter
of their jewelry. Just one bracelet—nineteen carats of old-
mine diamond and baguette rubies—on the plump arm of
Mrs. Vandervoort would have paid for an entire wing of
the hospital.

Yet because of the richness of the brocades and satins,
because of the dazzling glare from the diamonds, Sister
Serene attracted immediate attention in her black serge
robes, decorated only by the wooden crucifix on her breast,
and her flaring starched white headdress.

She had not wanted to come, nor had Mrs. Caylew been
at all pleased to have her former nursemaid assume Mother
Charlotte's role as guest of honor; but Mother Charlotte
had persuaded them that it was in the best interests of all.

Worse yet, Livvy, who was to have accompanied Sister
Serene, had been nursing a child whose case had turned
out to be measles; and she had come down with similar
symptoms and had been ordered to bed until either the
fever went away or the measles spots appeared. That had
not prevented her on the night before the event from
slipping out of her room to catch Sister Serene as she
returned from vespers.

"Guy is in New York, and I am quite certain Eustacia
will insist upon him being there tomorrow, Sister Serene.
Would you speak to him for me? He still opposes my

being here, you know, and while I don't want to hurt him, yet I'm determined to profess. It won't be long before I'm ready to do so, and it's important to me that Guy should support the idea.''

"What is it you want, Livvy, your brother's approval or a vocation with the sisterhood? That's the decision you must make.''

"I want to be a sister, you know that. But I can't hurt Guy.''

"Life's choices are never easy,'' Sister Serene agreed, her heart going out to the younger girl. "No one understands that better than I. I just wish I had some advice for you, something to help you make your decision. But only you can make it. Pray for guidance.''

"I have. That's why I'm asking you to talk to Guy.''

Sister Serene sighed. As an answer to a prayer she found herself with little ground on which to argue.

"If the opportunity presents itself, I shall see what I can do,'' she said with resignation. "Now do get back to bed before Mother Charlotte catches you up.''

"I'll say it was to wish you luck.''

"I'll need it. I've never looked forward to anything less in my life.'' Sister Serene thought, but did not say, that with Livvy's added request she anticipated the following evening with even less enthusiasm.

Guy Parrish was the first person she saw as she crossed the hotel's vestibule, which was crowded to overflowing. His tall gray-clad figure was immediately apparent, but it was not just his height or the color of his coat that set him apart; it was his air of belonging to the fashionable throng while being forever apart from it. He was listening to a large pearl-draped dowager. He must have been listening, for he answered her, and yet his expression was so distant that her remarks and the rising drone of chatter surrounding them, punctuated frequently by high-pitched laughter and even louder exclamations of greeting, somehow seemed to infringe on a certain sense of personal privacy.

As soon as he caught sight of Sister Serene, she saw him murmur something to his companion and then cross the lobby to greet her.

"This is a pleasant surprise. I didn't realize you would

be here. Livvy had said your Mother Superior was to attend.''

"I seem to have been railroaded. I was asked to write a speech; now I have to give it.''

"I suppose all of this must make you happy.'' He motioned at the crowd thronging around them.

"I'm happy for the money this will raise, but I must confess I am very unhappy at having to be here tonight.''

"Then we must stick together. I hate it too.''

She smiled. "You don't have to give the after-dinner speech.''

"At least you have a reason for attending. I don't; at least I didn't until now.''

He smiled at her, a smile that eased her awkwardness and made her feel that the evening might be bearable after all.

"Thank you for sending me Arnaud's notes and drawings.''

"I've been wanting to thank you for bringing him to Bellechasse. We've become the best of friends. He's very fond of you. When I told him I was coming to New York, he asked me if I would see you. I didn't think I would then. Now I'll be able to tell him I did, and that I found you looking as serene as ever.''

She laughed. "Concealment is one of the benefits of the habit. I feel far from serene this evening, I can assure you. But do, please, give Arnaud my love. Tell him I think of him often.''

"I shall.''

"My goodness, it really is you! I don't think I should have recognized you in all of that regalia, except Mama just mentioned that Mrs. Wickers's little helper would be here instead of Mother Charlotte.'' Eustacia's midnight blue satin glowed with the same brilliance as her dark hair, in which was perched an even more brilliant diadem of diamonds. She was, Sister Serene realized, as lovely as ever. No, she corrected herself, she was even lovelier; and though the pout to her curved lips had grown rather more petulant, it only served to enhance her air of sophistication. Time had left no other mark on her face, none at all. And yet, should there not be some expression other than boredom, some line to indicate how she had grown, changed?

As Eustacia turned to greet newcomers, motioning to her husband to follow her, Sister Serene wondered what their marriage was like. Guy Parrish shook his head in refusal and turned back to query, "I didn't realize you knew the redoubtable Mrs. Wickers."

"Yes, I used to work for the Caylews as a nursemaid when I was younger."

"That must have been fun." His sarcasm was evident.

"It wasn't so bad."

"I guess that's the explanation for your secret," he said abruptly.

"My secret?"

"It was Nanny Wickers or else the Caylews who drove you to a nunnery, rather than a broken heart as I imagined."

She found herself flushing, particularly since at that moment Templeton Caylew, in passing, paused to greet her. She nodded in return, then hesitantly responded to her companion's conjecture with "Not exactly, Colonel Parrish, though you're not entirely wrong."

Just as abruptly as he had raised the subject he apologized. "You must think me a boor. I've no right to pry, though you do make me curious."

"You're scarcely an open book yourself, Colonel."

"Is anyone?"

"Perhaps not, though what I meant was I noticed you as I came in; you seem to belong and yet not to belong."

"This is Eustacia's milieu, not mine."

"Perhaps, and yet to all appearances you seem entirely at home in this environment, a social creature like the others, at least in manner, in dress, in aspect."

"A social creature sounds proud and vain, empty-headed, unconcerned with social issues. Is that how you see me?"

"Not at all. From what I know of you, that is far from the case. Forgive me if I've offended you."

"Are you offended, Harwood? And over what? Or do you two have some secret?" Eustacia had returned, her eyes raking Sister Serene in unfriendly curiosity. "I understand that you're the one I have to thank for bringing the little boy to Bellechasse."

"Arnaud? Yes, it was so good of you to take him."

"You didn't ask me," Eustacia said pointedly. "I came back to a *fait accompli*. I do think you could have shown the courtesy of consulting me before approaching my husband."

"I'm sorry," Sister Serene began, only to be interrupted by Colonel Parrish.

"Eustacia! I'm only too glad Sister Serene did talk to me. Arnaud's a delightful child; we couldn't ask for a better."

Eustacia was clearly unhappy. "Well, Harwood, he's a nice enough little boy; but I only wish you wouldn't spend *all* of your time with him. You don't spend nearly as much with our little Bella."

"That's ridiculous!" he retorted. "Bella's always with that nurse your mother brought over from England. You don't want her to ride, in case she might fall; I can't take her to the warehouse, in case she'll get dirty; and as for taking her into Memphis—"

"I should think, Harwood, it would be obvious you can't take her to Memphis with those cotton merchants you mix with. Such language—not to mention their questionable friends. Like as not I'd find you'd taken her into that disgusting Cleopatra's Palace." She shuddered in horrified dismay.

"Really, Eustacia, of course I wouldn't take the child there." He looked around the room. "I might say, though, that I consider the crowd at Cleo's equal if not superior to the one here tonight."

"Harwood!" she snapped in indignation; then as his mouth twisted into a wry grin, she pouted. "Why will you insist upon teasing me so?"

"I really wasn't—"

"There you are, Sister Serene." It was a beaming Mrs. Caylew, the hostess at the grandest event of the year, who came bearing down on them. Sister Serene wasn't sorry to see her; she was disturbed to be privy to a domestic quarrel of which she felt, in part at least, to be the cause. "You must come and meet everyone. They're all dying to know absolutely everything about the hospital and the order and just what it is you do and well . . . just about everything. Do come along."

With that she took Sister Serene off to exhibit her like

the grand prize in a raffle. There were vapid questions from equally vapid lips; but Sister Serene discovered that only rarely was information requested, thus few answers were needed. For the most part she smiled and nodded, nodded and smiled, until her jaws ached, hating the superficiality, the meaningless noise, wishing every moment that Mother Charlotte had come, while reminding herself over and over that it was all for the cause.

She spoke no more to Guy Parrish, though she saw him across the room. Wherever he was, Eustacia was not far away. Sister Serene noticed again how little marriage and motherhood had altered her. Her face with its flawless skin and pink-tinged cheeks remained unchanged in expression, except for her eyes, which glowed whenever they fell on her husband, as they so often did, burning with a certain covetousness, inquisitively examining whoever he was in conversation with, glowering if it were a pretty woman.

She was relieved, when at last, the time came to sit down to dinner. As guest of honor, she was placed at the Caylews' table, seated across from Colonel Parrish.

The noise in the room had grown to a fever pitch. The flowing champagne loosened tongues even more; everyone wanted to talk, while no one appeared to be listening. Looking around at the glazed eyes of many of the guests, Sister Serene thought, with a sense of dread, of the speech she must give after the dinner was over. Her tongue grew heavy, and her throat thickened. How was she ever going to be able to utter a word? And if she did talk, how would she ever make them listen? They cared little for the reason they were there; but did that matter? It did, she knew, for if the evening produced insufficient funds it might all be in vain, in her eyes if not in the eyes of the revelers. The building of the hospital might be postponed indefinitely. More than ever she doubted the efficacy of the speech she had written to move these hearts.

"I had a letter from Dr. McChord," Templeton Caylew was saying. "He tells me the school has agreed to accept you. Quite an honor, I may say."

"Yes, Mr. Caylew. I was about to tell you the same thing, and to thank you for supporting my application."

"Might I inquire what this honor is that you have been

granted, Sister Serene?'' There was a hint of a smile in Colonel Parrish's eyes as he posed the question.

"My application to train as a physician at the University of Pennsylvania Medical School has been accepted. I shall be their first woman student.''

"My husband interceded with Dr. McChord on Sister's behalf,'' Mrs. Caylew explained.

"Good of him, I'm sure.'' Colonel Parrish was scrutinizing Sister Serene's face as he spoke; then he went on: "Will you like that?''

She nodded. "It will not be easy, but I'm very anxious to start.''

"And then what shall we call you, Sister or Doctor?'' Mrs. Caylew put in, laughing at her witticism.

"Sister. I shall always be a sister, Mrs. Caylew. Medical training doesn't change my vocation, but it will allow me to practice as a physician in the new hospital. Once the building is constructed, it is in trained physicians that our greatest need will lie.''

"Practice as a physician! A woman doctor! And you recommended a woman for such a profession, Templeton? I am surprised.''

More than surprise, there was shock in Mrs. Vandervoort's voice. Whatever her pronouncement, be it the weather, fashion, morals, or children's upbringing, she was an arbiter of all that was right and proper. The disapproval of a member of her own illustrious family cast a blight over Isabel Caylew's countenance, and it was her son-in-law who came to her rescue.

"Women served exceedingly bravely during the war as nurses on both sides, Mrs. Vandervoort,'' Colonel Parrish put in. "It was a woman who was responsible for saving my father's life when a bullet was lodged in his chest at Chickamauga. I see no reason why they should not most successfully practice medicine. Their hands are delicate, yet firm and strong; and they pay far more attention to precise detail than do we men. You cannot deny that women sew a finer seam than men. If on cloth, why not on flesh?''

"Harwood!'' Eustacia cautioned, catching her mother's pained expression; but Mrs. Vandervoort was eying him with renewed interest.

"I should have thought you, as a Southerner, would hold contrary views, Colonel Parrish. I'm sure we've all heard ad nauseam of the much vaunted delicacy of your Southern ladies."

"I assure you, Mrs. Vandervoort," he replied smoothly, "that rebels, both male and female, are quite as practical as Yankees, no matter what you may have heard to the contrary. Indeed, as conditions have been, our ladies can scarcely afford the luxury of delicacy. That doesn't prevent them from being entirely delightful, as are so many here tonight. I was remarking much the same thing to my wife earlier." He smiled at the older woman swiftly, even cajolingly, the sort of smile that made even her stern countenance crack momentarily into a grimace that might pass for an answering smile.

"Besides," he continued quite seriously, "I believe Sister Serene is eminently suited to the practice of medicine. They say that a good doctor should have the eye of a falcon, the heart of a lion, and the hand of a woman. From all I've heard of her work during the yellow fever epidemic in Memphis, she has these qualities."

Sister Serene's eyes met his in grateful thanks as he finished. That he acknowledged her glance with a slight nod of his head did not pass unnoticed by his wife.

Isabel Caylew smiled at him too, and Templeton Caylew was relieved that Mrs. Vandervoort appeared satisfied; otherwise she would be forever chiding him for espousing a cause of which she did not approve.

"I understand you are here tonight to sell bricks, Sister."

"That is so, Colonel. Each dollar paid for a brick replica will go to purchase actual bricks for the children's hospital. The state has promised to match whatever money is raised here tonight."

"Then I am quite sure that Mrs. Vandervoort intends to buy more than any of us. Were you not telling me earlier, Mrs. Vandervoort, of a magnificent gazebo you are designing for your summer place? How handsome it would be lined with these brick replicas, how impressive your guests would find it—simplicity and charity in the midst of splendor."

There was more than a suggestion of insolence in his tone. Sister Serene caught Eustacia's sharp glare at her husband and her mother's nervous laugh, but Mrs. Vandervoort nodded in satisfaction. "An excellent thought, Colonel. You know, I've had little chance to enjoy your insights until this evening. I must confess, I'm finding you a most interesting gentleman. It's clear to me now why our dear Eustacia chose you over all her other beaus."

"It was most certainly not for my fortune, Mrs. Vandervoort."

"Perhaps not, but obviously Eustacia saw other assets in you, Colonel. When my gazebo is finished, I shall insist upon your being my guest. You must let me have your opinion on it."

"I'm sorry; I come to New York seldom."

"Dear me, I do wish the orchestra would not play quite so loudly," Isabel Caylew complained; but in truth she wished they were playing a great deal louder. She was not at all happy with the turn the conversation had taken. She got along quite well with Eustacia's husband, but she never felt entirely comfortable with him; she didn't understand him as she understood Templeton. That note in his voice, for instance. And one should never speak of money under any circumstances; it simply wasn't done. What would Mrs. Vandervoort think? And nobody, but nobody, ever refused one of her invitations. The smile she extended to Sister Serene, who broke in to ask Drusilla Caylew about her new baby, was quite genuinely a smile of relief.

The dinner was more elegant by far than any that had ever graced the refectory table, but Sister Serene enjoyed it far less than their simple fare. She wasn't used to the number of courses, the richness of the meats and sauces. All she could think about as one plate after another was removed from her place, virtually untouched, was that after all this she had to stand up and speak to these people whom she understood as little as they understood her. She felt utterly sick.

Her speech began badly. Her hand shook so when she first picked up her notes that the words danced before her eyes and her voice quavered as she began to read. It might have been a good speech—perhaps it was; Mother Charlotte had thought so—but she had met these people who were listening to it and she knew the words would scarcely move them. Nor would her halting delivery help.

She paused, seeing Guy Parrish's eyes on her, encouraging

her to go on. She did, but then mid-sentence she stopped and put her notes aside.

"I have, as you see, prepared a speech for you, a speech approved by my superior. But these are words on paper; they cannot convey what this hospital will mean to the impoverished children of our city. I have worked in our small overcrowded, ill-equipped infirmary for several years, treating the children who come to us. I'd like to tell you about some of them."

She began with the story of Frank O'Connor. "He was the first patient I ever tended at Mercy House, a thin, pugnacious, half-starved child, caring for his mother and little sister at an age when boys should be in school. He stole some fruit. I'm not saying what he did was right, even though he didn't do it for himself, but for his mother." Here, quite by chance, Sister Serene's eye fell on Templeton Caylew. His countenance flushed and he hurriedly looked away. "Frank was punished for his act, horribly punished with a beating. It was one of many, the last so severe that he should have been hospitalized; but there was not a corner available at Mercy House to keep him. The wound was dressed, and he was told to return. He did not do so for several days, and by that time the leg was gangrenous. It had to be amputated. Some of you gentlemen may have have had your shoes shined by Frank, hopping around on his wooden stump. We got him the shoeshine box to keep him from a life of begging. A poor substitute for a leg that might have been saved, I think you'll agree.

"Vicky, his little sister, was the frailest, gentlest little child. Her lungs were weak; she was in need of constant care. She came down with a cold, but for fear of being a nuisance did not come to Mercy House until pneumonia had set in. The love of her life was flowers—flowers of all kinds—but her favorite was the little briar rose. As she was dying, she told me . . . " Sister Serene's voice cracked. She stopped and drew a deep breath before going on. "She told me that she will be waiting for me in heaven with flowers—lots and lots of flowers.

"The sisters have saved many lives, though many could not be saved because of the lack of beds, pharmaceutical and surgical supplies, equipment of every kind, a sterile area for operations, and physicians to perform them. Every time a child has died I think of Vicky, waiting for them in heaven, her arms full of flowers.''

Sister Serene went on to talk of other cases, of children with birth defects, of the lame, of the sightless, of those who spent their short span of life on the city streets. She paused, remembering Five Points, and her voice grew husky. "All this is happening right now, here in New York, not in some dark and distant land. These children are American children, our children. We of the Order of St. Catharine do what we can, but there is simply never enough of anything—nothing, that is, except love. That we give willingly, but I can assure you we give it in no greater degree than the children return it to us.

"That, in essence, is what the speech I was prepared to give was all about—that we receive so very much more than we give." She glanced briefly down at the paper she had set aside. "My notes say that God loves a cheerful giver. That, I am sure, is true; we ask for nothing to be given begrudgingly. I have noted also that the truly generous are the truly wise. I happen to subscribe to that belief, though there may be some here who would argue with it. But, in closing, all I really wish to say is thank you on behalf of all our children for listening to their story.''

There was silence as she sat down. While she had been speaking, the trembling of her hands had stopped; she had forgotten all about those listening and felt just as if she were back in the infirmary. Sitting back in her place at the table, however, looking around at the blank elegant faces staring at her, she realized where she was and felt her hands begin to tremble once again. Then the applause rang out, and first one gentleman rose, then another and another, until the entire audience was on its feet and clapping, clapping—and giving, giving.

Isabel Caylew was elated. A thoroughly worthy cause did so much to justify the lavishness of the evening. Sister Serene heard her loud whisper to Mrs. Vandervoort: "You know originally Mother Charlotte was to give this speech, but I'm so glad I persuaded her to allow Sister Serene to do it in her stead.''

If one were to judge the success of Sister Serene's speech by the amount of money raised in the sale of the brick replicas that followed it, it was a triumph. If one were to judge by the compliments she received afterwards, the same conclusion must be drawn. Sister Serene, however, judged its effect by one listener, and one only.

"Your words were truly moving." Guy Parrish was the first to congratulate her.

She smiled, raising her eyes heavenward for a moment. "I must confess, I did have help."

"Alas, we poor sinners have no such resources," he teased. "I've always been of the opinion that the gods answer our prayers only when they wish to punish us; but you're determined to shake all my convictions. It almost makes me wish you would pray for me.

"But I do, Colonel Parrish," she replied quite seriously. "Daily."

"You shouldn't have admitted that, for if that's so it weakens your case against the efficacy of prayer. But then, no doubt you'll counter with 'though a seraph may pray for a sinner, a sinner must pray for himself.'"

"No matter what you say, Colonel Parrish, I remain convinced that you are, at heart, a sincere and good man. Nothing will convince me otherwise."

"How little you know me!" he mocked, yet she thought she could detect a wistful note beneath the scorn.

Catching sight of Eustacia's eyes fixed on her with a far from friendly stare, Sister Serene turned to be greeted by a pale, effete gentleman.

"Nathan, Nathan Caylew," he reminded at her obvious lack of recognition. "You were magnificent, Mar—Sister, I mean." His eyes were fixed on her adoringly as he added, "Absolutely magnificent."

Sister Serene saw no more of Guy Parrish that evening. It was only after she had returned to Mercy House that she realized she had forgotten to argue Livvy's case.

SEVEN

Just as Dr. McChord had promised, from the moment of her arrival at the University Medical School Sister Serene began an education such as no other of her sex had yet received.

As Dr. McChord had also predicted, her fellow students heartily disliked her. Some disliked her because she was a woman, others because she was not woman enough. Some disliked her thinking her a Catholic; others, who were Catholics themselves, disliked her because they believed only Catholics had the right to take the veil. There was no pleasing them; nor did Sister Serene waste her energies in trying. A vote had been taken prior to her first lecture, mandating trousers for all. She took her place minus her flaring white headdress and squared white collar, but very definitely wearing a dress, black and decorated only by a crucifix. She ignored the muttered cries of derision, opened her notebook with precision, and concentrated all her attention on the lecturer.

There were times during that first year when she had cause to wonder whether the goriest, the least savory, the most intricate dissections were saved for her to perform; but one thing she had learned in the order was to obey without question or demur. Recognizing she would never be welcomed by either her fellow students or the physician-lecturers, she put all her efforts into her work, her reading, laboratory experiments, dissections, and memorization of names and definitions that Dr. McChord might call upon her to recite when she crossed his path in the hall or the classroom. In the operating room, other students might faint without undue criticism; she knew she could not. She never withdrew her eyes from anything, never flinched. Not a word of praise was ever directed to her, no matter how well she performed, but she did not work for praise; she worked only to achieve her goal: the diploma that would allow her to work as a physician.

Her fellow medical students might not jeer at her, as she had heard of other women in medical training being jeered, but they clearly delighted in telling coarse, lewd stories in her presence, their voices increasing in volume as their epithets grew more obscene. They were like naughty school-boys, she thought, trying to tempt the wrath of God. Their erotic imagination knew no bounds as they recounted in graphic detail their amorous conquests, slyly nudging one another while watching her out of the corners of their eyes, longing for her to protest; but she disappointed them by continuing to work alongside them silently, unobtrusively. Her lack of response annoyed them far more than their stories upset her, but still their attempts to humiliate her never ceased. Their obscenities, Sister Serene decided, were as much a part of their speech as the groans and oaths that accompanied each assigned laboratory task or reading.

If she won no friends by not reacting to their goading, she also won none by refusing to complain with the rest of the student body at the amount of work thrust upon them and the impossible deadlines set for its completion. Still, as time passed, though the other students might not like her, they came to accept her, perhaps because, as Dr. McChord had observed, she was a nun rather than a woman; and as a nun she placed no threat to them in the world they would eventually enter.

If their ways changed little, Sister Serene's changed not at all. Once, as a boastful Don Juan had finished a particularly graphic recounting of his previous night's performance—a superhuman feat—to her surprise, he had turned to her with a sheepish apology. "Sorry, Sister. Didn't realize you were there."

At her unperturbed response—"Sorry for what? Were you waiting to use the microscope?"—the student looked away, winking at his friends in bravado, but with a flushed face. That she never got angry or embarrassed, that she never rebuked them or tried to reform them was puzzling. They didn't know what to make of her.

"If you were a priest, I wouldn't hate confession half as much," a young Catholic from Chicago confided to her. It was the nearest any of them came to paying her a compliment.

She sometimes speculated whether the distant and pedantic Dr. McChord, who ruled his students with a rod of iron, had ever been as coarse and as lewd as these young men. Why, because their realm of study was the human body, must they dwell so often and so specifically on its excretory functions? Why must they lace all their remarks with references to those functions, or else the sexual organs and the acts they performed? Why did the brain or the heart never excite similar interest? She heard expletives freely used in those hallowed halls such as she had never heard uttered in the lowest corners of the Five Points district.

It was, indeed, an education.

One afternoon as she was observing an appendectomy, a message came that she was wanted immediately in Dr. McChord's office.

It was unusual to be called away from an operation. As she pulled off her overall, she searched her mind for anything she might have done wrong or omitted to do. Finding nothing, she became convinced that it must mean something was wrong at Mercy House, or with her mother in Newport.

She was quite breathless by the time she entered the room and not at all prepared to see the person who awaited her.

"Colonel Parrish!"

Her surprise was obvious and to be expected, but his hesitation at the sight of her was less understandable.

"I came to talk to you about Livvy, Sister Serene," he began and then stopped abruptly.

"Is she all right?" she asked quickly.

"Yes, yes, quite," he assured her.

"That's good." She breathed a sigh of relief. "We're not usually called in here except for some infringement, or an emergency of some sort."

"I'm sorry. I didn't mean to alarm you. I was passing through Philadelphia on my way to New York to see Livvy and thought to . . ." He broke off again, seeming distracted. Ever since she'd entered he'd been studying her with unusual concentration. "You must excuse me; it's just that you seem so different."

She put her hand to her head. "It's the coif. Dr. Mc-Chord didn't want me to wear it. I suppose he was right; it would be cumbersome here. We often have to crowd together in observing the physicians at work."

"Your hair is—"

"Messy, I expect." She brushed it back with her hand. "I came in a hurry. I thought something must be wrong."

"I didn't mean that. I meant . . . I'd always imagined it must be dark brown, the same color as your eyebrows, but it's . . . it's light, quite golden."

She flushed and said quickly, matter-of-factly, "You said you wanted to see me about Livvy."

"Yes. It's not that there's anything wrong, but I am concerned." He looked around Dr. McChord's neat office. "I don't know; I find it difficult to talk here, and I don't think you feel particularly comfortable. I wonder, would it be permissible to meet for dinner? My hotel is probably not the place, but perhaps you could suggest somewhere suitable." Seeing her hesitation, he reiterated, "I really do need to talk about Livvy."

She hesitated no longer. "There is a small restaurant where I go on occasion, the Old Heidelberg. It's plain but clean, and the food is good; and it has the added advantage, for me at least, of being inexpensive and close to where I board on Spruce Street."

He was there when she arrived, sitting in the corner at one of the checker-cloth-covered tables; but he got up as soon as he caught sight of her. As he pulled back her chair, he said, "I'm glad you came. I thought at the last moment you might discover something in your Rule to prevent it."

She laughed. "There's nothing in the Rule against eating dinner, and I do recommend the wiener schnitzel."

"Good, that saves me from having to study the menu." Instead he studied her face in the light of the candle in the middle of the table. "You seem pale. I noticed that when I saw you earlier. How are you finding it—difficult?"

"It's not easy," she admitted for the first time. "It's not only the studies, working till midnight and rising at dawn—that's the only way I know of to get everything done—but there's the loneliness of having no one to talk to. Still, I know that each day brings me one day closer to my goal.''

"And that is?"

"To be able to work—I refuse to say practice, because for me it sounds like experimentation—as a physician. Our new hospital's nearing completion. Mother Charlotte is ecstatic about the progress that's been made.''

"So is my *belle*-mère. From her impatience, I think she must be planning to open it with another of her gaudy galas.''

Though Sister Serene laughed, she reminded him, "You have to admit, Colonel Parrish, that without her help we would never be so close to having this hospital. Mother Charlotte's dreamed and schemed and prayed for it for years.''

He held up a restraining hand. "I know, I know. God works in strange ways.''

"Yes, He does.'' She smiled across at him. "Let me assure you that He does.''

He didn't reply at once; when he did it was to remark, "You've a very lovely smile. I enjoy pretty smiles, but yours is particularly intriguing. There's something secret about it. I keep wondering what's behind it.''

"A Buddha-like smile?'' She shook her head. "I'm no enigma.''

"I didn't mean that exactly, but sometimes it's as though you were sharing some quiet amusement with someone inside. It's like your name, Serene, though perhaps Serene isn't really your name.''

"As a matter of fact, it isn't. Mother Charlotte gave it to me when I came into the order, at a time when I was very far from serene. I think it was her way of reminding me that such a state was possible. It worked—I have grown into a state that might be described as serenity.''

"That must be nice.'' He ran his finger thoughtfully along the stem of his glass as he repeated, "That must, indeed, be nice. But your given name, your baptismal name, what is that? Or is that another of your deep, dark secrets?''

"Of course not. In fact, Dr. McChord refuses to call me

Sister Serene; to him I am Miss Fanshawe, or sometimes just Fanshawe." Then she added softly, almost shyly, "My Christian name is Damaris."

"Damaris, Damaris. Don't tell me." He thought for a moment. "I have it; she was the Athenian converted by St. Paul."

"For a man who's a nonbeliever, Colonel Parrish, you know a great deal about the scriptures."

"I was force-fed as a child, and unfortunately what we learn in those early years usually remains lodged in the brain to come back and haunt us when we least care about it, when we're older and, hopefully, wiser. All of God's religions have pulled man apart more than they've helped him put himself together."

"I know there are points on which we disagree, Colonel; that doesn't prevent me from liking you. It may even surprise you to know that there are aspects of your outlook on life with which I find myself quite in agreement. I do wonder, though, whether . . ." She stopped before completing the sentence.

"Go on," he prompted.

"Well, I've found myself wondering whether it was the war that changed your belief to disbelief, at the same time as it developed in you that mature judgment I so admire."

He remained silent.

"I know, I shouldn't have said anything, should I? You're going to say it's none of my concern, and you're right. I should realize from what I know of you that it's not something you care to talk about."

He pursed his lips, slowly shaking his head. "No, I don't."

A silence ensued, a silence Damaris broke at last with, "When we were at Mrs. Caylew's dinner at the Waldorf I heard you mention your father was wounded at Chickamauga. Mine was killed there. He was a chaplain with the Army of the Cumberland."

"I'm sorry. Chickamauga is an Indian word meaning the River of Death. Prophetic, the way things turned out, as the Indians so often are. My brother died there too. He saw my father fall and rode out to help him. A sniper got him as he bent down to pick him up. Any Reb was fair game, but I'm sure it wasn't Nicholas he was shooting at;

it was Father. The North had put an enormous reward up
for the man who could kill General Parrish. I saw what
happened, but I only had time to push Nicholas's body
aside and grab Father. Nicholas may have been dead then,
but I'll never know for sure. I did know I couldn't get
them both back. There was a hailstorm of fire; and by the
time I was able to make my way back to where he'd been,
there were bodies strewn everywhere. I couldn't find him.
His body wasn't identified till long after. I've often thought
about bringing back Father and leaving Nicholas. Those in
command were pleased, of course; they thought I'd shown
that mature judgment you just mentioned. Father mourned
Nicholas, but I guess he too thought I'd done right. But
I've always wondered. I probably always will.''

He stopped talking and looked down; they sat in silence
for a time, she watching his face in the flickering candlelight.

"My father's buried there somewhere," she said at last.
"It's strange he should have died in a battle for Tennessee.
That's where he was born, you see. When his parents
died, he came North to Rhode Island and became an
Episcopal priest, like the uncle who'd raised him. He
agonized over joining in the fight too; I remember the day
he made his decision to go.'' Her face grew solemn,
thoughtful. "I daresay, if he was to die in battle, he would
have preferred to lie at Chickamauga rather than Gettys-
burg. He always talked of going back, so perhaps it was a
sort of homecoming.'' She paused. "He promised he'd
take me there one day. I guess that's why when I was in
Memphis I had a sense of going home . . . of belonging.''

"I didn't, not even though I was born there, not until
these past few years—not, in fact, until after I began to
manage Bellechasse, to work the soil myself. Maybe I
made a deliberate attempt to separate myself from the
place. Father always made the point that Nicholas was the
one to take over; he trained him for that. I decided if he
didn't want me to work, then I'd have a good time, and I
did. That didn't sit well with Father. He didn't understand
play, not till the war. Then I always thought his greatest
game began. He loved it; I guess that's why he did so well
at it. Nothing would stop him; nothing did. He accused me
of being halfhearted. He was right; I was, at least at the
beginning. He said if I wasn't going to fight like Nicholas,

he didn't know why I'd bothered to come back from England.''

"Why did you?''

"Romantic notions, family pride, stupidity—call it what you will.'' He shrugged. "I struggled with my conscience over the problem of secession. I believed then and still do in a federal union of states; we've only got to look at the problems of Europe to see what division of territory brings. Having reached that sensible conclusion, I chucked it aside and threw in my lot with Father and Nicholas.

"I'd talked to men who'd fought at Waterloo, and I arrived with grand notions of war being a gentleman's game. That was crushed forever at Shiloh. I had to order green soldiers into battle. Some had never before held a gun; those who had often had never used one on more than a squirrel that couldn't fire back at them. There was no ammunition to spare for practice. They were a bunch of youthful innocents, and I had to order them to fight to the finish.

"I could scarcely blame those who ran, and an awful lot of them did; it was the ones who stayed and held on no matter what that surprised me. Everyone could see that the slackers got away with their hides, leaving the stalwarts to take on the enemy time and again; and each time more and more of them fell. Seventy percent of them died in the first hour of that battle. Those that came through, instead of being commended for their valor, given food and rest, had to go back in again. I watched those boys age in front of my eyes; I saw their bravery exploited, not rewarded.

"There were no civilized rules of warfare, the sort of thing I'd read about in history books, no moralities, no restraints; it was total war, one side bent on annihilating the other, and civilization was dead. It was sheer madness.

"Where was God, if there was a God at Shiloh? I thought a lot about it, too much, especially in the beginning. I kept trying to make sense of it; that was my trouble. War, like religion, is pure emotion; we can't think our way into it. Father and Nicholas didn't. It wasn't until I found out Mother had been killed, shot in our own home, that I stopped thinking and started acting. That was when Father began to like me more and I began to like myself less, a lot less.''

He stopped talking, and she reached across the table to touch his hand for a moment. He looked up, but neither of them spoke for a time.

"We all have to make choices—decisions that aren't easy—and we can never know for sure that they're right; we simply do the best we can at the time. Why are some saved while others die? I've agonized over that; it's really what brought me to the order and here to this training. It's something that haunts me, that will continue to haunt me. But the fact is that some do die while others survive. I was a survivor, and so are you. I have to believe there's a reason for being here."

She saw him shake his head in disbelief. "No, don't scoff! Someone once told me, after a dark night of my soul when I questioned my survival, that I was here for a reason, and I felt much as you do when I heard it. Now I know that was right. There is always something that can be done to make the world a better place."

He shrugged. "For you perhaps it makes sense. I can't see where my survival has benefited anything."

"You did save Bellechasse. Perhaps you did it better than either your father or Nicholas could have."

"I was full of plans. I was determined to make them succeed, and they did; but how much longer it would have taken without Caylew money. I'm not talking about my wife's dowry; that was hers, not mine. But I did force Caylew to make reparation for commodities he had purloined before I would agree to marry Eustacia."

"Does it really matter how you did it? The point is you made it happen."

"Yes, I made it happen," he agreed bitterly. "I guess, for better or worse, I do often make things happen. I made Eustacia fall in love with me by not becoming her adoring swain like all the rest. I married her knowing I didn't love her. I even told her as much, though then I did believe that would change, and that she would become less . . . less obsessive."

He looked over at her, realizing he'd never spoken of any of this to anyone before, wondering what it was about her that made him open his heart.

For her part, Damaris realized that time had not changed his relationship with Eustacia. Was it love, she wondered, that had made Eustacia's eyes follow him everywhere as they had on the night of the charity dinner, or was it because, though married to this man, she had never possessed him as she had that band of young men known as Eustacia's Castoffs?

"What would you have done if Nicholas had survived to run Bellechasse?" she asked.

"I'd have finished law, gone into practice."

"And then what?"

"Who knows? I might have ended up running for office."

She made no immediate reply. Then she asked, "Well, why don't you?"

"You may not be aware of it, but Republicans are not particularly popular in my part of the country. And my sympathies are still with Lincoln's party, despite the disasters wrought upon us by the carpetbaggers. That would never have happened had he lived; I'm sure of it."

"Lincoln made things happen, and you've said that you can also make things happen. You did it with Bellechasse, you could in Congress or in the legislature if you wanted to."

He smiled. "I suppose it's because of your desire to save people that you persist in trying to make me believe there's a reason for being."

"You've got lots of reasons. There's Bella, and Arnaud. You've given him a start in life few boys have. I'm not thinking of the material things you've given him, but the way you're bringing him up. He admires you tremendously; more than that, he loves you. His letters are full of you. You may impugn your own motives, but he sees you with the clear eyes of a child, and he likes what he sees. Livvy too—"

Laughing, he shook his head. "Do spare me. Your reasons for my survival are overwhelming."

"I'm serious, Guy. Why shouldn't you be encouraged just as much as you encourage others, like the boys at Shiloh, like Arnaud? You've said yourself that those who stay and fight, those who face up to things the way they are and don't run away, should be rewarded. Being strong doesn't mean we don't need encouragement and support too."

"Who supports and encourages you, Damaris?" he asked quietly.

That moment, when they called one another by their given names for the first time, signaled an abrupt and, they realized, perilous change in their relationship. It was a change they recognized as, across the table, their eyes met. It was a solemn moment during which they both knew that the next word might put them across the boundary of their safe world into a possibly terrible, possibly wonderful, but certainly untenable place from which there would be no returning.

"It's getting late. You came to talk about Livvy," she reminded him abruptly.

"Yes, that's right, I did. She's set on this life of yours; she tells me she is happy, but I wanted to hear it from you. You've called my judgment mature earlier; rather than argue the point, I'll accept that as a compliment."

"It was no more than the truth."

"Then you must take it as the truth that I respect your judgment too, and that is why I want you to tell me about Livvy."

"She is happy in what she's doing. I give you my word on that. And you can calm your fears of losing your sister. Mother Charlotte has told me that after profession she plans to send Livvy to take over St. Catharine's School in Memphis. She'll be close to you."

"And you?"

The question was simply put, but again she sensed the danger. "I shall never return to Memphis," she answered.

BOOK FIVE

Yellow Jack

'Tis the Destroyer, or the Devil,
that scatters plagues about
the world. . . . [He]
impregnates the air with such
malignant salts as, meeting
with the salt of our
microcosm, shall immediately
cast us into that fermentation
and putrefaction which will
utterly dissolve all the vital
ties within us.

Cotton Mather
The Wonders of the
Invisible World

ONE

Guy Parrish could pinpoint to the day, to the hour, when life with Eustacia had become unendurable for him.

What irony, he thought, that when he, who had never been in love, should at last succumb, it must be with one to whom he could never speak of it, one he could never touch, could never hold.

She had awakened feelings in him that he thought dead, not only those feelings he held for her, but those that were released for his daughter, for Arnaud. It was as though the floodgates that had long held back his emotions were suddenly opened. From that moment, he returned to life; he became capable of warmth, of delight, capable of love. But while he was able to open himself to others, he could not even look on the one who had made that happen.

He had wondered at his own perversity—falling in love with one so utterly unobtainable. Did he want only those things he could not have? But he knew it was more than that. His feelings for this woman were different from any he had ever felt before. He loved her, knowing he could never speak of it to her or to anyone; it had even been difficult to admit it to himself. He loved her because instinctively, without intent, she had touched some deep and hidden part of him and he would never be the same again.

Exactly how or why that could have happened in the few hours he spent with Damaris Fanshawe in that tiny Philadelphia restaurant, he couldn't say; he knew only that it was so. That she was forever forbidden to him, not just because of his marriage—somehow he never thought of his one-sided relationship with Eustacia as true marriage—but more particularly because of her own professed state, added poignancy but changed nothing.

It was Damaris Fanshawe sitting across from him that evening at the Old Heidelberg with the candlelight reflecting the gold of her hair, not the untouchable Sister Serene in her sweeping starched coif, who was imprinted on his memory. He had always been conscious of beauty in women. From the first he had been aware of the directness and honesty of her clear blue eyes, yet only when he saw her freed from that flaring headdress had he realized her special loveliness, not symmetric like Eustacia's, but impelling and exciting. What he remembered about her was far more abiding than mere physical attributes—her candid gaze and golden hair, tied back tightly yet with wisps escaping to brush her cheek, and that quiet, secretive smile. There was a maturity about her he'd never before seen in a woman, not maturity in years—he guessed her to be not very much older than Livvy—but she had the air of one who had faced life, come to grips with its problems, and taken her stand. He wondered what she had been like as a child, what path had led her to adopt the anomalous role of a nun. He remembered her slender yet capable hands moving to make a point in her discussion. He tried not to remember the crucifix that hung around her neck.

Ever since that morning at St. Catharine's School in Memphis when she had come in, her hand in Arnaud's, he had sensed she aroused something in him beyond the antagonism he felt. He had been puzzled by his feelings, by his growing interest when she had visited Bellechasse, which had been followed by an unexpected sense of pride at her triumph at the charity ball at the Waldorf. Then too he had had to admit to himself that his reason for stopping to see her in Philadelphia had not only been to talk about Livvy. He had never guessed, however, how devastating the effect of that visit would be.

The strange thing was that Eustacia, with an uncanny sense of intuition, suspected almost immediately that something had happened to him. How, he did not know; for though he was increasingly burdened by her cloying, suffocating affection, he reacted against it less than usual, perhaps from a sense of guilt at being unfaithful to her in thought, if not in fact. To him, their life seemed unaltered; he made no objection when Eustacia, sometimes with little Bella and her nursemaid in tow, rode out in the gig to watch him at work; indeed, he went out of his way to spend as much time with her as he could. When he made love to her, he thought he did so with equal fervor, yet he was haunted by an odd sense of infidelity. He cursed himself for a fool—how was it possible for a man to be unfaithful in making love to his wife—yet some part of him knew it was not of Eustacia he thought in those moments of intimacy. He wished he could forgo that marital duty that seemed to leave him with a nagging self-inflicted censure, yet that was the only way he knew to quiet Eustacia's suspicions.

Even so, she knew—he was sure of it—and she clung to him more tightly than ever, demanding explanations whenever he was away from her. The avidity of her possessiveness grew at equal pace with his own certainty of the utter futility of their marriage.

She needn't have worried about losing him, he thought with a sense of bitterness. There was no possibility of his being untrue to her with the only one that mattered. He resolved never to see Damaris again, never even to be in the same room with her. But no sooner was that resolution made than it had been set aside.

Eustacia had been surprised when, almost without demur, he had agreed to go to New York for the reception her mother was giving to celebrate the opening of St. Catharine's Hospital for Children. Eustacia had carefully gone over all the arguments he would raise against the journey and marshaled her arguments. Then, with scarcely a protest, he had agreed it would make a pleasant change.

Then and there Eustacia had decided that her husband must have become infatuated with someone in New York, not, as she had orginally assumed, some primping Tennessee belle. She knew that something had happened to change him; she could feel it whenever he touched her, and while he made love to her. Something was different in a way she found hard to define. She was sure that it was a woman who had made the change; she was equally sure that woman was not herself. She had tried so hard to make him love her, and she knew she had failed. She hated to fail. She would not fail. No one would ever take him from her.

In her mind she ran over the list of their New York friends, with particular attention to the prettiest women. It was not a short list; her husband attracted women, as she well knew. Hadn't he attracted her where others could not? Still, she could not remember when he had been parted from her for any length of time. In New York she saw more of him than in Memphis, where he so often spirited himself away all day in the fields or the warehouse or at the new Cotton Exchange. When she complained, he said it was his work; but she was sure that he did it to get away from her. She'd always been pleased when he was with her in New York, where she had less difficulty in keeping him close to her side.

For some time Templeton Caylew had repeatedly offered, even insisted, that Guy Parrish join him in his business. Her father, Eustacia knew, had a sneaking sense of her husband's worth, even though he'd never particularly liked him. She had repeatedly pressed Harwood to accept her father's offer, desisting only from a sense that her stringent advocacy might serve to strengthen his resolve against the plan. But she wanted it most dearly. She hated Tennessee. If it were not for Harwood she would never put foot in the state again; it was remote, uninteresting, and worst of all it lacked all the sophistication she had been born to. She waited for the right moment to argue for the move to New York, where, rather than making an annual visit to enjoy its cosmopolitan delights, she would be able to take her proper place in the Four Hundred, her dear Harwood at her side.

So far Guy Parrish had adamantly refused to consider it. Having tried so hard to persuade him to change his mind, she began to wonder whether he would now acquiesce, and, if he did, how she would feel. Not the joy of victory; she might prefer life in New York, yet it would scarcely be a fortuitous move if she risked losing the husband she had chosen and gone to great lengths to gain. Besides, the very thought of being set aside for another woman was insupportable.

As they were preparing for her mother's reception, she came up behind him as he was buttoning his shirt before the mirror, put her arms around him, removed his hands from the buttons, and began doing them up in his stead. He picked up his cravat and put it around his neck, and again she took it from his hands, arranged it under his collar, and tied the knot for him.

"Have you thought any more of Papa's offer, Harwood? He does so want you to go in with him. While I don't look forward to the day Papa is no longer with us, still, you must realize that if you accept you would eventually have everything. You know Lawrence is far too unsteady to take over, and all Nathan wants to do is to become a poet. I guess Mama wouldn't mind so much if only his verse weren't quite so . . . so plodding."

"It may improve, once some fire is lit inside him."

"How do you suppose that would happen, Harwood?" she demanded, suddenly very still, her hold on him tightening.

"I don't know, Eustacia. I'm a planter, not a poet. But I suppose that the greatest poetry has been written by men suffering under some affliction. Nathan at the moment is too comfortable. He gets just about everything he wants."

"Do you mean if he were in love?"

"Nathan always seems to be in love, but perhaps unrequited love might elicit some response."

Guy turned away from the mirror and gently removed Eustacia's hands from around him. "You'd better get dressed. You know how your mother detests late arrivals."

But Eustacia made no move to finish her toilette. Instead she returned to her original question. "Papa really wants you in with him, Harwood. Would you mind spending more time in New York?"

Guy turned away. More time in New York? He'd never thought of being anywhere but Bellechasse, but he remembered Damaris saying she would never return to Memphis. He had been wondering what he would say when he saw her that night; quite suddenly he found himself wondering how he could abide seeing no more of her than that.

"I'll think about it, Eustacia. Come along or we'll be hopelessly late."

It was the first time he'd offered to even consider her father's offer, and his concern about being tardy for the sort of affair he usually hated was cause for dismay.

Rather than being elated at having won, Eustacia became convinced that her suspicions were justified.

These suspicions deepened after their arrival as she watched his eyes searching the room. All evening he looked, but whoever he was looking for could not be there; she was sure of it. Yet that puzzled her even more. Everyone who was anyone was present. To be absent from such an occasion would have been a slight not only to her mother but to the entire Vandervoort clan; and she knew of no one, except perhaps her husband, who would have such fortitude. To be uninvited would have meant a deliberate snub on her mother's part. She would surely have heard of that. Eustacia studied the gathering with care, but noticed no obvious absences.

"Lavinia." Eustacia greeted her sister-in-law with a perfunctory kiss on the cheek. How odd these women were who took the veil, Eustacia thought as she surveyed her black habit. Still, Lavinia had always been one for causes. "I suppose I should call you Sister Lavinia now."

"Lavinia is fine." Livvy smiled, her eyes seeming larger than ever beneath the white wimple. "How are you, Eustacia?"

"Well enough."

"And my dear little Bella?"

"She's fine," Eustacia said, hurrying to change the topic to one that might lead to something more fruitful. After all, Harwood was so fond of his sister, perhaps she might know something. "Mother Charlotte says you're to take over the school in Memphis. That should make your brother happy."

"I think it does," his sister agreed.

"I've been concerned about him, though," Eustacia hazarded. "He seems distracted somehow; I can't understand why. Has he said anything to you?"

"No. Though now you mention it, I did sense something of the sort when I talked to him just now. Perhaps he's having problems at Bellechasse."

"Everything seems to be going swimmingly with his ventures on his dear plantation." Eustacia's asperity at having to share him, even with Bellechasse, surfaced in her voice.

"Well, that's a relief. Perhaps it's about Arnaud then.

He said he's been wondering what will be to his best advantage in arranging his schooling."

"That boy!" Eustacia exploded. "I swear he thinks more of him than our own little Bella."

"Oh, Eustacia, that's not so. He loves Bella. I just meant Guy's considering whether Arnaud should be prepared to enter the University of the South, or whether he would be better off with a Northern education. I asked what Arnaud would prefer, and Guy said he'd talked to him and for his part all he wanted was to remain at Bellechasse, but of course he must be properly educated. Guy doesn't want to make arbitrary choices for him. I can appreciate that, having been dispatched to England without being allowed to voice my own wishes. I was young, I know, but I hated having to go."

"I know. You've mentioned it before," Eustacia responded with disinterest, feeling this rambling conversation was getting her nowhere nearer to understanding the change in Harwood.

"Sorry, I suppose I have. Anyway, I suggested Guy talk the matter over with Sister Serene. Arnaud still writes to her. She found him, you know."

"I'm well aware that she did," Eustacia responded with some distaste, looking around the room. "I haven't noticed her here this evening."

"No, she's not. Mother Charlotte was rather distressed that she didn't come. She's getting very close to her final exams. She didn't feel she should leave. I hope your father, who was so helpful in getting her admitted to the medical school, understands and doesn't consider her absence a lack of respect."

"I don't suppose he's even noticed it," Eustacia responded unconcernedly, yet sensing it odd that Sister Serene, examinations notwithstanding, had not made every effort to put in an appearance. She was, after all, the star of the order, the one they had chosen to train as a physician especially for this hospital.

Was it possible that Harwood . . . The thought crossed Eustacia's mind for an instant before she dismissed the idea as not only implausible but quite impossible.

Though Eustacia wasn't aware of it, she and her husband were, at that moment, thinking much the same thing.

It was quite impossible, and it had been ridiculous of him to come all that way just to see her for a moment. They couldn't even have talked together except in generalities.

"I do hope you'll come to see me now the gazebo is completed, Colonel Parrish," Mrs. Vandervoort was saying. "You did help in the design, you know. I followed your advice and papered the walls with those brick replicas. It does give a rather nice effect."

"I'm sure the order must have found it beneficial too."

"Oh, they did—I can assure you that they did—most beneficial. I won't say that I alone was responsible for this hospital being built, but without my contribution I don't think this affair of Isabel's would be being held quite this soon." She beamed with satisfaction that someone, at least, had acknowledged her generosity. Mrs. Vandervoort only wished she had chosen to take up the order as her personal charity before Isabel had. She was beginning to put on airs about it and taking far too much credit.

"I'm quite sure everyone is well aware of your magnanimity, Mrs. Vandervoort." Guy smiled, and Mrs. Vandervoort decided yet again that Eustacia had known what she was about when she had chosen him as her husband.

"I haven't seen that nun Templeton was instrumental in having admitted to medical school. A foolish action on his part; I've told him so. I daresay she failed to stay the course."

"No." A shadow crossed his face for an instant. "No, she didn't fail. I understand she's preparing to take final exams. She'll come to the new hospital as a physician."

"Well, I still don't approve. I've told both Templeton and Isabel as much. A woman doctor, what next! She's sharp enough, eloquent in a way, but far too outspoken, particularly for one of her calling. I think the idea of a nun doing anything so worldly is quite disgusting."

"It's true, they're not a very worldly bunch," Guy agreed. The depth of his disappointment at not seeing her that evening had served only to re-emphasize the depth of his feeling for her. "In the world but not of the world," he murmured, half to himself.

"Oh, Colonel, isn't that a little sacrilegious, giving these ladies more than their due. Of course I know you always did champion her. What was that you said about her being eagle-eyed?''

"It's a proverb, Mrs. Vandervoort. A good doctor needs the eye of a falcon, the heart of a lion, and the hand of a woman.''

Eustacia came up, slipping her arm through his. "Falcons and lions, how frightfully medieval. I've come to ask your opinion, Aunt Vandervoort. Don't you think that Harwood should accept Papa's offer to go in with him?''

"I do, indeed. We would all delight in seeing more of him.''

"I'm sorry to disappoint both of you, but I've made up my mind against it. Bellechasse gives me quite enough to do. I shan't consider moving North.''

He mustn't come back to New York, Parrish thought. It was dangerous. He would only want to see her again, and he must not, not ever.

Eustacia was left with mixed emotions. She much preferred life in New York, yet she'd far rather see Harwood immersed in his beloved plantation than immersed in an affair with another woman. And she sensed from the finality of his words that he had thought it over and reached the same conclusion.

Guy Parrish returned to Memphis determined to bury himself in his work, but that was not enough. It was then he remembered Damaris's prompting and decided to throw his hat into the political arena by campaigning for a seat in the state legislature. Even a severe trouncing, which was likely given his known sympathy with Lincoln's party, would give him wounds to lick that would, for a time at least, take his mind from the wound that hurt him most.

He looked first at the Radicals, supposed supporters of Lincoln, but he suspected that Lincoln would have been horrified at the conglomeration of carpetbaggers, freedmen, and turncoats that carried his banner and subverted his aims. His fellow planters, in fact most of the gentlemen in Shelby County, were Conservatives, now coming to call themselves Democrats, yet their view was narrow too, and tainted by activities of the newly formed Klan.

In the end he had run as an Independent, which meant he received support from neither party. His friends could not understand why a son of General Parrish, and a man who had himself fought so long and so hard for the cause, would not align himself with the Conservatives. But because he was a Parrish, because he had staked his own life so many times for the cause, and because, despite this anomaly of political independence, he was one of them, people listened to him; and though they hated to admit it at first, what Guy Parrish said made sense.

The worst turmoil of Reconstruction was over, but Memphis was far from settled. Former slaves had been given their freedom, but little else. Those from Memphis, turning down the offer of a mule and forty acres of land, had preferred to stay in the city and were soon joined by thousands more who roamed the streets and fought with the Irish workingmen on the riverfront for the means to subsist. Parrish argued for their education; he argued for their employment; he argued for their acceptance. The North had freed them but left the South to resolve their future; then let the South show them the task was not too big for them. His opponents might deride him for appealing to the black vote, but they knew that after the first flush of enthusiasm for enfranchisement blacks stayed away from the polls in droves, especially after the closing of the Freedmen's Bureau and the return of its agents back North. Guy Parrish addressed the future of the blacks as well as the whites; but it was his fellow whites, knowing they were the ones who must somehow solve the problem of blacks and whites living together, who elected him to the state legislature.

Eustacia was pleased. It gave her the opportunity to entertain more often and more lavishly—far too lavishly, which did nothing to endear her to the wives of other senators.

"Why don't they like me?" she often pouted. "I don't understand them."

It was partly because she did not understand the South and was so obviously happier in the North, where he would never live, that he broached the matter that had been on his mind for some time; mainly, though, it was because he knew beyond a doubt that their marriage had failed.

The most violent scene between them had occurred at his refusal to summer in Europe with Eustacia and her family. The fact that he was preparing to run for a second term did nothing to alleviate her wrath. She had accused him of deliberately thwarting her wishes at every turn, and he had responded with the suggestion that they separate.

"There's someone else, isn't there, Harwood? I've known it all along." The accusation burst as swiftly from her lips as though it had been long poised there, waiting to be loosened. "You've got someone else and you want me to make way for her, whoever this little floozy is that you've fallen for."

She'd often accused him of infidelity before, but this was the first time he didn't laugh as he denied it.

"That's not true, Eustacia. I say it because, if you will be honest with yourself, you'll admit that this marriage of ours is not a satisfactory one. In fact, it's hardly a marriage at all. Marriage means joining. We haven't grown together; we've grown apart."

"You've grown apart from me, Harwood. All I've ever wanted is you; you know that. If anyone's unhappy with the marriage, it's certainly not me."

He shrugged. "Let's not argue the point, Eustacia. Have it that it's me."

Her eyes teared, as much in anger as regret. "You don't argue, because there's someone else you're planning to marry. That's it, isn't it? Who is she?"

"There's no one else I'm planning to marry, Eustacia. If we were to divorce, I should have no thought of re-marrying. I'm really thinking of you more than myself. You're young, very beautiful. Life with me can't have given you what you wanted or expected. You've never liked Tennessee. Don't protest; it's quite plain. I don't say it with any sense of recrimination. You've made no friends here—"

"I don't want friends; I want you."

"Good God, Eustacia, why must be you so single-minded!" He saw her mouth turn down at his outburst; and as her tearing eyes began to overflow, he went on in a softer tone: "You know, in the long run you would be far happier if we separated. I'm sure of it."

"And Bella?" Her words were muffled by the lace handkerchief held before her lips. "I suppose you're dismissing her too, now you have your precious Arnaud."

He sighed. "I'm not dismissing you, Eustacia, and I'm certainly not dismissing my own daughter. I don't deny loving Arnaud, but that doesn't mean I love Bella any the less. I do realize, however, that she has spent most of her time with you, with your family. I would never tear her from you."

"You won't tear her from me, Harwood, because she will be by my side; and I shall be where I belong, by your side. I shan't leave you, not for an instant. How could you suggest this terrible thing, knowing you're all I ever wanted? I love you, Harwood. I love you. I shan't go to Europe, even though Papa says I really need the change, even though it would be so good for our dear little Bella. I'll give up the idea of the trip entirely. I promise to stay here and never ever go away, not even to visit New York or Newport. I shall stay right here, with my dearest husband, always."

These words, muttered into his shoulder as she clung to him sobbing, were as much a threat as a promise. He had lost; he knew he had lost. She would never consent to a separation, let alone a divorce, though he had been sincere in his belief that it would benefit her as much as him. He could not reassure her of his love; but there was one way to soothe her, and that he had done by taking her to bed.

Afterwards, as they lay between the sheets, the afternoon sun streaming across the room, across her fair skin, her dark hair, she had again whispered, "I shan't go to Europe without you, Harwood. I shall tell Papa that I'm staying here with you."

It had taken both his own powers of persuasion and her father's to convince Eustacia that not only would her health and beauty benefit from being away from Tennessee's summer heat, but she should put aside her own wishes in order not to deprive Bella of the excitement of the journey. Nor should she deprive her father of his wish to purchase an entire new wardrobe for her from the House of Worth.

Guy Parrish had breathed a sigh of relief when at last she consented to go. The thought of Eustacia pinned to his side all day, every day of the year, never ever leaving him, was more than he could endure.

TWO

The summer of 1878 in Memphis was hot, humid, and like the languid flow of the great brown river passing alongside the bluffs of the bustling industrial city, lazy.

Even Guy Parrish, who had endured many a hot and humid summer there, found the heat that year discomforting. It hung in the atmosphere and clung to everything, making vegetation dry and people dripping wet. Even the early morning with its skies of unclouded blue and the late evening as the sun set low on the Arkansas side of the river were only tolerable.

Not till the long shadows crossed the lawn would Guy, with Arnaud by his side, wander out to sit beneath the copper beech. Bellechasse was so much more comfortable when Eustacia was away. He and Arnaud understood one another in a way he and Bella were never able to. Eustacia never permitted Bella to roam free in his domain—the fields and warehouses—while in the house, Eustacia reigned with an attitude of such dislike for Arnaud that Guy was determined to make up for it when he and the boy were alone.

Sometimes as they sat together they talked, but more often they were silent, listening to the whirr from the cicadas and the high-pitched drone of the mosquitoes.

"You're like me, Arnaud; the mosquitoes leave you alone. My father was not a man easily defied, except by the mosquitoes. How they used to pester him!"

Arnaud breathed a sigh of satisfaction; he loved to hear of anything that he and his adopted father had in common.

Livvy, now running St. Catharine's School, where Guy frequently stopped, agreed that not only were the heat and

humidity enervating but they boded ill. There were unpleasant rumors of another bout of yellow fever sweeping
up the river.

"They're speculating it may be as bad as in '73. Father
Quayle was by yesterday. He says the fever's rampant in
the Indies this year, and now cases have been identified in
New Orleans. He suggested we be prepared, just in case."

"Glad to see the Romans sharing something beyond
their Catholicism with you." Her brother grinned.

"Don't smite me with the branch of popery, Guy. I
have enough arguments on that score with others, I don't
need it from my own brother. I think Father Quayle,
Romanism notwithstanding, is a very sensible, very resourceful man. I've already written to warn Mother Charlotte that should the plague strike us as it did before I shall
be glad of extra hands to help."

Guy's face grew thoughtful for a moment before he
remarked, "I don't think she should allow Sister Serene to
come, not if this were to turn into an epidemic like last
time."

"Guy, you know as well as I that Sister Serene was the
one who really took over then. She would be the very best
one to have now, since she's not only been through it
before but she's a trained physician."

"It wouldn't do. What I mean is you should remind
Mother Charlotte her life shouldn't be risked, not now that
the order's invested so much in her training," Guy said,
looking away from his sister, afraid she might guess his
personal reasons for not wanting to see Damaris exposed
to the danger.

"You must be in collusion with Mother Charlotte. That's
just what she wrote. If it's necessary, she says, she'll send
Sister Agnes and Sister Bertha, and perhaps Sister Emmeline;
though I warned her it would be preferable to send those
who've been exposed to the fever before. She says she
realizes Sister Serene would be useful, but she simply
doesn't know how they could spare her. I'm concerned
about her being overworked. You know, last time I was in
New York she scarcely had time to talk, rushing from
bedside to surgery, with not a moment to herself. No
sooner did she stop to ask me how things were in Memphis
than she was called away. It made for most disjointed

conversations. I think they put too much on her. She's only one person; she's human. I don't know when she gets any rest. She can't go on like that.''

"She's a doctor; she must know what's good for her."

"A patient's a fool who has herself for a doctor."

"I don't think Sister Serene's anyone's fool."

"No, I suppose not." Livvy smiled knowingly. "Do you know what I think, Guy?"

Her knowing tone made him look up. Could she have guessed his feelings?

"What do you think?" he asked evenly.

"That you like Sister Serene a lot better now you know her."

"Perhaps." His voice was noncommittal.

"There!" his sister triumphed. "I always said you would. Remember?"

"So you did." Deliberately he changed the topic. "How would you like to come and watch the fireworks for the glorious Fourth with Arnaud and me? There's to be a dress parade of the Bluff City Grays that's sure to raise a nostalgic tear, but I imagine he'll find it fun."

"Will you be there as Colonel Parrish or as Senator Parrish?" Livvy teased. "You're becoming so prominent I'm finding it useful to remind people that I'm Guy Parrish's ister."

"No more useful than I find letting it be known I'm related to the worthy Sister Lavinia. It certainly helps overcome my lack of religious observance." He saw his sister's face cloud over. "Look, Livvy, the Fourth is meant to be fun. I just want to enjoy it, and what better way for both of us than in the company of a ten-year-old boy?"

"I've so much to do."

"Put it aside, for a day at least. Come along, join us!"

She did, stopping to watch the display of steam engines in Court Square, though, unlike Arnaud, carefully avoiding the water spray from their huge hoses.

"He's going to catch his death of cold," she warned her brother.

"Rubbish. Arnaud's as strong as I am, aren't you, Arnaud? A bit of water is what a boy needs on a hot day like this."

Arnaud gave Guy Parrish an answering grin. Seen together, they could quite naturally have been father and son. Livvy thought that maybe, because Arnaud spent every waking moment at Guy's side, he was growing up to be so very much like him.

"You're darned right, sir. A bit of water's what a boy needs. And I never catch colds, Aunt Livvy."

"There's Tom. Let's ask him if you won't believe me." Guy Parrish hailed the sturdy figure of Dr. Mitchum.

"Tom, I'm told you've taken over the helm of the Board of Health."

"I have, and a damned thankless task it's turning out to be." He caught sight of Livvy and, raising his tall hat, apologized. "Sorry, Livvy, but you've got to admit it's a scorcher this year. Hot enough to make a man forget his manners."

Guy Parrish motioned to Arnaud. "Livvy's been worrying about Arnaud catching pneumonia."

"Can't kill boys with water, Livvy," Mitchum said, "not boys like that one, at least. You're a lucky man, Parrish, having Arnaud for a son since your wife can't . . . Well, anyway, you're lucky. Parrishes always were lucky, though. And it's a lucky coincidence for me, running into you. I've been wanting to talk to you about the news that's leaking out on the outbreak of yellow jack this year. I'm getting mighty concerned."

"I know. Livvy and I were just discussing it. The religious orders are gearing up, as well as the Howard Association, of course, just in case."

"Can't be too soon, for it's my guess the help of each and every one of us is going to be needed for this one. I'm all for imposing an early quarantine in an attempt to ward off the worst of it, but the City Council's adamantly opposed. They say Memphis can't afford the loss of business. I told them in no uncertain terms that if they don't face facts and put it into effect soon, there may be no Memphis to do business in at all. I didn't make myself too popular, I can tell you. I could use your support."

"You have it, as long as you realize it may prove as much of a liability as an asset in some quarters. I may have gained office in the state, but it was scarcely by a landslide. There are many who don't appreciate my views."

"I do, though, Guy; you know that. I appreciate your understanding, no matter what others may think. Besides, whether they agree with your politics or not, you're a Parrish as well as a planter, and you stand to lose as much as anyone if Memphis is shut off from the rest of the country for a time."

Arnaud's face had clouded as they stood talking, and when Dr. Mitchum left, he asked hesitantly, "Will it be like before, sir, like when my mother died?"

Guy Parrish took his hand. "Not as long as we've got people like Dr. Mitchum watching out for us, Arnaud; besides, I shan't allow you to stay around if there's any danger."

"Will you go away too?"

"I can't Arnaud. I'll have to stay, no matter what. My place is here."

"If you stay, I shall also. My place is with you," he said staunchly.

"We'll fight about that when the time comes. Right now I hope you believe in magic, Arnaud. If you don't, be prepared, for that's what we're going to see."

"Do you believe in magic, sir?"

"You bet I do."

The fireworks set off from the bluffs, shooting high across the night sky, reflecting their lights in the still water beneath, were a magical display: fountains of every color, pyramids and palmettos, England's crown and America's eagle. They concluded in a hail of gold and silver stars tumbling majestically, silently, to die on the quiet surface of the river like so many spent bullets.

"Didn't I tell you you would see magic, Arnaud?" Guy asked, keeping his hand on the boy's shoulder so they wouldn't become separated in the crowd.

"It was grand." Arnaud nodded; but though he'd given every indication of having enjoyed the spectacle, his face was grave.

"Reminds me of England, Guy, when they celebrate your day." Livvy laughed.

"My day?" her brother questioned. "You mean they've named a day especially for me? By God, what are things coming to? Never thought the English would consider any 'colonist' worthy of such an honor!"

"Guy Fawkes Day."

"Ah, the day of the traitor. So that's it!"

"I didn't mean that," Livvy corrected hastily. "No one will ever get me to say our cause was treasonous. You fought for what you believed in."

"Did I?" He saw Arnaud's face questioning him. "Well, no matter."

And Livvy, feeling she had opened a wound, went on quickly: "I always thought of Guy Fawkes Day as your day. When I first saw the bonfires where they burned the Guy every year, I became furious. I thought it was you they were burning. Even when they explained, I could never join in and dance around the fire, singing along with the others, 'Please to remember the fifth of November, gunpowder treason and plot.' I'd never have felt comfortable about doing that."

" 'I see no reason why gunpowder treason should ever be forgot.' " Her brother finished the rhyme. "The English certainly have a way of making sure their people are never allowed to forget treason. Strange, isn't it, the power of a simple rhyme taught to generation after generation of children? Far more effective than threats or swords, and look at all the trouble it saves. You'd do well to remember that, Arnaud."

Arnaud had been unusually silent, and Guy demanded, "What's the matter, Arnaud, did you eat too much cotton candy?"

Arnaud shook his head. "It's the magic, sir."

"The magic?"

"Yes, you said you believed in magic. I was just wondering, could we invoke the magic to keep the fever away from Memphis?"

Guy shook his head. "Magic's powerful, but I don't know if it's that powerful. We may have to rely on Aunt Livvy's God for that."

"God's done greater things, Arnaud. I shall pray to Him, and you will too."

Guy Parrish might not attend church, but he made no attempt to prevent his sister from teaching her beliefs to the boy.

"I shall, Aunt Livvy, indeed I shall," Arnaud assured her.

But prayers were not enough. Though no cases were reported in Memphis, as July wore on they learned the fever had gained a firm hold in New Orleans. In an angry dispute over how the epidemic might be prevented from reaching Memphis, Dr. Mitchum resigned, to be replaced as president of the Board of Health by Dr. Saunders, who in lieu of quarantine advocated cleaning up the city by disinfecting streets with carbolic acid and lime, pouring a mixture of copperas, carbolic acid, and water down privies, and scattering lime around all building foundations. He also stopped northern-bound trains from entering the city until a thorough medical examination of their passengers had been conducted and all the cars had been disinfected.

Though newspapers continued to warn against panic, those Memphians who had the means were preparing to leave, packing clothes and supplies that would see them through the first frost.

The announcement of the deaths by yellow fever of two seamen on the *John Porter* in Vicksburg at last forced the Mayor to issue a proclamation designating President's Island as a quarantine station from which a harbor tugboat was dispatched to intercept the riverboat and prevent its landing at Memphis.

Daily the temperature climbed to over a hundred degrees. The acrid odor of carbolic acid filled the nostrils, and the cadent, stiletto blasts of cannon fire (designed to jar loose the poisoned miasma over the Mississippi Valley that was thought to be causing the disease) filled the ears. In this atmosphere that caused both people and vegetation to wilt, the first case of yellow fever was confirmed in Grenada, just a hundred miles to the south.

The exodus from Memphis began.

"Mother Charlotte writes that she is sending help," Livvy told her brother.

"Not Sister Serene?" Was his immediate response. "She hasn't changed her mind there, has she?"

"No, more's the pity. For my sake, I wish she had. She's sending Sisters Agnes and Bertha; and it seems Sister Angela is coming in place of Sister Emmeline." She looked questioningly at her brother. "I find it odd, Guy. During the last epidemic you were furious with Sister

Serene because she let me stay on here; now you seem afraid of her being exposed to the fever. I don't mind you liking Sister Serene better now, but I'll begin to be jealous if you take on the role of a big brother to her."

"Livvy, Sister Serene can never be a sister to me; you're the only sister I have. But a lot of good it would do for me to tell you to leave, so I'm not going to say anything on that score. That way it won't be obvious how little authority I have over my own family."

"Poof. Eustacia listens to your every whim. It's a good thing that she and Bella are away, though they usually spend the summers away from the heat in any event. What are you going to do about Arnaud?"

"I'm sending him to Knoxville, much against his wishes, I'm afraid."

"Poor Arnaud. He's so afraid of the fever, but he's more afraid of being separated from you. I wonder whether it wouldn't be better to let him stay on at Bellechasse. He's been exposed before."

Guy shook his head. "I'd prefer not, especially since I won't be there. I'm moving into the Peabody Hotel to work as liaison between the council and the Howard Association. We're all going to have to work together and use whatever resources we have to their best advantage. Let's hope we can somehow contain this and prevent it from being as bad as '73."

"Well, at least we've still some time. The fever's not here yet." Livvy pointed to the front page of the newspaper. "The *Daily Appeal* cautions us to keep cool. Avoid patent medicines and bad whiskey, it says. Go about your business as usual; be cheerful and laugh as much as possible. That's good advice. They say the public may rely upon it that whenever yellow fever shows itself, as is not at all likely, the Board of Health through the press of the city will promptly report it. At least that means we're safe for the time being."

"I'm afraid not, Livvy," her brother responded quietly. "A few days ago a deckhand slipped away from President's Island, saying he had to get something decent to eat. He stopped in one of those little places near the Gayoso Bayou, the kind that cater to rivermen. Afterwards he said he was ill. They thought he'd eaten something that disagreed with him and admitted him to City Hospital. Now they suspect the fever and have moved him to a quarantine hospital. If that weren't ominous enough, Mrs. Bionda, the wife of the snack-house owner, has come down too. Tom Mitchum told me in confidence that there's not the slightest doubt about the diagnosis of her case. I'm afraid we weren't successful in keeping it out. Yellow jack's already reached Memphis.''

THREE

*F*rom the moment the news leaked out that Mrs. Bionda had died of yellow fever, the death of the deckhand in the quarantine hospital following almost immediately thereafter, Memphis was in the grip of a panic.

Trains were jammed to capacity and beyond, with passengers savagely contending for every inch of space. Those unable to force their way on board through the doors tried to struggle through the windows, while those already inside fought even more desperately to protect their position, shoving the would-be intruders back out as fast as they got in. Every one of these overburdened, clanking, cranking conveyances left the train station of the plague-ridden city with people clinging outside to windows, doors, ledges, anywhere they could gain a hold, their efforts spurred by the sight of arriving trains bereft of passengers but loaded to capacity with coffins.

"Three things are best done in haste—escaping quarrels, catching fleas, and flying from the plague," sorrowed one wag who could not afford to leave as he watched one of the departures.

"Nothing should be done in haste except killing the fleas," his disgruntled friend asserted laconically as the overloaded train groaned and chuffed while the guard tried to wrench loose those who clung to the outside. "Looks to me as they're just trading one calamity for another."

"You ever seen anyone die of the fever? Might be better dying outright falling from a moving train."

Though those who remained were still being exhorted to protect themselves by killing vermin and scouring everything in sight, the number of cases of the fever grew despite these precautions; and hope dimmed that cleanliness alone would save their lives.

Some who talked as though they knew claimed the fever was transmitted by touch, so all infected bedding, clothes, and utensils, including mattresses the victims had slept on or, all too often, died on, were ordered burned. Others argued that the disease was carried in the miasmic air, and the Board of Health debated detonating fifteen kegs of gunpowder to cleanse it, finally deciding to burn a hundred barrels of pine tar instead. With this measure and the cannons, still being fired regularly, Board members argued that those who remained in the city could both see and hear they were doing *something*.

A suggestion that the fever might stem from animalcules following the course of the bayous was hooted down in derision.

Just as no one could agree on the source of the disease or the best measures for prevention, so none could agree on the most effective treatment. Many of the doctors at the Howard Association were advocating flushing out the patients' insides with emetics of ground mustard, salt, and warm water, followed by copious amounts of warm water once vomiting had begun, that in turn followed by cold water as a purgative to clean out the bowels.

Others thought the best method was the Creole treatment, keeping the bowels open with castor oil or calomel, the cure-all used in the war, mixing it with rhubarb root, and then dousing the patient in ice water. Following this merciless treatment, the chilled body was wrapped in many layers of blankets to induce sweating.

Dr. Mitchum was of the opinion that not only were these "cures" worthless, they could actually be harmful. When Livvy consulted him on the best course to follow, he shook his head sorrowfully. "Damned if I know the best course, not with any degree of certainty. Sorry. Guess I shouldn't cuss in front of you, but I'll do it till the day I die. I've been fighting this fever for so long it's like a personal enemy to me, but I've had to resign myself that since I can't cure it, all I can hope to do is alleviate the symptoms."

His advice was, as far as was possible, to give absolute peace to mind and body, reducing food and drink to a minimum and applying frequent spongings in an attempt to bring the fever down, and then to allow nature to do her part.

What Dr. Mitchum said made sense; since there was no known cure, why should the patient not at least be as comfortable as the agony of the affliction would allow? Livvy took his advice in organizing the sisters' relief efforts in the district surrounding St. Catharine's School, which the Howard Association had once again allocated to their care.

The arrival of three more sisters from New York had been welcomed wholeheartedly, though Livvy sorely missed the presence of Sister Serene among them. She was in charge and, given the seriousness of the situation, was not altogether comfortable with the responsibility. She offered to delegate her position to Sister Agnes or to Sister Bertha, either of whom had the right to supersede her since they had been with the order far longer, but both refused.

Livvy had not particularly welcomed Sister Angela, whom she thought stern and bossy. While it might be true that Sister Angela had known Sister Serene longer, Livvy always resented the proprietary attitude Sister Angela had adopted toward her own special friend and mentor, and she continued to regard her as an intruder.

Surprisingly, though, it was Sister Angela who quietly but efficiently took over the worst, the most difficult, the most menial tasks, without a word of complaint. While Nanny Wickers had had the reputation of being proud and haughty at the Caylews'—it was even said that Mrs. Caylew herself stood in awe of her—there was none of that in the demeanor of Sister Angela. Livvy learned she could always rely on her to make sure their supplies of clean linen, disinfectants, jalap, and quinine were adequate. She was the one who never refused to answer a call, no matter how late, no matter how exhausting her day might have been. It was her unfailing willingness to respond with that cadaver obedience they had been taught that made her indispensable.

"I never thought I'd live to see the day when I'd hate to hear church bells ring, but I'm beginning to loathe them. They've got my nerves on edge so, knowing each toll means yet another death." Sister Agnes groaned, looking up from the letter she was sending back to Mother Charlotte describing the gravity of their situation.

"I don't mind those so much; it's the cannons going off that have unnerved me. They startle me even though I know they're all the way over by the river. It's not as though it's unexpected. Even so, whatever I'm doing, I jump." Sister Bertha, folding clean linen, made her point by starting at the distant roar of yet another cannon.

"Don't worry, Sister Bertha," Livvy comforted. "We all felt that way at first, but you'll get used to it."

More alarming than the toll of church bells that announced death after death, tormenting their fraying nerves, was the cold fear that gripped them when, in mid-August, with the death toll higher than seventy a day and continuing to climb, the Civil Relief Committee ordered the bells to cease.

With both the Mayor and Chief of Police stricken, the Civil Relief Committee, headed by Guy Parrish, had assumed the responsibilities of safety and community services.

Whenever Guy could break away from his onerous and thankless duties, he would stop to see Livvy at St. Catharine's School. His visits were always hurried and of such short duration that Livvy began to fear for him.

"You're tired, Guy. Stay and eat with us. You mustn't run yourself so hard," she urged, noticing his eyes dulled and red-rimmed from want of rest.

"I'm not running myself any harder than you are, Livvy, or anyone else for that matter."

"But you look so wan; I'm worried about you. Dr. Mitchum says before anything else we must keep ourselves fit by eating regularly with as much nourishment as possible and sleeping properly. Then, even if the fever should strike us, we may be strong enough to combat it. We're so short-handed as it is, there's not one among us that's expendable, least of all you."

"My life's worth no more than anyone else's." Guy Parrish got up. As the days of fever wore on, he became increasingly unable to relax. Pacing the room with his hands in his pockets, he thought out loud. "We need doctors, nurses. As if things aren't bad enough, nine more doctors have fled. Nine, when we can't afford to lose one! Others keep threatening to leave. I've even considered

using force to make them stay. Not too rational of me, I
know, with the example set for them by Protestant ministers leaving their flocks to fend for themselves.''

He looked over at his sister. ''Not you; you know I
don't mean you. You and the Catholics have been taking
the brunt of the relief work. Those in the Irish sections
over by the river are hit worse than any. I've seen greater
valor in the Pinch than on any battlefield. They deserve
more praise than they'll ever receive, and all of you here
too.''

''We're not looking for praise on this earth, Guy.''

''I'll not argue the point. I'm simply saying it's deserved. Just as those who could help but instead run to
save their own skins deserve a bullet in the back,'' he said
bitterly.

''Guy, don't. They can't help it; they're scared.''

''Anyone with any sense is scared, Livvy; but if we've
been put in a position of trust, we have responsibilities to
others besides ourselves. Do you realize we've only got
seven police still fit for duty? I don't know where we
would be without the blacks who've taken on the job.
Again, whatever the reason, yellow jack's not decimating
their population as it is ours. Still, seven police are hardly
enough for a city of this size, particularly with so many
homes and businesses vacant. Looting's on the increase, as
well as assault. I was against doing so, but I've had to get
in militia to maintain order.''

He stopped, settling down at last in a chair opposite his
sister. ''Downtown it's like living in a cage, Livvy. Everyone inside wants to get out and those outside are adamant
they should stay in. I thought I'd seen the depths of the
human condition in the war, but somehow this is worse.
Maybe it's because we're fighting a natural rather than a
man-made disaster. Men's minds are diabolical, but there
are times when nature is even worse. There's not only the
problem of locating the dead—we've set up burial patrols
that seem to be working reasonably well—but there's the
matter of getting the bodies into the ground once we've
located them. Coffins are stacked like cordwood at
Elmwood. Under normal circumstances I'd be the last to
deny a person's right to a decent burial, but conditions
have forced us to dispense with individual graves and

markers and bury en masse. You can imagine the grief and complaint that's causing; some seem to think it's being done from spite. God knows why. I'm accosted at every turn about it. It's hard to understand why they can't see the fix we're in.''

Livvy nodded, saying slowly, ''I just wonder how many survivors there are going to be in the end, Guy. The fever's worse than I remember it from before; it's much more virulent. In '73 when it took hold we could count on about sixty hours for it to run its course, now it's little over a day; and the convulsions at the end are agonizing, really horrible.''

Livvy shuddered, and her brother looked over at her with compassion. ''Dear little Livvy, forgive me for airing my troubles. It must be terrible for you. To think you should have to go through this. What would Mother say if she saw you here?''

''Maybe she does, Guy, maybe she can see both of us. She'd think this was our place, you know.''

''Maybe she would,'' he mused. ''I know she would be as proud of you as I am.''

''You may think it odd, but I'm glad to be here. It's changed me, just as you were changed in the war.'' Noticing his questioning look, she shook her head. ''I don't mean that, Guy. No, this doesn't make me reject God, far from it. It's not His fault that all this is happening.''

''I won't argue the point. I'm just glad to see you taking all this on your shoulders and growing strong.''

''Father Daley died. I suppose you heard that. It means we can't take Communion unless another Episcopal priest is found. I doubt they'll discover anyone willing to come to Memphis at such a time. Mother Charlotte writes that the papers up North are full of the epidemic.''

''I should think anyone with a grain of sense would keep a wide berth.'' He looked out of the window at the empty street. ''From my room at the Peabody I can see the old *John Porter* plying the river; its crew is riddled with fever and no one will allow it to berth anywhere. Though the people here were violently opposed, I did manage to get some fresh supplies out to them. After all, there's no reason to pin the entire blame on them; an epidemic of this proportion would have reached us eventually, one way or another.''

"Do you remember the Matsons who live four doors down? The family went East weeks ago but left their servants behind—to guard the house, I suppose. I guess they thought that since the blacks had escaped the fever before they'd be all right. Sister Angela noticed there hadn't been any activity there for a while. She was used to seeing washing hanging out and that sort of thing, so she decided to call. They hadn't said anything to anyone, but I guess they'd been sick for some time. The old man was dead; not only that, he was in an advanced state of decay. We could still smell the odor on Sister Angela's clothes when she came back. I guess the others were just too weak to get help. She said the wife was going through her last convulsions when she went into the house, and the daughter was lying still, watching her. It must have been as bad as she'd seen. She's a stoic and rarely shows any emotion—that's what makes her so good to have around—but anyway, when she came in she just put her head down on the table and wept. In a way, I think the rest of us were glad to see it. It made her seem, well, human, I suppose.''

"Interesting. I remember the tales I used to hear about her ruling the Caylew nursery with a rod of iron.''

"Sister Serene used to work there with her, did you know?''

He nodded without answering.

"How I wish she were here,'' Livvy murmured.

"Well, I'm damned glad she's not,'' he responded tersely.

"I suppose it's wrong to wish this place on anyone, let alone someone I hold as dear as Sister Serene. It's just that she's such a comfort.''

"I know, Livvy, I know; but with the fever so much more virulent this time, as you've pointed out—killing more swiftly, affecting blacks as well as whites—even those of us who've been exposed to the previous strain may be placed in jeopardy.''

"Maybe. Though so far we're all pulling through.''

"Promise me you'll take every precaution. There are only two of us left, you know, and I value your life as much as my own.''

"Then I hope you'll take your own advice. Don't overdo things. Promise me you won't."

He laughed. "You sound like a mother instead of a younger sister."

"Maybe I shall be a mother someday," she said proudly.

He raised his eyebrows. "Don't tell me!"

"Not what you think, Guy. But eventually someone will have to replace Mother Charlotte."

"Ah, so my little Livvy has ambitions."

"Don't tease."

"I'm not. I'm just thinking how much you've changed."

"I'm the same Livvy I've always been." She went over and kissed his cheek. "Why don't you stay and eat with us today? I'll bet you're not getting the proper things to eat."

"No watermelon, I suppose. Someone came up with the idea that the disease was carried in watermelon—or had you heard that?—and now in the worst heat, when we could use something refreshing, watermelons have been banned."

"No watermelon, but we do have some good peaches, and Sister Bertha was talking of putting them into a pie."

"Mmmm, a good peach pie!" Though he licked his lips, he shook his head in refusal. "Tempting, but I said I'd call in at Cleopatra's and see Mrs. Laroche this afternoon." He caught sight of the shock on his sister's face and laughed. "I'm not seeing her in her professional capacity exactly, so don't get upset. With the drastic shortage of medical help, she went to Dr. Mitchum and offered the services of herself and her girls. They've been absolutely intrepid in working with the fever victims. Now she's turning the whole establishment into an infirmary. She's quite an organizer. I'm going to see what supplies she needs and give her what help the city can offer."

Livvy's face still wore a worried frown. "I suppose God works in strange ways."

"Seems I've heard that before," he said dryly, then added, "I'll be willing to bet you'd like Cleo Laroche if you knew her."

"Her name certainly fits her profession—Cleopatra Laroche." Livvy was scornful.

"If Christ was able to forgive Mary Magdalen, seems you might find a kind word for Cleo."

"Just because there's an epidemic doesn't mean we have to give up standards, Guy."

" 'Fraid I'm not much at upholding standards, Livvy, not today at least." He kissed her cheek. "I really must go."

Crossing the red-carpeted hall of Cleopatra's, Guy found Dr. Mitchum ensconced in an easy chair in Cleo Laroche's private office sipping a tall drink.

"Thank God she saved some Jack Daniel's. Here."

He pushed over a glass and the bottle to Guy; and as he poured his drink, Mitchum went on: "She'll be back. She's got Frank Johnson with her and don't ask me what they're about."

Guy laughed. "I wasn't about to. And I'd be the last one to question anyone with the sanity to do something enjoyable in this crazy inferno we're living in. I keep thinking about the war. Nothing could surpass the horrors of that, I always thought; but the other day I went into a house just south of here and found a woman holding a baby who must have been dead for days to her breast. She was rocking it and singing to it." He swallowed half of the drink he'd poured, was silent for a moment, then swore. "Christ, Mitchum, it was the most God-awful sight I've ever laid eyes on."

Mitchum nodded gravely. "Hear we lost more doctors. Still, if they wanted to get out we're probably better off without them; anyway, we're all helpless, physicians and laymen. We're doomed, Guy. Memphis is doomed."

"No!" Guy Parrish shook his head emphatically. "No, I won't go along with that. We're not doomed while we've got people like you and my sister. Even the Caylews' snooty nanny is turning into some sort of a heroine. And look at what Cleo's doing here. She's really organized her girls."

"Cleo's a businesswoman first and foremost. She was running a nice little establishment here, had it all together till this thing came. Maybe you didn't know her as I did. Didn't see you around here as much as some."

"I've had my share of her whiskey—good but over-priced. She's a businesswoman to the end of her long nails."

"Didn't mean that. I meant you weren't one of her

patrons, so to speak. Course, why should you be? You've been the envy of every red-blooded man in Memphis ever since you married.'' He studied Guy's unsmiling expression for a moment. "Odd thing is I've never been convinced you're entirely happy.''

"Who the hell is entirely happy, Mitchum? And what's the damned use of even thinking of happiness in the middle of this? It would make it seem even worse than it is.''

"You're right. And I should learn to mind my tongue. It's what comes of getting old and airing my opinions too freely.'' He slouched lower in his chair at yet another cannon roar. "I wish you'd get them to stop shooting off those damned cannons. They're not doing a thing except getting our nerves on edge. Yellow jack's not carried in the air, I'm certain of that. Something else is carrying it, but what the hell that is I'll be damned if I know. I've puzzled over it for so long I'm sick to death of thinking of it, yet I can't think of anything else.''

He pushed his hat back on his head, rocking himself to and fro and fanning himself with a newspaper, as Guy sat down opposite him, drink in hand.

"God, it's hot.'' Mitchum suddenly stopped fanning himself and swatted his wrist. "Gotcha!'' he yelled in triumph, holding up a dead mosquito. "That damned thing's been buzzing around me ever since I sat down. Don't know why he chose me over you.''

"Maybe it's a she, not a he, Mitchum, and she guessed your blood is sweeter than mine.''

"I'll not argue with that. You Parrishes have never been noted for being sweet—menfolk at least. Now Livvy—''

He was interrupted by a shout from the hallway. "Is Colonel Parrish around?''

"I'm in here,'' Guy Parrish called back.

It was the sergeant in charge of a detail posted to guard duty on the outskirts of the city. He'd served with Parrish in the war. As he entered the room, the soldier stuffed into his pocket the crumpled kerchief he'd used to mop the sweat from his brow and raised his hand in salute.

"Colonel, sir, there's some damn-fool nun trying to leave the city with a whole bunch of pickaninnies. We stopped her, but there's a crowd gathered and they're mighty unhappy. The nun's acting kinda high-handed. She insists they're going to leave, and that crowd's not about to let them. Thought I'd better come in and get you. Might be trouble. Way they looked when I left, they might have it in mind to lynch her.''

''Thanks, Sergeant.'' Guy Parrish threw back the contents of his glass and got up.

''Not your sister, is it, Parrish?'' Dr. Mitchum asked.

''I don't see how it can be. It's not an hour since I left her, and they were getting ready to sit down to dinner with one of Sister Bertha's peach pies.''

''Goddamn, it's a long time since I had a good piece of pie.''

''Then why not go on out and see them. Take the piece of pie I turned down to come here. But before you go, tell Cleo I'll be back once I see what this disturbance is all about. Probably one of the Catholic nuns from the Pinch. Doesn't exactly sound like a major skirmish.''

FOUR

It might have been no major skirmish, but by the time Guy Parrish reached the location of the disturbance, out beyond Elmwood Cemetery, his course hindered more than once by the huge furniture wagons converted into hearses, he found an angry gathering of people from the city outskirts, which had so far escaped the fever. They were clustered together so he could barely catch a glimpse of the cause of the disturbance in their midst, a wagon on which stood a black-robed nun surrounded by a group of small children clinging to her, while at her side was an old red-kerchiefed black woman.

As he began pushing his way through, Guy Parrish caught the sound of the nun's voice raised in pleading and protest; it stopped him abruptly in his tracks.

"I swear to you, I give you my word of honor, these children are healthy, free from the fever. I am a physician and I have examined each and every one of them. I assure you they are well and will infect no one. Their lives are in your hands. If you don't allow them to leave they'll very likely succumb as others have."

"It's our children that's dying, not theirs," an angry voice yelled out.

"I don't deny this fever kills more whites than other races. We don't know why. I was here in the '73 epidemic. Then we thought that the blacks were immune; now we're finding that's not so. They're dying too."

"Not like us."

"Not as many perhaps, but the fever's not discriminating anymore. Blacks and whites, old and young. These are children," she pleaded. "Whatever their color, they

315

are children. I've only just arrived in Memphis, but the sights I've seen in these hours I'll never forget as long as I live. Think of how it must seem to a child! They have long been promised a place of asylum in Cordova, but each time they try to reach it they've been stopped. Let them go on their way, I beg you. They'll go directly to the asylum, nowhere else. All they want is to be allowed to follow this road a few miles to their refuge. I assure you, I give you my word, God's word, that they are healthy. Let them remain so. I pray you, let them pass."

"Damned Catholics telling us what to do. Go to hell!" A scrawny man nearby spat at her; the sun caught the gleam of his spittle on her black robe. There was a guffaw from the crowd.

"Your halo slipped, Sister," a wag called out.

"If it makes a difference to you, I'm not Catholic. I'm from an Episcopal order, the Order of St. Catharine. We served here alongside our Catholic sisters, I am proud to say, in the last epidemic. Many from my sisterhood have been here ever since this one began."

"That's your funeral. If you want to act like heroines, go ahead. You take the little black bastards in, then."

"We would gladly, but they'd be no safer with us than where they were. They must get away from the city. What can I do to make you see that? I beg you, let them go.

"Damned woman, dressed up like a crow," a burly man shouted at her, raising his fist. "That harlot in town knows more about medicine than you, and she's a sight easier on the eyes."

Again the guffaws rose in appreciation, almost drowning out her reply. "I've already tried to explain. I've been trained as a physician at the—" At that moment a rock hurled through the air would have hit her face had not the old woman grabbed her arm and pulled her aside, so that it flew past and landed on the seat of the wagon, harming no one. She gathered the children closer to her, enfolding them in her arms.

"You great ugly bullies! Scum—"

Her angered cry was drowned by that of a gentleman who climbed up beside her. "For God's sake, stop! Stop this instant. What are you, a bunch of rabble? Stop, dammit. Do you hear me!"

"It's Parrish, Colonel Parrish," the wag close to the wagon shouted.

"You're right, it is Parrish. I'm charged with keeping law and order, and I intend to do just that no matter what it takes. Get that fixed in your heads. Now what's going on here?"

"Oh, thank God!" Damaris murmured.

But as he turned to her, his voice was still charged with anger. "I don't know what the hell you think you're doing here, Sister. They should never have let you come. For God's sake, why didn't you stay in New York where you belong? Only a fool would come into Memphis at a time like this."

"I'm sorry." Her voice was cool. "Maybe I am a fool. I won't argue the point. But I had to come."

"You shouldn't have." The anger faded from his voice as he looked into her blue eyes. "They should never have allowed you to come."

"It was my decision," she said quietly.

The tension in the crowd seemed to lessen at his upbraiding the intruder.

"That's it, Colonel, let her have it."

"That's telling her, Colonel. Thinks she can come down here and tell us what's what."

"Tell the do-gooder to go back up North where she belongs, Colonel!"

"Quiet! For Christ's sake, quiet. Shut up, all of you."

"Quiet. Shut up! Didn't you hear what the Colonel said!" This added command came from the sergeant who had fetched Parrish and was standing with a small knot of his fellow militia close by the wagon.

As he turned back to Damaris, Parrish saw the hurt in her eyes and sought to explain. "They told me there was trouble—something about a nun. I just never thought it could be you. I thought you were miles from here. Livvy said you were needed at the hospital, that you couldn't come. I didn't want you to come. Why did you?"

"I had to come, especially when I read of ministers quitting their flocks, doctors deserting. I couldn't stay away. I told Mother Charlotte I could never live with myself if I left our sisters to fight this alone, especially when I have the training, the knowledge to help. I broke my promise of obedience. I told her I'd come anyway, even if she wouldn't give me permission."

"A runaway nun!" A smile flittered briefly across his lips, then his brows furrowed. "But I saw Livvy only this afternoon. She said nothing."

"She knew nothing. There wasn't time. I only just got in this morning. I was looking for a conveyance at the train station; that's where I met Mrs. Timms. She told me about these children; she's been thwarted in all her efforts to get them out." She turned to the woman in the wagon. "Mrs. Timms, this is Colonel Parrish. I'm sure he can help us if anyone can."

"I wish I was as sure," he muttered.

"I knows it's the Colonel, Sister; I know who he is."

"Then why didn't you come to me, Mrs. Timms, instead of to Sister Serene? Civil Relief could have helped if you'd come about this sooner."

"Wouldn't've done no good. Wouldn't do nothing for these little' uns. They's for helping white folks."

"Mrs. Timms, the committee's there for everyone; that's its purpose. God knows we can't do everything, and we can't know everything. We're not mind readers; we've got to be told. If you'd come to us in the beginning, this evacuation would have been simple. Now the quarantine's tight; you can see for yourself how strict it is. These people don't want anyone from Memphis to leave the city. They're certain wherever we go we take the fever with us."

"It's not so. It's not people that carry the fever with them," Sister Serene put in. "The university where I studied proved that years ago, early in this century. It's been shown that nurses in hospitals have been exposed time and again to the fever and yet not come down with it. It's not spread by human contagion but by some other agent. Right now we don't know what that is. I only wish we did."

"Well, there's no time to argue medical research; it's not going to reach this crowd, I can assure you. Just who are these children, Mrs. Timms? Where did they spring from?"

"Orphans. They been in an asylum off of Beale, where I live with my daddy. Getting bad there, real bad. They been all alone. The one minding 'em run off, left 'em to fend for theyselves. Don't no one know where that one went. Don't make no difference nohow. I can't do no more than look in on 'em from time to time. I tried to get 'em out 'fore. Same thing happened. I can't help no more. My daddy, he's down with the fever; I got to stay with him. My place is by his side. Sister here said she'd help me. These chilluns got someplace waiting to take 'em, if'n they'll let them go. Else like as not they'll end up on the streets of Memphis. Never was no place for a little 'un, you knows that, Colonel sir. Now, well, you know what it's like same as I do.'' She shook her kerchiefed head. ''Lord! Lord!''

Parrish didn't answer immediately. When he did it was to ask Damaris, ''You say you've examined them?''

''I have, each one. I offered to help Mrs. Timms to get them out only after I'd assured myself there was no sign of the fever. I give you my word, Colonel, that they are healthy.''

Parrish looked at the disconsolate, frightened band of children and at Mrs. Timms guarding them like a mother hen.

''The city's under strict quarantine,'' he repeated, as though to remind himself as much as anyone.

''I know it is, but they're all right, amazingly fit, in fact, for the way they've been living. They've had little enough food from the sound of it.''

''And Mrs. Timms?''

''She's all right too.''

''No one's been allowed to leave the city for weeks.''

''I know. I'm sorry. It places you in a predicament, I know; but if they don't go where they have a place, I don't know what will become of them.''

Guy Parrish grew thoughtful. He turned back to look over the crowd that had quieted, perhaps certain he would turn the wagon back. For whatever reason, it had begun to lose some of its impetus.

''Most of you know me, or know of me. You, Dyer, we served together at Shiloh; and you, Snelling, you were with my father, weren't you?''

''With him throughout, Colonel. Daredevil, that General Parrish. Scared the britches off the Yankees, he did, right up to the end. Warn't afraid of nothing and no one.''

"That's so. I'm proud to be his son.''

"You're like your pa, Colonel; we're right proud of you too.''

'' 'Member that time at Shiloh when we got cut off? Yankees all around, thought we were done for. Rough, it was," Dyer yelled out, not to be outdone.

"I sure do, and I remember when we were down to less than fifty and positioned ourselves to sound like an army coming through the woods. I remember you there, Dyer; you made noise enough for a platoon all by yourself. If we hadn't been so occupied I would have recognized your valor then and there, but I'm glad to do it now. I see you've lost none of that strong voice of yours.''

Dyer's expression was pleased and puzzled at once, and Parrish hastened on. "It's not just Dyer here or Snelling. You were all brave. We fought together side by side. Lots died, just like we're dying in Memphis now, except then we fought back. Here we've got an enemy we can't see, we don't know, and we can't fight back. All of you have watched comrades die. I know I have. Saw my brother fall at Chickamauga; walked over mounds of dead to find him after. I don't have to tell you how it was. But as bad as it was then, let me tell you what's going on here in Memphis now is ten times—a hundred times worse. And it's happening day in, day out. And not just men dying in the worst circumstances, but women, children too.

"This lady here beside me—Sister Serene—is a nun of an Episcopal order who has been trained as a physician at what is probably the country's finest medical school, a school where they've made a special study of this fever. If any doctor knows about the dangers and immunities of yellow jack, it's going to be one who's been trained there. We still don't know how it spreads—the air, water, dirt, filth. We attack it on all fronts because we don't know. Sister Serene says these children are healthy, free from the yellow peril. I would entrust my life to her judgment, and I can tell you there are not too many people about whom I would say that.''

He paused, his eyes narrowed, scanning the crowd. "I put it to you, as one of you, let these children go to where there's a place for them. I'm satisfied there's no hazard to any of you. They'll go directly there, without stopping anywhere, I can promise you that. To make sure they do, I'm going to send along the sergeant and one of his men to escort them."

There were murmurs of dissent, but Parrish's voice rose above them, instructing the sergeant. "You're to see no one leaves the wagon under any circumstances, understand, Sergeant?"

"Yes, sir, Colonel." The sergeant saluted him briskly.

Parrish turned back to the children, giving them the barest perceptible wink. "They don't look much like a bellicose band, do they? But you're to take no chances. You're armed and they're to do exactly as you tell them."

"Yes, sir."

"Get on your way then, and report back any incidents to me as soon as you return."

"Right you are, Colonel."

"But, Colonel Parrish, sir," the scrawny man who had spat on Sister Serene interposed, "you're not going to let this Yankee nun come down here and tell us what to do."

"Stand aside, let the wagon through," the sergeant's voice bellowed as Parrish went over to the remaining dissident.

"You're damned right. Yankees don't tell me what to do. I'll bet you don't let them tell you either."

"Goddamned if they will!" The man let another wad of spittle fly.

"I know that the Sister here had the misfortune to be brought up in the North—we can't all be from God's country—but at least her father was born in Tennessee. Right here in Memphis, wasn't it, Sister? And I think we should hand it to her for coming back here to be with us in our hour of need. I respect her for herself and also because she represents an authority higher than any in this land. I imagine most of you feel much the same way on that score."

"Still . . ." the man began, but further protests were drowned by voices of others.

"Leave off, why don't you."

"Have some respect. She's a nun, after all."

Guy Parrish, seeing that the wagon was moving along

the road without incident, took out his handkerchief and
bent down to wipe the spittle that had fallen on the hem of
Sister Serene's robe.

There were further shouts. "You should watch where
you let that muck of yours fly. That's bad as spitting on
the cross."

"I'm sure it wasn't intentional," Parrish said. "No
harm was done. You are all right, aren't you, Sister?"

"Quite all right—now."

"Come along, then; I'll take you back to town. You'll
be staying with Livvy at the school, I suppose."

She nodded.

As he helped her into the light curricle, she said, "The
children would never have made it without you."

"They'd never have made it at all if you hadn't stood by
them, I can guarantee that." He glanced back. "Let's not
argue the point here. I know crowds, and I know how
fickle they can be." As he started the horses, he went on:
"Poor devils, I can't altogether blame them. We're all
struggling in this quagmire; don't know which way to turn.
They probably feel better for shouting and screaming. I'm
just glad we got there before any serious harm was done.
You really are all right?"

"Yes, I assure you, I am." She looked over at him.
"Do you think the wagon will make it?"

He nodded. "I know the sergeant that's with them. Tell
him to do something, and it's as good as done."

"Good!" She breathed a sigh of relief. "You were
wonderful."

"I didn't face them alone; you did. And I simply applied the advice I learned when first I became a political
animal: Use any and every argument that may work to gain
your point. It's not particularly brave or particularly candid, just expedient, practical."

"May I presume to disagree, Colonel." She smiled at
him; and though he had wished her miles from Memphis
and fever, he found himself overwhelmingly glad to have
her there at his side. Yet he spoke not of that, but of his
sister.

"I saw Livvy only this afternoon. She was just telling
me how she missed you. I can't wait to see her face when
she sees who I've brought with me."

"How is she?"

"She's amazed me. I would never have believed my little sister had it in her to do what she's doing."

Damaris smiled. "She's not your little sister anymore."

"No, I guess she's not, not little at least."

"I had a letter from Arnaud in Knoxville. He's not at all happy about your sending him there. But I guess he's never happy whenever he's away from you, especially now when he feels you're in danger. I tried to explain you had sent him away only because you love him and want to protect him, but I know he's so afraid you'll be taken from him as his mother was. I told him I was coming, that I'd watch over you for him."

"Well," Parrish replied lightly, "if I have you for my guardian angel, there can be nothing to worry about."

"I only wish I felt as sure."

"Damaris, just the sight of you makes me feel better; and yet I meant it when I said I wished you were miles from all of this."

"I had to come, Guy. Surely you of all people must understand. You came back from a haven in England to fight in a war, a war you didn't even believe in. I couldn't stay in New York and read about this, knowing Livvy and . . . knowing all of you were here, and I, a doctor, was doing nothing. You must understand."

"I suppose I do."

"I had to come," she repeated. "I came believing I was prepared for the worst. The daily accounts in the newspapers have been . . . well, ghoulish is the kindest thing I can say for them. Yet in spite of all that, when I walked out of the station to see this city virtually a ghost town with those few inhuman figures walking around with sponges tied across their faces, to see the coffins being loaded on wagons for burial like so much lumber, to hear the cries of 'Bring out your dead' (just like in the history books' account of the black plague that brought London to its knees), to smell the acrid fumes of carbolic mingled with the smoke of burning mattresses, to see the lime lying around the buildings like sprinklings of snow in the midst of this awful heat—I should have been prepared. I'd read all of that and more, yet being there in the midst of it—" She stopped, her voice overcome with emotion.

"Damaris! I wish you hadn't come," he repeated, "and yet . . . yet it's wonderful to see you again. I've thought so much about our talk together that evening in Philadelphia."

"So have I. I was pleased beyond everything when Livvy told me you were to run for the legislature. And when you won, I wanted to write and congratulate you, only—"

"Only? Why didn't you?"

"I . . ." She paused, remembering the number of notes she had written and not sent, and finished lamely: "There's really been so little time."

"Livvy says you're working like a Trojan."

"We're short-handed. It must be endemic in the profession."

"If you thought yourself short-handed in New York, I'm afraid you're in for a rude awakening here. We began with a deficit of doctors and nurses, and the numbers continue to dwindle."

"I just can't understand doctors leaving, Guy." She shook her head. "I don't understand it, especially at a time like this."

"Everyone hasn't your dedication, Damaris."

"Is it dedication? I think I'm just doing what's practical—as you said of yourself just now in getting the children out—just doing what one has the training to do. Maybe I'm not entirely free from vanity, though, for I've come hoping my being here will save lives and make a difference."

"Your being here makes a great deal of difference to me, Damaris," he said quietly.

Though he didn't look at her as he spoke, she studied his face intently. "How are you, Guy? I've been wondering about you."

"I'm fine—now."

"I'll be willing to bet if anyone's been working like a Trojan it's you." Then she stopped short, remembering the last time they had used one another's Christian names, remembering too how she had avoided Mrs. Caylew's reception for the hospital opening because she was sure he would be there—with Eustacia.

Her voice when she resumed was cool, professional, the

tone a doctor might use in advising a patient. "It is well to guard oneself when there is sickness about, Colonel, by not becoming overtired, getting adequate rest and nourishment to keep the body strong enough to withstand the strain."

He looked over at her, about to speak, then changed his mind, nodding. "I understand; it is well to guard oneself, Doctor."

They would see one another often in the days ahead; she was right in setting the tone of their relationship.

He said nothing more as he helped her down except to remark lightly, "I was promised a succulent peach pie here earlier today, made with the last of this summer's peaches. That sounds nourishing, something you'd approve of. I hope they've saved us some."

The peach pie, alas, was gone, for Dr. Mitchum had taken Guy's advice and was seated at the table finishing the last slice as they entered.

"You dog, I might have known." Parrish grinned amid the cries of welcome.

Though he'd been told more than once that he looked tired, for the first time the fatigue, the strain of long hours without sleep, the unceasing heat, the anguish of being a helpless witness to death and destruction, lifted momentarily.

As he watched his sister and the others hugging Sister Serene in greeting, it seemed, for a moment at least, that life had returned to some degree of normality. A wave of well-being swept over him.

Only Sister Angela seemed less than overjoyed at the new arrival; she kept repeating over and over again, much as he had when he first saw Damaris that day, "You shouldn't have come. You really shouldn't have come. You were safe in New York. You should have stayed there, away from all of this."

FIVE

D r. Mitchum had taken Sister Serene under his wing, showing her around the city's worst affected areas, indicating their attempts to combat the epidemic, most of which he labeled futile.

Under his aegis, she was introduced to the other members of their profession, yet despite his support and despite the dire need for physicians, from the very first they all but ostracized her. Whereas in medical school she had to some extent overcome the problem of being a woman by being a nun, in Memphis she found herself condemned on both counts. She fared little better among the nurses, who felt she should have been one of them and often showed resentment at her instructions, saying she was taking upon herself responsibilities that were not hers.

There were muttered complaints when she instructed them. "It's the doctor that tells us what medication to use."

"I am the doctor," she would respond patiently but firmly, "so no more calomel, and take off all these heavy blankets. Just leave one to prevent shivering. I'll look back in in the morning."

Gradually, though not willingly, they began to realize she was to be obeyed. By their actions they let her know they would not give her the respect they gave to her male counterparts; she would have to earn it.

"I can understand now why one of the the most effective doctors I came across during the war, who happened to be a woman, always dressed as a man," Mitchum told Parrish one evening soon after Damaris's arrival. "Make matters worse, she was a Yankee too, name of Mary

Edwards Walker, a graduate of Syracuse. They made her an assistant surgeon. Can still see her standing there in that uniform. Thought it was an affectation at first or some sort of aberration—one of those women born wanting to be a man. Our own Miss Tompkins—or Captain Tompkins, I guess I should say, the Confederates' only female officer—never went that far. God knows we men don't have it all our way, but watching what's happened to this woman doctor since she came to Memphis, I'm beginning to understand why Dr. Walker adopted that male attire—for protection, not from man's brute force but from his even more arrogant prejudicial bent.''

"We think of war as man's business. I say it with no sense of pride; but epidemics and acts of God, as nature's vengeance is so oddly called, belong to men and women alike. At least they afflict both sexes with indifference.''

"You're damned right they do. I never thought I'd ever find myself espousing any of the radical views of that wild Seneca Falls bunch; but after watching the reception given to a physician who, in my opinion, is professionally sound—I can give no greater praise than that, Parrish—I do have a sneaking sympathy for their cause. By God, you'd think they'd be only too delighted to take to their bosoms anyone fool enough to enter this inferno to help, let alone someone with Sister Serene's qualifications. But I swear she's treated worse than Dr. Tate.''

Dr. Tate was a black physician who had recently come from Cincinnati to offer his services. He had been assigned to an area known as Hell's Half Acre, just off Beale Street, a densely populated part of the city that no one was anxious to enter.

"I always thought the Fourteenth Amendment nothing but icing on the cake. Couldn't understand why women pressed to be included in it, but maybe they had a point,'' Mitchum concluded.

"I don't believe she had an easy time of it in medical school,'' Parrish responded thoughtfully.

"I'm damned sure she couldn't have, particularly at that sacrosanct school under that prissy McChord. She's calm, though, takes it in her stride, doesn't seem to let it bother her—on the outside, at least.''

Shortly after her arrival, Sister Serene attended a meeting of physicians at the Howard Association to assess their current strength and to plan future efforts. She sat in the back, beside Dr. Tate, who, unlike most of the others, treated her courteously but professionally.

When neither of them was called upon to contribute, he leaned over to whisper, "I guess we're both outcasts here."

She nodded. "Still, I intend to have my say." And though they tried to ignore her, she did.

"With our constantly dwindling numbers, I wonder whether the areas to which we've been assigned shouldn't be reassessed." She had risen to her feet and paused to look around at the others, either slouched in their chairs or deliberately looking away. "There does appear to be, in some cases at least, an unequal division of work."

"Why don't you let those of us who've been here the longest make those decisions, Sister," grunted a burly, red-faced doctor who had spent his time, from the beginning, in the eastern section of the city, an area far less affected than those near the river.

There was a chime of assenting voices. It was an accepted fact that the straggle of incoming physicians should be assigned to replace those who had died or else fled, which in either case meant their areas were the least desirable. They saw nothing wrong with that. After all, as one succinctly put it, "They'd only come from an innate desire to be either heroes or martyrs; far be it from me to stand in their way." Certainly none who had drawn a relatively safe district could see the need of sharing the greater risk taken by the newcomers.

"Since the majority have no quarrel with the areas assigned, I can see no need to discuss this further," Dr. Walters, who was presiding, declared.

"I, for one, am not quarreling with my assigned area. Beside the horror of Dr. Tate's, I find it relatively easy. All I ask is that we reassess our strength in the light of the districts hardest hit."

"I think Sister Serene has a point," Dr. Benson, another newcomer agreed, but he was swiftly overruled by Dr. Walters. Unlike Sister Serene, Dr. Benson recognized the futility of battling an unwritten, unspoken code according to which age and experience outranked youth and education, let alone race and sex. Still, he smiled sympathetically at Sister Serene, and that brought a cloud of disapproval to the face of his superior.

Undaunted, Sister Serene rose again to press her point. Dr. Walters was trying to decide whether to ignore or to ridicule her, when he was saved from his quandary by Colonel Parrish, whom he greeted with a fatuous smile.

"Is Dr. Mitchum here?" Parrish demanded.

Dr. Walters looked around. "That's odd, I guess he's not. I've been kept so busy answering pointless questions, I didn't realize that Tom hadn't put in an appearance. Must have been called out somewhere."

"Cleo Laroche is looking for him." Parrish ignored the guffawed comment, "Tom always was a lucky dog!" that greeted his remark. "There's some sort of medical emergency she wanted him to look in on."

He looked over indignantly in the direction of someone who whispered out loud, "Probably a case of clap."

"Dammit, that's unnecessary. The woman's doing a great job, and you know it. Since Dr. Mitchum isn't around, maybe one of you with a civil tongue in his head will come and see what it's about."

Sister Serene got up. "I'll come, Colonel. Maybe I can do more good there than I'm doing here."

For a barely perceptible moment Guy Parrish hesitated before thanking her and stepping aside for her to precede him to the dor.

"Hie thee to a nunnery, Sister," a wag called after her, laughing until, seeing the look on Parrish's face as he turned, he hastened to add, "Just quoting the old bard, Colonel—*Hamlet.*"

"Thou art too wild, too rude, too bold of voice. The bard again, sir, *The Merchant of Venice.* But he expresses my own sentiments most exactly," Parrish retorted as he foilowed Sister Serene outside.

"I must apologize for their boorishness," he began.

"Don't trouble. I'm quite used to it."

"Perhaps I should explain," he went on. "Cleo's— Cleopatra's—it's a house of ill-repute. Mrs. Laroche, the . . . the woman who runs it, has converted it into an infirmary."

"I gathered it must be a brothel," Damaris responded

calmly. "Don't worry, I daresay I may find more in common with the people there than with those I just left." She stopped suddenly and stood still in the middle of the sidewalk, facing him in sudden exasperation. "Wouldn't you just think, in the midst of this catastrophic situation, hard on everyone but harder still on physicians who need every hand they can get, that just for a time at least they'd put aside their prejudices, their bickering, their jostling for position? Dr. Walters, stressing his rights, refusing to listen to me simply because, as Queen Elizabeth succinctly but rather indelicately put it, I was born cloven rather than crested." She glanced swiftly at her companion before starting to walk on. "I hope I don't shock your sensibilities, as I seem to with these gentlemen; but I won't deny I'm angry, really angry at their parochial attitude, especially now. I'm even angry for all the times I was angry and said nothing."

He laughed. "Beware the anger of the dove. They'd better watch out."

And suddenly her anger too turned to laughter. "I feel dizzy with the freedom of saying all that. At least one thing I'm grateful to my medical training for is that it's given me the ability to speak out. I know that I know as much as they do, and they know it too."

"Of course they do. Why do you suppose they resent you so? You threaten them not only with your knowledge but with your womanhood. They know how to put down young Dr. Benson, and he knows how to play the game by the rules and sit down quietly when he's told. You don't play their game, so they don't know what to do with you."

"Oh, Guy! It's so good to talk to you. You listen; you don't judge; you understand. I don't know how or why, but I know you do."

"I don't think you've ever been slow to speak out when there was the need." He smiled suddenly. "Remember that speech of yours at the Waldorf, the one that brought down the house? Don't know if that's what she means, but the illustrious Mrs. Vandervoort still refers to you as 'the outspoken one'!"

She laughed again, feeling how good it was to laugh, how good to have someone to laugh with. "All I can remember about that dinner is how nervous I felt; but you gave me heart, especially when you said I'd make an ideal doctor, because a doctor needed the eye of a falcon, the heart of a lion, and the hand of a woman. I kept repeating your words to myself when times got tough in school.''

''Then I wish I could take credit for them, but it's an old proverb—Dutch, I think.''

He stopped before the smart gold and black doorway that marked the entrance over which the sign read PALACE OF CLEOPATRA.

''It doesn't make any difference where it comes from. The fact is you said it, and it was the remembrance of your words that comforted me,'' she responded as he held the door open for her.

Cleo Laroche, a white apron tucked around what was clearly a very expensive and very modish black satin dress trimmed with festoons of fine ivory lace, hurried out of her office as they walked in.

''Where's Tom? Couldn't you track him down either, Guy?'' she demanded.

''No luck, Cleo, so I brought along Sister Serene to look at your patient. She's just arrived and—''

''For Christ's sake, Guy, I need a doctor. There's a woman in labor. I could handle the usual thing, but this is a breech. You know as well as I do that I'm better than most nurses around here. I need a doctor, not a nun.''

Before Guy could reply, Damaris hastened to assert, ''But I am a doctor, Mrs. Laroche.''

The shapely redhead turned, one hand on her tiny waist, to scrutinize the face of the newcomer. ''By God, is it?'' She drew closer, looking directly into her face. ''I'll be damned if it isn't Damaris. Remember me?''

''Katie!''

And in the hallway of what had once been the most prosperous brothel in Memphis, where many a passionate and furtive embrace had taken place, there occurred a most unusual, most unexpected one between a curvaceous red-headed madam and a tall dark-habited nun.

''Fancy seeing you again,'' Cleo Laroche began, then she stood back to survey the black robes. ''They got you, didn't they? I was afraid they would; that's why I was so reluctant to go when you insisted on my calling in Mother what's-her-name.''

"Mother Charlotte.''

"I warned you, you know I did.''

"You did, I won't deny it.'' Sister Serene smiled. "I often thought of you. I wondered whatever became of you.''

"Remember how I always said I'd have a real swanky place someday, remember? Oh, you should have seen it before all this. We had music, good music, not honky-tonk stuff, not too loud, but soft and sweet and refined; not just now and then either but every night. Finest whiskey, champagne even, that's the sort of trade I catered to. And crystal chandeliers. Well, you can still see those. Gaming tables, properly run, nothing underhand, and a decent cook. That's harder to come by than the girls, I can tell you. Come on, I want to show you around. It's different now, of course, but I'll explain how it was, how it will be again.''

"The patient first, Katie,'' she reminded.

"Oh, yes, of course. You're really a doctor then? Well, I'll be . . . Guess I'd better watch my language around you now.''

"I'll bet after medical school I could teach you a few you haven't heard.''

They laughed together, and then both of them realized that Guy Parrish was standing there watching in puzzlement.

"We knew one another a long time ago,'' Damaris explained hesitantly. "You were Katie Dumont, wasn't it?''

"No, Duvere, though my real name was Framp; still is for that matter. But I met some man by the name of Laroche who staked me here, so I kept it. Sentimental of me, I suppose. It's French too; seemed right. And he told me about Cleopatra being from Egypt, like the first Memphis, so I changed my name to Cleopatra Laroche. Everyone calls me Cleo; it's years since anyone called me Katie. Let's see. How long ago was it, Dam?'' she ruminated.

"Ten years, exactly ten years, Katie,'' Damaris answered, her face growing serious.

"Oh, of course you'd remember that. I almost forgot about the poor little tyke. I suppose he died. I didn't think he could ever make it. Remember, I said as much when he was born—skinny he was, no color—but you would have it he'd live. You thought I was being hard-hearted. He didn't have a chance, did he, poor little thing?''

Damaris shook her head, repeating slowly, ''No, no, he didn't have a chance.''

She looked up, feeling Guy Parrish's eyes on her, and said, ''I'll go with Katie and take a look at the patient. You really don't have to wait. I know you're busy.''

''All right then. I'll run another check on Tom Mitchum. But wait for me. I'll be here to take you back.''

''Oh, God, hope I didn't talk out of turn. Guy Parrish's sister's one of you. I forgot,'' Katie said as she conducted Damaris to the room where the newcomer lay.

''No, that's all right, Katie. It's been on my mind. I've often wanted to talk about it.''

Katie had been right. It was a breech birth, and a difficult one for mother and for child. The girl was young; it was her first pregnancy, and the pain had terrified her. Damaris knew she must use forceps to get the baby through the pelvic canal; and for want of any other anesthetic, she allowed Katie to give the girl a little brandy to calm her. Even so, the patient fought against rather than assisted in the delivery.

It took time, far too much time, before Damaris could get a firm grip on the child to edge him carefully but firmly along the natural curve of the birth canal. When she at last held him up, she was sickened at the sight of his pallor, his stillness.

''It won't make—'' Katie began.

''Shut up!'' Damaris snapped fiercely, listening for a heartbeat. ''Get someone to take care of the mother, Katie, and come and help me. I need bowls of water—hot and cold water.''

She fumbled in her bag and breathed a sigh of relief to find she had some rubber tubing, one end of which she inserted in the child's throat, while sucking hard on the other in an attempt to open the windpipe.

''Now, Katie, hot water first, then cold. Hurry; don't stand there. For God's sake, pull up those lace cuffs.''

The baby was thrust from one bowl to another, and Damaris alternately sucked, then blew through the piping

to try to force air into his lungs. Again and again she
applied pressure to his tiny chest.

"It's no good, Dam, he's gone," Katie mourned.

"Shut up, Katie. Don't keep saying that! Have them
bring fresh water—hotter even."

But before the fresh water arrived there was a sudden
jerk, and color began to flood into the baby's face as
breathing began, not deep, not regular, but the child was
breathing nevertheless.

"Dam!" Katie was awestruck. "Dam, I do believe . . ."

Damaris smiled in relief. "Thank God, Katie, I think
he's going to pull through."

"I never saw the like," Katie said later to Damaris,
who, her hands cleaned, was buttoning her cuffs as they
walked back to the hallway where Guy Parrish was waiting. "I never saw the like," Katie repeated to Guy. "That
child was a goner, but she put life back into him. If only
I'd found someone that knew what they were doing when
your little one came, Dam, instead of that lousy student,
maybe things would have been different."

"Maybe, Katie, maybe. We'll never know." Damaris
shook her head, remembering that other child. Looking up
to find Guy Parrish's eyes on her brought her back from
that room in the Five Points district to the Memphis brothel.
"I just hope now the child's survived birth that the fever
won't get him."

"My girls'll give him every care."

"I know they will. I'll check on him tomorrow."

Guy Parrish's face as he helped her into the curricle and
unhitched the horses was impassive. Damaris discovered
that though she might have wanted to relieve her mind by
talking about her child, she really didn't know how to
begin. She turned her attention instead to the other birth.

"I think he'll make it. A breech birth is always difficult,
and he didn't breathe immediately; but as long as there's
no brain damage—and I could see no immediate sign of
any—he's going to be all right. Just as long as he escapes
the fever, that is. New life in the midst of death—strange,
isn't it?"

He nodded. "Yes, it is strange."

From the way he said it, she felt he was not necessarily
speaking of the birth that had just taken place. Her face

must have shown she had discerned his thoughts, for Guy Parrish added, "You don't have to say anything, Damaris, not if you don't want."

"No, I guess I do want to talk about it, Guy. It's just that it's been inside so long. I haven't talked of it to anyone, not since it happened."

"You once told me it did no good to keep things bottled inside."

"I did, and I was right in saying it, and there are times when I'd do well to listen to my own advice. This is one of them."

Still she was silent for a moment before opening the gates of memory that had been locked for a decade. Then, as he drove her back through the deserted streets, everything poured out. She told him everything, well, almost everything except the name of the father of the child she had borne. That she had told no one—not even Mother Charlotte, because Templeton Caylew was the order's benefactor. Nor could she tell Guy Parrish, who was related to him by marriage.

"Was it to exonerate yourself, then, that you decided to become a nun?" He was as much aware as she that she had omitted that one important detail. Though he felt a burning sense of curiosity about the man who had been her lover, an animosity toward this unknown who had possessed her, he was unable to ask her what he most wanted to know, and what she so obviously did not want to divulge.

"Exonerate myself from the sin of having had an illegitimate child?" She shook her head. "I would have given anything for him to have lived; illegitimate or not, that made no difference. I loved him above all else. I would have made a life for him. It wouldn't have been easy, but I would."

He made no answer, holding the reins loosely, looking straight ahead.

"You know, Guy, when I found Arnaud in Memphis, he reminded me of just how my child would have been, just about the same age, similar coloring even, and so dependent, so trusting. I knew I couldn't leave Memphis without being sure he had a home, a good home. I thought of you immediately. Livvy had said your wife . . . that it was unlikely there would be more children in your family, that you would have no son. Not only that. I thought of you because I sensed. . . . Well, I wanted him to be with you. I didn't really stop to analyze why; I just knew that I did."

"Have you since thought of the reason?"

"I . . . I don't know," she said.

"If having the child wasn't the reason you became a nun, what was then?"

"When my child died I didn't want to live. I felt I had nothing to live for. I even tried to kill myself. Mother Charlotte saved me; she saved me from myself. No matter how bad things are, Guy, I came to realize life is a gift for us to use as we will; but it's really not ours to take. Joining the sisterhood gave me a family; it gave me something to live for."

He stopped the curricle in front of the school by the Cathedral but made no attempt to alight.

"Damaris, there's something I have to say. I hadn't intended to say it ever; but you see, while you were with Cleo just now, I tracked down Tom Mitchum. He was at home—"

"And," she prompted.

"He has the fever."

An anguished look passed between them.

"Let me go to him," Damaris said quietly.

He shook his head. "I knew you were busy; I got hold of Dr. Walters. He's there now."

"I don't understand, though, what it is you must tell me, and why, because Dr. Mitchum is stricken."

"Mitchum has been through more epidemics than any of us; he's a tough old stick. If he's down with it, no one is safe—not me, not even you. That's why I have to tell you now what has been on my mind and remains in my heart. I've never said this before to anyone. I'll only say it once and I promise never to repeat it. But since we may not live through this thing, you must know how I feel."

She reached over to touch his hand momentarily. "Don't, Guy; don't say anything. I think I know."

He turned to her, saying nothing for a time. Then he shook his head. "I must say it. I have to. You were the one who told me it was wrong to keep things bottled inside. I may die; we both may. I couldn't bear that to happen without your knowing that I love you, Damaris; you're the only woman I've ever loved, the only one I ever will.''

They sat quite still, side by side, looking at one another without speaking, knowing that there was nothing either one of them could say.

"It's wrong, Guy; it's wrong," Damaris said at last.

"It may not be correct, but it's not wrong," he replied quietly.

She lowered her head and put her hand over her eyes.

"Look at me," he said.

She shook her head.

"You need say nothing, but I had to tell you."

He had reached over to take her hand from her eyes when he heard Livvy's voice calling. She was running down the path toward them.

"Oh, thank heavens, Sister Serene, there you are. I sent someone to find you, but they said you'd left the meeting. It's Sister Angela. She's . . . well, I was hoping against hope I was mistaken, but there can be no doubt of it; her complexion's already yellowing. She says she wants nothing, but she's been repeating the name Mary over and over again. She's got the fever.''

SIX

Sister Angela battled the fever in herself as stoically as she had battled it in others.

All of Sister Serene's coaxing could not make her stay in bed. She insisted on a simple pallet on the floor, arguing that whatever the outcome, the mattress would have to be burned. They were short enough of bedding without her adding to the problem.

The sisters took turns in sitting by her side, wiping her brow, giving her clear liquids to drink. As chills alternated with fever, as the pains in her head grew more severe, as Damaris, sitting at her side, recognized the symptoms, she recognized too her own impotence to do anything to prevent the inevitable outcome. That was a cross heavier than any she had had to bear.

"I came thinking my being here would help, would make a difference," she told Livvy. "What vanity! I'm not able to do anything to combat this scourge; not even for one of my own sisters."

Sister Angela too knew the signs; and as they progressed her cries of "Mary" grew more insistent, causing Livvy concern that Sister Angela, despite her frequent and outspoken attacks on the church of Rome, seemed to have all along cherished an innate desire to embrace mawkish Mariolatry.

Damaris could not allow what she recognized as an unwarranted criticism to pass and assured Livvy, "Nothing could be further from the truth. Mary was the name given to me by the Caylews, the name I used when I worked there with Sister Angela."

"Do you mean it's you she's been calling for all along?

I do think you should have told us earlier." Livvy's reproach was in her face as much as her voice.

"I'm sorry. I guess I should have. I didn't think it important."

Though Livvy tried to be satisfied with the explanation, it was obvious she was aggrieved, particularly when it became apparent that no one besides Sister Serene could answer Sister Angela's needs. It was not that Sister Angela made any complaints; it was simply that if Sister Serene was unavailable, she wanted no one.

"I don't understand why she insists you're the only one who can help," Livvy fumed. "She all but threw me out of her room."

"I suppose it's just that she's used to me. We shared the same quarters when we were at the Caylews'."

Though Angela had never again spoken of the conversation they had had when first she joined the order, Damaris had never forgotten it. At first she had been wary and uncomfortable in her presence, but as Angela gave every sign of having put her affection in proper perspective, so Damaris too put the matter behind her.

Now, however, in the throes of the fever, Damaris discovered that nothing in Angela's affections had changed, nothing had been forgotten. No longer, however, did this strange and perverse affection of one woman for another seem repugnant. All Damaris could think of was that one woman on the threshold of death was crying out to another for comfort. She was relieved to be there, to be able to hold out her hand.

After the convulsions began, Damaris knew the end was near and stayed with her. She had paid little attention to Livvy bustling officiously in the background, but once as she had been bathing Angela's brow, humming to her her favorite folk song, "Greensleeves", she had looked from the peace, adoration even, on Angela's face to the perplexity, even disgust, on Livvy's.

The moments spent at Angela's bedside had to be stolen from Damaris's busy day that now included Dr. Mitchum's rounds as well as her own. She could have spent her entire time at Cleopatra's since its conversion into a full-scale infirmary. Katie had every right to be proud of her work. Her girls worked as hard as, even harder than, other

nurses. They were clean, quick, and reliable, and followed
instructions to the letter. But of course, Katie saw to that.

Praise for Katie's efforts was forthcoming from all sides.
The Mayor, now recovered, was promising to name a day
in her honor after the epidemic.

"Maybe he thinks I won't make it, but I'm going to
survive if only so as not to allow the old bastard off the
hook. You know, Dam, deep down I've always hankered
for respectability." Her face grew serious, and she picked
up a letter and tenderly drew it from its envelope. "Just
look at this. Read it."

The letter, simply addressed to Mrs. Cleopatra Laroche,
Memphis, came from a group of women in Louisville,
commending her for her gallantry. "Every heart in our
great country responds with affectionate gratitude to the
noble example you have set for every Christian man and
woman."

"It's a wonderful tribute, Katie, but no more than you
deserve," Damaris said, handing her back the letter, watching as Katie folded it with care before returning it to the
envelope.

"I'm so proud of the damned thing, I want to shout it
out from the rooftops. Not that there's anyone around to
hear me in this godforsaken place."

"You should be proud, Katie. Frame it, hang it here on
the wall in your office."

"That's an idea. A gold frame, I think, wide and heavy,
but not too heavy to take away from its contents," Katie
mused. "And rather than hanging it in here, maybe I'll
move that painting of Venus out in the hall and put it
there. I only allow a select few in my office, but every
damned one of the bastards has to pass through the hall."

Though her time was full, it was not full enough to
prevent Damaris's thoughts from turning time and again to
Guy Parrish, to his feelings for her. She knew why she'd
been unable to look at him when he told her of his love; he
would know that she felt as much, even more, for him. It
was wrong; it must be wrong. She had forsworn such an
affection; and even if she had not, there was Eustacia.
Eustacia would always be there.

She made every effort to quash the emotions he aroused
in her, but the more she told herself she must forget, the

more she remembered. Resolutions to be strong, to resist, were broken as soon as she saw him, for inevitably their paths often crossed. Though only an exchange of necessary information or the barest commonplaces passed between them, whenever their eyes met it was as though they knew that any contact, even one so remote, was dangerous, and immediately one or the other would look away.

There came a day, however, at Dr. Mitchum's bedside, when they found themselves unable to tear their glances from one another. Damaris had been calling upon the doctor regularly. His case had gone beyond the initial chills and pain, and a subnormal temperature and pulse rate had set in, giving the appearance of convalescence. This was, however, the most critical stage. It could mean true convalescence or else be the prelude to the black vomit of blood and stomach acids that signaled the end.

"How is he?" Guy Parrish had come into the room just as she was about to leave.

"I can't tell. It's in abeyance. We must wait."

Dr. Mitchum opened his eyes. "Guy, thank God you got them to stop those damned cannons. I feel like dying in peace."

"We're not going to let you go so easily, are we, Damaris?"

"It won't be long now. You can't fool this old stick. Yellow jack and me, we're old enemies. I know this fever, and I know the end's not far."

"Don't . . . don't talk like that, Doctor," Damaris cautioned. "You know that part of the cure is to wish to be cured. I'm sure you must have told your patients that over and over again."

"Good old Seneca. Yes, I've repeated that old saw of his a thousand times."

"May be an old saw, but it works." She had brought fresh linen for him and had finished putting the pillow case on. Plumping the pillow, she slid it under his head.

"Mmmm, it smells like your mother's linen used to, Guy, and you, Sister. What is it?"

"Lavender." It was Guy Parrish who answered.

"Lavender"—he buried his face in the pillow for a moment—"lavender belongs to a civilized world, not in this mayhem; but it's nice to remember there once was such a place. Oh, but I'm tired, so very tired. I guess all I want to do is give in to gravity. All my life I've been fighting against that pull back into the earth where we all end up, just don't want to fight it anymore. I'm just going to lie back on my lavender-scented pillow and give up the ghost. I'm tired of this charnel house, sick and tired." His voice grew fainter. "Nothing will get better until the frost comes; and it's hot, still so damned hot. Never knew such heat in September, never did know such heat . . ."

His voice trailed off. It was then that Guy's eyes had met those of Damaris, in question at first, wondering whether Dr. Mitchum was even then dying. But when neither looked away, when gray eyes clung to blue, blue to gray, saying all the things their tongues could never utter, they acknowledged that their situation was as doomed as that of the city.

Momentarily they had forgotten the patient, everything but one another; but when at last Damaris tore her glance from his, she saw Dr. Mitchum's eyes were not only open but sharply aware of the intensity of that moment.

She got up. "I must go now, Dr. Mitchum. I'll be back later."

"I love it when you come to see me, Sister; but I know your time is spread thin. There are others who can use it to better advantage than me. I shouldn't say it, perhaps, but that God of yours is an enigma. If He, in all His wisdom, is going to visit us with plagues and pestilences, it does seem He might at least even the odds by sparing those struggling to combat adversity."

She made no reply. Each time she saw the horror that surrounded them—coffins piled everywhere like so many bales of cotton, decomposed bodies found so decayed that they were virtually unrecognizable as to race or sex, death being the ultimate leveler—then she found her heart filled with a disquieting sense of doubt that gnawed at her faith as relentlessly, as nauseatingly, as rats' teeth gnawed at dead and dying bodies. Rather than remembering the comforting words of the Beatitudes, she thought of Job. Why Memphis? Had it been so sinful that it deserved to be wiped from the face of the earth? Would God, in answer to their pleas, dare to answer them as He had Job, from out of the whirlwind, saying He had ordained this plague?

How had He dared allow it? she thought in anger, stopping short, remembering the rebuke Job had received for questioning. It was blasphemous to think as she did. Once she began to doubt, skepticism and a despondency even deeper than that suffered after the loss of her son engulfed her. As the days wore on and the death rate, rather than leveling off, continued to rise, she came to understand how Guy Parrish had lost his faith during the war. Without God the world made no sense; yet to look around and to believe that there was a kind and loving God and that He condoned what was happening made even less sense. Doubt grew, and with it desperation that all of her training had taught her nothing, except a realization of her own impotence. She was helpless, marking time, waiting, as they all waited, for nature to run its course, for the summer heat to fade, for the first frost.

She thought back on how confident she had been when she arrived, believing her presence would make a difference. What arrogance! She stood by with Mrs. Timms, able to do nothing more than watch as her elderly father succumbed to the fever.

Mrs. Timms knelt at his bedside, and bowed her head. "Would you say a prayer for him, Sister?"

Damaris hesitated, then knelt beside her. " 'I am the resurrection and the life, saith the Lord. He that believeth in me, though he were dead' "—her voice broke—" 'yet he shall live.' "

As she broke off, she felt the comfort of Mrs. Timms's arm around her shoulders. "There, there child. You tired and you seen too much. Never fear. He's alookin' down on us. I believe my daddy's with Him now, this very minute, and that make me so happy."

And slowly Mrs. Timms began to hum, and then to sing in a loud, joyful voice, " 'Swing low, sweet chariot, coming for to carry me home,' " and as the volume of her voice filled the room, Damaris began to weep as she hadn't wept since the death of her child, deep, guttural sobs. Mrs. Timms, without missing a note, pulled her head to her bosom, holding her close to her, so that the words and notes of the spiritual reverberated from deep in her diaphragm to echo in Damaris's ears and fill her head.

"Thank you." She wiped her eyes as Mrs. Timms

finished, though she continued to hum softly. The woman's faith humbled Damaris, who had no words of comfort to offer in return. She was empty, numb.

On her way back to St. Catharine's School, she heard the church bells tolling, an eerie sound echoing through an all but deserted city. Later she learned they marked the demise of the son of the leader of the Confederacy, Jefferson Davis, Jr., who had succumbed to the fever. He was mourned, but of more immediate concern was the fact that Sister Angela had begun to spew forth the black vomit. Damaris stayed by her side all night.

"Oh, Mary, I love you so . . . I've always loved you." The cry had reverberated throughout the building early the following morning as she died.

As Damaris helped Livvy to robe her body in her habit, she felt her eyes fixed on her, questioning her, but she offered no explanation. Going through Sister Angela's few personal effects, Damaris discovered she still had the copy of Mrs. Trollope's book about America, and on an impulse Damaris put it in her hands.

"But surely she has a Bible," Livvy objected.

"I didn't see one. This was her favorite book. When I worked as her assistant, she used to read it to me at night before going to bed."

Again the look of puzzled confusion was directed at her. She was thinking about Sister Angela's cry. Damaris knew she couldn't possibly understand. Maybe her obvious abhorrence was to be expected; the strange, the unusual, was always suspect. Perhaps she should have talked to Livvy about Angela, but she didn't; somehow she didn't care what others thought. It didn't matter. Nothing mattered.

For want of an Episcopal priest—the earnest young man who had come to replace Father Daley having succumbed to the fever within days of his arrival—Livvy asked Father Quayle to read the burial office. Generously he consented to leave the Pinch, where he had stayed throughout, where the Irish population was dwindling at a rate faster than any other. The toll taken on the priest was evidenced in his haggard face, his gaunt figure. He looked, as Sister Agnes said afterwards, like death itself.

" 'God is our hope and strength, a very present help in trouble. Therefore will we not fear, though the earth be moved and though the hills be carried into the midst of the sea.' "

As he spoke, Damaris remembered her first meeting with Nanny Wickers, their days at the Caylews', her strong opinions. What, she wondered, would she think of a Catholic priest officiating at her burial? Would her lips have tightened in disapproval? Would she have had some scathing comment for Father Quayle? No, as Sister Angela she had changed; she had softened. But then Damaris remembered that her affections had remained unchanged, that she had kept so much to herself. Had anyone ever really known her? Had Sister Angela known herself?

Damaris looked up as the prayer finished to find Livvy's eyes on her, questioning still. I suppose she knows, Damaris thought; I suppose she condemns Angela. Maybe that's what every normal woman should do, yet I can't find it in my heart. She turned away, to hear Father Quayle saying, "Sister Angela, a lovely name. Well, now she's with the angels."

Was she? Damaris wondered. She looked up, again acutely aware that Livvy's unflinching gaze had never left her. What was it she saw there—puzzlement, perhaps, or disappointment, or even hostility?

Suppose I were to tell her I love her brother. Would she detest me as much for that as for what she now believes? Damaris wondered.

I'm imperfect, Livvy, she wanted to say, but I'm not imperfect for the reasons you're thinking.

She said nothing.

Nothing mattered. Life was decaying all around her. Soon there would be nothing. None of them would survive.

The black vomit came to Dr. Mitchum too. She stayed with him as the convulsions set in. She listened to his rambling words.

"Got to be something, got to be some way. Not in the air. Not in the water."

It was, she thought, no more than rambling, a confused dream. But as she listened she realized he was still searching for the cause of the fever.

"One day they'll discover the cause, Dr. Mitchum; they will," she comforted.

"You will." His voice had become quite lucid, and that frightened her. It meant the end would be near.

"I don't know. I don't think I know anything."

"That's a sign you're a good doctor. You're not afraid to admit what we all know in our hearts. That will make you go on."

"I don't feel like going on with anything, Dr. Mitchum."

"Don't say that, Sis . . . Don't you have any other name besides Serene? It's damned silly, especially now when you're looking anything but serene." He spoke with such normal exasperation that she began to wonder whether he was going to cheat death after all. "What was that I heard Guy call you?"

"Damaris, Damaris Fanshawe."

"Damaris—that's a damned sight better. You'll come out of this, Damaris, and you'll work on this fever if it takes your lifetime. Do you understand? You're going to win where I have failed."

She smiled. "If you say so, Doctor."

"Guy Parrish is a lucky man, you know, a very lucky man. I never had a woman love me, not really love me. I wish I had."

She held his hand and his eyes closed. She felt relieved that his eyes closed, for they had told her more than his words that he knew everything.

"He's a lucky man," he said again, his voice growing fainter. "A lucky man. Even the mosquitoes don't bite him."

He was quiet, and she felt for his pulse, still there, but faint, very faint and growing fainter.

Unexpectedly his eyes opened, and he gave a guttural cry. "The mosquitoes, Damaris, the mos—"

He was silent, still. His pulse was no more.

Damaris sat still, watching, waiting, for what she did not know. Dr. Mitchum was dead. He would never again move or speak. His body seemed heavy as stone; without life it had indeed given in to gravity. As she sat quite still looking at a lifeless body devoid of soul, she thought of all the others she had seen, all those countless others who had been born and lived with hopes and dreams, only to finish in the agony of the putrid vomit of the saffron scourge.

They had worked and strived, yet nothing remained, not even a marker on an individual grave.

She thought too of her own dreams and aspirations. She had come to Memphis not only with hope but with the conviction that she could be of help. She had been able to do nothing. She was helpless. Worse yet, she felt betrayed. She had believed in God. All these years she had believed and served; yet if the God she had worshiped were there, what sort of a God could He be to look down on this inferno? What sort of a power would allow such evil?

She fell to her knees. She must force herself to believe. If she didn't, what was left? Nothing but a void. She tried hard to pray; she would catch a line of a prayer, but the rest of it would fade from her memory. She tried to say out loud the few words she remembered, but they wouldn't come.

Then, instead of praying, she was on her knees pounding the floor in front of her with her fists, crying, screaming, "God, oh, God, where are You? Where are You? If You exist, I command You to tell me why—why—why—why?"

Each repetition of the question was accompanied with an even fiercer pounding on the floor before her, yet even as her fists began to burn, sting, bruise, she didn't stop. She couldn't stop; not until she felt a hand on her shoulder.

"Damaris, don't. I beg you, don't. You mustn't let this happen to you."

Her hands fell still in her lap, and she lowered her wrathful, tear-stained face to them so that her cry of response was muffled by them.

"Guy! You, you of all people!" she accused. "You tell me I must not, you who long ago lost all belief and chided me for mine! I'd have thought you, above all people, would have understood."

"It's because I do understand that I can't bear you to go through this suffering. I can't bear you to have to experience the emptiness, the utter futility, the nothingness that I felt all those years until you brought meaning back into my life. Oh, Damaris, I chided you for believing, but I've been so relieved that you had that to hold on to in these past weeks. Without it, it's too easy to give in to insanity in this hell. I haven't believed, but having you here has kept me going when I thought I could go no farther. You must hold on to something, Damaris. I wish I could, but I can't ask that it be me.'' He raised her to her feet, and gently wiped the tears from her face. ''Come along. I'll take you back.''

SEVEN

September passed into October with little abatement in the heat, though the midday sun was no longer as high or as fierce. The deaths too continued, though the fatalities had diminished from the two hundred experienced on that darkest of days, the eighth of September. Just when the sisters began to feel that, apart from Sister Angela's death, they might remain without further casualty, Sister Agnes was stricken, the black vomit occurring so swiftly they believed she must have been carrying on with her duties without mentioning the early symptoms. Her demise was soon followed by that of Sister Bertha.

"Why is God sparing us?" Damaris demanded, as much in anger as sadness, as the nuns' bodies were consigned to the grave. "We've proved our ineffectiveness. We're no more than onlookers to death and destruction. Or is that what He wants—witnesses to disaster?"

"Hush, Sister," Livvy had cautioned sharply, looking around to see who might have heard. "Remember our position. Besides, haven't we done everything that we can possibly do?"

Relations between Damaris and Livvy had been strained ever since Sister Angela's death; and Damaris, who had fought to hold back the hot words as long as she could, bit her lip, resolving to speak no more.

Guy Parrish put a restraining hand on his sister's arm. "Livvy, please. Everyone knows you've done everything you can—all of you—more than is ever expected by one human being of another. Damaris speaks only for herself, and as a physician. She's blaming herself. She shouldn't, but let her speak; let her say what is in her mind and her heart.''

"It's all very well to excuse *Sister Serene*." Livvy pointedly emphasized the name to indicate that her brother's use of Sister Serene's Christian name had not passed unnoticed. "But we're supposed to set the example. If we lose hope, how can we expect others without the strength of our faith to sustain it?''

"Don't you think, Livvy," he intervened swiftly, remembering the scene at Dr. Mitchum's deathbed, "that you—all of you—may be expecting too much of yourselves?''

"Don't make excuses for me, Colonel Parrish," Damaris put in. "I apologize for my outburst, Livvy. It won't happen again.''

As he helped them into the carriage, Guy pressed her hand for a moment in encouragement. That, and the look that passed between them, was observed by Livvy and the sight of her own brother siding with another increased her annoyance.

Damaris sat back, saying not another word, yet her mind was in a turmoil. If only she could seek comfort in Guy Parrish, she thought, before realizing that of all the things that had crossed her mind that perhaps was the most dangerous. Had her friendship with Livvy been as it once was, she might have been able to confide in her; but since Sister Angela's death Livvy had become virtually unapproachable.

On her return from the cemetery, Damaris found a letter awaiting her from Arnaud. It came not from Knoxville but from Bellechasse. He pleaded with her not to tell his father he was there, for he would surely send him away again. He assured her he was quite safe; no cases of the fever had occurred there. He asked her for news and for her promise to come and see him before she returned North.

Before she returned North. . . . It sounded so normal. She never thought of returning anywhere; she never thought of a life beyond when it was all over. She often wondered whether it would ever be over. Once she even imagined that they were all dead and had been consigned to hell. She was glad to feel a mosquito stinging her face. Even the wretched itch it left made her aware that she was alive.

Still, she thought, the insect must have been desperate for someone to bite. Her mother used to say she lacked sweetness, for even the mosquitoes shunned her.

Her sense of futility, her loss of faith haunted Damaris. She sometimes found herself envying physicians who could hide their powerlessness in the oblivion of alcohol; yet the fact that she could even consider such an escape emphasized the depth of her failing, not only professionally but spiritually too.

Ever since Dr. Mitchum's death she had been unable to pray. She was torn between making excuses for avoiding chapel or attending with the others and going through the ritual while cursing her lack of integrity. Had there been a priest to turn to, she might have confessed her troubled state; but no replacement came for the last young priest who had been cut down within days of his arrival.

If only she could have talked frankly to Guy—surely he would have understood—but they were never alone together. That was, she supposed on further consideration, just as well.

Then in the middle of October, some days after the burial of their sisters, they awoke to find a frost, a heavy frost, covering the lawn before the house, on the branches of the trees, withering the last summer rose.

"Hallelujah!" Livvy's shout rose, echoing through the all but deserted rooms. "Hallelujah! It's over. It's finished. Yellow jack's gone."

It was the first good frost and a sure sign it was over. The fever had never survived a sharp frost. With her lips Damaris joined in the rejoicing, yet her thoughts were of the dead, those thousands who had died, many of them in her arms. She couldn't bring herself to give thanks to God. Thanks for what? her indignant heart demanded. Thanks for a graveyard overflowing; thanks for the destruction, almost in entirety, of the Irish population in the Pinch; thanks for a deserted, broken city; for families split apart; for the looting, the licentiousness, the lack of food, the avarice of gravediggers and suppliers who had demanded exorbitant recompense from survivors for simply doing their job.

Perhaps, she thought, she should give thanks for her own survival. A resounding *No* rose inside her. It was no victory to have survived to carry the memory for the rest of her life. Besides, why had she survived while others died? There was as little reason for that as for anything else. She was a sister of the Order of St. Catharine who had lost her faith; she was a physician who had been unable to do anything to save the lives of the victims of the capricious fever. Her anger and frustration grew; she knew none of Livvy's elation, and paradoxically she felt herself the lesser because she did not. All she knew was that she was tired in mind and body, tired down to the very marrow of her bones.

She decided to leave immediately; there was no longer any reason to stay. There had really been no reason to come; she had served no worthwhile purpose. Perhaps she had been able to make the last days of some of the victims more comfortable, but a good nurse could have done as much. All her studies, all her training had not enabled her to save one life.

It was only as she readied for the journey that she remembered Arnaud's letter and his plea that she see him before she left. Perhaps he had not heard the fever was at last controlled. She should give him that news and say good-bye. She might never see him again. She could never go to Bellechasse after Eustacia returned; nor could she have gone if Guy had been there, but Livvy had told her he had left for Knoxville, seeking aid for survivors and funds to raise a new Memphis from the ashes of the old. She was relieved she had not had to say good-bye to him.

Looking out from her seat beside the driver of the gig, whom she directed to take her to Bellechasse rather than to the station, she let her attention wander from the old man's continuous ramblings about the epidemic and its likely outcome. Her farewell from Livvy had been so unlike their other farewells, and she regretted the loss of her friendship. Perhaps she might have tried to explain about Angela, but it seemed like a great effort, and somehow she didn't care. In her own way, strange though it might be, she appreciated Angela's love. How could she condemn her for it? She remembered Mother Charlotte's cautions on "particular friendships." Yet Angela had done nothing wrong, to her or to anyone else. She had been made differently from others, that was true, but was she to blame for that any more than Damaris was to blame for her feeling for Guy Parrish?

She was a nun, bound to chastity, bound to deny affections. Even if that were not so, Guy Parrish was a married man. It was a passion doomed on every count. Yet if she did nothing, as Angela had done nothing, was that love wrong in itself? She suspected it was, as it had been wrong of Angela to love her. Yet how could a love be denied that was only too real, too alive to the one who bore it?

She was glad she hadn't seen Guy Parrish before she left, glad she had been relieved of having to appear cool and detached under his sister's eyes, burdened by the turmoil within. For his sake, for her own, she could never allow herself to see him again.

"Worse'n I ever seen," the driver was repeating, shaking his head. "I been here in '67, and then there was '55; I 'member that one. Nothing like this though. There was another way back, '28 I believe it was. Don't remember nohow—was nothing but a little biddy then, no higher than ma daddy's knee—but he used to talk 'bout that one. You know, Sister, in '73, I thought Memphis was done and gone, gone for sure, but it come back. Won't this time, though; they won't never rebuild this place."

"Perhaps. I don't know."

He was a nice old man, but she didn't feel like talking. Anyway, she didn't know anything, she thought diffidently, staring around her at the changing foliage of the trees. She'd always loved the colors of fall, the panoply of yellows and reds, nature's vibrant, heroic display before the inevitable sleep. The colors were exciting, full of bravado, not like the tranquil greens of spring, supple and tender with promise. They were a last outburst against the inevitable. They fitted her mood.

As she watched, the colors blended into one another and she saw flashes of vivid orange, vivid like something from a dream—or a nightmare. She tried to focus on individual trees, but found it difficult to do so. Every jolt of the gig on the corduroy road passed through her body, along her aching spine to her pounding head. She was exhausted, more than she had realized. Maybe she should have written to Arnaud instead of coming.

She thought of asking the driver to turn back, but they

had already reached the tall gates of Bellechasse. Arnaud would be so disappointed, especially if he were ever to discover she had been that close. She need only stay for a short while; there would be a conveyance to return her to the railroad station in time for the evening train.

"Drop me off here," she said. "I'll walk the rest of the way. It will do me good."

Anything was better than that jolting, she thought as she started out. Besides, she needed to clear her head; she mustn't let Arnaud see her in a state of confusion. The house came into view, and she was relieved to see there was no one outside, no faces looking from the windows. She must collect herself.

Midway down the wide drive she stopped, a terrible suspicion dawning upon her. The pounding in her head had grown worse; she felt very cold. In fact, chills were running through her body. She was shivering; her teeth were chattering. She looked back. The gig she had come in was long gone. She thought of going out to the road and waiting until someone passed to take her back to Memphis. It was not a well-traveled road. Besides, who would pick her up in that condition?

She changed her direction; instead of continuing along the drive to the house, she cut across the lawn behind the great copper beech, walking in the direction of the summer house. Now her face was burning. There was sweat pouring down her body under her robes, and her head was heavier than ever. She was relieved that she had not reached the house, that she had not seen or touched Arnaud. She turned the door handle of the summer house. It was open, and she went inside and sank to the floor.

As she lay there, she knew beyond any doubt that she had the fever.

EIGHT

What a travesty of fate to succumb to yellow jack now when the frost at last had come. Could it be God's punishment? Vaguely that thought crossed Damaris's mind as she lay on the floor of the summer house. To think she had carried the dreaded fever to Bellechasse, to Arnaud. Never must he know she was there. Perhaps later she could find a way to leave, to get back to Memphis, but first she must rest.

She lay still, remembering not to touch the day bed. That had belonged to Guy's mother; she must not contaminate it or it would have to be burned. She did, however, reach over to pull down a cover, for the fever she had felt crossing the lawn had turned again to violent chills that shook her body. She knew all the symptoms; she had watched them often enough.

All day, all night she lay there. She thought she heard a train whistle and wondered whether it was the train she should have been on. Once she opened her eyes to see a yellow arc in the dark sky. Was it a crescent moon or had someone upended the scale of justice? As time passed, she grew delirious; she was no longer aware of where she was, sometimes not even sure of who she was. Her mouth was parched; she thirsted for water. In a moment of lucidity she remembered that great river nearby. What irony! She remembered a story she'd read as a child of a man in a desert dying of thirst with an oasis close by that he hadn't the stength to reach. How frantically she had urged him to rise, to go those few steps, to drink and save his life. But he hadn't, and no more could she.

She remembered Dr. Mitchum talking of giving in to

gravity; she too had succumbed to its force, for even had she wanted to, she couldn't have risen from the floor. She didn't care; she didn't want to. Once she thought she heard voices, but she made no attempt to call out. She didn't want to be found. To die would be a relief. She wondered how long she had been lying there, how long before the black vomit would begin. She tried to remember. A day, sometimes more, then the final convulsions. Horrifying, yes, especially alone. She now knew how Angela had felt; she was glad she'd been there to comfort her, to hold her hand.

The fever returned; she fell into a coma; she was dying. She knew she must be dying, for she saw little Vicky, her arms filled with briar roses. She smiled. "I told you I'd be here waiting."

Damaris was comforted. Beneath her, rather than the hard floor she felt a softness that gave to the weight of her body; there was water on her parched lips, coolness on her fevered brow, the soothing scent of lavender in her nostrils. She even thought someone spoke her name, Vicky, perhaps, calling to her from heaven.

She found herself thinking of Guy Parrish, calling his name. Was that wrong? She was even at that moment dying. Would she be held accountable for having loved him?

She was delirious; she knew she must be, for she imagined she saw him. It wasn't simply seeing him that made her realize it was a hallucination; but she saw him beside her, on his knees, praying. The idea of Guy Parrish praying to God!

She was delirious, not yet dead, for as she had witnessed so often, the fever, the chills, the delirium passed. Lucid again, she opened her eyes. She was in bed, in the bed she had taken such pains to preserve from infection, beneath clean lavender-scented linen. Her robes were gone; she wore a fine cotton nightgown. She was in the summer house at Bellechasse. There was a table beside her and beside that a chair, but no one was in it. She looked down at her yellow-tinged hands and remembered the fever; so it wasn't over. She was waiting, waiting for the black vomit, waiting for the final convulsions.

She heard the door open. Surely it wasn't Arnaud; he

must not come near. She turned her head on the pillow; she was so weak that even that movement jarred her.

"Guy! Guy! It was you! I thought . . . I thought—"

"Damaris, you're going to be all right. Don't waste your strength trying to talk. I've brought some broth for you to drink. Come along. I won't take no for an answer. It's made with the best calf's-foot jelly, and it's a guaranteed cure for everything."

As she looked up at his face, he smiled, but concern was in his gray eyes. Was she dreaming or, perhaps, already dead and in heaven? But the feel of his arm placed gently around her neck to raise her head, the hard metal of the spoon against her lips, the warmth of the broth on her tongue, those were real enough. Slowly, one spoonful followed another, and all the time he talked of the swallows flying south, of the splendor of the copper beech on the front lawn, of Arnaud who sent his love and was longing to see her.

"He mustn't come, Guy. He mustn't come near."

"Not now, but soon; soon I'll be able to move you into the house."

"No, no. The fever's not over; it's only in abeyance."

"You're getting better, Damaris." His voice was determined. "Do you understand? You're getting over it; you're recovering."

She shook her head. "We both know this fever, Guy. It's just in abeyance until the vomiting and—"

"It's not always so." He put aside the bowl and took both her hands in his. "You're not going to die. I'm not going to let you die."

She looked out the window at the endless blue sky. "I don't really care. You know, we die hundreds of times in our lives, not just once. Every turn of the path, every encounter or event that shapes or changes us, each one is a death; but the last one must come." She turned back to him.

"I saw Vicky. She was waiting for me."

"Vicky?"

"Frank's little sister—the one who died. She said she'd be waiting for me with flowers, and she was."

"Damaris," he said firmly, "you've run a very high

fever. You're a doctor; you know a high fever causes delusions."

"But I—"

"Vicky can't claim you; not yet, not for a long time."

"I really don't mind. In fact, everything had become so complicated, it will almost be a relief. It's—"

"Don't," he interrupted sharply. "You're never to say that again—never. Do you understand? I care that you get well. Maybe that's the only thing I really care about. Because I care, you can't give in. Remember what you said to Tom Mitchum, that the greatest part of the cure is the wish to be cured. You're not to give up, Damaris. I won't allow you to give up. If you give up, then I shan't care about living; and just now, in this moment with you beside me, I care very much."

"Don't say that, Guy. You have Arnaud, Bella—"

"I know, I have the children; but you're the one who made life for me worth living again. I've told you how broken my spirits were after the war. It was something like what happened to you during this epidemic—seeing no hope, only despair, only the futility of everything—that macabre sense of futility. I wasn't living when first we met, not really; but you brought feeling back to my heart; you made me realize what warmth can come from caring for another. If you won't fight for your own life, fight for mine. I don't want to die again; and that's how it will be without you."

"You can't place that burden on me," she protested weakly.

"I can and do. I do so without compunction. If you die, you'll take part of me with you. I'm not ready for that. I don't want to hear any more about dying, understand?"

With that he took up the bowl and once more carefully refilled the spoon.

"This was your mother's bed. You shouldn't have put me on it. Now it will have to be burned."

"My mother would be glad to know her bed served such a good purpose." He held out the spoon. "No more talking now; you're to save your strength. What you need is sustenance."

He stayed with her, holding her hand, wiping her brow, touching her lips with cool water. By nightfall the vomit began, and he held the bowl catching the dark phlegm tinged with blood from the stomach, gently rubbing her back after each onslaught. It did not last long; then she waited for the convulsions to begin, feeling the warmth, the comfort of his hand in hers, feeling the strength of his body flowing into hers.

The convulsions did not come.

By the next morning even Damaris no longer doubted that she was on the road to recovery. She was able to take fruit juices and to keep them down.

"I think, perhaps—" she began.

"I don't think. I know. It's over, Damaris; the fever's over. You've come through."

"I guess so." She lay back, weak, living but lifeless. She had come through. She looked up at him. "I never would have without you. How did you come to be here? I thought you were on your way to Knoxville; at least Livvy said you were."

"That's right, I was. I'd thought to come by the school to see you, but frankly I couldn't stand the thought of saying good-bye, so I came directly to Bellechasse to pick up some things. I was surprised to find Arnaud here. He told me you knew, that he'd written to you, that you'd promised to see him before you returned North. I thought it odd you hadn't kept your promise. For whatever reason, that night I couldn't sleep. I got up and started walking. I came over to the summer house; I often come here to think. I opened the door . . . and there you were."

Damaris grew thoughtful. "I don't remember much, but if seeing Vicky was a delusion, the other must have been too." She looked at him steadily. "I thought I saw you at my bedside, on your knees, praying."

He didn't answer, and she said, almost with relief, "Then it was."

He shook his head. "No, Damaris, Vicky was, but that wasn't. I did pray at your bedside. I prayed because I was afraid you might die. I knew no doctor could help; I knew you couldn't fight for your own life; I knew I couldn't save you—so I prayed." Almost apologetically he added, "It was the only thing I could think of to do."

"But you told me you didn't believe."

"I know." He paused. "I've been rather proud in my

defiance. It wasn't an easy thing, I discovered, to get down on my knees and to pray. It forced me to admit that maybe God did exist after all.'' He paused before going on slowly, ''When my father was dying, he asked me to get down on my knees and pray with him. I didn't want to, but I did, repeating the words while hating myself for my hypocrisy. But when I knelt by your bedside, I did it knowing that even if you were conscious you would not pray for yourself. Very frankly, at that moment it was not only all I could think of to do but the most important thing I could think of to do.''

''I still don't understand. You've always said—''

''That there was no God, I know. Now I'm not sure. All I know is that when I prayed beside your bed, I knew at that moment you and I were not alone.''

Damaris shook her head angrily. ''No, don't. I won't have it, not from you of all people. You're the one who should understand.''

''I do. But I do.''

''Then why do you say these things that confuse me?''

''I'm equally confused, but I had to tell you what I felt.''

''There can't be a God,'' she reaffirmed. ''If there is, He's mean and vengeful. I'd rather have it that He doesn't exist than to worship a God who would allow things like this epidemic to happen.''

''I'd be the last one to argue with you, except to say we live in an unjust world. Maybe we shouldn't expect fairness, even from God, at least in the sort of human terms that we define. How or why God should allow such calamities as the war and yellow fever epidemics to happen I've no answer. I've long wrestled with that. I don't know the answer. Maybe He has no choice.''

''God told Job He runs the world, He makes the larks fly. If He can do that, if He is a God of love, why, why?''

''You're challenging Him, and that's not necessarily wrong. I believe a good honest doubt is better than blind, unthinking faith any day.''

''I don't know, Guy. I don't know.'' She shook her head.

He got up. ''That's quite enough theological reasoning.

Now I'm the doctor. Such power over others—you must love it, Dr. Fanshawe."

"I had little enough power during the epidemic."

"No one had. You must stop torturing yourself."

"If only we knew how it came, we might be able fight it."

"Dr. Mitchum had been trying for years to discover the answer to that."

"I know, even at the end, in his delirium, he was still wrestling with it until his mind grew confused. Do you know what he talked about, his last words?"

Guy shook his head.

"He was talking about you being lucky. He said not even the mosquitoes bit you."

He chuckled. "I remember that. We were having a drink together at Cleo's; right before he became ill, it was. He swatted a big one on his arm and held it up cursing. I think we ended up arguing about the sex of the insect." He grew serious. "I miss him very much. He was a good doctor, a good friend. But now I'm the doctor, and I'm prescribing for my patient laughter and fun, fine food and even finer company. I'll not brook any arguments. It's a doctor's prerogative to give orders—and to be obeyed."

He picked her up and carried her back home, to the main house, to Bellechasse, where a room had been prepared for her, filled with flowers and dresses of the most delicate voile. Though they were plain in style, Damaris feared at first they might be Eustacia's and was relieved to learn they had belonged to Guy's mother.

"Mother would have nothing but cotton," he remarked. "She used to laugh over Englishmen from the flax trade denouncing it as white vegetable fleece—too sensuous for a lady to wear."

Was it the feel of the soft cotton next to her skin that made her feel sensuous, or the pleasure of being surrounded by every care, of having Guy and Arnaud at her side, the sense of being wanted?

She had never known the fun of a childhood free from learning and responsibility; but in those days of her convalescence at Bellechasse, the three of them—she, Guy, and Arnaud—were like children together. All serious discussion was forbidden, all care and worry banished. They took turns in reading, choosing the peace of Thoreau or the swashbuckling dramas of Scott over the morality of Dickens. They played charades or beggar-my-neighbor, struggled over anagrams or attempted, quite unsuccessfully, to build a house of cards. Arnaud planned rides along the river to share with her his favorite haunts. She nodded, though such talk reminded her of Eustacia's inevitable return, of her own inevitable departure.

Symbolically, on Guy Fawkes Day, they burned the bed on which Damaris had lain in the throes of the fever. Consigned to the flames with it were the robes she had worn on her arrival. Guy and Damaris watched as the flames leaped higher and higher, reflecting out across the river. They watched Arnaud racing round and round the fire singing out the Guy Fawkes rhyme.

> Please to remember
> The fifth of November,
> Gunpowder treason and plot.
> I see no reason
> Why gunpowder treason
> Should ever be forgot.

"I won't ever forget this night," Guy said quietly as they walked back to the house together, Arnaud having run on ahead.

"Nor I," she answered. "But it's over, Guy; it's all over. I must go back."

"I love you, Damaris; I love you."

"I must go," she repeated doggedly.

As they reached the lighted portico, she lowered her eyes to look down as she walked.

Guy stopped and turned to her. "Look at me," he commanded. But she did not look up. "Why won't you look at me?" he asked.

She hesitated. "I can't."

"Why not?"

She hesitated again before going on. "In cloistered orders nuns are taught they must retain custody of their eyes; they keep them down as they go about their duties. It is necessary for me too, especially now, to have custody of my eyes."

"Why?" he asked, going on almost immediately: "You really don't have to answer that; I suspect you will not. But I've no need to ask. I know why. It's because the heart shines through the eyes, isn't it? The heart, childlike in its simplicity, not sophisticated and machinating like the brain. It can only say what it knows to be so. It can only blurt out the truth—just as yours would now if you were to look at me." He took her hand. "Please, Damaris, look at me."

Slowly, so slowly, she raised her eyes to his; and in the moment or the eternity that followed as they looked at one another, oblivious to all else, everything was known.

"I was right," he said huskily. "The eyes cannot lie. Maybe it is as well to have custody of them, but I'm glad you allowed yours to tell me what I most wanted to know."

"I must go soon, Guy."

"I know you must. I've been thinking about that. It's just that I don't know how I'll ever be able to stand life without you."

It was when they were at tea the next day, attempting to fit together one of Arnaud's jigsaw puzzles, arguing whether the section Damaris had assembled was part of the sky or the sea, that a visitor was announced—Bishop Turner.

"Just a quick call. I've come to check up on you, Guy. I've had a frantic letter from your wife. News of the seriousness of the epidemic has surfaced in the Paris papers it seems. She says you'd written there was nothing to worry about in the short notes you sent. Now she's been sending cable after cable without response. I was asked to track you down to ascertain you were all right—as I see you are. I thought it was so, for I talked to Livvy, though she was of the impression you had gone to Knoxville. When I couldn't find you there, I decided to call at Bellechasse. I'm on my way North, to New York, where undoubtedly, I shall be seeing the Caylews. I couldn't do so without conveying some definite news of you."

Bishop Turner's eyes fell on Damaris without recognition, for he nodded and said, "Good afternoon, ma'am."

"We're fine, sir," Guy said. "I thought I had assured Eustacia of that. I'm sorry you were troubled."

As Bishop Turner's eyes continued to rest on Damaris,

Guy added reluctantly, "You know Damaris Fanshawe, of course."

"I don't believe I've had the pleasure."

"I'm Sister Serene, sir, of the Order of St. Catharine. We have met."

"Sister Serene!" He was so clearly shocked to see her dressed in a light blue dress and, what was worse, so obviously at home beside the hearth at Bellechasse. His voice was chilly as he said, "I'm at a loss—I don't understand."

"Sister Serene," said Guy Parrish, with obvious distaste at the sound of that title, "came here to see Arnaud, not realizing that she had contracted the fever. She is only now convalescing from it."

"But your robes, Sister? What became of your robes?"

"They were infected; there was no alternative but to burn them."

Guy had responded, but still Bishop Turner addressed Damaris.

"Could you not have got others from Sister Livvy? In fact, would it not have been more suitable for you to recuperate there in Memphis with her?"

"Damaris— Sister Serene has been very weak. It would have been wrong to move her," Parrish put in firmly. "She is much better now."

"I can see that she is." The Bishop's response was touched with asperity. "I still think that Sister Livvy should have been told. She was under the impression that Sister Serene had already returned to the hospital in New York."

He looked from one to the other of them in a state of perplexed embarrassment. "Well, no matter. No harm done, I suppose. Since I am on my way to New York, I shall be able to conduct you there myself, Sister Serene."

BOOK SIX
Dr. Fanshawe

God who sends the wounds sends the medicine.

Cervantes
Don Quixote

ONE

Damaris's return to the fold of St. Catharine's was uneasy. She was haunted by her experiences in the epidemic, her shattered faith, and, most of all, by her love for Guy Parrish. The greatest relief lay in immersing herself in the work of the hospital, to the obliteration of all else. She pleaded the pressure of work to escape from reciting the Divine Office; her continued absence soon attracted not only attention but also dismay among the sisterhood. Mother Charlotte made no comment; and since she said nothing, Damaris said nothing. Perhaps she would regain her belief as Guy Parrish had regained his; but when her spirit continued in a state of turmoil, when the gnawing seed of doubt became a devouring torment, she knew matters could not be left in abeyance, that she must speak.

"It's no good, Mother Charlotte. I can't go on. It was Sister Serene who went to Memphis, but it is Damaris Fanshawe who has come back. I no longer belong in these robes; this crucifix hangs heavy on my neck. I can no longer take the host because it is bitter on my tongue. I've changed, Mother Charlotte; what happened has changed me. My faith is gone."

Mother Charlotte held out her arms to her, and gratefully Damaris flung herself into them.

"My dear! I've waited and waited for you to come to me. I guessed you were going through a personal crisis. But please, I beg you, don't allow it to crush you. All of us experience doubt at certain times in our lives, Sister. I'm of the opinion it is healthy that we do. Remember Tennyson's 'There lives more faith in honest doubt, Believe me, than in all the creeds.' Only one who is truly religious doubts.''

"I remember saying much the same words once to . . . to someone else.''

Mother Charlotte examined her troubled face. "It's more than your doubt that's upsetting you, isn't it, Sister?''

Damaris nodded. "Yes, there is something else.''

"Do you want to talk to me about it?''

"No, Mother, I'm not yet ready to talk about that to anyone.''

"Very well. But if I can help, you know I'm always ready to do so.''

"I know you are. I love you so much. I'd never do anything that would hurt you.''

"You're a fine person, Sister, and I love you dearly. Nothing you do could ever hurt me personally. The only thing that would matter is that harm should come to the order; and I know, whatever troubles you are now struggling with, you serve that as faithfully as I do. The order is my life; it's what I live for, and I pray it will live on long after I'm gone. That's the only legacy I leave to the world, to carry on with work that is God's work.''

"Mother, you have given me everything—even my life by saving me from myself. You gave me something to live for. But for you, I would never have had the chance to become a doctor. I owe you everything, and your work is my work, except''—she paused, her voice muffled with emotion—"except I'm not sure I can or should continue to do it within the confines of the sisterhood. Every day when I put these robes on, I feel, because of my doubts and for other reasons, a sense of hypocrisy that works to shatter my already uneasy conscience. I don't belong in them anymore, Mother. I earnestly wish to continue here at St. Catharine's, but as Damaris Fanshawe rather than Sister Serene.''

Mother Charlotte's face fell. "Oh, Sister, surely you're not going to disappoint me. You know how I've hoped and planned that it is you who will take over the reins from me as Superior.'' When Damaris shook her head, Mother Charlotte held up her hand to stop her. "No, now is not the time for decisions. Your soul is uneasy. Wait. Don't decide in the haste of the moment.''

"Mother Charlotte, I want to help you in every way, you know that; but things that happened in Memphis brought all of this turmoil to the fore. It is no hasty decision. There have been lurking doubts of my suitability to continue as a nun since . . . for a long time."

"But you're not still thinking of your reason for joining us. Surely that affair is not still on your mind, is it?"

"Not that, but I cannot say that part of my turmoil is not connected with a man." She raised her eyes to her superior, adding, "I've done nothing wrong, except perhaps even to think it is wrong. In that event, I have sinned in my mind."

"Oh, my dear, I'm so sorry." Mother Charlotte reached over to lay her hand on the younger woman's arm, giving her the strength to continue.

"I know you've talked of my taking over from you. Even when you first said it, I doubted my suitability to fill your shoes, and I said as much. Now I am certain that I am not the person for the job. You will be here for a long time yet, but if you must begin to look around for a replacement to groom, may I make a suggestion?"

"By all means. None of us knows the number of our days."

"I think Livvy—Sister Lavinia—would be ideal. She's devoted, faithful, and she's become a great organizer. I watched her when I was in Memphis; she has tact and ability."

"A recommendation from you is a recommendation indeed. I hadn't thought of Sister Lavinia, but perhaps . . . That is, if you don't have a change of heart."

"On that score, I shan't."

"We'll see. But let's have no more talk of your doffing the habit. You are, as you say, in a turmoil now; but all of this may pass. Promise me you'll wait; give it six months. Then if you are still of the same mind, I shan't argue with your decision."

Christmas came, with its bustle and confusion, causing an increase in patients at the hospital and not a minute for Damaris to think about anything but the work at hand, for which she was glad. She had sent a copy of *Surly Tim*, by Frances Hodgson Burnett, the English writer who lived in Tennessee, to Arnaud; from his reply thanking her she learned that Eustacia was back at Bellechasse. The letter ended, as all his letters ended, "Father sends his regards and hopes you are quite well."

She waited always for that stilted phrase; she read and reread it and chided herself for doing so, and for longing for him to be there saying even those few words to her himself. She had no right to think of him at all, most certainly not in the way she did. Even were she to leave the order, she would still not have that right, for Guy Parrish was married. It was sinful to think of him so often, more sinful when she reflected that she cared for him more than ever.

Work was the answer. No task was too difficult or too demanding; no hours were too long. If she worked she could think only of her work; she could not dream.

Yet in the early spring, as she was scrubbing her hands after finishing a tonsillectomy, a novice came with news there was a gentleman waiting for her in her office. The scrubbing brush flew at the task; she dried her hands and all but ran through the halls, robes streaming behind her.

The smile of welcome on her face froze at the sight of her visitor's stalwart back as he stood examining her framed diploma on the wall behind her desk.

"Ah, Sister Serene, or is it Dr. Fanshawe I have the pleasure of addressing? I have a difficult time keeping up with you." Templeton Caylew's tone was anything but pleasant. "I gather from the expression on your face that I wasn't the one you were expecting to find here."

"I didn't know who it was, sir; no name was given," she responded briskly. "What can I do for you?"

He walked over to stand before her, his hands gripping the lapels of his coat.

"What you can do for me, Sister Serene," he asserted bluntly, "is to leave Lucy's husband alone. I've no intention of leaving here until I have your promise on that."

"I don't know what you're talking about. I haven't laid eyes on Colonel Parrish since the Memphis epidemic."

"Don't give me that professional hoity-toity air you've taken on since you became a doctor. You may fool others, but not Templeton Caylew. Neither that nor those robes can hide from me the sort of person you are. You've always had it in for me. I knew it even when you demurely paraded around as 'dear Sister Serene,' so clever, so good, and now, since this epidemic, so courageous. I could tell things about you that would make your admirers falter in their paeans of praise."

"You are entitled to your opinion, Mr. Caylew, but I fail to understand—"

"I fail to understand," he mimicked, shaking his head. "No, that won't do. You understand very well what I'm talking about. I see it all. Parading around like some vestal virgin, you forced yourself on Parrish as a means of getting even with me. No one knows better than I do the extent of your *innocence*. From the beginning I had it in my power to destroy you, but I didn't, did I? Why, rather than disclosing your immorality, as well I might, I put my good name to work to get you admitted to the University Medical School. McChord would never have taken you without it."

"You did. I've never denied that. I thanked you for it, but since we're speaking frankly to one another for the first time, I consider you owed it to me."

"Owed it to you! I owe you nothing. You're a hypocrite, worse than that whore down in Memphis who was written up in the newspapers for her gallantry."

"Katie's a brave woman."

"I'm talking morals, not courage. You may have enough of that; I'm not here to argue that point. You certainly have the gall, but morally you're bankrupt. You had no compunction in forcing yourself upon Parrish as you did on me. You're nothing but a black-robed whore."

She struck him hard across the face, so hard that the red line made by her hand was visible on his pale cheek long after his curses ceased.

"Now your true nature is coming out, isn't it? Did it come out while you were seducing that worthless husband my daughter insisted upon having? Or did you give in to him as you did to me, pretending it was against your better nature?"

"I hate you!" Her voice was low and intense. "I hated you then; I hate you still."

"Fine words coming from one whose robes, at least, profess her virtue."

"It is unfitting to say it, dressed as I am, but how free I

feel for having admitted to you what I've so long felt in my heart.''

"Hate's not the feeling you hold there for Parrish, is it?'' he sneered.

"Nothing reprehensible has ever occurred between Colonel Parrish and myself. But if, as you say, you consider him truly worthless, I don't understand why you are here. I should think you would want your daughter to be rid of him.''

"So you admit your aim then is to get even with me by ruining my daughter's marriage.''

"I admit nothing at all. I've done nothing.''

" 'I've done nothing.' Listen to the little innocent! Dear sweet, pure *Sister Serene.''* He stressed the title. "Others may believe that, but not me, my girl. No one knows you as I know you. Oh, I can just imagine how it was. You sought him out. He was alone, vulnerable, and you saw your chance to hurt me by alienating his affections from Lucy.''

"I was in Memphis as a doctor, not for any other purpose,'' she argued hotly, but he ignored her.

"It hardly requires a sleuth to follow your path or to reach conclusions. What sort of a woman would stay alone at the home of a married man, any man for that matter? Bishop Turner found you there; and pretty hot under his clerical collar he was about it too, so don't try to deny it. Then no sooner did Lucy return to Bellechasse than Parrish began repeating his demands for a divorce.''

"A divorce!''

"Yes, a divorce, as if you didn't know. But it won't work, Sister. Your little plan won't work. My little girl is not going to have her name dragged through the courts, even as an innocent party. If she weren't so besotted with Parrish—and I'll be damned if I understand why—I wouldn't mind seeing a nun named as co-respondent. But it would put an end to this order once and for all, and I suppose my wife would hate ridicule falling on her favorite charity. Besides, Lucy wants him. I got him for her in the beginning, and as long as she wants him she's going to keep him. You're to stay away from him. I want your promise to leave him alone.''

"Mr. Caylew, I saw Colonel Parrish in Memphis in the

round of my duties. I did stay at his house because I came
down with the fever. I had gone there for the purpose of
seeing Arnaud. I've seen nothing of him since, nor heard
from him, nor do I expect to.''

"Not from him, perhaps, but the boy. You correspond
with one another through that boy you brought into his
household. I'm no fool; I know how these things work.
Lucy's been through your letters to him. Innocuous enough
in themselves, but she's convinced that since you can't
openly correspond with Parrish, they're written for him, to
prevent him from forgetting you. I want you to promise
those letters will cease.''

"That's unfair as well as untrue. Arnaud is my friend, I
love him—''

"Like a son, Sister?" His eyes pierced hers. "Like a
son, perhaps?''

"I suppose it's not wrong to say that.''

Caylew's eyes narrowed.

"I've often wondered ever since you took him there
whether he isn't really your son—your son and mine? He's
of the right age.''

Caylew was watching her so intently that he was unaware the door behind him had opened. Mother Charlotte
stood at the entrance to the room, a look of shocked
surprise on her face.

Though Caylew had not seen her, Damaris had; and it
was to the one she had long wanted to know the truth that,
with a sense of relief, she directed her response.

"No, Mr. Caylew, Arnaud is not the son I had by you.
Mother Charlotte buried him. You can ask her for yourself, since you seem to doubt my integrity.''

Caylew spun around, catching his breath at the sight of
Mother Charlotte's staunch form at the doorway.

"That is so,'' she said. "Damaris's child was baptized
and buried, Mr. Caylew; but until this moment I had no
idea who the father of that child was.''

He laughed, an uneasy laugh. "It was an accident.''

"I understand it usually is,'' she said calmly.

"She was a promiscuous girl, forced herself on me, just
as she forced herself on my daughter's husband when she
was in Memphis. Bishop Turner himself found her at
Bellechasse in Lucy's absence, alone there with Colonel

Parrish. I trust that he spoke to you about that sorry matter.

"I know she was there recovering from the fever, Mr. Caylew," Mother Charlotte said firmly.

"I hope you won't find yourself with a pregnant nun on your hands. That would be an embarrassment, wouldn't it? I dare say now she's wiser; her training's probably taught her what to do about such things. As for what you overheard just now, I'm not at all sure the child was mine; but I gave her money when she became . . . in the family way."

He avoided looking at Damaris as he spoke. She made no attempt to disagree but she kept her eyes firmly fixed upon him, and his cheeks grew even redder under her scrutiny.

"I think we both know the kind of person Damaris is, Mr. Caylew," Mother Charlotte said softly. "She came to you young and innocent. I knew her then; I knew what she was like. You did too, for you chose her to look after your own children."

"Well, apparently both you and I were hoodwinked by her. She took me in, and then she took you in. Now she's taken in my daughter's husband. She's dangerous. I'm sure if society was aware of the sort of women you receive into this order of yours, you wouldn't receive the support you now enjoy."

It was an unveiled threat, one that could not be ignored. Damaris looked sharply at Mother Charlotte as she affirmed, "You may be right." There was a thoughtful pause before she went on in a calm, quiet voice: "You're right. Perhaps, as Mrs. Caylew is our patroness, it is only to be expected that I should tell her everything." She paused thoughtfully, before repeating, "Everything."

Templeton Caylew's nostrils flared in anger. "You're almost as bad as she is; you're a blackmailing . . ." His voice spluttered as he bit his lips together to prevent the obvious epithet from passing them.

"Sir, you astound me. First you say the matter should be exposed, then when I offer to do so you accuse me of blackmail. Which is it, Mr. Caylew?"

"God dammit!" he cursed. Then looking up and seeing the crucifix on the wall, he turned back and reluctantly, though still angrily, apologized for swearing. "If you want to prevent yourself from being as big a hypocrite as she is, Mother Charlotte, I'd advise you to have this woman divest herself of the robes of your order. And I should appreciate your instructing her to have no further communication with married men, specifically with my daughter's husband. In return, you have my promise to say nothing further in the matter."

"A wise conclusion. As the sensible gentleman I know you to be, I thought you might reach it." Mother Charlotte smiled placidly.

He tipped his hat with the least possible courtesy and left the room, closing the door firmly behind him, as firmly as was possible without deliberately slamming it.

"Dear me," Mother Charlotte commented coolly, "I'm afraid Mr. Caylew is upset."

"I'm sorry, Mother. You must believe me. Nothing untoward happened between Colonel Parrish and me, nothing I have reason to be ashamed of. I—"

"You don't have to talk about it. You said you weren't yet ready to do so."

"But I thought I should explain about being at Bellechasse."

"I know why you were there. Bishop Turner, as Mr. Caylew implied, *was* a little hot under his clerical collar when he was here; but I told him that in my own mind I was satisfied that there had been no wrongdoing. I know you as he does not, and I think I managed to convince him. I am still of the same opinion."

"Nevertheless, Mother, to satisfy Mr. Caylew and prevent any further recriminations, perhaps it is best that while I continue to devote myself and my services to the order, I do so without being a part of it."

"I really don't think that necessary. I'm not concerned; and you owe him nothing, particularly when I consider the way you've guarded his name all these years."

"But in a way, his visit acts as a catalyst for something I've been wanting too. I can go on here as Dr. Fanshawe rather than Sister Serene. At the same time you can rely on Caylew's support. He'll feel he's won his point; we all get what we want."

Mother Charlotte's face grew thoughtful. "Oh, I don't

know that the order would lose it in any case," she mused.

"I don't understand," Damaris began in puzzlement. Then her face cleared. "Oh, you mean that his conscience might prompt him to greater generosity."

Mother Charlotte smiled. "I always knew you had the makings of a superior in you; it requires an ability to study human nature as well as the divine. Take off the robes then, if that's what you wish; but for yourself, mind, not for Caylew's benefit. And remember, that still doesn't mean I'm giving up hope of you becoming my successor."

TWO

The matter of where she would live had been solved for Damaris by one of St. Catharine's supporters who had committed the folly of building a huge apartment house on the west side of the newly completed Central Park, in a location so remote that it had earned the name Dakota, after one of the country's remotest territories. He offered her a tiny apartment under the eaves, one constructed perhaps for servants but quite adequate for her needs. The rent he asked—whether because he was anxious to fill the building, or as a charitable gesture—was one she could afford, and she had been able to move in immediately.

She enjoyed the solitude of the area; and whenever time permitted, she walked the twenty-block distance to the hospital each morning and back again at night, unless there was a critical case that required her attention. Then, more often than not, she stayed on to catch what rest she might on the sofa in her office.

Discarding the habit she had worn for a decade had not been without an emotional wrench. Indeed, the clothes she adopted, though lacking the veil, were not so very different, being plain and dark in color. Even so, wearing them gave her an immediate and overwhelming sense of freedom, like a schoolchild finding herself unexpectedly on holiday. She would have liked to wear the new bloomers that were much talked about but little in evidence. They seemed infinitely more sensible than voluminous skirts for an active woman, but to have done so would have drawn undesired attention. She compromised by keeping the length of her skirts long enough for modesty but short enough to

377

free her ankles and reveal nothing more than her high-
button boots.

Her cloak had large inner pockets that allowed her hands
to be free of any cumbersome purse; thus she could maintain a steady stride on those days when she eschewed the
dubious comfort of the Ninth Avenue elevated railway for
the walk to St. Catharine's. Then she would arrive, cheeks
pink, eyes sparkling, muscles relaxed, with both body and
mind ready for the day ahead that was in its duties not so
very different from those past.

The members of the sisterhood were puzzled by what
they construed as Sister Serene's defection. Though she no
longer occupied the narrow cot in the cell that had been
hers and eschewed prayers or attendance at chapel, she
often joined the refectory table for the sisters' silent midday meal; and even her severest critics had to admit that
she worked harder than ever for the small sum she was
now paid in lieu of board and lodging.

Freed from the obligation of having to maintain the
posture of a religious, Damaris found herself attuned to
life around her as never before, not in a worldly way, but
with a renewed sense of joy in simply being alive. She
delighted in the first jonquils to appear in the park, the
robin nesting in the tree beneath her window, the spring air
soft and tender on her face, the calls of the flower vendors
on the avenue, the salute of the policeman on the beat,
even the rain splashing her face as she walked home; and
then getting in and closing the door of the first home that
had ever been hers, changing into dry things, lighting a
fire, and sitting before it with her tea. Her life was no
longer ruled by the clamor of bells marking the offices.
Away from the hospital, it was her own to do with as she
would; and she found for the first time that life was to be
enjoyed for itself alone. It became filled with things that to
her were luxuries, simple perhaps but filled with comfort.
She had a room of her own to furnish as she wished,
sparse though the furnishings might be. Her clothes and
possessions were of her own choosing, meager perhaps,
but to one who had had nothing to call her own, the
smallest item selected and purchased with her own money
generated a sense of excitement and discrimination. Through
her purchases she learned about herself—her likes and

dislikes. Life she found full. Her pleasure was so apparent in the glow on her face that even the most surly strangers passing her as she strode on her way would be forced to return her smile.

But that did not mean her life was free from problems. Her mother, a recipient of a widow's pension, no longer relied on Caylew for support, though she continued to occupy the house that he owned. Might he not, now that his secret was known to Mother Charlotte and with a desire to even the score, demand that she quit his house? On the amount she received, Damaris was hard-pressed to supply her own living; she could not take on that of another. And the idea of having her mother share her sparse quarters was unappealing. Though joined by a blood bond, they were virtual strangers.

Then there were Arnaud's letters that haunted her, unanswered. She had given no promise to discontinue writing to him, yet she could not do so without mentioning she had left the order. Would that not be construed as telling Guy Parrish as much? And if he knew, what then? Would he come to her? Did she want him to come to her? She knew the answers to all these questions, and it was for that reason she dared not write. If he came to her she would throw aside everything for him, and scandal must result; Eustacia and her father would see to that. And worse yet, if he did not come . . .

She was as perverse as woman ever was! Be not anxious for the morrow, for the morrow will be anxious for itself. Sufficient unto the day is the evil thereof. The wisdom of these words from the Sermon on the Mount, her lack of faith notwithstanding, could not be denied.

Then on an evening in early April as she started out from St. Catharine's Hospital walking toward the park at her usual brisk pace, she felt someone fall into step beside her.

Looking up, she spoke the name that never left her mind. "Guy!" And then she repeated it: "Oh, Guy. You came."

"Of course I came."

They stood still in the middle of the busy sidewalk, and he took her elbow to shield her from the heavy traffic of

horses and carts and carriages and the jostling of passers-by hurrying home.

"You shouldn't have," she said softly.

"You didn't want me to come?"

"I . . . I don't know."

She looked away, but he reached over to turn her face
up to him. "I won't allow you custody of the eyes."

And then she looked up at him, and he smiled. "That
point is settled at least."

"I wanted you to come. I longed for you to come, and I
knew you would if you knew."

"So that's why you stopped writing to Arnaud. I couldn't
understand it. I was worried, afraid you might be ill again.
I asked Livvy, and she said that there had been changes. I
had to come and see for myself if those changes were what
I hoped them to be."

"Livvy told you?" she asked in surprise.

"No, she simply alluded to changes. But knowing of
your doubts, I thought . . . and hoped, and what I hoped is
so. Are you happier?"

"Yes . . . yes, I am. Livvy is too, I think."

"Because you're no longer in the order now?" he asked
in surprise.

"Perhaps that, perhaps for other reasons."

"Livvy's changed. She's been remarkably close to
Eustacia for some unfathomable reason. They were less
than bosom pals during the early years of the marriage
when I was still attempting to come to terms with Eustacia's possessiveness."

"Livvy will be the next Mother Superior of the order
when Mother Charlotte steps down. I don't say this from
any sense of malice, but I am sure she's aware of the
importance to the order of keeping the Caylews' friendship."

"Well, that explains part of it. It's a very political
position, and maybe Livvy is being practical and approaching
it that way. That sister of mine never ceases to amaze me.
She did during the siege of yellow jack; she does now. I
think she learned from you. She idolized you, you know. I
was wondering why—" He broke off.

"Why she no longer does?" Damaris shrugged. "We
change, I suppose." Yet she had grown thoughtful, won-

dering whether to tell him about Angela, whether he would understand.

"I don't change, Damaris, and I never shall. I love you. That's the reason I came—to tell you so once again, to tell you like this, without the burden of seeing you in that hideous habit that made profanity of my sentiments."

"It's not a hideous habit," she protested.

"On Livvy perhaps not, but I much prefer seeing you dressed as you are now."

"I seem to remember a time you thought the opposite."

"Never. I might then not have wanted my sister to wear it; but when first I saw you in it, something inside warned me that in addition to other encumbrances the fact that you wore it was going to cause me grief. It has made Livvy a different person—stronger, more sure. But how it gladdens my heart to see you set it aside."

They found a small Bavarian restaurant that reminded them of the Old Heidelberg in Philadelphia. Both ordered the bratwurst, and neither of them ate anything, much to the consternation of the red-aproned restaurateur, who insisted upon giving them the house's own apple strudel with their coffee, which they also left untouched.

But they feasted their eyes on one another, feasted their hearts on being together.

"I've asked Eustacia for a divorce. Did you know?"

She nodded, thinking of Caylew's visit. One day she must tell him, but not then. "I had heard that things had not gone well since Eustacia's return."

"She won't agree to a divorce. She refuses to let go; she is obsessive in her passions. I guess I should have realized that at the start. I believe the fact that I wouldn't allow her to possess me as she has possessed everyone and everything else in her life is what prompts her to hold on to me as fiercely as she does. It's not love. Love is something she doesn't understand. She's not to be blamed; her father is much at fault. This marriage of ours never worked. She's an intelligent woman, and I suspect underneath all her obstinacy she is as much aware of that as I am."

"Eustacia is at Bellechasse?"

"No. She is here in New York. I forced her to agree to a trial separation. That, in itself, was ugly; and I'm quite sure the acrimony will grow far worse before the matter is resolved. That is why I won't have you involved in any way. But I had to come to see you, to see for myself if it was true." He reached over to enclose her hand in his. "You are free, and eventually I shall be too."

"I love you, Guy."

"I know I shouldn't have come, but I just had to. I had to hear those words from your lips."

"I love you so very much," she repeated.

"You know how I feel about you."

"I know, but tell me anyway."

"You are my life; you mean everything to me. I didn't believe it was possible to love another person as I love you."

"Guy. Oh, Guy." Though her voice trembled with emotion, it was strong and clear. "Can you possibly realize what it means to hear you say that and not to have to deny the way I feel for you? I know you're still married, but somehow that doesn't matter."

"I shan't always be, but you must understand that getting a divorce from Eustacia is going to be a long and tedious affair. Will you mind waiting?"

"I'm willing to wait forever. I'm happy simply knowing you feel for me as you do. I'm happy even though we can't be together except for a few stolen moments."

"I want to be with you openly, freely. And that is how it is going to be one day. You brought love into my life. I never intend to lose you."

"You never will."

"Eustacia's determined that the marriage remain intact. I'm equally determined to pursue the separation to its inevitable conclusion. Even getting this far was like winning a major battle. Eventually she will realize that it is for the best. She much prefers life here in New York. I realize that she will try to take Bella from me completely. I don't want that, and I shall fight it when the time comes. I know Caylew will throw his wealth and position into the fray to ruin me financially and politically. I know this, and you must know it too."

"I love you, Guy, not for any reason other than yourself. I knew it that evening in Philadelphia. Maybe I even guessed it before then but wouldn't admit it, even to myself. I'll always love you, no matter what."

"Eustacia must never know," he warned. "She can be ruthless. If she suspected, she would try to ruin you."

"I don't care."

"But I do."

He paid the bill and they left the restaurant, puzzling the owner by telling him how much they had enjoyed their untouched meal.

They walked together in the freshness of the spring evening, no longer briskly but walking close to one another, holding hands. Passers-by coming upon them as dusk turned to darkness imagined at first it was one and not two.

They spoke little; it was enough to be together, together in that close sense of acknowledged intimacy for the first time. But at the doorway to the apartment building Guy Parrish stopped. "My train doesn't leave until tomorrow evening, but it would be unwise to see one another again."

"Please come up, just for a little while. You must. I have some good English tea—from Ceylon, I think. I don't know why it's called English tea. It was the kind Angela always sent home for. I saw it in a store and treated myself to a quarter of a pound. Do come up, just while I brew a pot." She kept talking to prevent him from leaving.

"I must go. If I come up, it could compromise you. I don't want that, and I know you don't either."

"No, no, of course not."

She couldn't afford to be compromised. Even though no longer a member of the order, still she was St. Catharine's trusted physician. Yet somehow at that moment that seemed of scant importance. Tomorrow he would be gone. She looked around at the empty streets; the wind was growing chill.

"I can't bear for you to go," she whispered urgently.

"I can't bear to go."

"Then come up, please. Just so I can see you in my apartment and remember you there."

He knelt before the hearth building a fire while she put the kettle on the two-ring stove. Then she came and knelt beside him, watching the first flames cast their flickering golden light across his pensive face.

"You realize what will happen if I stay longer, don't you?"

She nodded.

"Hold me, Guy. Hold me close, so close nothing can ever come between us, not ever."

His arms closed around her, holding her as she had wanted him to hold her for so long. His lips fluttered softly over her eyelashes and eyebrows as he loosened the knot in her hair and ran his fingers through its long strands before kissing the top of her head.

"I never knew what being in love was like before," she whispered.

"Damaris, I love you so utterly, so hopelessly."

"Not hopelessly. It can't be hopelessly."

They knelt together before the fire and she watched the reflections of its flames in his eyes as he began to unbutton her high-collared waist and then slipped aside the straps of her white linen camisole.

"Damaris, you're everything to me."

She put her arms around his neck and kissed him softly.

"I'll never stop loving you, ever. You know . . ."

But his lips met hers, muffling the words; and she no longer knew what they were, for she wasn't thinking of speaking. In fact, she wasn't thinking at all; she was filled with a sense of wonder that flooded her as relentlessly as the swing of the sea at mid-tide—lips on her mouth, assuaging a hunger no food could fill, lips on her eyes, her brow, her throat, lips at her breast so she forgot everything, everything—who she was, even who he was.

I love you, I love you, I love you—the refrain echoed from the room's blue and white wallpaper, from the panes of the window overlooking the park, from the heavy wooden door that shut the world out. Though not all the world, for they reached the ears of one intruder standing in the hallway. Neither that stranger nor Guy Parrish left until early the following morning.

Inside they made love. Not once; once would scarcely suffice for two who had waited so longingly, so impatiently for one another. For the first time in her twenty-nine years Damaris gave herself to a man, gave herself willingly, lovingly, releasing desire that had burned long and deep in her soul for him. And in giving herself, she became so much more than she had been; in losing herself she became part of something greater by far.

Years before, the only man she had ever known had taken her against her will, and she had felt violated by an act she found crude and unfeeling. And when at the university her fellow medical students had described in coarse and lascivious terms their sordid, furtive amorous forays, it was, she had thought, all part of the same ugly experience. But there was no similarity between that and what passed between the two of them that night. Love changed everything.

They lay together holding one another tightly still, as though to prove it was real, not a dream. Then unexpectedly he shattered her peace with "Do you ever see the other man, Damaris—the father of your child?"

She shuddered, nestling her head into his shoulder. "I don't want to think of him, especially not now."

"I'm sorry. It was wrong of me to speak of it. Except, ever since you told me about him, I imagine some rival with godlike attributes, someone you must think of—"

"You've no reason to. I don't think of him, not willingly at least. He's . . . he's quite unworthy."

As she lay beside him she put aside the thought of Caylew. She couldn't waste a moment of their time, for soon, too soon, he would be gone from her. She would lie alone.

"I said before that I would be happy with only a few stolen moments, Guy; but now . . . now I'm not sure. You make me greedy. I'm not sure I can bring myself to say good-bye when you must go."

"Don't let's talk of that, not now," he said, pulling her to him.

Later she wondered why she, who less than two months earlier had cast aside a religious order, who had just made love to a man still encumbered by marriage to another, should at that moment feel more pure than ever before. Why was there no guilt, no sense of shame? And she sat up suddenly, her long hair falling around her shoulders, her knees bent, clasping her arms around them.

"It's strange, Guy," she mused. "Why is this so right? So very, very right?"

He sat up beside her, putting his arm around her bare

shoulders. "It's right because it's what we've both waited for all our lives. Two solitary souls coming together, touching, holding, meeting one another in a moment of inexpressible happiness."

"Yes, that's it. There's something almost spiritual about it."

"If not spiritual, certainly the most perfect thing in creation."

She was silent for a moment; then she said slowly, huskily, "If I never had anything but this one moment to remember, it would be enough."

He gathered up her hair, loosely twisting it in his hands and softly kissing the nape of her neck. "No, I can't agree. There's more for us—much, much more."

Very early in the morning he dressed, even before the sun cast its first glow across the park.

"I must leave. I never meant to stay all night."

"I never wanted it to end. I'll come to you even if Eustacia refuses to divorce you."

"If you do, it would ruin you—as a woman, but most particularly as a doctor," he warned.

"I don't care. You're not concerned that Caylew will ruin your political career; how can you believe I would worry about mine?"

"There's only one way that Caylew could ruin me, and that would be by making me lose you."

"That will never happen," she whispered, lifting his hand and pressing it against her cheek. "Never."

"I'll do everything I can to make sure you're not implicated."

"I expect I already am. Bishop Turner has told everyone about my being at Bellechasse."

"But you were ill. Nothing happened, not then."

"I know, but others think otherwise. I don't care, especially now I've had the joy of loving you in the way that they were already convinced I had done."

"If the Caylews are certain, though, they'll try to put pressure on you," he warned. "Promise me you won't give in."

"Never. How could you think I would! There's nothing in the world that could ever make me give you up, Guy."

"Eustacia hasn't won, not yet at least. She may boast

that she always has her way in the end, but not this time. I don't know yet how I'm going to get free of her, but I know that I am.''

He picked up a green clay figure that one of the children at the hospital had made for her and rubbed its protruding belly with his hand. ''I know you've been going through a period of doubt, but do you think you might, like me, occasionally believe in magic.'' He rubbed the belly again before passing the figure to her. ''Make a wish, Damaris. Who knows what may happen? Not today, perhaps, not tomorrow, but sometime it will. Together we're going to win. In fact, in a way we've already won. In this strange world, where so little makes sense, we've found all that matters—one another.''

THREE

Guy Parrish was wrong. Damaris didn't have to wait for something to happen. It did that very evening.

He had asked her not to see him off, but as the afternoon wore on, as her eyes watched the continual progress of the hands on the clock, knowing that each second ticking by was one closer to his leaving, that she didn't know when she might see him again, her resolve to allow matters to take their own course weakened. She heard the bell announcing tierce and had an unexpected and almost irrepressible desire to join the sisters, to pray for his safety and for their future together. Though she chided herself for the selfishness of her wish, her longing to see him again that evening turned her steps toward the Erie Railroad's Pavonia Ferry on Twenty-third Street rather than toward the park.

All was confusion at the ferry building. A porter indicated where passengers for St. Louis and onward connections might be found, and she jostled her way through the teeming crowd, thinking how impossible her mission must be. Then suddenly, through a momentary gap in the surging throng, she saw him waiting, leaning against a pillar, newspaper in hand yet looking beyond it, lost in thought.

"Damaris!" He threw the paper aside and caught hold of her hands, raising them for an instant, palm up, to kiss them swiftly, first one, then the other. Then he let them fall and looked around before saying, "You shouldn't have come."

"I know." She smiled up at him.

"But how glad I am you did."

"You said that once before, in Memphis, remember?"

"I've been thinking about that—about everything."

"So have I."

They stood close to one another, hands barely touching as they watched the railroad ferry on which he would all too soon have to leave. They stood together, silent amidst an orchestrated chorus of final farewells, the cries of "Write, please write," those last fervent kisses.

"I must go now," he said as the call of "All aboard" reverberated again and yet again.

"I know."

"I won't say good-bye."

"Nor shall I."

"Leave, leave before I do."

She turned, but couldn't prevent herself from looking back to watch his disappearing figure and the raising of the gangplank. She stayed as the lumbering ferry pulled out into the river to cross to the Jersey shore to connect with the train. When its shape became indistinct in the growing dusk, she turned to go.

As she slowly made her way through the crowd toward the entrance, she heard her name, or a name from the past that once had been hers: "Sister Serene!"

She turned quickly and there at her elbow was a fashion plate in an azure promenade dress with a modified bustle to emphasize a tiny waist, a smart toque trimmed with ostrich feathers that brushed a pink and white cheek. What Damaris noticed more than the matching pearls at the neck was the gleam of gold on the third finger of Eustacia's ungloved left hand.

"Or is it *Miss* Fanshawe, or perhaps you prefer Dr. Fanshawe?"

"Damaris will be fine, Eustacia."

"*I* am Mrs. Parrish. I'd prefer you not forget that."

"Very well."

"Very well, Mrs. Parrish," Eustacia corrected.

But rather than repeating it, Damaris shrugged. "Have it your way."

The crowd leaving the ferry building parted around them like a stream flowing around an obstructing boulder in its path.

"I think we have some talking to do, Sister," Eustacia said, gripping Damaris's forearm.

"Either Miss Fanshawe or Dr. Fanshawe. I'm no longer in the sisterhood, Mrs. Parrish."

"That's true. How conveniently you worked everything out, didn't you? You plotted and planned. Mother Charlotte told Mama they didn't want you to go to Memphis, but you went, didn't you? You went because he was there, alone and vulnerable. I can just imagine it! You had your claws in him long ago. I guessed someone had, just by his touch. A woman senses these things without being told. I knew immediately someone had come between us, but I never thought to look among the cloisters for her. And then you had the gall to insinuate yourself into my house, my own home, and put on my clothes, and, I suppose, sleep in my place by his side—"

"Please, that is untrue, completely untrue," Damaris protested, aware of the turning heads of the people swarming past them. "It's true I was there, but I was ill with the fever."

"Have it your way. I won't argue the point; I don't need to. You may have been chaste as Diana, but your own bishop certainly didn't think so. He had to come to escort you back or you'd probably be there yet. He's been kept busy trying to explain away the matter ever since. As for you, you didn't trouble yourself with anything so mundane. You came back and neatly divested yourself of the encumbrance of those robes and your pretended chastity and waited for him to come to you. And like a fool he came. Men are so innocent, so trusting, aren't they, Mary? And yet we're helpless without them."

"You're not helpless, Eustacia. You never were."

"Perhaps, perhaps not." She smiled demurely. "My carriage is outside. Allow me to give you a ride back to your apartment. I know you came a far distance to be here; and dedicated soul that you are, you have to be up early." She smiled knowingly. "You can't afford too many of these late nights, can you, Doctor?"

Damaris's eyes narrowed. "I don't care for a ride. Say what you have to say to me here and be done with it."

Eustacia looked down at her wedding ring before slowly pulling on her glove. "For what I have to say, I would advise you to accept the privacy of the carriage. I think you will find it preferable.''

"Very well.''

They set off in the smart black barouche, sitting as far apart as possible, though the width of Eustacia's skirt took up much of the vacant seat between them.

"What is it you want?'' Damaris demanded.

"I want you to give me your promise that you'll never see my husband again.''

"If you made me come with you for that, it's a journey made in vain. I'll never make such a promise. If that's what you wanted, you should have said so at the station; I'd have told you so then. I love Guy, and he loves me. I'll never give him up.''

"Yes, I watched that touching little parting scene between you just now. And as I watched I vowed I'd have my revenge, and I shall.'' She paused as though to give added significance to her next words. "I've had Harwood followed. I know he stayed with you last night—all night.''

Damaris's reply was equally deliberate. "That doesn't surprise me in the least. I'd expect something like that of you. I'm not ashamed of it, nor would I ever deny it. Don't you understand? We love one another.''

"Love!'' More scorn could not have been put into an entire soliloquy than Eustacia managed to convey in that single word. "Love! This from Sister Serene, only just released from the bonds of a holy order! Sister Serene, who disavowed all men, promising herself only to God! Dear me, it seems nothing in the literature of what goes on within convent walls—the stuff your proponents label as scurrilous—can be in the least exaggerated.''

"Don't threaten me, Eustacia. I'm no longer a member of the order, and what I do is my own affair!'' Damaris's voice rose in exasperation. "Again, what is it you want? I shan't give up Guy no matter what. You can expose the fact that I've slept with him; I don't care. I love him; there was nothing indecent about that.''

"But it wasn't the first time you'd slept with a man, was it, Sister?'' Eustacia's voice was soft, almost cajoling. "In fact, your fertility is not a matter of doubt, is it, Sister? You've had a child. I had that from a certain *lady* in Memphis who seemed to know all about it. For a nun, you've made some very colorful friends.''

Damaris had been looking away from Eustacia out at the traffic surrounding them, but she turned back. "If we're playing to kill, let me warn you that your family stands to lose quite as much by exposing that matter as I do.''

"Subterfuge, Sister, I expected some sort of protestations or countercharges,'' Eustacia purred.

"I suggest you ask your father about the child, Eustacia.'' Damaris snapped. In the dark she heard a sharp intake of breath. "And if he denies it, you might take your query to Mother Charlotte; she can corroborate what I have said, for she heard it from your father's lips. I was young, innocent, a servant in his house, and he seduced me. It's a common enough story, but no more pretty for its lack of originality.'' When Eustacia made no response, Damaris went on in calmer tones. "I would not have told you had you not been prepared to use it against me. But you must realize I'm quite as determined as you in this matter.

"You can put to work all the wiles that only someone with your inventive mind could devise to make things difficult for us, but you'll never browbeat me into giving Guy up. There's nothing you can say that would even make me consider it. Certainly not the fact that your father seduced me when I was little more than a child. You'll have to find something better than that.''

Eustacia was silent, and Damaris settled back in her seat and turned her gaze outward again, deciding that perhaps, after all, the ride back was not going to be as difficult or as ugly as she had imagined. It was allowing the matter to come to light, and that would be beneficial. No longer would there be a need for subterfuge. She was as strong as Eustacia, and quite as determined. She had had no wish to destroy Templeton Caylew in his daughter's eyes, but if it came to a choice between that and being blackmailed into severing her relationship with Guy, she had no compunction to use every weapon that was at hand.

"Perhaps I will find something better than that, Miss Fanshawe,'' Eustacia proclaimed abruptly. "There is another incident in your past that I think might make even spicier reading for the insatiable perusers of our tabloids—

something I am quite sure that Mother Charlotte, who prides herself on the morality of her order, does not know—something that could put an end not only to your career but hers also.''

Again there was silence, but this time Damaris could feel her heart pounding in her chest, pulsating in her neck until the noise of its beat became deafening in her ears, though not deafening enough to cover Eustacia's prompted ''Well, aren't you interested to know what it is? You were quick enough to respond over the child, but now you say nothing.''

''If this concerns Sister Angela—''

''Aha!'' Eustacia triumphed. ''It does indeed concern Sister Angela—dear Nanny Wickers, as she was known to us. She was so kind to you, wasn't she, when you were undernursemaid in our house. She took pity on you, didn't she? She took you into her room so you wouldn't have to sleep with the other servants, didn't she? She took you in so you would sleep only with her!''

''For God's sake, Eustacia, I may have stayed in her room, but I never ever in my life slept with Angela Wickers. Nothing happened between us ever. I swear it didn't.''

''You're doing a lot of swearing, Sister. It marks you as a woman of the world. Did you pick it up in the Five Points district or from your companions at medical school? I know all about you, you see.''

''I simply had to make you listen to what I'm telling you. Angela Wickers never did anything that could be construed as immoral to me or in my presence.''

''That's not what Lavinia thinks. Little Livvy, who is—or was—your dearest friend, said our precious nanny died with your name on her lips. She too was swearing, swearing her eternal love for you. Or are you calling Harwood's sister a liar?''

''No, what Livvy said is true. I know the fact that Angela fastened her affections on one of her own sex is unnatural. I'm not denying that or even condoning it. But since it happened I have tried to understand, and I know that in her way Angela really did love me.''

''You have the gall to admit it. Well, well, I wonder

what Harwood would think to find his woman does not limit her sexual preferences."

"We were speaking of Angela Wickers. I have done nothing except to try to understand her. I swear nothing unnatural ever occurred between us. Hers was, in fact, quite a pure emotion."

"Pure! Pshaw! I've made inquiries about that lady too. I've found out that when she came to us it was because she had to leave the Rossmores'. She'd been found in bed with the new parlormaid. How's that for a pure emotion? Do you think the tabloid headline writers will share your views of purity? The Rossmores kept it quiet; she came of quite a decent family. They palmed her off on us. I can hardly condone their act, especially since it allowed a woman of distinctly questionable character contact with my young sisters."

"Angela was a martinet for discipline, but she never did anything immoral in your household—to me or to anyone. You're being unkind and unfair."

"Unkind! Unfair! Listen to the support you give this woman, and then deny being involved in an unnatural affair with her. Make up your mind, Sister! I'm content to leave it at that; I wouldn't disturb Beatrice or Eleanor by questioning them about such disgusting debauchery. I shall, however, not hesitate to raise the matter with others—Mother Charlotte, for one, who should have been told a long time ago. Lavinia says it was on your recommendation, and yours alone, that Nanny Wickers was accepted into the order. Mother Charlotte made no other inquiries as to her character, as she would have done otherwise. She never contacted the Rossmores, who would, I trust, given the circumstances, have been more open with her than they were with us."

It was dark outside now, with only an occasional carriage passing by. They must be close to her home, for the driver began to slow the horses' pace, but Eustacia rapped on the window, instructing him to circle the park until she told him otherwise. Then she turned back to Damaris.

"Your bravado fails you at last. Your silence indicates you must have changed your tune. Perhaps now you'll be willing to agree that I have won, after all. You see, I have documented proof—in fact, everything that's necessary to ruin not only you, Dr. Fanshawe, but Mother Charlotte as well, and to bring down her whole house of cards about her head. You're so loyal, aren't you? Leos are always loyal; it's in your astrological sign. Don't be surprised; I told you I know all about you. Loyalty is thought to be a virtue, but sometimes it can be such a burden, can't it?"

"What is it you want?" Damaris demanded quietly.

"You know very well what I want."

"For me to promise never to see Guy again."

"Yes, that goes without question, but it's not quite that simple. He would come to you and you would swear your innocence as you have earlier tonight. Men, as I said before, are such gullible fools, most particularly when they are infatuated. I want you to tell him, as only you can, that you will never under any circumstances have anything more to do with him."

"He won't believe me."

Eustacia's face grew thoughtful. "I realize that, and that's why it has to be put in such a way that he will. You must use that fertile imagination of yours. You earned very high marks in medical school. I've checked everything, you see."

"Whatever I say, he will suspect you're at the bottom of it."

"Of course he will; I know that. I don't care. He knows I want him; he knows I'll do anything to get him back. But what I want most is for him to hate you." She was silent, ruminating, then she gave a cry of triumph. "I have it—your career. I shall help you in your career. That's very important to you, isn't it? Of course it is, and rightly so. You must tell him that you've thought things over and that if you are involved in this divorce you may never be allowed to practice again—which is no more than the truth—that you can't give it up, that he must never see you again."

"No! I can't."

"Oh, but you can." Eustacia sounded considerably cheered by the desperation in her companion's cry. "Indeed you can. You can say that should he succeed in extricating himself from the marriage without implicating you—which, of course, he never will—then you may consider marriage to him, but otherwise it is out of the question. Let him realize how very selfish you are!" She sat back in obvious pleasure. "You're not the only one with brains, Sister. I think if I'd gone to Harvard I would have done much better than my brothers did."

"I have no doubt of it," Damaris said bitterly.

"And I'd like to see your letter before it is sent, just to make sure."

"No!" Damaris said sharply. "You have my promise that I will write it in such a manner that he will hate me when he reads it. That's what you want; it will be done. There's an end to it."

"Don't sound so downhearted. I'll support Mother Charlotte and her order and see that no scurrilous gossips are allowed to tarnish its reputation. And I meant what I said about helping your career."

"Please, Eustacia, spare me your kindness. I prefer your natural feline nature."

"I won't deny, Sister dear, that vengeance is sweet; but I would hope to be able to count on you to render a civil face to me in public at least. To do less might give rise to the suspicion that your letter was written under duress, in which case I might as well tell everything, and all of your nobility, your loyalty, would have been for nought. You know"—Eustacia leaned forward confidentially—"I'm almost beginning to like you. We have much in common. We're both strong women in love with the same man. I even believe your lofty principles may eventually allow you to forgive me for having won."

FOUR

The memory of Guy Parrish in her apartment, that Damaris had so longed for, became a torment. Having written a letter that could only earn his disgust, she wished he were not there everywhere. When she came home at night, before she went to sleep, when she awoke, each time she lit the fire or put water into the copper kettle that had blackened from having boiled dry while they made love, his presence so surrounded her that when at last she did fall asleep, he came again to haunt her dreams.

All too well she knew her own anguish in writing the letter she had been forced to write; she could only imagine the anguish its receipt must have caused.

He made no reply; she did not expect he would. She had worded it so as to leave no doubt in his mind that she meant what she said—that her career came before everything else in her life, and though she had given him her promise to stand firm, she had not then considered the impact that any connection with divorce must have upon her standing in the hospital, particularly since it was sponsored by the family of his estranged wife. It was not only her name that would be besmirched but her entire future. She apologized; he had swept her off her feet, but she was to blame for allowing it. She wished him good fortune, but made it clear that she never wished to hear from him again.

Once she had written the letter, perhaps the most difficult task she had ever performed, she could not bring herself to reread it. She folded it and inserted it into the envelope she had earlier addressed. As she licked the flap of the envelope, her eye fell on the green clay figure whose protrud-

ing belly Guy had rubbed for luck. At that moment it
embodied all her frustrated hopes and dreams. In a fit of
passion, she picked it up and flung it against the wall. It
fell in the corner crushed beyond recognition—a shapeless,
formless thing—much like her spirit. There it lay, a reminder that there never was and never had been a magic
power that made wishes come true.

The morning sun lit the sky, as it had the morning
before when Guy had left her. That the earth had made
only one rotation between that morning of hope and this of
despair seemed inconceivable to Damaris, wearily rising
from the table at which she had passed the night. She
mailed the letter on her way to the hospital, arriving to
assume her duties with the spring gone from her step, the
light gone from her eyes.

Because she couldn't bear the memory of Guy in her
apartment, she stayed at the hospital longer at night and
arrived earlier in the morning, so that Mother Charlotte,
hopeful perhaps that she wished to rejoin the order, suggested she might prefer to move back in with them. It was
a suggestion Damaris considered but refused. Even the
hospital had become a bleak reminder of why she had had
to give him up. In itself it served as no comfort. Only her
work did that.

A letter came from Arnaud. She felt hope on seeing it
that at least Guy had not forbade him to write to her. She
tore it open and turned immediately to the end, noting that
that last stilted line, "Father sends his regards and hopes
you are well," had been omitted. The omission said far
more than the line itself ever had.

Livvy arrived from Memphis. She had come to stay, for
with the sharp drop in the city's population—more than
five thousand was the conservative count of those who had
died in the yellow fever epidemic, a total of 75 percent of
the white population that had stayed in the city—the fate
of the school seemed sealed. Of those who had fled the
fever's scourge, many had decided never to return to a city
cursed by God and nature and had established themselves
permanently elsewhere. The city of Memphis was bankrupt. Its charter had been revoked, and it had been relegated to the ignoble status of a taxing district administered

by the state. Many doubted it would ever become anything more, but not Guy Parrish.

"He's thrown himself into its cause. He swears Memphis won't die while he has breath to save it. I've never seen him so determined." Damaris had been there when Livvy regaled the sisters with her news. "He's stepped down from the legislature. I really can't understand why; he was doing so well, and I always thought he enjoyed the political fray. But anyway, Governor Marks said he wasn't about to let him off that easily. He said if Guy's that determined about Memphis he'd better see what he can do about it, so he appointed him to preside over the Taxing District. Now all I've been hearing about is sewers and garbage disposal, food inspection, street cleaning, and the hazard of the open bayous. Guy says give them five years and the city will be greater than it ever was. When my brother puts himself into anything and drives himself as hard as he's driving himself now, I wouldn't want to take odds against him."

Damaris listened avidly whenever Guy was mentioned, but she never spoke his name to anyone, especially not to Livvy, who always seemed ill at ease in her presence. Perhaps she wondered how much Damaris knew of the things she had told Eustacia.

But if the relationship between Damaris and Livvy was cool, Eustacia appeared to be courting the sister-in-law she had once scorned, for no sooner had Livvy arrived in New York than Eustacia's ceremonial hospital visits began. She would arrive, accompanied by some fashionable acquaintance, to be met by a swirl of black robes and conducted to the wards, where for five or ten but rarely for fifteen minutes she played the role of Lady Bountiful with the children. To Damaris's high dudgeon, Eustacia gushed almost as much over her as she did over the children.

"You simply must meet our dear Dr. Fanshawe," she would say to whatever witness she had brought to watch her play her part. "She's simply too brilliant. We are really quite proud of her. Papa was able to get her admitted to the University of Pennsylvania Medical School, the very finest, as you probably know. Dr. Fanshawe was the first woman to graduate from there. They would never have taken her without Papa's say, isn't that so, Dr. Fanshawe?''

It was a fact Damaris could not deny.

"Still, Papa always says all the credit is hers. He never was one to talk about what he does for others. Of course, as Dr. Fanshawe knows, we follow her career with the greatest interest, and she knows she may count on our support always,'' she would conclude, throwing a fatuous smile at Damaris, while her companion might wonder at a lack of any responding warmth.

"She may be smart, but she's a cold fish,'' Damaris heard one of them remark as she walked away.

"I wouldn't say that exactly,'' Eustacia had answered forgivingly.

"That's because you're too kind.''

Eustacia's sudden and official, if often officious, interest in the hospital was seen as a sign of the Caylews' unflagging interest and was, therefore, appreciated by all, including Mother Charlotte.

"We're lucky to have Mrs. Parrish as an active supporter of our cause, especially after the speech Mrs. Tracy gave to the Ladies Missionary Relief Society, in which she demanded the General Convention look closely into our order. Mrs. Tracy is demanding that I obtain a guardian's consent for each entrant under five and twenty, and keep complete testimonials as to character and fitness for every entrant. As if I would take in anyone who is unwilling or of questionable character! Mrs. Tracy would love to lay her hands on anything that might discredit us, but she won't find it. I assured Mrs. Parrish myself that there was no possible fear of that. We need the patronage of people like the Caylews to defend us in circles where we cannot easily defend ourselves.''

Spring became summer, bringing with it an exodus of the fashionable from the New York heat. Damaris sighed with relief when she learned that the Caylews were to leave for Newport. They decided to mark their departure, however, with a large charity ball in support of the hospital, an event that became a point of staff discussion.

"It's so kind of Eustacia—Mrs. Parrish,'' Livvy said. "It was her idea. She said she was sure there were things we needed, and this would be the chance to get them. It's to be at the Waldorf again, quite a gala event. Mrs. Caylew's allowing Eustacia to plan it this time, and Eustacia is anxious that it be the biggest party of the season. Her plans may seem a little opulent—three full orchestras seems excessive—but it's not for us to cavil over such matters. She expects all of us there; she particularly asked for you, Sister—Dr. Fanshawe.''

Mother Charlotte noticed that Sister Lavinia always had trouble remembering Damaris's name and she was the only one among them who never used her Christian name. In the light of their long association, it was a matter on which she could not avoid speculating. Though, as neither of them spoke of it and neither one confided in her, she had no right to raise the matter.

Another matter on which she had conjectured was the friendship that had sprung up between Sister Lavinia and Eustacia Parrish, especially strange now that Eustacia was separated from Lavinia's brother. Mother Charlotte never remembered them as having been particularly friendly before. Caylew's assertion of an affection between Damaris and Guy Parrish, she felt certain, must provide the explanation of the rift between Damaris and Lavinia and the friendship of Lavinia and Eustacia. Indeed, Bishop Turner had grown quite apoplectic at the thought of such a thing. Damaris never spoke of it. Mother Charlotte, remembering how she had kept the secret of Templeton Caylew, wondered whether she would ever know from her lips what had happened. Her eyes, however, could not hide her unhappiness.

Mother Charlotte was concerned about Damaris, so concerned she even suggested she consider an offer made to her to join the medical staff of a new marine hospital being established near Memphis; an offer she refused.

"Perhaps one day I may make a change, but not to go there. I'll never go there, never."

The vehemence of her refusal seemed to indicate whatever there may have been between Damaris and Guy Parrish was no more.

"It has unhappy memories, I suppose." And in answer to Damaris's sharp questioning glance, Mother Charlotte added, "The yellow fever epidemic."

"Yes, that too."

She was to wonder about the meaning of "that *too.*"

Mother Charlotte was drawn back from her conjectures by a sharp exchange between Damaris and Sister Lavinia over Eustacia's planned event.

"I'm sorry, but I must decline Mrs. Parrish's invitation," Damaris had said, to which Livvy sharply retorted, "Oh, but you can't. I told her you would be there, and the Caylews are most certainly counting on you. In fact, they specifically mentioned you by name. It's to your advantage as well as ours, Sis— Dr. Fanshawe. You can speak both professionally and as one who knows the sisterhood intimately."

"I don't give a rap for my personal advantage," Damaris responded tersely.

"I thought that must be the reason you left the sisterhood," Livvy returned equally sharply.

"Now, please don't argue." Mother Charlotte turned her attention to Damaris. "I understand how you feel—to some extent at least—but let us at least remember the good the Caylews have done. If you could bring yourself to attend, I would count it a personal favor. I'm sure there's no need for you to stay all evening if you don't wish to; just put in an appearance, please, for me."

The invitation, Damaris found, was not so much a request as a command to be reiterated by Eustacia on her next visit, when she arrived accompanied by a titled visitor to America.

"Lord Gilvray, you must meet our lady doctor, Dr. Fanshawe. We are so proud of her." And Eustacia went on at great length and with even greater sweetness to extol her virtues as the visitor looked her over casually yet assessingly, with a half-smile flickering across his mustachioed lips.

"I've never known a lady doctor before," he said with the slightest lilt to his clipped English voice. "Rather unusual occupation for a woman, what?"

"Since members of both sexes require medical attention, it appears sensible that there should be physicians of both sexes," Damaris replied laconically.

"I'm afraid, Dr. Fanshawe, though I know you to be excellently qualified, I should find myself lacking the same confidence in the opinion of a woman doctor as in

that of a man; but I hope you take no offense." Eustacia
smiled sweetly. "I can't speak for Lord Gilvray, of course."

Her companion examined Damaris speculatively, stroking his mustache as he did so. "Hard to say, don't you
know. A woman doctor would be, well . . . different,
don't you know." He laughed, without particular mirth.
"Rather exciting."

"One doesn't go to a doctor for excitement, Lord
Gilvray," Eustacia reminded coldly, "but to be cured of
an ailment."

"To be sure, to be sure. Have you skills at mending
broken hearts, Dr. Fanshawe?" As Lord Gilvray asked
this question, he looked soulfully at Eustacia, who tapped
his arm with her neat white glove. "Come, come, my dear
man, we mustn't take any more of Dr. Fanshawe's time.
We expect you on Thursday," she reminded as Damaris
gathered up the patients' charts.

"I'm not sure—" she began.

"We're expecting you. Remember, Dr. Fanshawe"—
Eustacia looked at Damaris purposefully—"you promised
to give your personal as well as your public support to
our efforts to assist the order. We count on your presence.
Come along, Lord Gilvray. I'd love to spend hours here—I
usually do—but I can't forget my promise to show you the
city."

Watching Eustacia's retreating figure in its immaculate
form-fitting plum coat trimmed with scarlet—who, but
Eustacia, would have thought of putting those magnificently
glaring colors side by side and succeeding in the effect?—
Damaris wondered about Lord Gilvray's broken heart.
Had Eustacia done the breaking, and if so, would she
effect the cure? Was it possible that she had given up hope
of getting Guy Parrish back?

Damaris turned away. It really made no difference if she
had. Her own words—"must protect my position," "you
must understand that I live for my career, I can't allow
anything to jeopardize it"—rose up once more from the
paper on which she had written them. He'd been willing to
give up everything, and it must appear to him that she
would give up nothing.

If she had had any doubt that it was Eustacia who was
the cause of Lord Gilvray's broken heart, that doubt van-

ished at Thursday's charity ball. Everyone was talking of
Eustacia's conquest.

"So handsome, so elegant, and a marquess. My dear,
do you realize that means that his wife would be a count-
ess?" A stout overdressed lady in a pink ball gown adorned
with far too many frills was examining herself approvingly
in the full-length mirror in the ladies' room where Damaris
had sought refuge from the crowd and one member of it in
particular.

"He has a fine figure, it's true," agreed the lady's
companion, of similar build yet less overpowering, since
her dress lacked such opulent trim. "Stiil, one would think
that by this time he would have found a wife. I'd judge
him to be forty at least." She lowered her voice. "I've
heard that many Englishmen are odd."

"Odd? What do you mean?" her friend inquired avidly.

"You know—odd in their preferences. They like their
own sex."

"Oh, how disgusting of you to even mention such a
thing!"

Her friend's titillation was short-lived, however, as the
speaker went on. "But I suppose that could hardly be true
of Lord Gilvray. Haven't you seen the way his eyes follow
Eustacia Parrish everywhere—such dark, passionate eyes
they are too."

"They say she's still mad for that husband of hers,
who's nowhere to be found. I always thought he was a
charmer. Besides, she's not the only one his eyes follow.
Of course," she added as though to explain everything,
"it's an Irish title, isn't it, not English?"

They left together, sailing through the door side by side
like two ships steaming out from harbor after having been
refueled.

That Lord Gilvray was a philanderer Damaris had discovered for herself. Since her arrival at the ball he had
pinned himself to her side for far too long, and she'd
found his conversation most offensive.

She hoped he had attached himself to someone else in
her absence. But despite passing close to half an hour in
the ladies' room waiting for the moment she could op-
portunely depart, she was confronted by him again when
she returned to the ballroom.

"Tell me, Doctor, what do you require your patients to wear when you examine them?" he began lazily.

"I fail to see the relevance of your question," she answered coldly, looking around the room.

"I was merely seeking information."

"It would depend, Lord Gilvray, on the reason that necessitated an examination."

"I see." He laid ringed fingers lightly across his waist. "Pains in this area, for instance. Would you require a gentleman to remove his pantaloons for such an examination?"

"Really, sir, this conversation is not only irrelevant but very silly," she snapped in annoyance, her voice so loud that she saw several people looking askance in their direction. She made to leave, but he detained her.

"Not really so irrelevant, Doctor. You see, I am having some slight disturbance. I was wondering if you would examine me, privately."

"Sir, if you require medical attention, I'm sure you'll have no difficulty in discovering a physician to help you. I am not that physician. Now if you'll excuse me—"

"You're not leaving, are you, Doctor? Mrs. Parrish asked me specifically to see that you did not leave. I was trying to make conversation, but I see you're not in particularly good humor."

"You're quite right; I'm not in good humor. May I suggest you look elsewhere for a more convivial companion."

"I don't mind, really. I find you quite fascinating. I never met a lady doctor before."

"So you've already said."

"I wonder . . . I realize you practice at the hospital, but perhaps we might have some private arrangement. I could come to your place sometime. You can rely upon my discretion. I should say nothing to anyone."

"You will say nothing, sir, because there will be nothing to say," she snapped. "I am sick to death of your childish innuendos. I would think more kindly of you if you left me alone."

She turned on her heel so swiftly that she walked directly into a pale gentleman who had been standing behind her and who said quickly, quietly, "Let me know if he's annoying you, Mary."

She sighed in relief at the sound of his voice. "Nathan—Nathan Caylew."

He smiled at her, responding with an odd triumph, "That's right. You did remember me this time!'

She did remember, and at that moment, compared with the companion she had just left, the sight of Nathan Caylew came as a welcome relief.

"How are you, and what are you doing? Please do tell me all about yourself."

He put his head down, almost apologetically. "I'm still writing poetry—bad mostly, at least that's what Mother says."

"Have you any of it with you? I should very much like to see it." It was said as a means of escaping from undesirable company, but when she saw Nathan's face light up at her interest, she decided that she really did want to read his poetry.

"I only have one that I started this evening, just since you came in, as a matter of fact. I jotted it down on the back of the menu. It's incomplete, just a few ideas really, but if you're *really* interested—" He broke off, looking at her doubtfully.

"I am. I am, indeed."

"Come along then. I'll get you an ice and go over it with you; but don't judge me by this, for, as I said, it is only a fragment; though I'm rather proud of some of the metaphors I've drawn—the fresh milk and gold honey of the placid Memphis skies looking down on the gall beneath—but I must allow you to be the judge."

"I didn't realize you were interested in Memphis."

His face flushed. "I wasn't—not until I heard you'd gone there, at least."

As he held out his arm to escort her from the ballroom, Damaris sensed rather than saw Eustacia beckoning in her direction. She was unsure whether to acknowledge the gesture or to leave with Nathan and pretend she hadn't noticed it. Her quandary was decided by a drum roll from the orchestra and an announcement summoning her, among others, to the platform.

Damaris, standing beside Mother Charlotte and Livvy,

had no idea why she was there. She listened to Mrs. Caylew speaking of the hospital and its continued need of support, of the work done by the order not only in New York but during the terrible yellow fever epidemic in Memphis. There were a few remarks, mainly laudatory, and then a vote of thanks proposed by Mother Charlotte for the Caylews, without whom, she said, the order's achievements would not have been possible.

Then Eustacia Caylew Parrish came forward, standing without speaking for a moment so that all might admire her slender figure in its Worth creation cut *à l'impératrice* from shining white satin festooned with garlands of the finest silver Alençon lace mounted over Milanese bands of dove-gray velvet.

She began by speaking of her consuming interest in their "dear little patients," each of whom was just like a son or daughter to her. Her eyes glistened as she spoke of her life's desire to bring just a moment of happiness into their hearts.

"How deeply I love each one of them!" she said with such feeling it appeared that those glistening eyes of hers must let loose a veritable flood, a flood she so bravely blinked back in a tremulous smile at her audience, such a charming, comely smile.

"I mustn't let my emotions overcome me, especially on this occasion when my remarks concern not only those I hold so dear to my heart but also one whom my father helped to gain admittance to our country's finest medical school so she might bring the benefit of that knowledge to assist these poor waifs. Though that person is no longer a Sister of St. Catharine, for reasons that need not concern us tonight"—she pressed her delicate hands together, looking down at them for an instant, with her lips pursed, as though those reasons, unpalatable as they might be, would never be dragged from her—"we overlook that change in her status and recognize only the fine work she has done and continues to do. She worked admirably under the devoted direction of dear Sister Lavinia and alongside our former nanny and her very special friend, Sister Angela, during the Memphis yellow fever epidemic.

"When Sister Serene, as she was then, left the order, my father promised he would continue to follow her career with interest and would do whatever he could to promote it on her behalf. Papa has tonight given to me the privilege of announcing that he has put forward to President Hayes the name of Sister Serene—or Dr. Fanshawe as she is now—to sit on a commission that is being formed under the new National Board of Health to study the cause and effect of yellow fever. I am pleased to tell you that the President has seen fit to respond to my father, officially extending that honor to Dr. Fanshawe.''

She waved aloft a telegram. ''It is the first time such a distinction has been conferred on one of my sex; and it is perhaps appropriate that a woman should be the first to congratulate Dr. Fanshawe on her appointment.''

At this point a smiling Eustacia, telegram still in hand, extended her arms to Damaris, while a round of applause, aimed as much at the speaker as the recipient, judging by the scattered cries that echoed throughout the ballroom of ''Isn't she simply charming!'' ''What a lovely dress!'' ''Must be a Worth.'' ''How well she spoke, so sincerely, so eloquently.''

When Damaris made no move, Eustacia went over to her and put her arms around her, bussing her cheek and, as she did so, whispering, ''You kept your word. Now I've kept mine.''

It was at that moment the photographer from *Harper's Weekly* came forward with his contraption to drape the black cloth over his head and capture the moment for the readers of his magazine. Despite that distraction, it did not escape the notice of the assembled company that in her reply Damaris had thanked the President and the commission, with scarcely a mention of the Caylews' name.

FIVE

The etching made from the photograph that appeared in *Harper's Weekly* was captioned, "Lovely New York socialite Eustacia Caylew Parrish congratulates Dr. Damaris Fanshawe on her appointment to the President's Council on Yellow Fever." The magazine article noted the role played by influential financier Templeton Caylew in securing the appointment for the woman doctor, and described in great detail Eustacia's appearance and dress, her vital interest in the children's hospital, as well as her concern about the yellow fever epidemic in Memphis, her husband's home town.

"I would do anything to benefit my husband and his people," Eustacia was quoted as saying. *Harper's* also took the opportunity of noting her husband's absence, while at the same time commenting on the presence of Lord Gilvray, and finished with a lurid account of the previous year's yellow fever epidemic in Memphis.

A copy of the magazine had been sent to Damaris. She had picked it up with her mail, but it had lain unread until the following Sunday, when she opened it to see the depiction of the perfectly groomed Eustacia in her magnificent Worth gown, and her plainly attired companion on whose face the artist had somehow managed to affix a fawning smile. A copy of the issue would, Damaris was sure, also find its way to Bellechasse, to lend credulity to her letter by illustrating the Caylews' willingness to further her career and her own willingness to accept their help.

She was about to throw the magazine aside when she heard a knock on her apartment door. She rarely received visitors and hurried to answer, thinking it must be a mes-

senger from the hospital. The last person she expected to
see leaning against the doorjamb, a large cigar protruding
between unusually pink lips that matched his equally florid
cheeks, was Lord Gilvray.

"Dr. Fanshawe, how glad I am to find you at home.
Feeling particularly unwell, I decided there was nothing
for it but to seek professional advice. May I come in?"

He hiccoughed, and without waiting for a response—she
had been too astonished even to greet him—he pushed past
her to enter her tiny apartment. There he took his cigar
from his lips and exhaled the smoke before training an
unsteady glance around the cramped quarters and then
appraise its occupant, still standing by the open door.

"If you're in need of a doctor, Lord Gilvray, I can
direct you to one. I cannot help you. Though from a brief
observation it would appear that what would most answer
for you at the moment is a cup of strong black coffee."

"Coffee? Who wants coffee when they can have champagne?" He drew forth from the deep pocket of his over-
coat a large gold-tipped bottle. "It's a superior vintage,
highly recommended. Here." He went to remove the seal
from the bottle. "You have two glasses? Flutes would be
preferable, but anything, tumblers even, will do. Any port
in a storm, eh, Doctor?"

She held out her hand to stop him opening the bottle. "I
don't drink it; I don't think you should drink any more
either. That is a personal as well as a professional opinion."

"Don't be such a spoilsport! You're not in the nunnery
now. And do shut that damned door!"

"I didn't invite you in here. I am asking you to leave."

"But I came all the way from town, miles and miles.
Besides, I've dismissed the cab I came in."

"If you don't find another, the walk back will have a
good and sobering effect. I recommend it."

"God, you're a hard woman," he said, plopping himself down in the only armchair, clearly undeterred by her
lack of sympathy.

"You will leave my house; you will leave now," she
ordered, yet a strain of uncertainty crept into her voice as
she wondered just how she could force him to leave.

"Do shut the door, for God's sake. There's a bloody
draft!" When she made no move to comply, he got up,

crossed the room, and, removing her hand from the door, slammed it shut. "There, that's more in accord with your much-vaunted American hospitality."

"I have no reason to offer you hospitality, Lord Gilvray; you are no friend of mine. Nor, from the little I know of you, can I say that I enjoy your company. If you don't leave of your own volition, I shall be forced to call help to make you leave."

"Who would you get all the way up here? Instead of being so unsociable, I should think you would thank me for making all this effort to see you. I swear, I never climbed so many stairs in all my life. They must have intended these places for the pigeons to nest in. Still"—he pulled aside the curtain at the dormer window—"must admit it gives a decent good view of the park." He turned back and saw the open issue of *Harper's*. "Excellent likeness. You look so . . . so sure of yourself, so efficient. I never met a lady doctor before."

"So you've said repeatedly," she responded icily before reminding him, "You're a friend of Mrs. Parrish. I doubt she would appreciate knowing that you impose your presence upon other women."

He stroked his mustache, half smiling. "Come now, a gentleman goes where he's invited, don't you know?"

"But I didn't invite you."

"Your word against mine. Besides, your fine eyes did. They're your best feature. I'm quite a judge of women; you should be proud."

"Undoubtedly you keep horses also."

"As a matter of fact, I do."

"Well, I'm neither a mare in your stable nor a filly in your bedroom. I'm ordering you to leave, or I'll—"

"You'll what?"

He grinned lazily, but when she moved to reopen the door he grabbed her hand, holding it behind her and pinning her against the door. "Don't want to let everyone in on our little secret, do we?" His liquor-laden breath wafted down upon her as she tried to free herself. "Having a former nun and a woman doctor all in one—exciting prospect. You must know more about a man's body than a whore."

For response, quite suddenly, quite lethally, she lifted

her knee to kick him sharply in the groin. He released her immediately, groaning in agony. "Damn you!"

Still she had not hurt him sufficiently to prevent him from pulling her to him. "That's enough of that, Madam Doctor. Now you've removed any compunction I may have had in taking what I came for."

He pressed her back against the door, bringing his mouth down on hers, bruising her lips against her teeth as she resisted his attempts to make her open them. He might have had too much to drink, but she discovered that he was far from incapacitated. She attempted to kick him again, but realizing this, he pulled her down to the floor, pinning himself on top of her. Though she was neither particularly small nor weak and was armed as much with anger as with fear, she knew he was overpowering her and hated him more than ever. He disgusted her in himself, and also because his onslaught brought back to mind the indignities Caylew had forced on her. She hated to realize she was still vulnerable to such attacks.

He lay on top of her, holding her head down by her long hair that had become loose in the fight. "Might as well lie still and enjoy it." He grinned. His face, inches from her own, looked to her like that of a satyr about to devour his prey.

For answer she spat at him. That was when he began slapping at her face, swearing as he tore at her skirts.

She hadn't thought it of any use to scream, there being no one in her part of the building to hear, but it was her only recourse. She screamed, not expecting help but hoping her screams in themselves might deter him.

It was hard to say which of them was most astonished by the sudden timid knock at the door, followed by a cautious inquiry: "Dr. Fanshawe, are you all right?"

With a shamefaced though warning look, Lord Gilvray clambered to his feet, allowing her to get up and fling open the door.

"Are you all right, Mary? I thought I heard a scream."

She pushed back her disheveled hair as she looked on the pale concerned features, like those of a heaven-sent messenger, of Nathan Caylew.

"Oh, Nathan, thank God!"

Lord Gilvray, his expression aloof, was unconcernedly straightening his coat and tie.

"I do think it would have been decent of you to have let me know when I came that you were expecting someone," he reproached, as though she had done him harm. "One gentleman never intrudes on another's turf, Caylew. I owe you an apology. I didn't realize that you had a prior claim. Sorry, old chap. Won't happen again." He picked up his hat and waved in the direction of the champagne. "Enjoy it on me. Périgord, and a very good year. I'd appreciate it if you didn't mention this to your sister." With that he was gone, his steps heard long after as he disappeared clattering down the spiral staircase.

"Are you all right?" Nathan repeated. For now it was over Damaris found herself trembling.

"Did he . . . did he hurt you?"

She shook her head, her breast heaving. "I'm all right now. Let me wash my face." She looked down at her hands; everything he had touched seemed soiled. "My face, my hands."

When she got back, her hair pinned back up, her face composed, Nathan Caylew was at the window looking down on the park.

"I didn't thank you, Nathan. I was never so glad to see anyone in all my life. I never expected anyone to come— least of all you. What on earth brought you here?"

His pale face flushed. "I was outside in the park. I saw him come in, and then I saw him at your window. I thought perhaps that you . . . you had invited him, but then I remembered him pursuing you the other evening, and you hadn't seemed to like that. I decided to come up. When I did I overheard what I thought was conversation, so I intended to leave. I was just about to go back down the stairs when I heard you scream and I knew you must be in difficulty. I'm glad he left as he did. I'd have had some trouble throwing him out."

"What happy chance that you should be in the park, all this way out too!"

He looked down at his feet. "It wasn't chance exactly. Since I discovered you lived here, I've spent more than one afternoon there, hoping to catch sight of you coming or going."

"Oh, Nathan, that's so kind, except—"

"Don't worry, I didn't have any ulterior purpose. At least . . . well, I suppose I did, but nothing like Gilvray's. You have nothing to fear from me. I did it just because I wanted to talk to you, not for anything else. I guess I'll leave now you're all right."

But he stood still, looking unusually young despite his years, and decidedly awkward, so that she felt a wave of gratitude as well as one of sympathy toward him. "Could I at least offer you a cup of tea before you go? And you did want me to read your poems the other night. I never got the chance. I'd like very much to see them, if you have them with you."

"As a matter of fact . . ." He reached into his pocket and pulled forth a sheaf of papers, then laughed with embarrassment. "As a matter of fact, I have."

As she poured the tea, Damaris was glad she didn't have to talk, for Nathan, once begun, expounded unceasingly on the use of words for sound, meaning, emotion, and intensity. He was like a dam suddenly loosed, one thought tumbling after another, with only an occasional respite when a sudden phrase occurred to him and he would pull a notebook from his pocket to jot it down. He spoke sometimes like a professor instructing his class, sometimes like a priest exhorting his flock, more often like a child who after years of talking to an imaginary friend suddenly finds that friend in the flesh.

When at last he stopped, apologizing for having monopolized the conversation, Damaris asked him to read from his work.

"Do you really want me to? Mother won't have it, and Lucy says it's boring."

"Being read to is among life's greatest pleasures. One of the things I enjoyed most about being a nun was not having to talk at meals, but instead having someone read aloud."

He began self-consciously at first, but gained courage as he went. He finished with "The Maid of Memphis," the poem he had begun the night they'd met again.

"That's good. It's very good, Nathan." She applauded.

"Do you like it, really? I mean, you're not just saying that."

"I never just say anything for the sake of just saying it. I think it's good, really good. You should submit it for publication."

"I've tried. No luck. I sometimes wonder whether it's detrimental for a poet not to be poverty-stricken."

The sky over the park was reflecting the dying glow of the sun, when at last he rose to leave.

"I like you, Mary. I guess you know that," he said with outward diffidence. "You needn't ever think I would do anything . . . anything like father accused me of years ago. You've probably forgotten the time when you took care of my foot. I was an obnoxious brat, I know, but I didn't mean any harm. I did like you, though. I guess he must have guessed that."

"Maybe he did. That was a long time ago." She shuddered slightly, remembering again the resemblance of Gilvray that afternoon to Caylew. And then she looked over at the rug before the tiny fireplace remembering another man and how different that had been.

Nathan Caylew, seeing her pensive face, assured her. "Please, don't ever think I'll force myself on you, or anything like that. I should like to see you again, just to talk, that's all. It's like I said—because I come from a rich family no one takes me seriously. Stedman—Edmund Clarence Stedman, I guess you've heard of him." When Damaris shook her head, he explained, "He's just about the greatest influence there is in the world of American poetry. He's denigrated almost everything I've done. It's so hard on the spirit when there's not a word of encouragement from any quarter."

"Nathan, I don't have a great deal of time to call my own; but when I do, you may most certainly read your work to me. I'm not sure I can be constructive or helpful, like this Stedman, but I can promise you I'll listen."

"If you'll listen, if you'll just listen, that's all. The words come alive when they're said out loud, when they fall on another ear. It's not so much a question of giving constructive criticism as allowing me to make my own. If only you knew . . ." Impetuously he clutched at the sheaf of papers in his hand. "I'm leaving here with so many ideas. You've been so wonderful—a real angel."

"You were the deliverer today, Nathan. I don't know

what would have happened this afternoon without your help."

"Make me a promise." He took her hand. "Promise you'll let me know if you ever want or need anything."

"Nathan, Nathan, you're so kind, so very kind."

He smiled. "I'll be satisfied with being kind, for now at least. I don't think Gilvray will come back."

"No, thanks to you, I don't believe he will."

Nothing more was heard from Lord Gilvray. It had not been the sight of Nathan Caylew's frail figure that deterred him, Damaris suspected, as much as the fact that Nathan was Eustacia's brother; for as time went on Gilvray's attentions to Mrs. Parrish became the subject of public speculation. Nevertheless, the incident had unnerved her; and she never heard a knock on the door without thinking of it, and never answered without first finding out who was there. It was with some relief she heard that Gilvray had left with the Caylews to spend the summer in Newport.

Just when her life seemed to be settling once more, a troubled demand for her help came from her mother. The Caylews might have played her benefactor at the charity ball, but Templeton Caylew, it seemed, had not forgotten his promise to get even with her for intruding on his daughter's marriage.

Mrs. Fanshawe wrote to say Caylew's agent had called with a client. The house she had been living in all these years had been put up for sale, and without so much as a word to her. When a buyer was found, she'd been told, she would have to quit it immediately. She was distraught; it was her home; she would be on the street without a roof over her head, with only her widow's pension between herself and starvation. The only person she had in the world was her daughter, her dear daughter who had helped her before.

"Come, please come without delay to aid your loving mother." The letter closed with a series of violent dashes.

Damaris went. She felt she could do nothing, but she went. Perhaps her presence might help, the fact that she was there, that her mother was not alone in the world. She went, but once there she discovered that while her own life had undergone so much turmoil, her mother's had not changed one whit, unless it was that her complaints had become more strident.

"Ten years I've lived here, more than that, more than a decade. Everyone I know refers to this as Mrs. Fanshawe's. It's my home, Damaris, not just the place where I live. I have everything here, arranged just as I want it. See the way my armchair fits just neatly into the window, and I can sit there behind the curtain and watch who comes up the path. It's so convenient, for if it should be someone I don't particularly want to see, then I don't have to be at home. And my flower beds, all planted and cared for by me. Think of my prize begonias going to another. No, don't. It doesn't bear thinking of. And the peaches, how I've enjoyed the peaches. And my pictures and photographs" —she gesticulated toward the picture-crammed walls—"that one of your father over the mantel, taken the day he was ordained, it's been in that exact spot ever since the day I moved in. Just imagine having to take it down, and all the rest—my ornaments, my china. What's to become of my china? And what's to become of me? Worse yet, what will people think!" Her mother began to cry, and Damaris put her arm around her, feeling guilty because of her inability to feel pity in her heart.

"I'll find something. I'm sure I can find something, perhaps not quite this big; but there's bound to be something that's available that can be made suitable."

"Made suitable! I don't want something makeshift," her mother admonished sharply, before her voice became plaintive and wheedling again. "Do go and talk to Mr. Caylew, Damaris. You did before, you remember. I'm sure if you talked to him he wouldn't insist upon selling."

Her mother began to cry in earnest, and Damaris, looking around the room, remembered how she had given in to her mother's pleas once before. What would her life have been like if she'd stood her ground then? she wondered. She most certainly wouldn't be where she was today, a woman with a career before her . . . and the love of her life behind her.

"At least ask him to wait for my . . . my demise." Her mother became distraught at the very thought.

"Now, Mother, you're a strong, healthy woman, and amazingly agile for your years. It's a long time since I've seen you, and I'm delighted to find you so fit. There's no need to talk or even think of your demise."

"I just *seem* fit, Damaris. I'm a poor, frail old lady. That's why people take advantage of me."

"I don't think anyone's ever really taken advantage of you, Mother," Damaris said, her voice unusually hard.

"But they'll listen to you. The Caylews think highly of you. Why, I saw that picture of you in *Harper's*. I was so proud. . . . I have it here somewhere." Her mother began rustling through a stack of papers.

"I know the one. I've seen it," Damaris interposed.

"Well, it's obvious from that if nothing else that they think highly of you. Mr. Caylew put you through medical school"—she pursed her lips doubtfully—"not that I think that a particularly suitable thing, for a lady, that is. Still, I suppose it is preferable to that awful business of the religious order. Your father must have turned over in his grave at that. The church is a gentleman's province."

"I wasn't a priest, Mother," Damaris said sharply.

"Well, a nun. It was awful. I really didn't care to talk about it. People were always asking if you'd gone over to Catholicism. But quite a few of my friends are impressed now you're Dr. Fanshawe. It does sound rather . . . rather professional. You must be earning good money too, Damaris. At least I'm told doctors earn good money. Perhaps you can buy this house from Mr. Caylew."

"I'm still a physician for the Order of St. Catharine. The order was more instrumental in my being trained than Mr. Caylew. I receive very little beyond what I require for my room and board. My apartment in New York is tiny." She paused before adding reluctantly, "But perhaps we could share it."

"Newport is my home, Damaris; surely you know I couldn't move from here. Besides, what about this commission you've been appointed to?"

"Honorary, except for expenses when the commission meets, and that won't be until next year some time from all indications."

"But can't you do something—anything!" her mother burst forth in exasperation. "You're my only hope; that's why I wrote to you. They've taught you how to heal bodies. Well, Damaris, poverty causes troubled minds. There's just as much anguish there, I assure you."

Damaris thought back to Memphis, to all those for whom she'd been able to do no more than close their eyes before their bodies were coffined. "I'm not even sure I can heal bodies, Mother. As for troubled minds"—she shook her head, thinking of her own—"the only cure I know for that is keeping occupied. At least that's what I prescribe for myself ."

"Just as if I'm not busy every minute with the Garden Club—I'm secretary this year, and I've been president twice—there's so much work attached to that, people never realize. And there are my friends. Friendships take time and effort, Damaris. And goodness knows I would never let the maid dust my china; I couldn't trust anyone with that. And there are my African violets; I water them myself once a week. I'm busy all the time. But if I have to move into some awful little place, like the one you found for me when I had to leave the rectory, well, I just wouldn't have any of that. I'd be too ashamed to receive anyone. It would be such a . . . such a disgrace. You must do something. What's the use of having a child if she can't help a mother in distress? You're my daughter; you owe it to me that I be allowed to finish my days in peace."

"You're my mother. Didn't you owe me something when I was a child—care and protection?" It was the first time Damaris had ever spoken so directly to her mother. She hadn't intended to, any more than she'd intended to tell Caylew how much she hated him; but the words that had often crossed her mind were out, and despite the shocked dismay on her mother's face, she didn't altogether regret them.

"Damaris, what's come over you! It's this education. Women were never meant to be educated. You should never—"

"I'll see what I can do, Mother," Damaris broke in abruptly. "I can promise nothing."

"Just talk to Mr. Caylew, like you did last time, that's all I ask," her mother cajoled.

"That is absolutely out of the question, but I will have a word with his agent."

"That won't do any good," Mrs. Fanshawe scorned.

In that she was right. The agent only confirmed that the house was for sale, and upon completion of the sale it was to be vacated by its occupant. He already had one or two interested parties. It was a good house, well-maintained, well-situated, and priced to sell. He emphasized this last, indicating if Dr. Fanshawe was interested in her mother remaining there, she could do worse than buy it herself.

She promised to consider the suggestion, telling him to be sure to consult her before selling the property to anyone else. Halfheartedly he agreed, though even as he did so she was quite certain that he would sell without a single qualm to anyone with money in hand. Besides, hers was a futile gesture. She had no savings of any kind, and the only people she knew with money were the Caylews. They were the least likely to help her in this predicament.

In this she was wrong. Less than a month after her return to New York, she received in the mail the deed to the house on Catherine Street where her mother lived.

The accompanying letter read: "My father's agent mentioned your visit. Why didn't you come to me? I asked you to whenever you needed anything. While I'm not independently wealthy, I had enough from my trust fund to do this for you. Nathan Caylew."

Immediately she returned the deed to him. The house was his, she wrote. The agent had assured her it was a good investment. If he would only allow her mother to remain in it she would be forever in his debt.

"I don't want you in my debt," he replied. "I only want you to be happy."

Nathan Caylew might have wished her to be happy, but not all the members of his family were of like opinion.

Templeton Caylew, visiting New York in midsummer to attend to business, called on her at the hospital with a stern warning.

"Stay away from my son. You've tried to separate my daughter from her husband—without success, I might add. Now in your vindictiveness you've turned yourself on that fop of a poet of mine, insinuating yourself, as is your way, with one who's weak and vulnerable. You may have wrapped him around your little finger, but I have to warn you he's got no more money of his own—he spent most of what he had on that house your mother's in—and I'm prepared to cut him off completely if he seeks to marry you.''

"I have no thought of ever marrying Nathan. I will tell you this, though, Mr. Caylew, you may call him weak and gullible, but he's a finer person than you ever were or could ever hope to be.''

"You'd call anyone fine who does your bidding." He rammed his tall hat on his head. "Leave him alone.''

From her mother came a letter of effusive thanks: "The agent says I may stay. I knew if you spoke to Mr. Caylew that you could arrange everything. You are such a dutiful daughter, Damaris.''

On reading this note, Damaris crumpled it in her hands and stared into the fire. She had been used, manipulated, exploited—by her mother, by Caylew, by Eustacia. But as her anger rose, so did the realization that she had only been used by them because she had allowed it. At any point she could have denied them that right and taken the consequences. She smoothed out the note to read again her mother's phrase, "a dutiful daughter." Her duty, she realized, was as much to herself as to anyone else. She crumpled the note. Never again would she allow herself to be exploited, for whatever reason. She was her own woman, no one else's. She threw the note into the fire and watched the flames devour it until nothing remained of it but blackened ashes.

SIX

The commission to examine the spread and propagation of yellow fever in the United States, formed under the aegis of the National Board of Health, did not meet until 1880, a year after it had been set up. It might not have met then, except that President Hayes, who had called for the commission to be formed, had become a lameduck President by announcing prior to June's Chicago Republican Convention that he had decided against seeking a second term, whereupon the commission's chairman, Dr. McChord, decided equally abruptly to call his commission together for the purpose of discussing the form their study should take. Certainly the study must be under way before a new President had a chance to disband the commission for serving no useful purpose.

That summer in Washington was one of the hottest on record, and by Independence Day the capital was all but deserted. No one remained there from choice; those who had to be there moved in laggardly fashion through air that was humid, oppressive, without a stir. It was, to say the least, an unpropitious time to call together a body to embark on a difficult and what had so far proved a baffling study.

Because of the pressure of work and the late arrival of the young physician Dr. Dalcourt, who was to replace her at the hospital during her absence, Damaris was the last to arrive and meet the others who were to sit with her. Besides herself and Dr. McChord, there were two other physicians—Dr. Sylvester, an old colleague of Dr. McChord's; and Captain Reed, an Army doctor on leave from frontier garrison duty. There was also a public health official from Philadelphia, a former congressman from Ohio who was a personal friend of the President, and finally a New York banker who knew nothing of the fever and who had, it seemed, been appointed to the commission to repay an obligation.

Throughout most of the meetings he slept, and whenever asked for his opinion he would always say he agreed in principle if not in fact with the speaker, with an occasional variation to agree in fact if not in principle. He never, however, agreed with anything in fact as well as principle, which allowed him, if cornered, to change his mind without appearing to do so. It was perhaps a sign that the country was not yet reunited that no member from the South had been appointed to the commission, even though that part of the country had been most affected by yellow fever.

Everyone, even to some extent the chairman, though he would never have admitted it, hated being in Washington that summer; and the committee room from the first was charged with heat from short tempers as much as from the atmosphere.

Damaris Fanshawe's entrance had not been auspicious.

"Lordee . . ." The former congressman was mopping his neck with a large handkerchief when he spied her. "Would you see we get plenty of iced tea, honey, and I like lemon as well as sugar with mine. Don't know about the others."

"I am Dr. Fanshawe," she responded, watching his geniality fade.

"But Dr. Fanshawe is a member of this commission, and you're—"

"I know, I'm a woman. And I am Dr. Fanshawe."

"Well, I'll be . . . Glad to meet you," he finished lamely.

Her greeting from other members was scarcely more affable, though least affable of all was that from the only member she knew, the chairman. It soon became obvious to all that Dr. McChord went to some pains to take out his own disgruntlement, and the disgruntlement of other members, on his former student.

Damaris bore a dual stigma. First, she was the commission member who was most knowledgeable on the subject. Not only did she have firsthand experience in the most recent and most virulent epidemic, but she had spent the period since her appointment studying the work of Louis Pasteur and Robert Koch on preventive medicine, and of William Osler and William Welch on bacteriology. In addition, she had been in correspondence with a Cornell graduate student, Hermann Biggs, who had extensively studied the role of public health in preventing epidemics, and had commented incisively on yellow fever in Memphis. Secondly, and even more to her detriment, was the fact that she, a woman, had been appointed at all.

It was the first such commission Dr. McChord had been called upon to chair, but the pride he had felt had been blighted by what he viewed as a personal affront. Women were putting their noses into everything, even agitating to vote; next they'd be running for Congress. Dr. McChord had arrived in Washington with one idea foremost, the determination to quash all such ideas by proving how ineffective a woman was in any except the role to which God and nature had assigned her, that of wife and mother.

Perhaps if Damaris had remained silent, taking notes, as Dr. McChord had suggested she should, she might have saved herself from the brunt of his ire; but she had point-blank refused to keep the minutes, pointing out that a secretary had been assigned to the commission and they might as well avail themselves of his services.

And if that weren't bad enough, no matter that the chairman made a point of never calling on her or even looking in her direction, she insisted on being heard. She was prepared for the meeting; she knew of studies being undertaken and studies that had failed to produce results. She had done her homework, and she refused to sit silently by and keep her knowledge to herself; she made every effort to share it and was not averse to coupling the information she imparted with her own comments and criticisms.

Apart from young Captain Reed, her fellow physicians looked grim but said nothing. The public health official and former congressman might nod from time to time, though they would never bring themselves to voice either opinion or comment. As for the banker, he would awaken occasionally with a start to announce that though he might be inclined to agree with her in principle, he could not in fact. Dr. McChord, however, could never bring himself to agree in any respect with anything she said.

Her most ludicrous statement had been her opinion that the fever might be spread by the mosquito. It had provoked some hilarity, more so when she had backed up her argument with the experiments being conducted by a doctor in Cuba, Carlos Juan Finlay.

"My dear Dr. Fanshawe, I hate to hear anyone who has studied at a school with which my name is associated citing as an authority someone from an obscure Caribbean island who probably hasn't been out of the jungle, let alone received any creditable degree."

"Dr. Finlay resides in Cuba, Dr. McChord, but he is of Scottish-French descent, and his education and research methods, from all I have discovered, are impeccable. I would also cite Dr. Mitchum, a former president of the Memphis Board of Health who died in the 1878 epidemic. He spent his professional life searching for the cause of this fever. I was at his bedside when he died, and his last words, which mystified me at the time, I now believe indicate that he had reached the same conclusion—that the fever may, in a manner we don't yet fully understand, be spread by the mosquito. It is an acknowledged fact that the fever and the mosquito appear simultaneously; they also disappear at the same time, that is, with the first heavy frost. This is only one point, but a not insignificant one. How the mosquito might carry it, which species, why all are not afflicted—there are many unanswered questions. The research is in the earliest stages. I would add, for what it is worth, that though I am usually spared by the mosquito, I was bitten prior to coming down with the fever."

Here the Ohio congressman chuckled benignly. "My dear lady, which of us has not suffered from mosquito bites in the summer. If what you say were true, we would all have been downed by the dreaded fever."

"That is so; that is why I say these are early days to make any assessment. It is a theory, only a theory perhaps. But it happens to be the theory I am interested in following for want of any other that appears significant."

"Perhaps, Dr. Fanshawe, you will allow us to proceed to matters more relevant to the work of this commission,

the uses of calomel as a preventative by purging. Dr.
Sylvester has some words on the subject, I believe.''

Dr. McChord turned his back on Damaris, which put the
sleeping figure of the banker clearly within his line of
vision. His brows contracted. Still, he thought, at least he
preferred that recumbent member to the woman doctor's
unshakable calm.

At the conclusion of that day's session, Captain Reed
caught up with Damaris as she was leaving the room.

"Dr. Fanshawe, I would really be interested in hearing
more about Dr. Finlay's theory on the mosquito as the
propagator of yellow fever. I don't quite know why I was
appointed to this commission, for I have little experience
with the fever; but since I have been, I would like to learn
as much as possible. May we meet to discuss it?"

Damaris, delighted by Captain Reed's show of interest,
invited him to join her for dinner that evening at her hotel.
She returned there in a more pleasant frame of mind than
on any other afternoon, to be startled to find Nathan
Caylew in the lobby. She had made every effort to dis-
courage him since his father's irate call, but unlike him in
his youth, when he had heeded his father's every injunc-
tion, paternal displeasure now seemed only to renew his
interest. Apart from the matter of buying the Newport
house so her mother might continue to live in it, there had
been a steady stream of flowers and chocolates and bon-
bons addressed to her at the hospital, all of which she had
given for the enjoyment of her young patients. Enclosed
with these gifts had been poems, dedicated to her and
distinctly amorous in tone, which she had not shared.

"What on earth are you doing in Washington, Nathan?"
Damaris demanded, sharpness exceeding cordiality as she
suspected what his answer might be.

"I came to see you were all right."

"Nathan, of course I'm all right. Really, you shouldn't
have come. You know how annoyed your father would be
if he knew. If he discovers you're here he'll draw all kinds
of illogical conclusions.''

Nathan shook his head. "There won't be any misun-
derstandings on the old man's part. It can only confirm
what he already suspects, that among women you have the
highest place in my regard.''

"But think, Nathan. He might easily conclude this was a preconceived plan."

"He wouldn't be wrong—in part at least—for as soon as I heard you were to come, I immediately decided I would come also. I couldn't allow you to be alone among strangers."

She looked into a face whose youthful pallor denied its years. "It's kind of you, Nathan; but had I known, I should certainly have dissuaded you. Your being here places me in a predicament, besides risking your own future."

"But, Mary, you are my future."

"Nathan, I'm not." Her voice was that of a kind but firm mother, which was very much how she felt toward him. "You've been nicer to me than anyone in your family—I'll always be grateful to you—but you know your father will cut off your allowance if you continue to see me. I don't want to be the cause of that."

Nathan's face fell. "I know, but I don't give a damn about his money."

"You only say that, Nathan, because you've never known a life without it. Poverty is not a disgrace, but I can assure you it is disagreeable beyond belief."

"But I could work. Look"—proudly he drew a copy of *Puck* from his pocket—"my first published poem, 'Damaris, Fair Maid of Athens.' And Stedman's talked of putting me up for his Century Club, and Henry Holt read it and he's indicated a willingness to look over my other work with a view to compilation."

"Nathan, I'm glad. Really that's wonderful. I honestly believe you are firm in your resolve to be a poet; that I wholeheartedly applaud. I've no doubt that one day your poems will be assigned to lazy children in school to memorize in an effort to give them greater appreciation of words and ideas. They may hate you at the time, but when older they'll come to love you for the joy you brought to their lives. Think, though, Nathan, that of all people, poets need an income. Poetry is not easy to write under the very best of circumstances, but to try to write it hampered by want and insecurity is to risk losing the muse forever. It would be foolish to annoy your father now, especially without reason."

"But it's not without reason. I love you, Mary; you know I love you."

He had raised his voice, and several heads turned in their direction. She lifted a finger to her lips to silence him; and looking beyond Nathan across the foyer, she noticed the stride of a tall figure leaving the hotel, the carriage, the stride reminding her once again of Guy Parrish. So often that happened—the turn of a head, a manner of listening, a gesture of surprise, or a sudden laugh in a stranger would bring him to mind—just as it had then. Why must she think of him still? Would it always be so?

The memory, however, served to strengthen her reply. "Please, Nathan, you mustn't say that. You have an infatuation that very frankly I believe is enhanced because your father is so strongly opposed to it."

"It's not infatuation, Mary; it's love. And it's not rebellion from my father I care about but submission to you." She shook her head, but he insisted. "Don't say any more now. I've made reservations for dinner; we'll discuss, it then."

"I can't, Nathan. I've arranged to have dinner with Captain Reed." And seeing his disappointment, remembering his kindness, she explained: "He's on the commission and has an interest in Dr. Finlay's research on the fever."

"Well, if you must put your old commission before me." He pouted, much as Damaris suspected he had pouted as a little boy in order to get his way, but she was resolved not to give in.

"Tomorrow, then. You can't refuse me when I've come all this way."

"No, Nathan, I can't and won't. I think it's time we have a good talk so we clearly understand one another's intentions. You've been kind to me; I wouldn't want you to be hurt."

"Dammit, Mary, I'm tired of being kind."

"Then you must try to understand how I feel."

"And you must realize my feelings too. I shall come to meet you."

"We're hearing testamentary evidence in the afternoon; it may run late," she warned.

"I don't care. I'll come anyway, and we can go on directly from there."

She saw Nathan enter the hearing room soon after the session began, and while the president of the National Board of Health droned on at some length in what seemed more of a political harangue than relevant testimony, she considered that during the course of the evening she must forever dispel any hopes Nathan held of an eventual marriage between them. His floral and candy tributes—but more than those, his poems—had been impossible to reject, especially coming from one so sensitive who had shown such a keen desire to please her. Even so, she had never expected he might follow her to Washington. Perhaps it was as well, though, for they would have the opportunity, away from inquisitive eyes, to clear the matter of where they stood with one another.

"Thank you, sir, that was most helpful, most helpful indeed." She heard Dr. McChord pause, as though wishing to sum up what had been said without knowing how. Instead, he looked expectantly around the table. "I daresay my fellow members are anxious to pose questions. Well, now's the time."

There was silence, a silence that awoke the banker, who commented immediately, "I agree completely in principle, if not in fact, with everything the learned gentleman has said."

"Well, er, well, yes, indeed, we all do. We've learned a great deal about . . . about a great deal. Thank you, sir, for sparing your time to give us such lucid comment. And now . . . let me see . . . now we are to hear from . . ." As Dr. McChord studied the paper before him, Damaris glanced across at Nathan. He was dozing, probably the best thing during what was proving to be a boring session on an afternoon even warmer than usual.

She was suddenly jolted by hearing Dr. McChord demand: "Is Colonel Parrish here?"

Her eyes, even more anxiously than Dr. McChord's, searched the room. Could that really have been Guy Parrish in the foyer of her hotel yesterday? She breathed a sigh of relief that he wasn't there, but no sooner done than the door opened to admit the tall figure she had imagined to have recognized a thousand times in others. He crossed the room to sit in the chair so recently vacated by the previous pompous witness, returning the chairman's greeting with a general salutation to the commission, not singling her out, not even looking directly at her.

She made a determined effort to concentrate on his words rather than on his face, which was grave and unsmiling, or on his hands with their long fingers, now bereft of any ring.

He spoke clearly, factually, without any notes, of the measures the Taxing District had taken following the epidemic to prevent a recurrence. Food inspection had been established; systematic garbage disposal was under way; the Nicholson blocks, which some thought had carried the miasma into the air, were being replaced by hard pavement; and Waring's new sewer system was to be installed. He himself had invested in a new hospital that would be equipped with the latest equipment and the best staffing affordable. At their instigation, the federal government had instituted a system of marine hospitals for the sailors who plied the river, to insure that never again would seamen experience the plight of those on the *John Porter*, who had everywhere been refused care. These were measures taken to notify the world that the Memphis of the future would be a place of healing and renewal.

"There was another outbreak of fever last year, only sporadic compared to the horror of '78. Far fewer lives were lost, but given the depleted population, there were far fewer lives to take; thousands who fled earlier never returned. I don't give up hope of others replacing them. And I can assure you that though Memphis may have had to surrender its charter, the city will rise again. No step forward is ever made without pain."

As he said those words, he glanced for the first time directly at Damaris, and then almost as swiftly he looked away again. "Tennyson has said we must trust that good will be the final goal of ill, and overcome the pangs of nature, sins of will, defects of doubt, and taints of blood. I prefer to remember *his* words of hope rather than those of another Englishman, a journalist who came to mock us with 'I wonder why they gave a name of old renown to this dreary, dismal, muddy, melancholy town.' I would remind that gentleman, and this commission, that we took a name of old renown for our city, and we've since earned that name by a baptism of fever rather than water. Having been baptized, Memphis refuses to succumb but earnestly awaits confirmation. You can help us by throwing whatever light you can on the fever that attempted to but did not succeed in destroying us. That's where our battle still lies, in preventing the catastrophe of '78 from ever happening again."

"Thank you, Colonel Parrish. Eloquent words indeed. As you so rightly point out, we are here to be of assistance to you." Dr. McChord smiled benignly. "You are, I know, related by marriage to my good friend Templeton Caylew."

"I was, sir," Parrish replied abruptly. "If it is in my power to tell you any more on the subject at hand"—he emphasized those last words—"I shall do whatever I can."

"Yes, of course." Dr. McChord was clearly perplexed as well as displeased, and he showed his displeasure by snapping, "It was generous of our President to appoint us to look into a fever that primarily has scourged that section of our nation that so recently sought to forever divide us."

Parrish fixed his eyes on McChord as he answered with equal deliberation, "I think no part of this great land to which we were both born has a right to pronounce judgment on the other in a matter of natural disaster. Twenty years ago the South did take up arms, the South was overcome, the South has paid and continues to pay for that act of rebellion. But to suggest that the President is generous for being willing to look into the scourge of yellow jack because it has primarily afflicted the South is unworthy on your part, Mr. Chairman, and seeks to detract from what I believe was his honest intention, to prevent what happened to Memphis from happening again—to anyone, anywhere."

At this rebuke Dr. McChord shuffled papers in front of him in indignation. He turned to the commission to announce abruptly, "I think that is all we need to hear from Colonel Parrish. That will be all, sir."

The banker, awoken abruptly by the angry tone of this dismissal, hurriedly put in, "I agree with the witness in principle, if not in fact."

Parrish raised his eyebrows. "Would you mind, sir,

elucidating those facts with which you find yourself in disagreement? Perhaps I can then explain further.''

''Well, what I mean is . . .'' The banker cleared his throat and looked to Dr. McChord, who sought to save him from embarrassment by throwing ridicule in another area.

''Our work, Colonel Parrish, is only at its inception. We shall consider all avenues of approach, even those that seem ludicrous. One member, whom I shall not mention by name''—nevertheless, he looked pointedly at Damaris —''is of the opinion that that infernal mosquito is at the root of the problem. We must all from time to time have been annoyed by its sting, so to theorize along those lines seems irresponsible and a waste of time. The mosquito is and always will be prevalent during the summer months. Should that insect be the cause, we should all be dead of the fever. Nevertheless, ludicrous as it seemed, we have not refused to listen. As I said, we intend to leave no stone unturned in our study.''

''I'm glad to hear that, Dr. McChord,'' Damaris said. ''May I take that as your consent to pursue my theory and to include my conclusions in the commission's study?''

''Well, I haven't yet decided on the final form our study will take,'' he blustered.

Colonel Parrish intervened. ''There have been others who were of the same mind as Dr. Fanshawe, Mr. Chairman, but unfortunately their ideas were hooted down. I'm glad to find you are willing to study all approaches. It makes me realize the sincerity of your intention. You must forgive my outburst just now.''

''Yes, yes, indeed. Well, if there are no more questions—''

''I do have one for Colonel Parrish,'' Damaris broke in. Guy Parrish turned to her, his expression inscrutable. ''I was wondering, Colonel Parrish, since you don't scoff at the idea, whether you have given any thought to the control of mosquitoes during the summer season.''

She ignored the guffawed aside from Dr. McChord to his friend Dr. Sylvester: ''Just as soon control the house fly.''

''That, Dr. Fanshawe, is an enormous problem in an area such as the Mississippi Valley; given our hot, humid climate, it is a perfect breeding place; but I have, nevertheless, been giving the matter consideration. For instance, I have recommended the draining and filling in of the Gayoso Bayou. I don't have the agreement of everyone to this plan, and it will be costly. But I intend to press for it."

"If there is any help that the commission can give in strengthening your argument, Colonel Parrish, I am sure that Dr. McChord will be glad to be of assistance." Damaris made a note on the paper before her as Dr. McChord made irritated comments on the usurpation of his duties as chairman.

"I am sure I had no such intention, sir," Damaris replied, "but if you care to argue the matter, I see no reason we should hold up Colonel Parrish while we settle our dispute."

"It's just that you so often forget your place, Dr. Fanshawe," the chairman responded testily.

"Before I go, Mr. Chairman," Parrish intervened, "I wonder if I might make a matter of record a long overdue recognition? I should very much like to, if I have your leave."

"By all means." Dr. McChord was eager to change the subject, though his pleasure did not last long.

"The work of the religious orders in my own city during this devastating epidemic—I speak of both Catholics and Episcopalians—was truly above and beyond anything that might be expected. Where others—ministers as well as doctors—fled, they stayed to work long and valiantly, many, far too many, succumbing to the fever. I should also like to put in a special word of thanks from the city of Memphis to Dr. Fanshawe, who is a member of this commission. She came to Memphis of her own volition; she fought alongside her fellow physicians, willingly helping wherever she was sent rather than taking offense at their ungracious reception of a female in their ranks. It was an act of true courage, and I am glad to have this opportunity to acknowledge it publicly." He rose from his chair. "I shall await the commission's report with great interest."

As he turned to go, Dr. McChord, with a sigh of relief, declared the session closed for the day. Damaris rose from the table to catch up with Parrish just as he reached the door.

"Guy, that was kind and generous of you just now. I didn't expect it; I thought you must despise me."

"You're correct, Dr. Fanshawe; personally I do." His face was impassive, his voice cool. "What I just told the committee was an official recognition that was, as I indicated, long overdue. I wanted to make it a matter of record, that's all."

Her face had paled. "Oh, I see."

As he moved to leave, she stopped him. "I'm sorry, really sorry."

"For what?"

"For the letter. I had to write it."

He motioned to her empty place at the table as he responded coldly, "Yes, I see that you did. I read the article on your appointment. I suppose I should have sent my congratulations. I was remiss. Allow me to convey them now."

"I know what you must think, that Eustacia used this appointment as a means of—"

"A means of what, Dr. Fanshawe? Buying you—is that the phrase you're searching for? I thought she had reached her nadir when she sent a team of workmen to Bellechasse in my absence to cut down the copper beech my mother had planted."

"Oh, Guy, I'm so sorry . . . so sorry. I know how much that meant to you."

"So did she. It was loathsome and willfully malicious—not only for my sentimental attachment but because the tree was beautiful in itself. Still that was nothing to the pain I felt when she managed to buy you. You see, I never thought you, of all people, were for sale. But I suppose each one of us has a price, and she found yours. I was a fool to think you any different."

"It wasn't like that, Guy."

"Wasn't it?" He looked across the room to where Nathan Caylew had awoken and was beginning to realize the meeting must be over. "She told me that you were her father's mistress, that he was the one who had fathered your child."

Under the cold ferocity of his attack, Damaris was

taken aback; yet it was perhaps only to be expected that Eustacia, adept at using every weapon, would have told him. "I never thought of myself in those terms; however, what she told you was right. Templeton Caylew was the father of my child."

"And now his footsteps are being followed by his son. You're keeping things in the family, I see. Well, good luck to all of your ambitions, Doctor. I always said Nathan might become a decent poet if he met with unrequited love, but his presence here seems to indicate a more happy state."

"That's unfair and untrue," she answered hotly.

"Is it?" Eyes granite gray and just as hard met blue eyes deep and distraught. "Eustacia's despicable, but I despise you more, Damaris. You made me vulnerable, capable of being hurt as only a man who has loved can be hurt. That I can never forgive."

Damaris blinked to prevent tears; she never wanted him to know how much he had wounded her.

"As for that benefactress of yours, you can tell her from me that she can rot in hell before I'll lift a finger to give her anything she wants, anything at all. She's running around with Gilvray, and if I know Eustacia, eventually she's going to want that title of his. Years ago when I introduced her to him, I suggested it. What agony might have been prevented if she'd only taken that advice. But now, through you more than any of her other callous acts, she's cut me too deeply to allow me to ever forgive or forget. I'll be the thorn in her side that she's been in mine all these years. She may have bought your support, but with that she played her last ace. It was a case of bad timing on her part, I'm afraid. She's used all her weapons; there's no way she—or you—can hurt me now."

He nodded abruptly to Nathan as he joined them, a nod that served as greeting and farewell, for without another word to either of them he left the room.

SEVEN

The meeting of the commission was to be a turning point for Damaris. There had been a definite break with Nathan Caylew; that had come as a relief. There had also been the finality of Guy Parrish's angry words and the pain they caused.

It had been difficult to make Nathan understand that she had never contemplated marriage with him, so firmly was that idea fixed in his mind. He had been kind to her; she could not forget his kindness. How he had disliked her calling him kind! He had been hurt by her refusal to reconsider his offer, though his hurt in no way affected her as had the anguish she'd seen behind the anger in Guy Parrish's eyes, or her own anguish at knowing how deeply he despised her.

She had looked forward to returning to New York, to work, to her apartment. But there change, in the form of tragedy, awaited her. Mother Charlotte had been stricken by an attack quite soon after Damaris had left for Washington.

Dr. Dalcourt's concern was evident. "I thought it was the heat at first, but soon realized it was much more serious than that. Her heart must have been weak for years."

"But she said nothing. She never complained."

The young doctor shook his head. "I called in a specialist. I insisted on getting a second opinion though she didn't want it. She said she'd known about it all along; it wasn't necessary. He agreed with my diagnosis and was surprised that she had continued to work as she had; he said she should have had complete rest. I wanted to send for you. While I realize you can do no more than has already been done, I thought your presence would comfort her. But she wouldn't hear of it."

"Even so, you should have, I would have come; you know I would."

"Don't fuss, Damaris," Mother Charlotte's normally hearty voice was barely above a whisper. "If you had come sooner, I would have died sooner. I asked God for time enough to see you before I go."

Damaris stood beside her, her hand on her pulse, trying not to let her concern at its irregularity and the pallor of that usually robust complexion show on her face.

"Don't talk like that."

"I know what you're going to say—part of the cure is to wish to be cured—but it's not a matter of cure, Damaris. You know that as well as, probably better than, I. As soon as this attack struck, I realized that my life was all but over."

"You've had them before?"

Mother Charlotte nodded.

"And you kept them from me? Why?"

"Because I thought you'd fuss the way you're fussing now and try to prevent me from doing my work. I'm not sorry to die now, but earlier it would have been a terrible blow, to start and be unable to finish what I'd begun. Now I feel I've done the work God put me on earth to do. I've done it as well as I could; maybe another might have done or will do better, but still I am satisfied. I can say no more than that. I asked only for time to see you before I go; and, you see, even that was granted me, so I am happy."

"Oh, Mother Charlotte." Damaris knelt beside her bed as the Mother Superior reached out a hand to her, a hand once so strong, so capable, now thin, unusually frail. "I love you."

"I know you do, and I've loved you like the daughter I never had. There have been so many novices who've come to me and placed their lives in divine hands through the means of my all too human ones, and I've loved them all; but you've always been special to me. I'll never forget that time on Long Island as we walked along the beach, I was so afraid you would walk into the water again. I don't know what I talked about, but all the time I was praying,

praying. Maybe it was wrong of me, to love you more, but as I said, I am only human; and it is a human trait, or perhaps a weakness, to love one above all others.''

"I know,'' Damaris answered softly.

"I know you love someone very specially, not in the way you love me, not that way. I've known it. I've watched you. You haven't been alone in your suffering; for though you may not have wished it, I've prayed for you. Now don't shake your head. To pray for another is a privilege God grants that cannot be taken away, even by an unwilling recipient. Loving is the most beautiful, yet so often the most dIfficult, part of life. I don't know why it should be so. It's a paradox, but so much of life is paradox. Maybe I'll find out why soon enough. You've been brave, Damaris, and I only wish that somehow you may find the happiness you deserve.''

She paused to draw breath that no longer flowed with ease, but she refused to stop talking. "No, I wanted you to come so I could say to you what has been on my mind. Now is the only chance I shall have. I am fond of Sister Lavinia—she'll soon be Mother Lavinia—but though I shouldn't say it, I wish it were you I was passing the reins to. You've handled things so beautifully—like that business with Sister Angela—no one else could have done as well.''

She saw the startled look cross Damaris's face. "Didn't you know that I realized she loved you? I told you a superior must be aware of these things. I knew you were troubled by her affection, yet you never cast scorn upon her for it, nor did you ignore her, nor did you put the matter to me. If you had, in my position I should have been forced to ask her to leave. You knew that. Instead you tried to understand, you realized that what had brought her to the order might become an opportunity to do something really worthwhile with her life—and that was what happened. She became one of the best sisters the order ever had. That was because of you.''

As Mother Charlotte's breathing grew more labored, Damaris bent her head over that frail hand she held between hers. "I shall miss you, Mother.''

"No, no you won't, because I'll be with you wherever you go. There will be choices, chances waiting for you.

You'll see." The voice was quieter than ever, so quiet, in fact, that Damaris wondered whether she had only imagined it.

"Mother Charlotte?" she ventured, afraid there might be no reply.

"I'm praying. Damaris, pray with me, please. It's the last thing I'll ask of you."

And together they prayed. It was the first time Damaris had prayed from her heart since Memphis; but before the prayer was done, by the time she reached "Thy will be done on earth," she realized that only one voice was saying the words, not two. Still she finished, and only after the final amen did she look up to see that life had indeed departed from the figure in the bed; it was no longer Mother Charlotte who lay there, but only the body that had once held her spirit. She reached over and, as she had done with so many fever victims, closed her eyes— eyes that had twinkled and shone their way through life, now dulled and stilled by death.

She hadn't realized that Livvy was in the room until she looked up and saw that she too had knelt to pray on the other side of the bed.

"It's over, Livvy. She's dead."

Her heart was cold, heavy. She wanted to be alone, yet she saw Livvy was stricken not only by the death but by the mantle of responsibility that had in that moment fallen on her shoulders.

"I'm not worthy to follow her, Damaris."

"Livvy, of course you are."

Livvy shook her head. "I'm not. I don't have her understanding."

"You will, Livvy; that will come."

"Do you think so?" Livvy looked at Mother Charlotte's face, placid in repose, and shook her head again. "I wish I had your faith—in people, I mean. I owe you an apology."

"Why?"

"I heard what Mother Charlotte said about Sister Angela. I always thought that you and she were . . . that you were particular friends. I didn't understand that you were not at fault."

"Sister Angela was not at fault either, Livvy; she felt differently, that's all."

"You see what I mean; I still don't understand."

"You will, Livvy; you will. Understanding, compassion—it all takes time. You're still young, but you have great common sense; you keep your head in a crisis, and you have faith in God."

"I heard you praying. Does that mean . . . ?"

Damaris shook her head at the unspoken question. "Not yet, but perhaps that too takes time."

All the pomp of the church was put into Mother Charlotte's funeral. Three bishops were present, each of whom gave a eulogy. Templeton Caylew and his wife, with Eustacia Caylew Parrish, were chief mourners; and Sister Lavinia, as the next recognized recipient of the Mother Superior's abbatial seal ring of office, stood beside them.

The death, unexpected as it was, was a last blow to Damaris, leaving her completely alone. Even in her darkest moments, though she might not have gone to her, she had always known that Mother Charlotte was there, that she would understand. She thought of Mother Charlotte's words: "I'll be with you wherever you go." Perhaps that was so; still she felt alone, so alone. As for those choices and chances, she could see nothing but emptiness ahead.

She knew, despite Livvy's attempts to restore their friendship to its former footing, that it would take time for the wounds to heal. Maybe it would happen only when Livvy stopped trying to make it happen.

She had no one in whom to confide, and for the first time work did not provide the answer. The hospital had so completely embodied the spirit of Mother Charlotte that every day Damaris expected to see her figure hurrying down the corridor, waving greetings at the entrance to the ward, comforting children who were sick, or parents who waited. She looked for it, even though knowing it would never be there again.

Livvy would be a good Mother Superior; Damaris didn't doubt that. Yet she could never replace Mother Charlotte in her life. The hospital was firmly established; there would be no difficulty in finding another doctor. Damaris began to consider doing something else with her life, not seeking another appointment but a cause to which to devote herself, to absorb her mind, her energy—the choice and the chance Mother Charlotte had promised.

When she first spoke of her intention, Livvy, as she knew she would, dissuaded her from the idea of making a change. However, she hadn't expected one of the most insistent dissuaders to be Eustacia.

"You owe it to my father to stay on." Eustacia saw a look of exasperation cross Damaris's face and hurried on. "If not to him, then you owe it to Mother Charlotte's memory."

"I stayed with Mother Charlotte in her life. The hospital is now sufficiently endowed, thanks to the support of your family and others, to allow Livvy a choice between several well-qualified replacements."

"But if you stay we can continue to help your career."

"Eustacia, really!" Damaris made no attempt to hide her exasperation. "I never wanted your help. You know very well it was a source of embarrassment to me. That was your intention. Had the appointment you secured for me not been to a commission on a subject in which I am vitally interested, I would have refused out of hand to sit on it at all. I confess to being chagrined that I found myself unable to refuse it, but I suppose you knew that. You're astute. Who knows what you might have done with that perspicacity of yours if it had been directed into useful channels."

"There are angels of mercy, and then there are simply angels." Eustacia smiled.

"I'd never describe your qualities as angelic."

"But yours are; that's why we can't afford to lose you.

Damaris put aside the chart she had had open before her when Eustacia had come in. "What is it you want, Eustacia? I fail to understand these arguments you are putting up to insure that I stay on here. Why is it of any importance to you?"

"I wish you would stay . . . because of Harwood," Eustacia began hesitantly.

"Guy!" Damaris was astounded. "If I failed to understand before, now I am utterly confused. You forced me under the worst of pressures to put into words a falsehood that caused me more pain than you'll ever know, Eustacia. When I wrote that letter I knew it must guarantee that he would hate me always—just as you wanted. I can assure you that he does."

"I was wrong to have done that, Damaris. And I know from what Livvy has since learned that my accusations about your conduct with Angela Wickers were untrue."

"I told you that at the time," Damaris said coldly. "You knew it was untrue then."

"You did; I should have listened to you. I know you love Harwood. I wish you would write and tell him so."

"What am I, your amanuensis? Write this, Damaris, write that!" Damaris's astonished anger changed to distrust and finally outright suspicion. "All right, Eustacia, what is it you want this time? You've no wish for my happiness, and you've treated a man who deserved far better with the malevolence of a witch. How could you—ordering that copper beech his mother planted at Bellechasse to be cut down!"

"I know, that was a mistake," Eustacia put in quickly. "But you see at the time I was angry, very angry."

"It wasn't the act of an angry woman but a malicious one."

"How dare you!" Eustacia responded heatedly, before ameliorating her tone to press, "Do write to him, Damaris. You may tell him I made you write that other letter."

"Why do you want me to?" Damaris demanded. "The truth Eustacia; I won't accept anything less. I recognized the crocodile tears you shed so sweetly on the night you made the announcement of my appointment to that commission—an announcement guaranteed to convince Guy of my selfish concern for my career. You succeeded on both counts then—in captivating your audience, in forever alienating him from me. When you did that, you made my career my life. At least I have that; you can't take it from me. But don't try lies and falsehood now. Tell me the truth and I'll listen, but that's all I promise to do. I won't jump around like your puppet, waiting for you to pull my strings, never again."

Eustacia's smile disappeared. "Really! You're a slut. I knew you were when you boasted of having slept with my father."

"You told Guy that too, didn't you? Well, Eustacia, when you did that you played your last card; there are no others up your sleeve for you to flourish and threaten with. As for being a slut, call me what you will. You are certainly qualified to recognize the qualities of a slut, since you're so admirably endowed with the traits. If you're through, you may leave. I'm quite busy.''

"You professional trollop, how dare you speak to me like one of your minions! My family can buy and sell your sort a dozen times over." Eustacia swore and flounced toward the door, drawing her fox fur close around her neck; but once there, she turned back, her angry face suddenly wreathed in a smile.

"Well, Damaris, we are a pair, aren't we? Let's call a truce, shall we? You see through my act, and I see through yours.''

"Mine?" Damaris raised her eyebrows. "You're the actress. I have no act.''

"Oh, but you do. This one of your career being your life. It's important to you, that I'll grant, but my guess is there's something or someone you would place before it.''

"What is it you want, Eustacia? I suggest you get to the point and admit the truth or leave," Damaris snapped, ignoring the implication.

"I'd like you to tell Guy you still love him, that I made you write the other letter. It's no more than the truth.''

"Why?" Damaris demanded. "Tell me truthfully why.''

"Because I'm sorry for the way I've treated him, and you.''

"Get out! You're wasting my time with your lies. You've never been sorry for trampling anyone under those tiny pointed feet of yours. You're not woman enough to admit what it is you really want. I've nothing more to say to you. Get out!''

"All right, Damaris, you don't have to shout. The fact of the matter is that I realize that my marriage to Harwood is over, that even Papa can't get him back for me, and now Lord Gilvray has asked me to marry him.''

"So, the truth at last! If you're asking my opinion on the match, I think it excellent. You will make a good pair.''

"I daresay we will," Eustacia said, adding diffidently, "or would. But the thing is that I can't marry him until I am free to do so.''

"Oh," Damaris observed without looking up from the chart in her hand.

"And Harwood is being difficult. First he was so anxious to have a divorce that he would have allowed anything. I realize that was because he wanted to marry you. Now, though he insists on separation, he says he no longer cares anything about a divorce. If I insist on going back to Bellechasse he tells me he'll do nothing to stop me, but he won't be a husband to me. He is so cruel, so unkind! As if I'd want to live in that godforsaken place. He well knows how I've always hated it." She paused, her face flushed with resentment. "He's being diabolical. I hate him."

"I imagine your father can get the divorce for you, Eustacia, just as he got you the marriage."

"Of course he can, but we can't have our name dragged through the courts, muddied, besmirched. We hold a position in society that must be protected, and Harwood knows that. He knows too that I can't continue to remain in this anomalous state—married but not married—and he knows Jack Gilvray has been . . . well, he's been attentive. So now Harwood's making demands. I've given in on practically all of them, even agreeing that he may see Bella, but still it's not enough. He's determined to be difficult. I want the matter concluded with the least possible difficulty. There have been so many scandals lately; I won't become part of yet another one, but he insists he doesn't care how much publicity results. I thought if he knew you care for him as much as ever—"

"No, Eustacia," Damaris snapped. "No!"

"But you do."

"Whether I do or not is my business, not yours. "You'll not use me to get your own ends—not now, not ever."

"I'm being nice in suggesting that you do this, thinking of your future and Harwood's. It's that"—she paused dramatically before concluding—"or else I'll name you as co-respondent. You know I have proof of his infidelity with you, proof I was willing not to use because it would ruin you; but if you won't do this, I may have to."

"Use it by all means," Damaris replied coolly. "You don't have to ask my permission to do that. I wouldn't expect you to. Do exactly as you wish."

"It will prevent you from being offered any decent position, anywhere. Think of that."

"It may, for a while, but you see, Eustacia, I just don't

care. Use your dirty little proof, and I hope Guy fights you every step of the way. I won't plead with you to save my reputation, and he doesn't give a brass nickel about it, thanks to that letter you forced me to write. You can't always have everything your way. Many things are beyond your power. Nothing you can do will join back together the copper beech you had cut down, and nothing can ever restore the feeling Guy had for me. You brought this all on yourself—with your father's help, no doubt—now even he can't fix things for you, can he?" She saw Eustacia's lip begin to quiver, but rather than stopping her harangue it served to add impetus. "You haven't an honest bone in your body. You're twisted and conniving, and, worst of all, though you're an intelligent woman, you hide behind that father of yours like the spoiled child you are. When are you going to grow up?"

"How dare you?"

"I dare because there's nothing you can do to hurt Mother Charlotte now; you can't hurt Guy anymore; and there's really nothing you can do to me that would matter, not now. If you'll excuse me, I have a great deal to do."

"You think you've won, don't you? Well, you haven't, I'll—"

"Do whatever you want. There's been an ongoing battle between us; but as with most battles, winners often turn out to be losers in the end."

With that, since Eustacia showed every sign of carrying the argument to greater length and no sign of leaving her office, Damaris herself quit not only the room but the hospital.

She walked and walked, not noticing or caring in which direction her steps led. She bumped shoulders with passers-by and didn't pause to apologize. She was filled with wrath at Eustacia; she was filled too with uncertainty at her own future. It stretched before her, not filled with hope, with steps to climb, matters to be accomplished, but flat, empty, devoid of any landmark.

A shadow fell across her path, a shadow cast by the steeple of St. Stephen's; and without thinking, as though willed to do so, she climbed the steps to the church.

Inside it was dark, calm, airless. In the loft the organist was practicing for the Sunday service and the resonant tones reverberated through the tall building, bouncing down from its resplendent stained-glass windows.

Damaris sat in the first pew she came to, as far from the altar as it was possible to be. Here she had once sat as nursemaid to the Caylews, a participant in the service, allowed to partake of Communion, though only after all those who sat before her had done so.

The last shall be first, the first last, it was said. She wasn't first or last; she wasn't really anywhere. She wasn't the nursemaid who had once sat in that pew, but who was she? Was she a better, stronger person than that girl had been? She wasn't sure. That outburst with Eustacia. It had made her feel better to say things at the time, but it had solved nothing.

She felt so alone.

She stopped thinking, allowing the notes of Brahms to carry her far away. The darkness was peaceful. All around her was calm—tranquillity, darkness, music. She allowed them to carry her back, back, far, far back into a sea of sound, red and yellow and blue reflected sound. She closed her eyes, but the colors stayed. She was surrounded by color, by sound that grew in crescendo, and above it she heard a voice, a voice she knew.

"I'm with you, Damaris. You mustn't worry. There will be choices, chances . . . you'll see."

"Mother Charlotte, Mother Charlotte!" she called.

She opened her eyes with a start. It was quiet inside the church. The music had stopped. But someone was beside her. Her heart thumping, she turned to look into her face—

His face. It was an elderly man, the organist, she realized, who stood there looking at her strangely, nervously.

"Do you need help? A drink of water perhaps?"

She got up hastily. "No, no, I'm quite all right."

"Stay, I'll call the rector."

"No, I'm all right, I said."

Without another word, she brushed past him to hurry out into the sunlight without so much as a parting word of thanks for his solicitousness. She felt guilty, ashamed. She was a practical person, not given to hallucinations. People didn't speak from the dead. She had allowed herself to become carried away by the music, the atmosphere. Her mind must be wandering.

She shook herself and glanced at the watch hanging from the chain at her neck. She'd been gone two hours; she'd never done such a thing before without saying where she could be found. Her heart beat faster in time with her hurrying steps.

But at the hospital, in answer to her immediate inquiry, she found nothing had arisen to demand her attention. She breathed a sigh of relief as she went through the mail on her desk. Nothing of importance, except—She noticed one envelope with unusual stamps and tore that open first.

It was from Dr. Carlos Finlay in Cuba. He had heard of her advocacy of his work before the commission in Washington, and he thanked her for her support. He would very much like to meet her; more than that, though, since she did not scoff at his theory that yellow fever might be propagated by the mosquito, would she, he wondered, consider joining him in his research?

EIGHT

*L*ivvy had wanted to arrange a splendid farewell for
Damaris, but Damaris preferred a party with the children on the wards—a celebration with balloons and cake
and no dignitaries and most certainly no speeches.

She was pleased that the children liked Dr. Dalcourt,
who was to step into her position. He was young and
charming and extremely patient, and they responded well
to his frank and open approach. She was leaving without
any doubt that her young patients, for whom she cared
deeply, would remain in excellent hands.

She had pointed this out when Livvy had attempted to
make her change her mind about going to Cuba to work
with Dr. Finlay.

"I've been here long enough, Livvy; it's time for a
change, for me, for you, for everyone. The children adore
Dr. Dalcourt, and there has been no resistance from any of
the sisters."

"You wouldn't have gone if Mother Charlotte were still
alive," Livvy pointed out.

"I know. But I hope you don't think I'm leaving just
because she's no longer here. There comes a time for
everyone, as you know, when change is necessary. It is for
me now. You're doing so well, Livvy, in taking over a
difficult position; you have the respect of everyone."

"But not their admiration," Livvy responded.

"Maybe not in the same way Mother Charlotte did, but
it will come; admiration will follow respect. A religious
order is conservative by nature; any change must be carefully assimilated. Now you have the loyalty and obedience
due a superior. When the sisters have become accustomed

to the change, you'll have their personal regard too. I know you will, but I'm looking in from the outside now. It makes a difference."

Livvy's hands caressed the polished surface of the desk that Mother Charlotte had brought to New York from her Virginia home.

"I never thought I'd ever be sitting here, Damaris. I can't deny how much I relish the challenge."

Damaris smiled. "I'm glad, Livvy, really glad."

"She wanted you here, you know that."

"You're much better at the task than I'd ever have been. I'm not an administrator. You are, and a very good one."

Livvy looked down at the large abbatial seal ring on her left hand. "Will you ever really forgive me, Damaris, for what I did to you?"

"There's nothing to forgive."

"I think perhaps there is. I sometimes wonder whether I told Eustacia about Angela so that I would sit here instead of you. At the time, I believed I was simply angry with you for having rejected me as a friend, but my disloyalty to you has come to haunt me. I've thought about it, prayed about it, and I think that I may have reacted as I did because I knew something like that would preclude all possibility of your taking over. Mother Charlotte had made no secret that that was what she wished."

"Don't torture yourself, Livvy. We can't always understand our reasons. If it's of any consolation, I firmly believe that things have turned out as they were supposed to. I'd never have had this opportunity to do research in which I have a vital interest if I were sitting where you are; in fact, I know I'd hate it. You enjoy it, and though no one will ever forget Mother Charlotte, you will make a wonderful successor to her in your own very special way." Damaris put her arm around Livvy and kissed her cheek. "I'd better go. I've a million things still to do. I don't know how I'll get everything finished by Thursday. You see"—she laughed—"unlike you, I'm a rotten organizer."

"There is one thing before you go. Though perhaps you may not want to talk about it, I must ask. Eustacia told me that there was some . . . some feeling between you and Guy. Was she . . . was that so?"

Damaris hesitated. Livvy was right; she couldn't talk about it. It still hurt too much. Besides, it was all over. She shook her head. "There isn't anything to talk about, Livvy, not now. I really must go."

She left, but instead of going through the records in her office she sat thinking of the new direction her life was taking. Dr. Finlay's invitation had seemed like an answer to a prayer. Was it? Was that what she had prayed for that afternoon in St. Stephen's? Had Mother Charlotte intervened? She'd heard her voice; she was sure she'd heard her voice. There will be choices, chances. She was pleased with the invitation to take part in research that might eventually solve the blight of yellow jack; she could ask for no greater challenge. Yet why did she stil awaken each morning with a gnawing sense of unhappiness?

One afternoon, in gathering together the belongings in her apartment, she'd come across the misshapen green clay figure in the corner where she'd tossed it; she'd put aside her packing to try to reconstruct its odd shape and rounded belly before realizing the afternoon had gone by with nothing done. Opening a file drawer to pull out a handful of charts, Damaris mentally shook herself. Time was drifting by again; she must concentrate on all that had to be done.

The cake was enormous, white icing with trellised pink roses all around the border and an inscription: "The Children of St. Catharine's will miss you, Dr. Fanshawe." Around the inscription was a circle of stars, one for each of the patients.

"It's so beautiful I don't want to cut it," Damaris complained, "but you'd never forgive me if I didn't. And I'd never forgive myself, come to that. I'm dying to have a piece."

So the heavy knife cut through the letters, and she gave the first slice of cake to the patient who'd been there longest, eight-year-old Louise, hospitalized since she was six with a hip injury that refused to heal properly. Damaris was especially fond of the little girl, who reminded her of Vicky.

"I don't want you to go, Dr. Fanshawe," she whispered.

"But you like Dr. Dalcourt, Louise; you told me you thought he was so handsome, and he's very fond of you."

"Is he?" she questioned doubtfully.

"He told me so himself."

"He's not like you, though."

"He'll take good care of you."

"Will he give us flowers and candy the way you used to?"

"Now you know I haven't had any flowers or candy to send you for ages."

Those gifts had ceased coming soon after that meeting with Nathan in Washington. Their cessation, Damaris suspected, had been promulgated not only by her rejection of him but also by Nathan being taken up by Edmund Clarence Stedman, who had written an effusive critical appraisal of his work for his massive opus *Poets of America* and had graciously allowed Nathan to join his charmed Saturday night group at the Century Club. Since then, Nathan's poetry had appeared regularly in such prestigious publications as Howells's *Atlantic Monthly* and Gilder's *Century*.

"I always loved the flowers better than the candy," Louise said wistfully. "They reminded me of how it used to be playing outside in the sun."

"You will again. It's hard to wait, even when you're as old as I am, but the one who knows how to wait without losing hope is the one who wins out in the end."

The child studied her face. "Do you really believe that, Dr. Fanshawe?"

But Damaris had to look away as she answered, "Of course . . . But come along, do eat this delicious cake. I won't forget you, Louise. I'll come back, and when I do I expect to see you walking. And I promise I'll send you postcards of the flowers in Cuba. I'm told they have the most exotic ones there."

That was when her eyes fell on the young gentleman carrying a huge mixed bouquet of white carnations, pink hibiscus, and what she thought was spiraea, until, as he came closer, she saw it was her favorite lavender. Though the bouquet was so large that it almost completely hid the bearer's face, the presence of the lavender and an unmistakable stride made her exclaim immediately, "Arnaud! What a wonderful surprise! What on earth are you doing here? I know, don't tell me; Mother Lavinia planned it."

She would have hugged him, except the bouquet was in the way.

"You see." She turned back to the little patient. "You didn't have to wait too long for that wish to come true. I'm going to put some of these in a vase just for you. Come along, Arnaud, and tell me what brings you here. Did you really come all this way to say good-bye to me?"

"In a way, though not altogether. But I wouldn't have wanted you to leave without my seeing you," he added hastily as they walked down the corridor in search of vases and water. "Father had to come to New York on business, and he asked me to come with him."

"I see." Damaris saw too that Guy had not come with Arnaud to the hospital. "I'm glad you came. How you've grown! You must tell me what this fine young gentleman has been doing."

"Oh, we've been having such a grand time. Father took me to a wrestling match at Madison Square Garden, and we had dinner at Delmonico's. And he's taking me to see Coney Island. We're going on a steamboat from the Battery and I've ridden a Pullman car on the elevated and we walked in Central Park and he pointed out to me the building where you live."

"Why didn't you come up and see if I was home?"

Arnaud looked uncomfortable. "Father thought you would be busy packing."

"I see. Well, of course, he was right. I have been very busy. But anyway, I'm so glad I got a chance to see you today."

They had found a cupboard with vases and selected two, one large, one small, and arranged the bouquet in them, with Arnaud plying one question after another. As they finished, Damaris stood back to examine the result.

"Very nice," a voice over her shoulder commented. Guy Parrish was approaching with Livvy.

The greeting was awkward, stilted. Almost as soon as their eyes met, each looked away again.

"Livvy tells me you're leaving for Cuba," he said.

"Yes. At the end of the week. I'll be working with Dr. Finlay."

"So I understand."

"It's what I want to do." For some reason her voice

sounded defensive, and as though she owed an explanation, she went on: "I'm very interested in his theory about mosquito propagation of yellow fever."

"Yes, I remember."

The atmosphere grew even more strained as that brought to mind their last angry meeting in the committee hearing room.

"Dr. Dalcourt will be taking over here. He's excellent." The conversation did not flow; it sputtered. Damaris looked at Livvy for help, remarking, "Livvy's becoming a wonderful Mother Superior. I'm very proud of her."

"So am I."

"Well, I'd better get these flowers Arnaud brought out to the ward. It was very kind of him to think of them. I love lavender."

"I know," Guy said.

That was all.

"Good-bye, then." She picked up the large vase and handed the smaller one to Arnaud, but just as she was about to go Guy asked quickly, "I was wondering whether . . . whether you might have dinner with Arnaud and me tonight."

Damaris was silent for a moment, then she shook her head. "I'm awfully busy—packing and everything—I've left so much until the last minute."

"Yes, of course, I understand."

"But thank you."

"I understand," he said again.

"Besides, Guy," Livvy put in, "you seem to have forgotten that this is the evening I set aside to entertain Arnaud and Bella. I have tickets for the circus, but only three."

"Of course. I had forgotten. Well, I suppose I shall have to eat dinner alone then."

"You do have to eat, don't you, Damaris, even if you are busy?" Livvy pressed. There was a sense of urgency in her voice, a look of pleading in her eyes.

"I suppose I do," Damaris wavered.

"I know a little Bavarian restaurant not too far from here," Guy said, his eyes meeting, holding, hers. "We could have an early dinner. You'd still have time to pack.

The food is good." He stopped, then added, "At least, I believe it is."

"I don't think . . ." Three pairs of eyes were fixed on Damaris.

"You do have to eat," Livvy reminded her again.

"Yes, yes, of course."

So they walked together, as they had once before, toward the Fifty-ninth Street restaurant with its blue painted trim and red and white curtains. Guy Parrish talked a great deal, as though it were better than silence, telling her about Memphis and the Tax Board, the new bank he and his friends had set up to help fund new residents— immigrants for the most part, but diligent, hardworking people— about the dinner given for General Grant, who'd volunteered his support.

"It sounds as though you're doing wonderfully well," Damaris congratulated. They had been shown to a corner table, where both studied the menus assiduously, even gratefully, for it was a task that required attention and precluded the necessity of having to look at one another across the narrow confines of the small table.

"I don't know that I've been doing anything especially wonderful, but it has been an all-consuming job, and that was what I needed—something that would take every minute, every second of my waking thoughts. I felt myself so thoroughly in sympathy with Memphis—both of us in dismal straits, we needed one another."

When she neither responded nor looked up, he went on in a lower but insistent tone. "I'm glad you agreed to come this evening, Damaris. I was afraid you wouldn't after my furious tirade in Washington. You had every right to refuse. I wanted to apologize to you for the things I said. I was angry at the time. I wanted to hurt you because you'd hurt me. I didn't really know how wrong I was, though, until now. Livvy has told me about the way Eustacia had used her and used things she'd told her about Angela Wickers."

Damaris put the menu aside to look at him directly for the first time. "You know why I wrote the letter then? Eustacia was threatening to ruin Mother Charlotte and the order by exposing what she claimed to be an unnatural relationship between Angela and me."

"I gathered that's what must have happened."

"It wasn't true, though I don't deny Angela was fond of me beyond the affection one woman normally gives to another. Angela did nothing wrong; but because there was some truth in Eustacia's allegation, I knew she could—and would—use it. You said in Washington each of us has a price. Mine wasn't the appointment to that commission, as you thought. But I did have a price. I couldn't stand to be the cause of bringing down what Mother Charlotte had built and cherished."

"I apologize for saying you'd thought only of yourself. The things I said to you in Washington have weighed heavily on me. I wish I could say now that they were untrue, but your rejection hurt me so deeply, more deeply than any hurt I'd ever known, that when I said them, I meant them. You were the only person who ever really knew me, the only one to whom I'd allowed myself to become completely vulnerable. Your rejection was unbearable."

"I'm sorry, so very sorry."

"Why couldn't you have told me—explained just to me?"

"If I had, you'd have come, wouldn't you?"

"I suppose I would."

"You know you would; I know you would; Eustacia knew you would. She'd have exposed Angela, and the order would never have recovered from such a blow. The hospital would have lost its support. The truth of the matter would never have been understood." She looked over at him. "Maybe you yourself don't even understand."

"I suppose I don't, not entirely. It's not important to me, though."

"Angela wasn't a bad woman, Guy; she did nothing wrong. I didn't like her in the beginning, not because she was different in that way—I didn't know that then—but because she seemed to hate America so. I think what she really hated was not America but herself, for feeling as she did. She died so admirably. I only hope that I shall be as brave when that time comes."

"Don't speak of dying, Damaris. I thought I'd lost you once—I suppose more than once—though that time it seemed so final."

The waiter came for the order.

"What would you like?" Guy asked.

"Anything."

For all their study of the menu, neither seemed aware of its contents, and both seemed relieved when the waiter recommended the bratwurst.

"That's what we'll have then." Parrish closed the menu.

"And a nice Rhine wine or liebfraumilch perhaps."

They drank the wine, while the food, placed before them with a flourish by the chef himself, remained untouched.

"So what brings you to New York?" Damaris asked as conversation flagged.

"I'm here to see Eustacia's lawyers. She wants a divorce, a nice clean divorce where she will be blameless. It's what she could have had a thousand times before, but it's too late for that now. She won't have everything her way any longer. I want to assure you, despite the threats I know she's made, that your name won't be mentioned. It's one of my stipulations. I know quite enough about Eustacia and Jack Gilvray to make it unwise for her to tarnish your reputation."

Damaris shrugged. "I doubt it would matter much to me. I'll be far away."

"It matters to me though," he said. "She will get her divorce—I want it perhaps more than she does—but now it will be on my terms. I know a great deal about her affairs that she wouldn't want to become public knowledge. Maybe that makes me sound as rotten as she is, but she's left me very bitter."

"You're nothing like Eustacia, Guy, nothing at all. You're so thoroughly . . . decent."

"I suppose I should be glad that you think at least that much of me. I can hardly expect much more after calling you Caylew's mistress. I thought afterwards of how callous that was. You must have been so young then, so innocent, you in his household. He had absolute power over you. I never liked him, but thinking of that has made my dislike turn to hate. I'm sorry for adding to what must have been painful."

"I don't deny it hurt, but only because it came from you. After all, I suppose that's what people would have called me. At the time, though, I was very innocent, and very confused, as well as utterly dominated by my mother's needs that he said he would supply, and of course by him. I was, in fact, the very opposite of being mistress of what happened. He was all master, and not at all kind.''

"I'm so very sorry.'' His eyes more than his words spoke the depth of that sorrow.

"That was a long time ago. I'm quite far from that helpless innocent now. I thank God I'm my own woman at last. Even so, I've hated Caylew, and I've hated the fact that I hated him. Somehow that belittled me. I'm only now overcoming that, putting the matter in perspective. It will be even better when I'm at a greater distance from him. Cuba, my work there, it will all be new. It's never too late to start over. Just as you've discovered in helping to rebuild Memphis.''

Her eyes followed his hand, slowly swirling the contents of his glass. His too followed the circling motion of the wine as he remarked, "I keep seeing Nathan Caylew's poetry in print. It's really improved a great deal.''

"You said a poet needed unrequited love to succeed.''

"Then it's all over between you?''

"Not exactly. It never really began. He was kind to me, very kind. He helped me more than once when I most needed help, but I never thought of him as anything more than a friend.''

"His poetry indicates that he must have felt otherwise.''

"He may have done; I suppose he did. But he's happiest doing what he wants to do, which is writing poetry.''

"Maybe in time he'll become renowned. I hope he does.'' Smiling, Guy lifted his glass. "To Nathan Caylew, poet laureate.'' Then his face grew serious. "You asked why I came to New York. It was to see Eustacia's lawyers, to retain certain rights over my own daughter, to make sure your name was kept out of it. But I could have done all that without coming myself. There was another reason.''

She said nothing, not asking the reason, not even looking at him as he continued. "I knew you were leaving, and I had to tell you before you went away how much I love you. I know this seems contradictory after what I said in Washington. I did try to hate you; in fact I convinced myself for a time that I did, but all along inside I knew I loved you, that I'll only ever love you. I came to tell you that, but when I got here all I could think of was the hurt in your eyes when I'd been so harsh, and so unjust. I love you, but you'd have every right to hate me. You must tell me so, though.''

She'd lowered her eyes as he was talking, and he reached across the table to raise her chin, forcing her to look at him.

''Again, I refuse to allow you custody of the eyes, Damaris. They must tell me what I need—but may not want—to know.''

Slowly she raised her eyes to meet his.

The waiter came to remove their untouched bratwurst. Neither responded to his concerned inquiries at first; but when he repeated them, Guy Parrish smiled and said, ''Excellent, everything is excellent.''

''Some strudel, perhaps? The chef's very proud of the apple strudel.''

''Excellent,'' he said, and again, ''Excellent.'' And when the man had gone, he said, ''Thank God, Damaris. I was almost afraid to look. Your eyes don't lie; they can't.''

''You're the only man I've ever loved, the only one I ever shall.''

He reached across the table to take her hands in his. ''Must you go, then?'' he asked.

''I must. I've promised I would. But it won't be forever.''

''As children we used to say, ''Good night, sleep tight, don't let the mosquitoes bite.' I might say as much now.''

''One case of the fever builds immunity.''

''We thought before that exposure to it gave immunity. That turned out not to be so. You'll have to put up with my concern, I'm afraid. Take care of yourself for me, if not for yourself.''

''I promise.''

''You'll have to forgive me. You're independent, I know, but I can't help wanting to protect you.''

Damaris remembered that first time she'd seen Isabel Caylew motioning for her husband to take care of things for her. She'd often wondered how it would be not to have to bear responsibilities alone. She never wanted to be like

Isabel Caylew, but just imagined having someone who really cared what happened to her.

"I really don't know. No one's ever done that for me." She smiled. "It sounds rather wonderful."

"I shall force myself not to ask you to stay. I know how important this is to you. Since it's also of such importance to Memphis, maybe it will be necessary to come over to see what progress you are making."

They left the restaurant at last, thanking the proprietor for the handsome dinner, assuring him no future visit to New York would be complete without dining there.

He watched their figures melding into one as they disappeared along the gaslit street; then, looking back at the untouched strudel, he shrugged, shaking his head in puzzlement. *"Ach Du lieber Gott!"*

He shrugged again before removing the strudel from the table and carrying it back to the kitchen.

About the Author

DIANA BROWN, a librarian who now devotes most of her time to writing, set her previous novels, which include *The Emerald Necklace, Come Be My Love,* and *The Sandalwood Fan,* in the Regency period of her native England. She is a book collector, primarily of women's journals and letters. She lives in San Jose, California, with her husband, Ralph, and daughters, Pamela and Clarissa.

Signet will sweep you off your feet . . .